AMERICAN LABYRINTH

AMERICAN LABYRINTH

Intellectual History for
Complicated Times

Edited by Raymond Haberski Jr.
and Andrew Hartman

CORNELL UNIVERSITY PRESS   ITHACA AND LONDON

Copyright © 2018 by Cornell University

All rights reserved. Except for brief quotations in a review, this book, or parts thereof, must not be reproduced in any form without permission in writing from the publisher. For information, address Cornell University Press, Sage House, 512 East State Street, Ithaca, New York 14850. Visit our website at cornellpress.cornell.edu.

First published 2018 by Cornell University Press

Printed in the United States of America

Library of Congress Cataloging-in-Publication Data

Names: Haberski, Raymond J., 1968– editor. | Hartman, Andrew, editor.
Title: American labyrinth : intellectual history for complicated times / edited by Raymond Haberski Jr. and Andrew Hartman.
Description: Ithaca [New York] : Cornell University Press, 2018. | Includes bibliographical references and index.
Identifiers: LCCN 2018031296 (print) | LCCN 2018032447 (ebook) | ISBN 9781501730221 (pdf) | ISBN 9781501730238 (ret) | ISBN 9781501730214 | ISBN 9781501730214 (cloth ; alk. paper) | ISBN 9781501730986 (pbk. ; alk. paper)
Subjects: LCSH: United States—Historiography. | United States—Intellectual life.
Classification: LCC E175 (ebook) | LCC E175 .A4545 2018 (print) | DDC 973—dc23
LC record available at https://lccn.loc.gov/2018031296

We dedicate this book to Charlie and Leo, our history teachers.

Contents

	Introduction: Intellectual History for Complicated Times *Raymond Haberski Jr. and Andrew Hartman*	1
Section I	**MAPPING AMERICAN IDEAS**	
	1. Wingspread: So What? *James Livingston*	11
	2. On Legal Fundamentalism *David Sehat*	21
	3. Freedom's Just Another Word? The Intellectual Trajectories of the 1960s *Kevin M. Schultz*	38
Section II	**IDEAS AND AMERICAN IDENTITIES**	
	4. Philosophy vs. Philosophers: A Problem in American Intellectual History *Amy Kittelstrom*	55
	5. The Price of Recognition: Race and the Making of the Modern University *Jonathan Holloway*	71
	6. Thanks, Gender! An Intellectual History of the Gym *Natalia Mehlman Petrzela*	86
	7. Parallel Empires: Transnationalism and Intellectual History in the Western Hemisphere *Ruben Flores*	104
Section III	**DANGEROUS IDEAS**	
	8. Toward a New, Old Liberal Imagination: From Obama to Niebuhr and Back Again *Kevin Mattson*	119
	9. Against the Liberal Tradition: An Intellectual History of the American Left *Andrew Hartman*	132
	10. From "Tall Ideas Dancing" to Trump's Twitter Ranting: Reckoning the Intellectual History of Conservatism *Lisa Szefel*	146
	11. The Reinvention of Entrepreneurship *Angus Burgin*	163

Section IV CONTESTED IDEAS

12. War and American Thought: Finding a Nation through Killing and Dying *Raymond Haberski Jr.* 183

13. United States in the World: The Significance of an Isolationist Tradition *Christopher McKnight Nichols* 198

14. Reinscribing Religious Authenticity: Religion, Secularism, and the Perspectival Character of Intellectual History *K. Healan Gaston* 223

15. "The Entire Thing Was a Fraud": Christianity, Freethought, and African American Culture *Christopher Cameron* 239

Section V IDEAS AND CONSEQUENCES

16. Against and beyond Hofstadter: Revising the Study of Anti-intellectualism *Tim Lacy* 253

17. Culture as Intellectual History: Broadening a Field of Study in the Wake of the Cultural Turn *Benjamin L. Alpers* 271

18. On the Politics of Knowledge: Science, Conflict, Power *Andrew Jewett* 285

Conclusion: The Idea of Historical Context and the Intellectual Historian *Daniel Wickberg* 305

Contributors 323
Acknowledgments 327
Index 329

AMERICAN LABYRINTH

Introduction

INTELLECTUAL HISTORY FOR COMPLICATED TIMES

Raymond Haberski Jr. and Andrew Hartman

The intellectual historians who gathered at the Frank Lloyd Wright–designed Wingspread House were not there to admire the architecture. They were worried. The year was 1977, and the discipline of history was being overtaken by social history.

Unlike the type of intellectual history in fashion during the middle of the twentieth century, which focused mostly on the ideas that animated the world of the political and economic elites, social history unearthed the histories of peoples long neglected by a discipline over-attuned to elites. Social historians, who were explicitly motivated by the liberation movements of the 1960s, sought to prove that even oppressed peoples helped determine the warp and woof of history: even the wretched had "agency."

As social history emerged as the dominant trend in the discipline of history in the 1970s, intellectual history faded from view. Intellectual historians persisted in producing great scholarship, but it became obvious even to them—especially to them—that their work had to take stock of the new social history, which truly did represent a revolution in professional history. History was now to be written from the bottom up.

Against the backdrop of the social turn in the discipline, many prominent American intellectual historians gathered outside Racine, Wisconsin, at the Herbert F. Johnson House—better known as Wingspread—to discuss the state of their subfield. The Wingspread Conference—which included as participants David Hollinger, Henry May, Gordon Wood, Dorothy Ross, Laurence Veysey, Thomas Haskell, David Hall, Thomas Bender, Warren Susman, John Higham, and Paul Conkin, among other intellectual historians—was clouded by anxiety. Could intellectual history maintain its vital place in the historical discipline in the wake of social history's explosive emergence? How would intellectual history respond? These tense questions also shaped the collection of essays that grew out of the Wingspread Conference, *New Directions in American Intellectual History* (1979), a volume that became a standard text for specialists in the subfield.

During the middle of the twentieth century, Richard Hofstadter wrote sophisticated historical inquiries, including Pulitzer Prize–winning books like *The Age of Reform* (1953) and *Anti-intellectualism in American Life* (1963), that offered counterintuitive explanations of the crucial ideas that animated postwar American culture. But after Wingspread, intellectual history turned inward. Just as social historians tended to focus on marginalized, often small communities of people, intellectual historians turned away from broad explanations of political culture and instead focused on what Hollinger termed "communities of discourse," or the culture of intellectuals qua intellectuals. Some historians, like Christopher Lasch, persisted in writing broader studies of the "American mind" of the Hofstadter type—and the fact that Lasch's *The Culture of Narcissism* (1979) sold hundreds of thousands of copies proved that a readership for such books continued to exist. But in general, the subdiscipline deemed such approaches passé, not to mention methodologically unsound.

Then, in the 1980s, *cultural* history arose as the history discipline's new lodestar. In addition to excavating marginalized human experiences in order to revise a narrative about America—the mission of social history—cultural historians decoded the meaning of cultural practices in order to understand how human beings adjusted to their situations. Most historians embraced what came to be called the "cultural turn" and acknowledged just how vast their reservoir of sources about life had become.

Intellectual historians could work with cultural historians. Both were invested in decoding meaning, and as such both were interested in language as a historical source. In other words, cultural history emerged as a way to combine the insights made by social history—that nonelite historical actors mattered—with intellectual history's fascination with texts and the reception of ideas. Intellectual and cultural history developed as discrete subdisciplines, to be sure. Intellectual historians remained interested in the history of formal thought—like philosophy and the social sciences—while cultural historians primarily focused on informal gestures of signification. But there were overlaps that expanded the range of both. Just as cultural historians could learn from the methods of intellectual history when analyzing formal expressions of culture such as the visual arts, intellectual historians could learn from the methods of cultural history when seeking to understand the thought worlds of people whose ideas did not fill the pages of journals, books, and letters.

The upshot of intellectual history's engagement with the cultural turn is that its practitioners increasingly began to operate under a bigger and bigger tent. All peoples have ideas, and intellectual historians began to seek out ways to understand, analyze, contextualize, and historicize ideas wherever they could be found. The history of pragmatism, which had previously been a history of formal thought as laid out by William James and John Dewey and other giants of American philosophy, expanded to include histories of the ways in which pragmatism flourished in film, in public schools, and in the workplace—pragmatism from the bottom up, and all the way to the top. Intellectual history, in short, learned its place in a discipline that no longer focused solely on elites, and it was much improved for it. Even scholarship that continued the important work of historicizing formal, often elite thought demonstrated the significance of social and cultural dimensions. It turned out that those who write about elites need not be elitist.

However, even as intellectual history profited from its encounters with social and cultural history, as a subdiscipline it suffered from relative obscurity. Many historians avoided claiming that they did intellectual history, because to most of the profession it seemed nothing more than a mere afterthought. But perhaps times are changing. As measured by the enthusiastic response to the birth of two new academic societies—the Society for U.S. Intellectual History (S-USIH) and the African American Intellectual History Society (AAIHS)— many young scholars have embraced intellectual history as their academic calling, even though there are very few precious academic jobs for intellectual historians (or any kind of historians, for that matter). More important in terms of gauging the renewed interest in intellectual history has been the fervor with which a general reading public has consumed books of intellectual history, beginning perhaps with Louis Menand's 2001 book about the origins of pragmatism, *The Metaphysical Club: A Story of Ideas in America*, which won a Pulitzer Prize and had surprisingly robust sales. Since then, intellectual history has moved closer to the zenith of the history publishing business. Recent books such as Ibram Kendi's *Stamped from the Beginning: The Definitive History of Racist Ideas in America* and Nancy MacLean's *Democracy in Chains: The Deep History of the Radical Right's Stealth Plan for America* have won big awards and made a bunch of news.

One prerequisite for intellectual history's growing prominence is clear: intellectual historians have taken seriously the lessons of social and cultural history. Wingspread kick-started these changes, and since then intellectual history has gradually evolved into the big tent that now defines the subdiscipline. Despite this gradual evolution, which would suggest that nothing is novel about our current moment, something new is afoot.

As was the case when Hofstadter wrote his award-winning books, when McCarthyism seemed like an irrational current of ideas—at least to a liberal academic like Hofstadter—our current political culture is riven by strange, anti-intellectual, almost inexplicable ideas. More and more people—a general reading public disturbed by these developments—are seeking out answers to vexing questions about a nation riven by war, economic turbulence, social dislocation, and the persistence of racism and sexism. Intellectual historians, sensing this craving, have attracted larger and larger audiences that are hungry for explanations about the origins, contexts, and consequences of ideas that seem more powerful than ever. How do we understand a society riddled by profound contradictions—a society that transitioned, during the time this book was written, from Barack Obama to Donald Trump?

Ideas matter. A lot. Most people recognize as much. Intellectual history—the study of ideas in the past—thus has a lot to offer people. This collection is conceived with this basic fact in mind.

This volume of essays has brought together intellectual historians to contribute original essays on topics that interest many audiences. We asked the authors to consider the following question: How might the methods of intellectual history shed light on contemporary issues with historical resonance? Their answers, while rigorous, original, and challenging, are eclectic in approach and temperament. This book does not claim to be a comprehensive representation of intellectual history, but rather seeks to illustrate how intellectual historians can operate in many different registers at once: from the theoretical and philosophical to the literary and theological to the popular and political.

The first set of essays, from James Livingston, David Sehat, and Kevin M. Schultz, map American ideas. By interrogating ideas that illustrate the intersection of popular and elite history, these writers help define the contours of the subfield itself. Livingston investigates the irrepressible logic by which American intellectual history has returned and will always return, because ideas are the American currency. Sehat's essay is a genealogy of constitutional originalism, or what he terms "legal fundamentalism," and a convincing argument that intellectual history is the antidote to such fundamentalist thought. Schultz's essay, a post-Hofstadteran exploration of the "American mind," analyzes the recent history of "freedom," an idea that overwhelmed other concepts, such as "community" and "love," that promised more radical social change during the revolutionary 1960s.

The second set of essays contends with relationships between ideas and American identities. In excavating how race, gender, and nationality shape identity, these chapters by Amy Kittelstrom, Jonathan Holloway, Natalia Mehlman Petrzela, and Ruben Flores exemplify the ways in which intellectual history has responded to the social and cultural turns. In her chapter, Kittelstrom uses the dynamics of gender as a lens by which to complicate the "philosopher" and to expand the breadth by which we might conceptualize philosophy as a historical subject. Holloway, in an essay that goes far beyond earlier scholarship that simply recognized the contributions of black intellectuals, mines the intellectual history of college campuses to investigate how racial recognition comes with a steep price. Petrzela's chapter reflects on the ways in which gender as a historical category has multiplied the range of topics and approaches open to intellectual historians; she demonstrates this by investigating the intellectual history of wellness. And Flores, in an essay about how the flow of pragmatism to Mexico and other Latin American nations has been neither one-way nor predictable, shows that ideas are not so easily attached to national identities—*and* that ideas move among national identities.

We call the third set of essays "Dangerous Ideas." Chapters by Kevin Mattson, Andrew Hartman, Lisa Szefel, and Angus Burgin demonstrate how intellectual history illuminates the context of American politics and economy—a minefield for politicians and a gold mine for intellectual historians. In a forceful essay that foregrounds the 2016 Democratic primaries, Mattson illustrates that the intellectual history of liberalism, exemplified by Reinhold Niebuhr, endowed Barack Obama (and to a lesser extent Hillary Clinton) with the right mix of hope and humility to carry liberalism forward in a way that the author could support. In a chapter that agrees with Mattson's categories but reverses his judgment, Hartman provides a genealogy of the Left that traces its origins to its late nineteenth-century adoption of Marxism and argues that the American Left has always existed in creative tension with liberalism and is in fact defined by that tension. Szefel, pointing us in a historiographical direction suitable to the Age of Trump, follows the big-tent approach by suggesting that the best way to understand conservative thought is to focus not on intellectuals but rather on the demotic sensibilities of the conservative base. In Burgin's essay, his dissection of the overused word "entrepreneur" shows how an impersonal concept like "the economy" can be made to seem more contingent, more human.

In the fourth section, "Contested Ideas," Raymond Haberski Jr., Christopher McKnight Nichols, K. Healan Gaston, and Christopher Cameron showcase the ways consensus histories of things like war or religion cover up deep divisions over the traditions that shape American life. Haberski, in a chapter on the meaning of war in American culture, argues that because Americans have come together around war like nothing else, the very nation might not exist without it. In an essay grounded in the recent transnational turn in historical scholarship,

Nichols contends that an apparently provincial idea like isolationism, which has been much abused by pundits and historians alike, has a surprisingly complex history that teaches us about both the national and transnational flow of ideas. Gaston, in her chapter on religion in postwar America, grapples with the very word "religion" and argues that the intellectual historian's perspective complicates normative uses of that term. Cameron, on the other hand, finds a normative conception of religion useful in his argument that the intellectual history of black atheist thought has largely been ignored precisely because so many historians have been invested in the narrative of black religion that, supposedly, provided African Americans agency against the racist structures of American society.

In this volume's concluding section, "Ideas and Consequences," Tim Lacy, Benjamin L. Alpers, Andrew Jewett, and Daniel Wickberg explore how ideas get used, abused, and confused. Lacy provides a counterintuitive reception history of Hofstadter's *Anti-intellectualism in American Life*, arguing that even though the book was riddled with problems, including elitism, no writer has yet improved on its provocative argument. Alpers demonstrates how working at the intersection of intellectual history and cultural history helps him think through the use of 1950s nostalgia by American filmmakers of the 1970s. Jewett challenges the common assumption that recent intellectual history sits nicely alongside cultural history by arguing that much of the best new scholarship in the field is better identified as the "politics of knowledge," or the act of denaturalizing supposedly timeless concepts like "economic laws." And last, Wickberg engages "historical context," a phrase that has become too pat for historians, by showing the plurality of ways in which historians put "historical context" to use and by arguing that more methodological clarity would make a big tent even bigger and more capacious.

We hope to perform a literary excavation, getting behind a disparate array of things—law, philosophy, economy, war, power—to identify the ideas that make them meaningful. We suggest that there is a constant interaction between things made apparent in our world—things often documented by social historians—and the ideas that gave rise to the material existence of history. For example, historians study social movements as different as civil rights and white nationalism, but they also study ideas like religion that fed these opposed movements. Intellectual historians, then, tend to embrace the way some ideas, such as Marxism or liberalism, can lead to diverse, even contradictory, consequences. In this sense, intellectual historians often produce work—books and essays and lectures—that appears contrapuntal. They acknowledge things that capture popular attention but also bear witness to the ideas that few might recognize lurking behind the social history of their time.

The chapters in this volume do not pretend to align with each other or with an overarching argument. They do not speak from a dominant school in intellectual history and are not the product of a specific influence in the subfield. What unites these essays is that they get readers to think more creatively and expansively about the assumptions they hold. Thus, James Livingston wonders in his essay why he cannot be both a historian of ideas and an economic historian: who gets to determine the categories, or even the difference? Amy Kittelstrom forces us to rethink what a philosopher is when that philosopher is a woman. The things we study as historians are never completely stable, of course, because they are also open to interpretation and revision. But this volume does not pretend to jettison the idea of reality—there is no appeal to the social construction of everything. Rather the authors argue that there are very good reasons why we collectively take things for granted—why we imagine that war can be good for a democracy or that exercise is good (physically and morally) for our bodies—because those narratives, those things, are based on ideas that travel so well across time that they grow dangerous.

Intellectual historians have learned some lessons, but now they have lessons to impart in turn. And the central lesson is that if you want to understand why people do things, if you want to understand why people get so animated about statues and symbols, if, in short, you want to understand the world, then you must understand ideas. Maybe not exclusively, and certainly with due attention to the role of interest, but still . . . you must understand ideas, because ultimately there are no things—no human things—but in ideas.

Section I
MAPPING AMERICAN IDEAS

1

WINGSPREAD
So What?

James Livingston

When the Wingspread conference convened in 1977, departments of history were already exporting economic history to departments of economics, political history to departments of political science (the "new institutionalists"), and intellectual history to departments of English / comparative literature, in an academic replay of deindustrialization, sending jobs to places that, when the disciplines first formed in the early twentieth century, had been less-developed outposts of the metropolitan origin.

These three fields had once been the core of the history curriculum as such. Now they were beginning to look less interesting and important than the new social history, indeed almost peripheral compared to this usurper. Cultural history was the answer to the perceived crisis in all three fields—perhaps a way to repatriate the jobs lost to the new, invasive species of academics who crowded the field. The Wingspread volume, *New Directions in American Intellectual History*, was an early symptom of this perception, and perhaps also its cure.

I think that's why the memorable essays, the ones we still read and put to use as intellectual historians, are those that recapitulate the new rhythms of social history—and the similar cadences of new social movements in the late twentieth century—by locating the source of ideas in cultural ferment, "from the bottom up," as it were. Thomas Haskell's essay, for example, begins by asking how to teach intellectual history as it has been transformed by Thomas Kuhn's arguments about scientific revolutions. But "we" is surely too strong a pronoun. I'll speak just for myself.

I remember the essays by Haskell, David Hollinger, and Warren Susman because they read like catalogs for an exhibition at an art gallery. They're full of wonder, to begin with. They also *situate* the objects of their scrutiny, but they refuse to reduce these objects to the situation of their composition (context, as we used to say). And, even more significant, they refuse to assign responsibility to one social stratum or another—say, intellectuals—for the articulated effects of the ideas in question.

I lived through this moment as a graduate student, so I can—if I may—share a sense of the panic that set in as it happened, as once discrete fields realigned and recombined. I thought of myself as an economic historian because I had written an MA thesis on Russia's early modern backwardness (one dimension of the "second serfdom" in Eastern Europe), and I was writing a PhD thesis on the origins of the Federal Reserve. But I knew I couldn't compete with the economists who were flooding the field with graphs, charts, counterfactuals, and regressions. I also knew the numbers they compiled from, say, the nineteenth century, were created by economic theories and their statistical armature—they were produced, not discovered; they were nothing like mere facts that registered an inert historical reality. The intellectual history of political economy, as Angus Burgin rightly and pointedly notes in this volume, is the hidden transcript of capitalism: it's the account book where the significant economic changes are recorded, sometimes avant la lettre.

In that limited, inchoate sense, even before my encounter with Friedrich Nietzsche and my engagement with Thomas Kuhn, I already knew that no economic transaction or change happened in the absence of language, thought, and purpose. *No things but in ideas*, I said to myself, inverting William Carlos Williams's dictum.

Still, what was to be done? Hell if I knew. Then I received an invitation to give a talk at Princeton, in early February 1981. I had defended the dissertation on the Fed the previous June and was working two part-time jobs, one as a ghostwriter for a profoundly stupid dean, the other as a history instructor in a maximum-security prison—Stateville, in Joliet, Illinois (if you've seen *The Blues Brothers*, you've seen the north wall). When it dawned on me that this call might be about a job, I asked the professor on the other end of the line, Stanley N. Katz, why I was being invited. "Is this about a job?"

"Yes, of course, I'm sorry, we're looking for a young economic historian. Hal Woodman recommended you. He says you're writing on the Federal Reserve."

"A job at Princeton, you mean?" My recently minted PhD was from Northern Illinois University. Oh, and in 1981 I was a serious, sectarian Marxist, and quite possibly a maniac. Princeton had come calling?

"Yes, we're looking for unorthodox perspectives, younger people."

So I flew from Chicago to Princeton by way of Newark and Teterboro, to do an on-campus interview for the first time in my brief academic life. Dinner on Thursday night with John Murrin, Sean Wilentz, David Abraham, Tom Slaughter, and Lou Masur, lunch the next day with Arthur Link, Robert Darnton, and James McPherson—old Arthur stamped his cane on the floor and demanded sherry—then the job talk on Friday afternoon.

I was always underdressed. At dinner on Thursday night, I had to be equipped with a greasy sport coat from the restaurant's inventory because, well, because that was the rule in Princeton, and at lunch the next day I was just naked because we discussed my two extant publications, the first in *Socialist Revolution*, the second in *Marxist Perspectives*. Yes, this happened in Prospect House, at Princeton University. Arthur loved the *SR* piece on revolution as such, Bob hated the *MP* essay on "Romeo and Juliet," Jim was dubious about both.

On Friday morning over breakfast, Stan Katz says, "I want you to know, you're the only person we're interviewing for the job. The thing is, the colleagues aren't sure you're an economic historian."

"Ah. What do they think I am?"

"They think you're an intellectual historian. You write about ideas. There's not much about the economy per se in the dissertation."

"Even the stuff about the corporations, how they changed the economy?"

"I like that part, we all do, but then you write about economic theory, crisis management, what people were saying *about* the economy. You see the difference? That's what worries the colleagues."

"But Stan, the economy isn't an externality"—I could speak the language—"because the origins of economic change are social, and intellectual as well. Marx taught us that! Like, social movements aren't just permeated by ideas, they're constituted by ideas. These guys who invented the Fed, they understood that." I was more or less quoting myself from the dissertation. "I mean, economic history isn't just what happened to people, it's what people were doing and saying. We separate business history from economic history, but how does that work? Here's what the managers said, kind of intellectual, here's the effects they had, kind of economic? It makes no sense."

Katz shrugged, in what I took to be agreement with me. "We'll see."

The first question after the job talk, from the resident intellectual historian, was, "So, did the economic history of the United States change because the Fed was founded?" I could have repeated what I said to Stan Katz: "It all depends on what you mean by economic history." At the moment, however, that answer sounded obscure, evasive, and metaphysical, even to me.

As I fumbled through a different answer, I was pretty sure I wasn't getting the job. I was right. Instead, I got a job as a copy editor at Scott, Foresman, & Co., the textbook publisher, where I worked for six months, and then started teaching full time as a visiting assistant professor at North Central College. When I was fired from that job the following spring, I collected unemployment long enough to rewrite the dissertation for publication.

As I did so, in the long aftermath of that question in the bowels of Firestone Library, I realized that I was, in fact, an intellectual historian, down bone deep and for good. *I realized that we all are*: we're all trying to understand the difference, and the relation, between material circumstance and intellectual inscription. We can't help it. But the question lingered because it restates the classical conundrum of intellectual historians: how and why did this idea make a difference? Notice that we ask it because the pragmatists forced us to.

After Princeton, I was able, if that is the right word, to see why the new economic history was a dead end, where the old intellectual history had failed, and how they might be brought back together under that impossible rubric of cultural history—and to revise the dissertation accordingly. But I was able to see these things only because I was meanwhile reading the young Hegel, he of the seminary in the 1790s, the big arguments with Schelling and Fichte (1800), and finally *The Phenomenology* (1807). And it's only in light of that reading, I believe, that the Wingspread volume makes sense and remains useful.

The "discipline of culture," Hegel argued in *The Phenomenology*, was a matter (almost literally) of work and language. I read this argument as an uncanny premonition of Roland Barthes's *Writing Degree Zero* (trans. 1967) and Fredric Jameson's *Political Unconscious* (1981), because, like these successors among literary critics, Hegel insisted that form or genre—you might say paradigm—is a social convention that mediates between language (the broad history of its speakers) on the one hand and style (the narrow biography of the writer) on the other, thus determining the accessible intellectual content of all speech and writing, regardless of the subject. Form doesn't merely reveal the content of thought, it determines that content as well. But the choice of form is an expression of social and historical solidarity with certain readers and writers—it creates or validates a constituency. Notice that this is a genuine choice among many plausible alternatives: context is a pluralistic universe, as Daniel Wickberg insists in his chapter for this volume.

So the question Hegel asked was not "How do I know what I know?"—as if that "I" was a transcendental ego exempt from the vicissitudes of time—but rather "What have we said to each other about what we have known, and why did we say it then, in that form as against any other?" Suddenly epistemology became the history of how certain ideas acquired meaning in the world. *How did they become things?* What made them material, and thus intelligible? Metaphysics became intellectual history.

Let me translate. Work and language were, according to Hegel, means of self-estrangement, and therefore paths to the kind of self-consciousness that wouldn't settle for the "spiritless formal universality" attained by the mere assertion of natural right—this consciousness had "undergone development" and was therefore "concrete and actual," not merely abstract. The "formative process of Culture" was composed of these acts of self-estrangement. The *content* of self-consciousness, of ideas themselves, could be known only insofar as it took tangible, external *form* in such acts, in the sublimated desires we call work and in the submission to inherited rules and icons required by language—only then could this content be observed, understood, and evaluated by others, who would validate your possession of ideas, by their observation, understanding, and evaluation, for only then could you become intelligible to yourself. In this sense, the only way to attain self-consciousness is to become something you're not, to depart from what you already are, to be estranged from what you have been.

In other words: the history of ideas just was the formative process of culture. Work and language weren't higher or lower levels on a philosophical, epistemological, or curricular hierarchy; they were equivalent, often simultaneous moments in a developmental, historical sequence. The most ineffable ideas were indecipherable absent knowledge of the material circumstances that permitted their articulation—and vice versa. Language and work were different but related ways of realizing consciousness of self, and that self was subject, in every sense, to change.

With *The Phenomenology*, Hegel dismantled the distinction between philosophy and social theory, as Herbert Marcuse would have it, but he also erased any defensible boundary between the history of ideas and the history of work—or between intellectual and social/economic history. The two most important nineteenth-century results of this uncanny new cultural atlas were *The Philosophy of Right* (1821), where Hegel cites Adam Smith, Jean-Baptiste Say, and David Ricardo to demonstrate that modern liberal bourgeois politics were no less interesting and potentially virtuous than those invented in Athens, and volume 1 of *Capital* (1867), where Marx cites the same sources to demonstrate that the beliefs we call Protestantism were the chalice that held the promise of liberty, property, and Bentham. Marx showed that the law of accumulation would someday extricate human labor from goods production, leaving us with nothing to do but think deep thoughts. At that point, intellectual history would be the only work left to us.

Work was central to both these volumes, of course, but, for two reasons, Hegel's late text was more original. First, he amplified his treatment of work as the scene of self-consciousness: *The Philosophy of Right* is the completion of the intellectual agenda set out in *The Phenomenology*, not a repudiation of it.

Second, and more important, Hegel jettisons the ancient and medieval valuation of meaningful, consciousness-producing work as *poeisis*, which Emerson would revive, twenty years later, as the "Doctrine of the Farm." Drudgery of the kind found in factories—"the moving life of the dead," Hegel called it—and even slavery, these were forms of social labor that created self-consciousness.

The Wingspread volume is a distant echo of these literary or theoretical events, I believe, because its presiding spirit is Thomas Kuhn, whose great work on scientific revolutions was animated, you might even say motivated, by his encounter with Continental philosophy in the form of Stanley Cavell, when they were young assistant professors at Berkeley. The memorable essays I mentioned, by Hollinger, Haskell, and Susman, take Kuhn for granted in the sense that, like him, and like Hegel, they assume that cultural change is the groundwork of intellectual innovation.

But what exactly does it mean to say that intellectual innovation presupposes cultural change, in the sense, say, that the Copernican revolution was animated by the ferment of the Reformation? Isn't this mere reversion, a way of saying that base and superstructure are related precisely as the vulgar Marxists always claimed? It all depends on what you mean by cultural history. Barthes taught us that any text is composed of language, form, and style, to which, he suggested, the categories of history, society, and biography corresponded. The cultural historian will be more interested in the mid-range choice of form and its social, objective correlatives, than in the stylistic specifics that a given writer's biography permitted or demanded—the specifics that a literary critic, say, would foreground. But that historian will also be aware of the styles determined by the prior choice of form. And that historian will ask about what forms the language made available, and how the language itself was transformed by the invention of new forms. Knowingly or not, he or she will be a string vibrating to the tuning fork of Continental philosophy.

Thomas Haskell's essay is a good example of what I'm getting at here. Like David Hollinger, but in a drastically different minor key, he explains what Kuhn has accomplished, and why it matters—or doesn't. It's a muted yet powerful meditation on the philosophy of history, or rather philosophy *in* history, a rehearsal, if you will, for the brilliant essays on capitalism and humanitarianism that would appear six years later in the *American Historical Review* (by my reckoning, there are more footnotes here, in a sixteen-page essay, than in the *AHR* series). In the end, R. G. Collingwood stands in for Thomas Kuhn!

Like every other contributor to the volume, and every historian who's ever had an idea about ideas, Haskell asks, What is the relation between social thought and social context? He uses Kuhn to answer the question, but, unlike Hollinger, he ends up more skeptic than sponsor: "It is not at all clear that Kuhn has any useful message for us about the relation between thought and social setting," Haskell concludes, unless that message amounts to something intellectual historians have known time out of mind, namely, "mankind's most fundamental assumptions—the 'paradigmatic' ones—are normally immune to the experiential evidence that might modify or falsify them."

By this accounting, intellectual history was in no danger from social history (or its heir apparent, cultural studies), because it was reading between the lines all along, trying, like analytic philosophy, to decipher the inarticulate presuppositions that permit the most simple of declarations. "Intellectual history has repeatedly taught that the deepest layers of assumption in human belief systems [notice: not ideology] are so tenacious that they shape experience far more often than they are shaped by it." *No things but in ideas.*

But of course the Wingspread volume still exudes anxiety about the standing of intellectual history—that's why John Higham and Paul Conkin convened it. Who cares? So what? Merely ideas! But nobody except the old-fashioned Rush Welter actually explains why intellectual history is unavoidable in and indispensable to the study of *American* history—and therefore modern history as such. Everybody else, Hollinger, Haskell, and Susman included, invokes theoretical models or philosophical idioms to close the distance between popular culture or social history, on the one hand, and educated utterance or intellectual history on the other. Only Welter assumes that precisely because the people "out of doors" had taken things into their own hands and made the revolution we call modernity, it followed that public opinion—the marketplace of ideas—became the site of political possibility and the residence of recollection that matters.

Here is how Welter puts it. "To the extent that the United States has been egalitarian in its social aspirations, to the extent that its educational institutions and media of information have been popular rather than elite in their bias, to the extent that popular opinion (however misinformed) has been a given within which its political leaders were forced to work, the ideas current in the society at large have had more to do with how it conducted its affairs than have comparable ideas in other societies."

Here is how Abraham Lincoln put the same proposition in the first debate with Stephen A. Douglas at Ottawa, Illinois: "In this and like communities, public sentiment is everything. With public sentiment, nothing can fail; without it, nothing can succeed. Consequently, he who molds public sentiment goes deeper than he who enacts statutes or pronounces decisions. He makes statutes and decisions possible or impossible to be executed."

Intellectual history matters here more than elsewhere, in short, because consent is the regulative principle of governance—the supremacy of society over the state, or the sovereignty of the people, requires the well-placed and the well-educated to *persuade* their potential constituents, to make their ideas clear to everyone, even the least informed of us. You might even say, on the same grounds, that intellectuals matter here more than in, say, France.

Intellectual history, and intellectuals as well, matter here more than elsewhere for another but related reason. Americans have never shared a national origin, a linguistic affinity, a religious devotion, or a racial stock. We're orphans or mongrels all the way down. All we've had in common is the stories we tell each other about where we came from, and these stories—about the founding, about the Civil War, about whatever—are various, to say the least. To be an American is to argue about what it means to be an American, and intellectual history, no matter how you define it, is the essence of that argument. The marketplace of ideas is the habitat of every American. Those of us with professional credentials are visitors, not arbiters, because ideas matter here as they do nowhere else.

And yet twenty years after the Wingspread conference, what do we witness? Deeper anxiety! In 1996, the *Intellectual History Newsletter*, the proximate cause of *Modern Intellectual History*, the staid new journal that now has to compete with the unruly start-up S-USIH, ran an issue about the threat of cultural studies to the field.

How and why did this strange event happen? I'm still mystified after all these years because, as I said in my little contribution to the issue—my credentials as an intellectual historian were by then in order—cultural studies had enriched the field by letting us understand ideas differently, in Foucauldian or Nietzschean terms. A lousy movie is no less an intellectual product or purpose than a great novel. The most degraded commodity, say a used car, is no less a psychological fetish than an expensive wedding band. The power of an idea has nothing to do with its origin, because an author is always already a historical artifact. But the methods and manners of intellectual history still apply.

Notice, too, that this *Intellectual History Newsletter* issue came *after* the publication of seminal works in American intellectual history—books that re-electrified the field, as it were, by designating new lines and locations of inquiry. I'm thinking here of James Kloppenberg, *Uncertain Victory* (1986), Casey Blake, *Beloved Community* (1990), Robert Westbrook, *John Dewey and American Democracy* (1991), the usual suspects, but also of Judith Butler, *Gender Trouble* (1990). Go ahead, make your own list. These books made us rethink the intellectual history of the entire twentieth century from an "American" standpoint, by which I mean only that they begin or end with the revision of an ostensibly European canon.

Only? The beginning and the ending of these indispensable works is either Friedrich Nietzsche or William James, the two figures that early twentieth-century European intellectuals, from Bertrand Russell to Émile Durkheim, saw as the same species of nihilist. To put it more stridently, pragmatism is the beginning and the ending of these books, Butler's included. It served the same purpose across the disciplines in the 1990s, from literature to philosophy, from Morris Dickstein to Richard Rorty.

And now, speaking of such endings and their beginnings. The Wingspread volume concludes with Warren Susman's strange little essay, in which he quietly announces the extinction of intellectual history as we knew it. If you want to understand the meaning and significance of the ideas that matter at any moment, Susman insisted, find out what the larger, lowly culture was up to. This procedure will force you into the realms of myth, religion, and metaphor, where the unwashed and the uneducated reside.

Pay particular attention to the metaphors everyone takes for granted, because these words carry the weight of intellectual change across boundaries of class, race, gender—and generations. They are the linguistic *and therefore* social intersection where intellectuals and the rest of us meet to decide on what has transpired, and what will remain important. They're not mere registers of material reality because they solicit expectations. Nor are they the "presuppositions" that Haskell, following Collingwood, urged us to penetrate; they run deeper, and they're not made of logical steps.

Susman famously distinguished between *character* and *personality* as the metaphors through which Americans of all kinds glimpsed the difference between the old economic necessities of the nineteenth century (the "pain economy," as Simon Patten named it) and the new social imaginary of the twentieth century (the "pleasure economy," according to Patten). Any number of historians have claimed that it was more complicated than that. Their criticisms are beside the point because, like Richard Hofstadter twenty years earlier, Susman was trying to decipher the intellectual transition to what we have come to know as corporate capitalism and/or consumer culture. Noticing and explaining the shift of metaphors was one way to do so.

Let me cite another example that comes from the same period Susman studied. As the early critics of pragmatism from Lewis Mumford to Theodor Adorno and Max Horkheimer remind us, both John Dewey and William James deployed the metaphor of credit or finance to explain their new theories of truth. Of course the critics were right. But they never asked *why* that metaphor—what work did it do that no other could? And why did James and Dewey fall back on it at the most pivotal, crucial moments of their arguments, for example in lecture 6 of *Pragmatism*, and before that in the first two essays in radical empiricism?

I have elsewhere argued that they borrowed this metaphor from the rhetoric of the "Money Question," the popular political discourse of the late nineteenth and early twentieth centuries, to emphasize their departure from a correspondence theory of truth, and, in Dewey's case, to signify his acceptance of large business enterprise. It was a perfect fit because "money was a sign of real commodities, but credit was but the sign of a sign," as Edward Bellamy explained in the bestselling *Looking Backward* (1887), a book James and Dewey knew well. The metaphor worked because it expressed the new vertiginous contingency in the relation between subjects and objects, ideas and realities, thoughts and things, which had been created by the advent of a "credit economy"—as its critics (the labor movement, the Populists) *and* its advocates (the usual suspects) agreed it had. If the lawyers could redefine private property to include intangible or immeasurable corporate assets such as "good will" or a stream of future income, why couldn't the philosophers redefine truth to include the "existing beyond"?

What Mumford, Adorno, and Horkheimer never understood, and what more recent students of pragmatism cannot fathom, are the simple facts. James and Dewey were social democrats, each in his own fashion. They neither worshipped "business culture" in the United States nor preached a pragmatic acquiescence to the existing realities of corporate capitalism and imperialism. They deployed financial metaphors taken from the popular political discourse of their time not to validate capitalism but to explain how truth works in our time.

So what? Hell if I know. Except that after Wingspread, everybody seemed to understand, along with Haskell and Susman, that significant intellectual change presupposed cultural revolution. Me too.

2
ON LEGAL FUNDAMENTALISM

David Sehat

Critics have always beset legal originalism, the doctrine that the original meaning of the Constitution should bind subsequent interpretation. One of the most powerful objections against originalism has been that it is, in fact, a form of legal fundamentalism. Critics point in particular to the originalist understanding of texts as evidence of its fundamentalist character. Rather than assuming, as many modern observers do, that interpretation involves a creative process in which the cultural understanding of the interpreter controls or creates meaning, originalists rely on a strict literalism in reading the Constitution. Their literalism is actually a form of biblicism, frequent among fundamentalists, which assumes that the text's meaning is stable, that it is easily accessible to the common reader, and that it serves as the final and perhaps only authority in the formation of legal doctrine. To many critics, the spirit of biblicism discredits originalist theory. For some supporters, especially the many conservative religious writers who adhere to the doctrine, the common method of reading both the biblical and the constitutional text is a testament to the integrity of originalist practice.[1]

Yet this understanding of originalism perhaps too readily grants originalism's self-conceit. It concedes the idea that originalism is, above all, an interpretive approach. In other words, the difference between originalism and its critics, in this line of analysis, is a set of interpretive rules and practices that can be dissected, subjected to scholarly dispute, and ultimately made to terminate in a jurisprudential orientation. But behind these rules and practices, or perhaps beneath them, is a more profound disagreement that makes it difficult to carry on discussion between originalists and their critics. The deeper rupture involves a fundamentalist posture toward time and change that critics of originalism in large measure reject. That posture becomes especially apparent when we consider the development of originalism and the way that its proponents have used history.

As an impulse within constitutional jurisprudence, what we might call the originalist orientation goes back nearly to the beginning of the judicial tradition, if not before. In 1803, when John Marshall emphasized in *Marbury v. Madison* that the Constitution was an expression of fundamental law more consequential than any particular statute, he expressed a core originalist notion. Because the Constitution was of a more foundational character than a mere statute, Marshall argued, it deserved special care within judicial interpretation as the ur-expression of the people's will.[2]

The originalist orientation was not a fully formed originalism, partly because it was not usually thoroughgoing. Jurists, politicians, and others who participated in public debate might in one breath invoke an originalist understanding of a constitutional doctrine, sometimes by referencing their own experience in constitutional formulation or by appealing to the testimony of other still-living framers. Then in another breath they might invoke a different understanding entirely. Quite often, the still-nascent originalist impulse was used as a defensive maneuver to hold back political change. The rhetoric could be, and often was, easily discarded once the threat had passed.[3]

With the death of the founding generation, the originalist impulse became even more ambivalent. Although politicians continued to invoke an original meaning to the Constitution, that tendency was often balanced by a countervailing force that looked at the American constitutional tradition as living, capable of emendation, and able to be transformed according to time and circumstance. The more liberal tradition had distinguished proponents, many of whom were exasperated with the latent originalism that had shaped American political and legal discussion since the Founders' deaths. Henry Clay, for example, complained that the popular worship of the Founders, especially Thomas Jefferson, made "all Mr. Jefferson's opinions the articles of faith of the new Church." Abraham Lincoln, who referred constantly to the founding era and the Declaration of Independence to justify his position on slavery, still rejected the idea that "we are bound to follow implicitly in whatever our fathers did." "To do so," he said, "would be to discard all the lights of current experience—to reject all progress—all improvement." Ulysses S. Grant, after the Civil War, went still farther in dismissing the Founders' constitutional understanding. The nation had been transformed between the founding era and the Civil War. The war itself had changed the Constitution. The legal, political, and cultural moment that had generated the Constitution's original meaning, Grant claimed, had passed. But that fact did not trouble him. "It is preposterous," he said, "to suppose that the people of one generation can lay down the best and only rules of government for all who are to come after them."[4]

By the Progressive Era, the originalist impulse was losing ground. Theodore Roosevelt, who would later become president of the American Historical Association, used his 1905 inaugural address to articulate what was becoming a widespread sense of historical anachronism that plagued the original meaning of the Constitution. "Our forefathers faced certain perils which we have outgrown," he said. "We now face other perils, the very existence of which it was impossible that they should foresee. Modern life is both complex and intense, and the tremendous changes wrought by the extraordinary industrial development of the last half century are felt in every fiber of our social and political being." A sense of historical change fed into Roosevelt's progressivism and his distance from the Founders' ideas. As he said a few years later, political development could not "be a mere submission to the American ideas of the period of the Declaration of Independence. Such action would be not only to stand still, but to go back."[5]

The Progressive idea had many proponents besides Roosevelt. No one articulated it more clearly than Woodrow Wilson, who in 1908 published a groundbreaking book called *Constitutional Government in the United States*. Although the idea of a living constitution had been circulating since Henry Clay, Wilson was one of the first people to use the term. He also gave the notion a theoretical elaboration far more sophisticated than it had received to date. "Our life has undergone radical changes since 1787," he wrote, "and almost every change has operated to draw the nation together, to give it the common consciousness, the common interests, the common standards of conduct, the habit of concerted action, which will eventually impart to it in many more respects the character of a single community." The historical development of the past century was at odds with the original constitutional ideas of federalism, of the separation of powers, of the limitations on executive actions, and much more, Wilson believed. But that was not a problem, he argued, because the Constitution was living, partly through the subsequent growth of constitutional law that emerged out of a century of legal decisions and partly by the contemporary adaptation of constitutional doctrine and ideas to new contexts. The original constitutional ideas were, he wrote, "sufficiently broad and elastic to allow for the play of life and circumstance" regardless of their original meaning.[6]

To a considerable extent, living constitutionalism underwrote the entirety of Progressive reforms, which sought to create a more democratic republic and a more equitable economic system. As these reforms went forward—through constitutional amendments, political changes on the state level, and a variety of civil and municipal innovations—progressive writers provided legal and political justifications through a new jurisprudential approach, known as legal realism or, sometimes, sociological jurisprudence. The approach assumed, first, that judges sought to use the law to achieve desirable social ends and, second, that the ends varied with the time in which interpretation took place. Many who supported the new sociological jurisprudence were flatly skeptical that the ideas of the founding era, with its rank illiberalism, could be readily appropriated into a more progressive era without change. And many agreed with the claim of Louis Brandeis and Samuel Warren, who argued in a famous 1890 *Harvard Law Review* article that "political, social, and economic changes entail the recognition of new rights." The frankly modernist and modernizing perspective of sociological jurisprudence began to sweep through legal and political circles in the first two decades of the twentieth century.[7]

It was at this point that the originalist impulse began to turn into legal fundamentalism, though it did not occur instantaneously. As the religion scholar Martin E. Marty has explained, fundamentalism involves a multifaceted embrace of the past that expresses itself in a militant opposition to the modernization movements characteristic of contemporary life. Fundamentalism is, in Marty's words, "always reactive, reactionary" in attempting to return to "some earlier, presumably primal and pure, and thus normative stages in one's own sacred history." When thought of in that way, Marty stresses, fundamentalism is not an approach to texts or a commitment to a specific set of doctrines, though it involves both of those things, but a social phenomenon that rejects many aspects of the modern world.[8]

In legal circles, the fundamentalist approach began in the early twentieth century with the growth of so-called constitutional conservatism, which was dedicated to the suppression of many changes promoted by progressive politicians and jurists. As the political scientist Michael Lienesch has shown, constitutional conservatives mobilized after Woodrow Wilson's 1912 election to the presidency to inculcate a reverence for the Constitution among the people as an antidote to changes within American society. Working through such elite civic organizations as the National Security League (NSL), the National Association of Constitutional Government, and the American Bar Association, constitutional conservatives sought to brand their arguments as "non-partisan" and even "non-political" so as to avoid, in the words of Robert McElroy from the NSL, "even the appearance of being reactionary."[9]

Yet they were undeniably reactionary. The goal of constitutional conservatism was, according to Lienesch, "to create a campaign to educate citizens in the fundamentals of the American Constitution, thereby instilling patriotism in the general public and inoculating it against radicalism and progressive reform." That goal, in turn, required defining the Constitution in a way that supported conservative legal doctrine and that promoted what might be called the conservative political disposition among the American citizenry. Constitutional conservatives boasted a reverence for the Constitution as a sacred political text. They often quoted Gladstone's description of the Constitution as "the most wonderful work ever struck off at a given time by the brain and purpose of man." Their reverence for the Constitution, and their belief that it was perfect as a national governing document, made them critical of amendments, particularly those made during the Progressive Era that allowed for an income tax, that required US senators to be elected directly by the people, that allowed for the national prohibition of alcohol (although there was some disagreement here), and that gave women the right to vote. Constitutional conservatives often characterized their reverence for the Constitution in explicitly religious terms, speaking of "the articles of our political faith," "our holy of holies," and our "pillar of cloud by day and of fire by night." As James M. Beck, one of the leading constitutional conservatives, explained, reverence was necessary because "if free government is to function, man must have a deep and abiding respect akin to a religious feeling for the authority of the state."[10]

One thing that constitutional conservatives did not do, though, is to put forward a theory of judicial interpretation. Although they believed that the Constitution had conservative political import, and although they asserted that progressive talk about changing time and circumstance undermined the Constitution's general framework, they still did not take the next step of laying out a theory of original meaning to enforce judicial restraint. Part of the reason was simple: the threats to the Constitution were not, at the time, coming primarily from the judiciary. They were coming from politicians and through political parties that could, constitutional conservatives hoped, be fought through traditional political means.[11]

Their perspective would change with the Great Depression and, especially, with the election of Franklin Delano Roosevelt to the presidency. Roosevelt followed the progressive idea in upholding the notion of a living constitution. But he took it much farther than progressives had previously been able to go. Throughout the 1932 campaign, he argued that the crisis of the Depression revealed just how much the nation had transformed since the time of the founding and just how much the government needed to change to meet those challenges. He told the crowd at the Democratic National Convention that he was not one of those "who squint at the future with their faces turned toward the past, and who feel no responsibility to the demands of the new time." That new time, he said, required "a new deal," a different arrangement between the government and the people. Although he declined at that point to specify what the new arrangement might be, his dedication to a modernist political sensibility was quite apparent. He was calling the party to be, he told them, "prophets of a new order."[12]

Once in office, Roosevelt set about bringing the new order into effect. The New Deal, in all its various programs, simply assumed that the full power of government needed to be brought to bear in order to battle the Depression. The scope of governmental innovation, with its alphabet soup of new agencies, promised to transform the framework of government in profound ways. Conservatives were despondent. In a letter written the summer after Roosevelt's election, Beck confessed his fears that the movement for constitutional conservatism was, now, "hopelessly lost." A few years later, in a speech for the anti–New Deal organization the American Liberty League, he lamented the widespread belief "that truths are only relative and conditioned upon time and circumstance." Such thinking had allowed men like Roosevelt to abandon the "eternal verities" of the Constitution and led "to the unceasing destruction of its basic principles."[13]

To the extent that constitutional conservatives had any bulwark against the New Deal, it was the US Supreme Court. And initially that bulwark held, with Roosevelt at one point threatening to pack the court in order to get his way. The court-packing effort failed. But beginning in 1937 and growing in intensity over time, the court acceded to the new political reality by moving in two directions that outraged conservatives. It signed off on various liberal economic measures by adopting an expansive reading of the commerce clause, which allowed Congress to regulate interstate commerce and, by implication, to regulate business practices that affected the nation as a whole. Shortly thereafter, it decided to conduct, in its words, "a more searching judicial inquiry" into political arrangements that negatively affected religious, national, and racial minorities.[14]

It was the latter commitment that drove the Supreme Court, starting in 1938 and intensifying through the 1940s, into what critics called an activist attempt to change American society. The court elaborated what it meant by a "more searching judicial inquiry" by applying various parts of the Bill of Rights to the states, often for the first time, in an attempt to curb state-level discrimination. In 1953, with the beginning of the Warren court, the trend intensified still further. The court's decision in *Brown v. Board of Education* (1954), and then in the many follow-up decisions throughout the decade, took it deeper and deeper into regulating state and local communities. By the 1960s, the trend went into overdrive. The commitment of the court to protect civil liberties had led it into increasing legal thickets, to which it responded by hacking away at large portions of settled law that had, it argued, sustained illiberal and illegitimate policies for much of American history. The modernizing impulse within the court made it into one of the central sites for the liberalization of American public life. Within a decade it overturned prayer and Bible-reading in schools, struck down laws regulating contraception, declared a general right of privacy, rejected laws that prohibited obscenity, quashed antimiscegenation laws, and more. It continued the campaign against segregated schooling that it had begun with *Brown v. Board*. The entire program was staggering in its scope and in its pace of change, a forthright attempt to apply the Constitution in a way that recognized the new realities of the twentieth century.[15]

Although the political loss that constitutional conservatives felt was tough, the court's abandonment left them in frenzy. A new generation of conservatives grew up fulminating, in the words of Robert Bork, against the court's overthrow of "constitutional text and structure, judicial precedent, and the history that gives our rights life, rootedness, and meaning." And it was in that environment that conservatives began to take the reverence for the Constitution, which earlier constitutional conservatives had hoped would motivate the electorate, and to turn it into an originalist theory of judicial interpretation in order to hold back the court.[16]

Led by Raoul Berger, Robert Bork, and, to a lesser extent, William H. Rehnquist, originalists asserted throughout the 1970s that the modernist impulse within American law was entirely wrongheaded. In contrast to liberal constitutionalists, who said that they were merely adapting the Constitution for a modern age, originalists maintained that the Constitution did not grow. Its meaning was fixed at the time in which it was drafted, and the goal of interpretation was to recognize the limits inherent in a fixed meaning. If judges would simply remember that fact, the process of judging was simple. A jurist sought to understand what the framers had meant in particular clauses at the time the Constitution was drafted—they sought, in Bork's words, to extract what "the Framers intended to project" with a particular clause—and then, once they had done so, they applied that rule to the case and decided accordingly. But because the court had failed to exercise such rigor and restraint, originalists complained, new rights were invented in almost every term and the government continued to grow. Only a return to the original intention of the Founders could hold back the unchecked power of government through the maintenance of constitutionally established boundaries.[17]

Yet, at least initially, originalism failed to overcome a lingering air of disrepute. It often went unnoticed outside of academic theorizing, and when the theory did break into public debate, it did so in unsavory ways. In 1977, for example, Raoul Berger published *Government by Judiciary*, which took issue with the Warren court's reading of the Fourteenth Amendment and asserted that the framers of that amendment did not intend to forbid segregated schooling or, really, any sort of segregation at all. Many of the decisions that flowed out of the Warren court, including *Brown v. Board*, were wrong.[18]

In the resulting controversy, critics of originalism smelled blood. Legal scholar Paul Brest, reviewing the book in the *New York Times*, noted that Berger was in the position of condemning nearly every important decision involving the Fourteenth Amendment since it was enacted in 1866. The frank rejection of settled law was startling enough. But it was a certain intellectual sloppiness, an inability to specify precisely how the original intention of the framers was to be applied to a later period or even why it should be, that Brest found particularly disturbing. Instead of a rigorous method or even a reasoned argument, Brest claimed, Berger offered "a collection of quotations more or less favoring the author's view" and called it historical research. Other writers made similar points, questioning the basic historical integrity of Berger's analysis.[19]

But in spite of the criticism, originalism was gaining ground in conservative circles. It fed into conservatives' grievance with the political direction of the past seventy years and promised a method by which conservatives could mobilize voters beyond their base and, hopefully, to restrain the court. It did so by offering a story, ubiquitous among fundamentalists, that true principles were once upheld but had been subverted at some point in the past. The exact moment of betrayal varied—it was either in the Progressive Era, or during the New Deal, or in the 1960s, or maybe all of the above—but the story suggested that what was required was a recommitment to core values and a return to faithfulness in order to preserve the political community. Only by honoring what James Beck had called the "eternal verities" first put forward by the framers could the original genius be preserved.[20]

Yet the call of renewal was a partial one, in keeping with a dynamic within fundamentalism. As Martin Marty has said, fundamentalist leaders almost always deal in a selective recuperation, picking and choosing among fundamentals, because "not all such fundamentals are equally serviceable for mass-movement formation." The past was messy, and in the American political context, some fundamentals were especially not acceptable. Constitutional originalists did not call for a return, for example, to the framers' original ideas about slavery, women's political participation, the treatment of children and the insane, or other such issues. That was why Raoul Berger's book was so controversial. It forthrightly accepted the illiberalism of the past and plunged ahead with an originalist argument anyhow.[21]

In response, academic critics began sharpening knives. In a widely influential law article published in 1980 that set the stage for much future critique, Brest expanded on his criticism of Berger by taking aim at originalism more broadly. The problem, as he saw it, was with originalism's claim that it offered a clear interpretive method. The method begged several questions. Brest pointed out, for example, that in claiming that original intention controlled subsequent interpretation, originalists presumed that there was a singular intention for a collective enterprise. In fact, various individuals who took part in constitutional debate had different intentions in a way that made it difficult if not impossible to determine what their collective intention might be. As such, originalism failed to acknowledge cases in which the framers adopted language that cloaked interpretive disagreement behind an agreed-upon but vague set of words. It further failed, Brest argued, to provide a basis by which to apply the purposeful use of open-ended language that some framers hoped would be malleable over time. These collected problems were fatal, Brest thought. Although the theory of original intention sought to provide straightforward interpretive rules, it offered no way to work through historical complications without denying the simplicity that originalism was supposed to provide.[22]

But that was not its actual purpose, which became clear once Ronald Reagan took office in 1981 and especially once Edwin Meese became the attorney general in 1985. Reagan had long been concerned about what he considered the drift away from the genius of the Founders' vision of constitutional government. By the time he achieved the presidency, constitutional originalism had morphed into a central tenet of the conservative political revolution. Reagan then used his power of legal appointment to further that conservative agenda. In 1986, for example, when Chief Justice Warren Burger retired, Reagan nominated Associate Justice William Rehnquist to the position. Although Rehnquist was not entirely consistent, he did advocate, as he had said in one 1977 opinion, for understanding the Constitution in the way that "the Framers obviously meant it to apply." Reagan's nomination of Rehnquist then opened up another seat, which he filled by nominating Antonin Scalia, an even more outspoken originalist. Although Scalia would later call himself a "faint-hearted originalist," because he could not always bring himself to roll back two centuries of interpretation when he thought the courts had departed from the original text, he did believe that originalism provided a clear plan for judges. Since words had a limited range of meaning, Scalia argued, the judge read the law, understood the case, and responded accordingly. There was little discretion for judges, and most matters were very clear. As Scalia would later say, "The originalist, if he does not have all the answers, has many of them."[23]

At Rehnquist and Scalia's swearing-in ceremony in September 1986, Reagan made explicit his purpose in nominating them. Their appointment offered an opportunity to reflect, he told the audience, on "the inspired wisdom we call our Constitution." And he looked forward to the beginning of "a time of renewal in the great constitutional system that our forefathers gave us." The agenda continued the next year, when he nominated one of the formulators of originalism, Robert Bork, for the next Supreme Court vacancy. The nomination did not go well. Bork's criticism of *Brown v. Board*, his naked contempt for the Warren court, and his general intellectual temperament doomed his candidacy. But originalism's new salience in American political life was now apparent.[24]

In response, liberals began to probe the intellectual and political impulses that gave rise to originalist theory. Some of the highest-profile criticisms came from jurists. William Brennan of the US Supreme Court criticized the jurisprudence of original intention as "arrogance cloaked as humility" because it sought to overturn decades of decisions on often inconclusive historical evidence. Others went farther. Richard Posner, a Reagan nominee on the Seventh Circuit Court of Appeals, pointed out that the rules of originalism offered plenty of room for a judge to arrive at any conclusion that he wished, regardless of the originalist rhetoric about judicial limits. What originalism actually was, he said, was "a summons to holy war" that had a narrow conception of constitutional faithfulness and that sought to excommunicate everyone else who had other ideas.[25]

It also suffered from a categorical confusion, critics pointed out. In speaking of original intent, both originalists and some of their critics tended to mush together various and often-discrete levels of meaning. One could speak of the original intent of the framers, the original meaning of the text itself at the time in which it was written, or the original understandings of then-contemporary readers of the text, particularly the ratifiers in the state ratification conventions. The first was a subjective sort of meaning. The second was semantic. The third was cultural or perhaps intersubjective and arose out of the readers' response to the text. As Jack N. Rakove pointed out in his Pulitzer Prize–winning book, *Original Meanings*, these distinct interpretive registers might not always align. The framers might have had one set of intentions (or not), but various people interpreted the text itself in wildly different ways at the time of ratification. Current-day interpreters then ought not speak of original meaning but, as the title of Rakove's book suggested, original meanings that shifted depending on the interpretive context.[26]

Rakove was essentially arguing for the contextual approach to understanding meaning that has become the dominant mode within intellectual history. As Rakove would later say, "the only possible way in which one could satisfactorily reconstruct the original meaning of a constitutional text must necessarily involve an essentially historical inquiry." But this was what originalists almost never did. Nor could they. To turn to intellectual history, as legal historian William W. Fisher pointed out in 1997, would have impossibly muddied originalist jurisprudence. In addition to exposing the various meanings of the Constitution that were present when it was drafted, the contextual approach tended to highlight "the differences between the contexts in which provisions were drafted and the contexts in which they are to be interpreted." Put simply, the United States at the end of the twentieth century was very different from what it had been at the end of the eighteenth. Being aware of the disjunction between time and context thereby made the originalist judge's task even more difficult, if not impossible. He had to translate ideas from one context into another in a way that would necessarily depart from the framers' intentions simply because they could not be said to have had intentions toward something that did not exist when the Constitution was framed. In cases involving, for example, the Internet, jurists were forced to draw upon, depending on the issue, the eighteenth-century law concerning personal papers, or free speech, or search and seizure, none of which really conformed to a means of electronic communication facilitated by a network of computers, whose technical, institutional, and legal infrastructure did not exist in the eighteenth century. The only solution then would have been to adopt the notion that the Constitution's meaning changed according to time and circumstance, which was the exact conclusion that originalists sought to avoid.[27]

The effect of such criticism was crippling to originalist theory, exposing it as, variously, a political approach that pretended to be legally neutral, an intellectually incoherent set of claims, or, simply, as an expression of rage against the modern world. The fundamentalist origins of originalism were all too apparent, though they were still often misdiagnosed as an incoherent approach to texts. But because acknowledging these criticisms would have been fatal to originalist thought, rather than making a more careful historical turn as many critics had urged, in the mid-nineties originalists responded by moving in a different direction entirely. They remade originalism into a form of textual analysis that marched alternatively under the banner of "semantic originalism" or "public meaning originalism."[28]

The goal seemed to be to turn originalism into a respectable mode of academic inquiry. Yet the result was no less fundamentalist than earlier versions of originalism, even if it was more constrained in its approach. The new originalism continued the idea of an authoritative text that was incapable of evolution. Most crucially, it also adopted a consistently anti-hermeneutical posture that tended to elide the difference between past and present. The core idea behind the new originalism was that language is an intersubjective phenomenon that relies on shared meanings generated by the objective rules of grammar and syntax. A new originalist would seek to interpret the text according to its original meaning by figuring out "the communicative content" of a constitutional utterance. "As competent speakers and writers of the natural language English," the new originalist Lawrence B. Solum has explained, "the Framers are likely to have understood that the best way to convey their intentions would be to state them clearly in language that would be grasped by the officials and citizens to whom the constitutional text was addressed." The goal then was to study the framers' words with great care in order to parse what they might have meant at the time.[29]

The approach did not require historical inquiry or contextual analysis of the sort done by intellectual historians, new originalists maintained. To the extent that they acknowledged context, or what they called the "contextual enrichment" of an utterance, it was again as a linguistic process that disambiguated multiple linguistic meanings through analysis of other parts of the constitutional text or through other texts that existed at the time of the drafting. It did not usually involve looking at what the actual people who debated or ratified the Constitution thought, because doing so would expose a range of meanings that, again, would not be useful in judging. In other words, as Rakove has recently suggested, new originalists steadfastly refused to recognize the Constitution as a political text that was the product of disagreement and compromise during the drafting process and then subject to further disagreement during the ratification and initial amendment processes. The new originalists read the Constitution, above all, as a binding legal text whose meaning was clear and must be fixed. Then they went about finding that meaning.[30]

But the new originalist reformulation has not quelled criticism, particularly in the last few years. In 2013, the early American historian Saul Cornell published a blistering attack on what he saw as the simpleminded and intellectually disingenuous method of the new originalists. Having written a book on the Anti-Federalists, Cornell was sensitive to the interpretive disagreement of the founding era. His sensitivity led him to point out that contemporary intellectual historians reject a core assumption held by all originalists, namely that cultures are so fully integrated that it is possible to speak of a collective mind or a shared set of meaning and values, which would be necessary in order to achieve a return to those values. Because originalists make such a foundational error, Cornell argued, they "gather evidence in an arbitrary and highly selective fashion" that only reinforces their faulty assumptions.[31]

Cornell suggested that if originalists wished to discover original meaning or, more accurately, meanings, they ought to look to the leading practitioners of intellectual history as a methodological guide. He pointed in particular to David Hollinger, who has argued that intellectual historians study communities of discourse that are united by a shared set of questions rather than answers; James Kloppenberg, who has argued that intellectual historians situate texts in a shifting array of contexts and seek to understand the dizzying range of intellectual practice and interpretation at various times; and Quentin Skinner, who used the speech-act theory of J. L. Austin to suggest that meaning was determined by some combination of authorial intention and the limited range of words at a particular moment. Because originalists refused to do any of this, Cornell concluded, originalism in all forms was a "flight from historical reality" and a "constitutional scam."[32]

In 2015, Lawrence Solum responded to Cornell's criticism in a long article asserting that intellectual history had only limited relevance to originalist practice. In the process, he confirmed the essentially fundamentalist quality of originalism in its denial of historical time. Throughout, Solum distinguished between constitutional interpretation (when a judge determines the communicative content of a text) and constitutional construction (when a judge develops legal doctrine that applies to a particular case). The distinction is an important one, because it suggests that constitutional interpretation is not really interpretive but an empiricist exercise with an objective set of findings. In that process intellectual history might be useful, Solum conceded, but a quick survey of the works of Hollinger, Kloppenberg, and Skinner led Solum to conclude that "the contextualist methodology of intellectual history ... is underspecified, if viewed as a method for determining the communicative content of the constitutional text." Working with an analytic precision that he thought intellectual history lacks, Solum then laid down a set of distinctions and methodological rules for interpretation that would, he believed, constrain the judge from bringing his or her own perspectives to the process. Yet Solum ignored or rejected Cornell's claim that constitutional terminology was contested in the founding era. He presumed instead a stable linguistic meaning that stretched across two centuries, except for isolated cases of what he called "semantic drift."[33]

Solum is not alone among new originalists in his persistent refusal to see the difference between the past and the present or to see disagreement among people in the past. As the legal scholar Stephen Griffin has recently pointed out, "The essence of contemporary originalism is the privileging of evidence from the past in the determination of constitutional meaning over evidence from the present." But in committing themselves to that foundational assumption, Griffin continued, originalists still have not "come to grips with the idea that there are better and worse ways to do history." In many cases, precisely because they assume that the past and the present are basically alike or, if there is a difference, that the past was simpler and with less disagreement than the present, their attempts at history are facile, ad hoc, and selective, or they rely on contested linguistic theories rather than historical knowledge to justify an elaborate set of anti-hermeneutic rules.[34]

Their unwillingness to make any kind of persuasive historical turn is suggestive of the more fundamental issue. The problem, at bottom, comes down to an inadequate historical consciousness and a discomfort with time and change. As Thurgood Marshall, the nation's first black Supreme Court justice, explained in 1987 on the two-hundredth anniversary of the Constitution, "When contemporary Americans cite 'The Constitution,' they invoke a concept that is vastly different from what the framers barely began to construct two centuries ago." The search for original meaning then could only be problematic because the original Constitution was, Marshall said, "defective from the start." It required "several amendments, a civil war, and momentous social transformation to attain the system of constitutional government, and its respect for individual freedoms and human rights, that we hold as fundamental today."[35]

Intellectual historians, like all historians, recognize this reality, which is why they have tended to be some of the strongest critics of originalism. They know that the past is different from the present; that time is corrosive of meanings, arrangements, and cultural ideas at particular moments; that its corrosiveness leaves only remnants from the past that historians must pick over to make sense of now-lost worlds; and that the reconstruction of the past is always, as a result, only provisional and partial. As such there is not, historians have suggested, a set of interpretive rules to be followed by which original meaning will be revealed, since that meaning was contested at the founding and has evolved over the centuries. But originalists have been seduced, in the words of the intellectual historian Daniel T. Rodgers, by "the idea of penetrating time, folding history over upon itself so that one could slip out of its complexities." That is the ultimate fundamentalist position. It is an attractive but reductive solution. And like most reductive solutions, it continually crashes against the complications of the world.[36]

NOTES

1. On originalism as a form of fundamentalism see, for example, Peter J. Smith and Robert W. Tuttle, "Biblical Literalism and Constitutional Originalism," *Notre Dame Law Review* 86 (March 2001): 693–763; Cass R. Sunstein, *Radicals in Robes: Why Extreme Right-Wing Courts Are Wrong for America* (New York: Basic Books, 2005), xiii–xiv; Morton J. Horwitz, "The Meaning of the Bork Nomination in American Constitutional History," *University of Pittsburgh Law Review* 50 (Winter 1989): 663–64; Johnathan O'Neill, "Constitutional Maintenance and Religious Sensibility in the 1920s: Rethinking the Constitutionalist Response to Progressivism," *Journal of Church and State* 51 (Winter 2009): 24–51.

2. See Marbury v. Madison, 5 U.S. 137 (1803).

3. For examples of this tendency see David Sehat, *The Jefferson Rule: How the Founding Fathers Became Infallible and Our Politics Inflexible* (New York: Simon & Schuster, 2015), 3–105.

4. Henry Clay to James F. Conover, May 1, 1830, in *The Papers of Henry Clay*, ed. James F. Hopkins (Lexington: University Press of Kentucky, 1959–), 8:200 (first quotation); Abraham Lincoln, "Address at Cooper Institute, New York City," February 27, 1860, in *The Collected Works of Abraham Lincoln*, ed. Roy P. Basler (New Brunswick, NJ: Rutgers University Press, 1953–1955), 3:534–35 (second quotation), 535 (third and fourth quotations); Ulysses S. Grant, *Personal Memoirs of U. S. Grant* (New York: C. L. Webster, 1885), 1:221 (all remaining quotations). On the overlapping methods of constitutional interpretation see Johnathan O'Neill, *Originalism in American Law and Politics: A Constitutional History* (Baltimore: Johns Hopkins University Press, 2005), 4–5.

5. Janet Podell and Steven Azovin, eds., *Speeches of the American Presidents* (New York: H. W. Wilson, 1988), 325 (first two quotations); Theodore Roosevelt to Hugo Münsterberg, February 8, 1916, in *The Letters of Theodore Roosevelt*, ed. Elting E. Morison and Alfred D. Chandler (Cambridge, MA: Harvard University Press, 1951–1954), 8:1018 (third quotation).

6. Woodrow Wilson, *Constitutional Government in the United States* (New York: Columbia University Press, 1908), 46 (first two quotations), 57 (third quotation).

7. Samuel D. Warren and Louis D. Brandeis, "The Right to Privacy," *Harvard Law Review* 4 (December 1890): 193.

8. Martin E. Marty, "Fundamentalism as a Social Phenomenon," *Bulletin of the American Academy of Arts and Sciences* 42 (November 1988): 20.

9. Michael Lienesch, "Creating Constitutional Conservatism," *Polity* 48 (July 2016): 390.

10. Ibid., 391 (first quotation), 402–3 (second quotation), 404 (third through fifth quotations), 405 (sixth quotation).

11. See ibid., 394–98.

12. Franklin Delano Roosevelt, "The Governor Accepts the Nomination for the Presidency," July 2, 1932, in *The Public Papers and Addresses of Franklin D. Roosevelt*, ed. Samuel I. Rosenman (New York: Random House, 1938–1950), 1:649 (first quotation), 659 (second and third quotations).

13. Lienesch, "Creating Constitutional Conservatism," 411 (first quotation); Beck, *What Is the Constitution between Friends?* (Washington, DC: American Liberty League, 1935), 2 (fourth quotation), 4 (second and third quotations).

14. United States v. Carolene Products Co., 304 U.S. 144 (1938), at 152n4. For a longer explanation of this shift see David Sehat, *The Myth of American Religious Freedom*, updated ed. (New York: Oxford University Press, 2015), 216–26.

15. See Brown v. Board of Education, 347 U.S. 483 (1954); Torcaso v. Watkins, 367 U.S. 488 (1961); Engel v. Vitale, 370 U.S. 421 (1962); School District of Abington Township v. Schempp, 374 U.S. 203 (1963); United States v. Seeger, 380 U.S. 163 (1965); Griswold v. Connecticut, 381 U.S. 479 (1965); Loving v. Virginia, 388 U.S. 1 (1967); Stanley v. Georgia, 394 U.S. 557 (1969).

16. Robert H. Bork, *Tradition and Morality in Constitutional Law* (Washington, DC: American Enterprise Institute, 1984), 8.

17. Robert H. Bork, "The Constitution, Original Intent, and Economic Rights," *San Diego Law Review* 23 (July–August 1986): 826.

18. Raoul Berger, *Government by Judiciary: The Transformation of the Fourteenth Amendment* (Cambridge, MA: Harvard University Press, 1977).

19. Paul Brest, "Berger v. Brown et al.," *New York Times*, December 11, 1977. See also Robert M. Cover, "Books Considered," *New Republic*, January 14, 1978, 26–28; "An Exchange of Views: Raoul Berger and E. Richard Larson," *Nation*, February 25, 1978, 217–20; Robert J. Kaczorowski, review in *American Historical Review* 83 (June 1978): 811–12.

20. Beck, *What Is the Constitution between Friends?*, 4.

21. Marty, "Fundamentalism as a Social Phenomenon," 20.

22. Paul Brest, "The Misconceived Quest for the Original Understanding," *Boston University Law Review* 60 (March 1980): 204–38.

23. Trimble v. Gordon, 430 U.S. 762 (1977) at 777 (first quotation); Antonin Scalia, "Originalism: The Lesser Evil," *University of Cincinnati Law Review* 57, no. 3 (1989): 862 (second quotation); Antonin Scalia, *A Matter of Interpretation: Federal Courts and the Law: An Essay* (Princeton, NJ: Princeton University Press, 1997), 46 (third quotation). See also Edwin Meese III, "Interpreting the Constitution," in *Interpreting the Constitution: The Debate over Original Intent*, ed. Jack N. Rakove (Boston: Northeastern University Press, 1990), 13–21; Sehat, *Jefferson Rule*, 197–204.

24. Ronald Reagan, "Remarks at the Swearing-in Ceremony for William H. Rehnquist as Chief Justice and Antonin Scalia as Associate Justice of the Supreme Court of the United States," September 26, 1986, in *Public Papers of the Presidents of the United States: Ronald Reagan* (Washington, DC: Government Printing Office, 1982–1991), 1986:1270.

25. William J. Brennan Jr., "The Constitution of the United States: Contemporary Ratification," in Rakove, *Interpreting the Constitution*, 25; Richard A. Posner, "Bork and Beethoven," *Stanford Law Review* 42 (1990): 1369.

26. Jack N. Rakove, *Original Meanings: Politics and Ideas in the Making of the Constitution* (New York: Alfred A. Knopf, 1996). For an excellent account of the many different meanings ascribed to the Constitution at the time of ratification see Pauline Maier, *Ratification: The People Debate the Constitution, 1787–1788* (New York: Simon & Schuster, 2010).

27. Jack N. Rakove, "Joe the Ploughman Reads the Constitution, or, the Poverty of Public Meaning Originalism," *San Diego Law Review* 48 (May–June 2011): 577n11, 580 (first quotation); William W. Fisher III, "Texts and Contexts: The Application to American Legal History of the Methodologies of Intellectual History," *Stanford Law Review* 49 (May 1997): 1106 (second quotation).

28. For a helpful overview of originalism, old and new, see Keith E. Whittington, "Originalism: A Critical Introduction," *Fordham Law Review* 82 (November 2013): 375–409. The November 2013 issue of the *Fordham Law Review* prints several articles from a two-day symposium on the New Originalism and offers a good starting point for understanding the current state of second-wave originalist scholarship.

29. Lawrence B. Solum, "Originalism and Constitutional Construction," *Fordham Law Review* 82 (November 2013): 457 (first quotation), 462–67 (second and third quotations on 464). See also Randy E. Barnett, "Interpretation and Construction," *Harvard Journal of Law & Public Policy* 34 (Winter 2011): 66.

30. Solum, "Originalism and Constitutional Construction," 465 (quotation); Rakove, "Joe the Ploughman Reads the Constitution," 584–88. See also Fisher, "Texts and Contexts," 1103–8.

31. Saul Cornell, "Meaning and Understanding in the History of Constitutional Ideas: The Intellectual History Alternative to Originalism," *Fordham Law Review* 82 (November 2013): 724.

32. Ibid., 733 (first quotation), 740 (second quotation). Also see David Hollinger, "Historians and the Discourse of Intellectuals," in *In the American Province: Studies in the History and Historiography of Ideas* (Bloomington: Indiana University Press, 1985), 130–51; James T. Kloppenberg, "Thinking Historically: A Manifesto of Pragmatic Hermeneutics," *Modern Intellectual History* 9 (April 2012): 201–16; James Tully, ed., *Meaning and Context: Quentin Skinner and His Critics* (Princeton, NJ: Princeton University Press, 1988).

33. Lawrence B. Solum, "Intellectual History as Constitutional Theory," *Virginia Law Review* 101 (June 2015): 1156 (first quotation), 1160 (second quotation). See also two responses to Solum: G. Edward White, "Intellectual History and Constitutional Decision Making," *Virginia Law Review* 101 (June 2015): 1165–78; Saul Cornell, "Originalism as Thin Description: An Interdisciplinary Critique," *Fordham Law Review Res Gestae* 84 (2015–2016): 1–10. Jack M. Balkin has pointed out the porous boundary between constitutional interpretation and constitutional construction in a way that, to my mind, is subtly devastating for semantic originalism. See Jack M. Balkin, "The New Originalism and the Uses of History," *Fordham Law Review* 82 (November 2013): 641–719.

34. Stephen Griffin, "The New Originalism and Living Constitutionalism: A Reconsideration," *Balkinization*, August 11, 2015, http://balkin.blogspot.com/2015/08/the-new-originalism-and-living.html. Also see the forum "Historians and the New Originalism: Contextualism, Historicism, and Constitutional Meaning," in the December 2015 issue of *Fordham Law Review*, which has essays by Martin S. Flaherty, Saul Cornell, Jonathan Gienapp, Helen Irving, and Jack Rakove.

35. *Thurgood Marshall: His Speeches, Writings, Arguments, Opinions, and Reminiscences*, ed. Mark V. Tushnet (Chicago: Lawrence Hill Books, 2001), 282.

36. Daniel T. Rodgers, *Age of Fracture* (Cambridge, MA: Belknap Press of Harvard University Press, 2011), 241. One possible exception to the originalist disavowal of time is the so-called framework originalism or living originalism of Jack M. Balkin. Given the history of originalism, it is likely that Balkin's originalism is not really an originalism at all. But it is certainly not fundamentalist. See Jack M. Balkin, "Framework Originalism and the Living Constitution," *Northwestern University Law Review* 103 (Spring 2009): 549–614; Jack M. Balkin, *Living Originalism* (Cambridge, MA: Harvard University Press, 2011).

3

FREEDOM'S JUST ANOTHER WORD?

The Intellectual Trajectories of the 1960s

Kevin M. Schultz

When, in 1970, Janis Joplin sang the iconic lines of "Me and Bobby McGee," she was singing a wistful tune of good times gone. The song, written by Kris Kristofferson and Fred Foster and first recorded by Roger Miller in 1969, tells the story of a pair of drifters who hitch a ride through the American South on their way to California. The pair are drawn closer and closer to one another through the journey, but Bobby eventually tires of the freewheeling life and settles down in Salinas, California, leaving the narrator/singer to regret his or her addiction to the freedom of the road: she (or he) would "trade all of my tomorrows for one single yesterday" but knows that the past is the past, the good times are gone, the journey is over. One can hear the wistful note in the song's most remembered line: "Freedom's just another word for nothin' left to lose."[1]

Freedom and love, love and freedom: the two themes that arise most prominently in the intellectual history of the 1960s, with, as Bobby McGee learns, freedom's triumph equaling love's demise. In general, the 1960s have been well served by historians. Scholars have done admirable and often excellent work on many of the decade's most vital events: women's liberation, the Vietnam War, the civil rights movement and the black power movement that followed. Scholars have examined the role of music, of youth culture, of suburban conformity and its relative white anticonformist anxiety. They have looked at the decade's poetry, its literature, its language, its television, its movies, all in order to tell us what kinds of change happened throughout the decade. They have also, now as much as anything else, examined the conservative backlashes to the various visions for a new world proposed by those demanding so much change so quickly.[2]

For intellectual historians, though, if we take our tasks holistically, our job is slightly different, and indeed, is twofold. First, alongside the other kinds of historians, we are supposed to analyze and explain the ideas and intellectuals of the period, from Thomas Kuhn to Susan Sontag, from "general systems theory" to *Silent Spring*. In this, our work is similar to social historians studying social movements and political historians studying politics. And intellectual historians have done a good job on this front. Books and articles appear frequently detailing the life and lessons of many of the key thinkers and ideas of the 1960s. Betty Friedan has had her day in the sun, as has Daniel Bell, W. W. Rostow, William F. Buckley Jr., Amiri Baraka, Mary McCarthy, Hannah Arendt, Milton Friedman, William Sloane Coffin, the Berrigan brothers, and many, many more. Themes and events like authenticity, modernization, and decolonization have also been well covered.[3]

But it's in a second realm that intellectual historians have done less sparkling work. Quite simply, this second realm pertains to our responsibility to come up with a large-scale and systemic way to understand the dramatic changes that took place during any given period. Yes, lots happened in the 1960s (and in almost any decade one can think of). But what were the large-scale changes that help us make sense of any broad collection of those more particular transformations, of, say, women's liberation, the black freedom struggle, the anti–Vietnam War protests, and the return of laissez-faire economics? And, more than that, how can we historians offer some synthetic way to explain *why* those changes took place when they did, and in the way they did?

This gap is evident in the titles of the intellectual histories of the period. For example, the best intellectual history of the period is probably Howard Brick's *Age of Contradiction*. It is a remarkable book that manages to be both brief and encyclopedic at the same time. But what it does not offer is a synthetic way to understand the underlying changes that mark the decade. The title of Brick's book, for example, is not terribly helpful. *Age of Contradiction* could work for almost any decade at which one chooses to point a finger. And the book's central premise—that a wide variety of binary opposite ideas formed the ideological underpinnings of the decade—is too diffuse to offer much explanatory power.[4]

One potential model of the kind of history I am suggesting we write for the 1960s comes from several generations earlier. In 1959, Henry F. May published his now-classic work, *The End of American Innocence: A Study in the First Years of Our Time*. The task May set for himself in that book was to study the changing set of assumptions held by most American literary and political intellectuals in 1912 or so, and then again after World War I. He, of course, tied together structure and superstructure in the way they must be tied together, aligning political and social history with that of ideas. But the book focused mostly on grasping the water in which most literary intellectual Americans swam, the ideas that grounded their thoughts and even, if one is bold enough to say it, their existence. It described, in short, the basic assumptions possessed by most literary and political elites in American life throughout the 1910s. And to know those assumptions allows us to understand at a deep level their actions, their politics, and their art.[5]

That such an overarching book does not exist for the 1960s is troubling for several reasons. For one thing, many other periods or eras or decades (a marker seemingly especially useful for twentieth-century historians) are clearly marked by identifiable events. One, for instance, cannot write about the 1930s in good conscience without describing the Great Depression. The 1940s are necessarily dominated by the Second World War. The 1970s are punctuated by the country's declining economic status in the world. In the 1960s, however, despite the fact there were indeed wars and troubling economic signs, the changes that took place during the decade were not overwhelmingly consumed by those facts. The economy remained strong throughout most of the decade, and wealth was divided as equally as it had ever been in the history of the United States. The Vietnam War, while clearly visible in many of the battle lines drawn throughout the decade, was not nearly as all-consuming to the life of the nation as the Second World War had been. This latter fact was by design, of course, as the federal government never initiated the kind of all-out war the country witnessed during World War I or World War II. Regardless, one could plausibly conclude that the changes of the decade emerged more in the realm of superstructure than in structure, and this, one would think, would be where intellectual historians could do their best work. If the changes weren't wrought by war or economic collapse, what provoked them?

The lack of any overarching intellectual explanation for the period is even more ironic considering that so many of the writers of the 1960s were so greatly preoccupied with defining their own intellectual atmosphere. One can't flip through an article by Norman Mailer, Joan Didion, Gore Vidal, Truman Capote, or James Baldwin without encountering a diatribe against broader currents within American life. Baldwin wrote essays and novels practically begging, nay demanding, that Americans push beyond their sense of self-congratulation in order to eradicate what he called "the national innocence."[6] Norman Mailer was preoccupied to the point of exhaustion with the set of assumptions buried inside postwar America, and although he and Baldwin differed on what each man deemed the root causes of those assumptions, both men were remarkably aligned in their diagnoses.[7] Betty Friedan similarly sought to illuminate the societal assumptions that curtailed the possibilities of half the nation.[8] Surely there is plenty of raw material, then, to help us better understand the set of assumptions that provoked so many calls for change so suddenly, and then if those assumptions changed during the decade: from what to what, and why?

It is also well worth noting that it is an open question if historians can do this kind of work anymore. Is it possible to define the intellectual contours of an age, any age, that most citizens of a nation, state, city, culture, subgroup, etc., agree upon? The single best exploration of this question came, properly enough, from an intellectual historian. In 1986, Thomas Bender wrote a thoughtful piece in the *Journal of American History* titled "Wholes and Parts: The Need for Synthesis in American History." In the face of the numerous "new" histories that had proliferated since the 1960s, Bender worried that, with the rise of group-based social histories, "what we have gotten are the parts, all richly described." Unfortunately, though, because of this newfound focus, "we get no image of the whole, and no suggestions about how the parts might go together or even whether they are intended to go together."[9] Bender then called for a better national history, with the idea of the nation understood "as the ever changing, always contingent outcome of a continuing contest among social groups and ideas for the power to define public culture, thus the nation itself."[10] Focusing on the ranges of acceptable ideas within public culture, then, with an understanding that they are always contested and being challenged, could be one way intellectual historians might be able to conceptualize the range of possibilities in American thought at any given moment, to make a whole out of all those parts that constitute a society. Whereas Henry May focused largely on literary intellectuals, Bender's urge was that historians focus on public intellectuals, policy makers, academics, and other public figures, suggesting that, by studying them collectively, it might be possible to illuminate the set of assumptions that grounded the public culture of an era. And by doing that, we might be able to add up all those parts to get a sense of the whole, keeping in mind, of course, that public culture is always contested until, ultimately, it breaks, and the set of assumptions changes.

The beginnings of such work for the 1960s might be to pick up on May's structural model and imagine, with May, a triptych of assumptions underlying postwar America, before all the transformations took place (keeping in mind of course that these assumptions were always contested).[11]

The central plank of this postwar, pre-1960s order might be a profound belief in rational thought. Americans knew that problems were out there in the world, sure, but the public culture operated in a way that was premised on the fact that these problems could be detected, debated, and then coolly dispatched with technological precision. Give President Eisenhower a map, and he would fund the interstate highway system that systematically carved up the nation into a variety of straight lines, with highways ending in 5 going north–south and those ending in 0 going east–west. Give Robert Moses a map of New York City and he would rationalize the best place for a road, a ballpark, a concert hall, regardless of whether there were organically grown neighborhoods there already. Technology was a handmaiden to this lionization of rational thought. The country had built the atomic bomb just in time to win the war. Polio had been beaten. Open-heart surgeries were now available. Who was going to say we couldn't get to the moon by the end of the decade, or develop faster, more efficient automobiles, or be able to travel across the globe in just a few hours? Yes, humankind, when freed from the dogmas and mythologies of the past, could be systematized and improved upon to the point of near perfection. As Robert Moses memorably put it, "Our usual method of remedying wrongs is to create new agencies ... to provide some service for which there was a popular demand or *to complete the perfection of mankind.*" Through their agencies, bureaucratic rational thinkers could "complete the perfection of mankind." And, in part, modern New York City owes its shape and texture to Moses's postwar vision. Rational thought was the central plank of the postwar triptych.[12]

The second article of faith in postwar, pre-1960s American life—let's put it on the right of our triptych—was a strong belief in the moral righteousness of corporate capitalism. Following the Great Depression, it wasn't communism that swept into power (as Karl Marx imagined it would have), but rather a crew of government bureaucrats who showed up to save the day, arriving in Washington, DC, to rationalize the economy and save capitalism from itself. They eventually succeeded (with the help of the Second World War), but as they did, they realized along with John Maynard Keynes the vital importance of the federal government in tipping the scales when things looked bad for corporate America. Understanding this, they all became Keynesians, and a friendly kind of corporate capitalism carried the day. When there was a slump in the economy in 1953, for example, the first measure President Eisenhower took was to increase defense spending. The whole economy was buoyed. Friendly relations between the government and corporate America became vital to the life of the nation. Taxes were high, sure, but so was economic security. Corporations could trust that the federal government would step in when things might be heading south, so corporate leaders chafed at but did not actively discredit contributing to the commonweal. This is what president of General Motors and newly named secretary of defense Charles Erwin Wilson suggested when he said he couldn't imagine how any decision he made on behalf of the country would be detrimental to General Motors, "because for years I thought what was good for the country was good for General Motors, and vice versa." A friendly kind of corporate capitalism, with high taxes and high economic security, was a key pillar of postwar America's primary set of assumptions.[13]

The third assumption within postwar, pre-1960s American life—and let's put this one on the left of our triptych—is what I have come to call the Rules. The Rules were easy to locate if one was looking. They were the norms of society, the rules of acceptable public culture. Proper Americans were supposed to dress properly, which meant a collared shirt and tie for men, and dresses for women, with sweaters or shirts whose necklines were well above the cleavage. Hemlines had to be modest, at the knee or below, and there were organizations that would help you understand that guideline more precisely if you needed help. Hair was to be cropped short for men, above the neck and ears. Women typically wore their hair long, but could get away with short hair if they looked and dressed like Audrey Hepburn, which is to say, still feminine. Most important, authority figures—husbands, bosses, politicians, clergymen—were to be respected and obeyed—even your school principal. Emotions were to be controlled and outbursts minimized, and always apologized for later. Adults were to be addressed as Mr. or Mrs., and treated with respect. Obedience was the key virtue.

There were more Rules, of course, and the list could continue. And the Rules were codified by a collection of organizations, through churches or Boy Scouts or Little League or charity organizations. And of course, buried within the Rules were the basic assumptions of society. Proper women were to be respected, but men were the strong caretakers, the primary, decision-making figures, rightfully in powerful positions. Anglo-Saxon Protestants, and their rules and authority, were to be unquestioned, or at least questioned with great care. White Americans were situated above African Americans and other minorities, not so much because they were biologically better but because they practiced the Rules better. Rights claims from outsiders often went unheeded if they violated the Rules. The Rules were easy to flout and poke fun of, but it carried consequences if one did so too brazenly. Challenges were therefore executed with minimal regularity.

As static as some of the Rules were, they did serve a purpose: to maintain a sense of common cause and common struggle in the national project. The Cold War looms heavily here, as perhaps the gilded framing around each image of our triptych. To step outside the norms of acceptable public culture was to risk being cast out beyond the pale, to be not taken seriously. And anyway, the assumptions seemed to be working for many Americans. The economy was mostly strong throughout the 1950s and early 1960s, and wealth was distributed fairly equally. The educational system was the beacon of Western liberal achievement, available to most, and at very little cost, supported as ever by the commonweal. Social mobility was possible. And increasingly, minorities like Catholics and Jews were earning a seat at the welcome table, which was, as a beacon of power holders in American life, slowly expanding to include some minorities.

Throughout the 1960s, each of the assumptions in our triptych came under attack. Some were challenged completely, some just a bit. But after the 1960s, the set of assumptions that most Americans lived with were quite different. The two obvious questions that follow, then, are: first, why did they change when they changed? And second, what replaced them?

The second question is easier to answer than the first. In short, what replaced the triptych of ideas were starker, more individualized versions of what came before. The Rules tumbled first. By the early 1970s, no one was surprised to see not just miniskirts but pants on a woman, or bearded men not just without neckties but maybe also without collars on their shirts, or without shirts at all. Coarse language appeared in public and in popular culture. Pornography was legal to view and participate in if you were older than eighteen. Perhaps most profoundly, sexual behavior changed, as people waited until they were older to get married, but nevertheless had more premarital sex. And anyway, contraceptives were legal and widespread by the end of the decade, validating the notion that sex could be had just for pleasure, without procreative consequences. Meanwhile, and just as profoundly, many Americans openly flouted convention. A popular bumper sticker appeared: "Question Authority." It didn't take much to see that the norms of acceptable behavior within American public culture had changed dramatically between, say, 1962 and 1969.

And of course as with any set of normative behaviors within a public culture, the changes reflected transformations taking place below the surface. The Rules, it turns out, had proven unworthy. They had masked hierarchies and structures of power. Long-excluded minorities pointed out that playing by the Rules had gotten them nowhere meaningful. Many young Americans argued that the Rules were little more than a means to perpetuate a society premised on eternal war. Worse, the Rules were perpetuating a society that was aimed, at root, at unfulfilling goals.

What replaced the Rules-based society was one premised on rights, as American society moved from a rules-based society to a rights-based society. People from all walks of life began borrowing from the civil rights movement and proclaiming rights for themselves. Americans had a right to wear their hair however they wanted; or to protest in the streets, whether against the war in Vietnam or against property taxes. The "black is beautiful" campaign of the late 1960s was nothing if not a rejection of postwar cultural norms about how black people should proceed if they wanted to get ahead. The "gay is good" campaign from 1968 made a similar argument with its title alone. Individual and group rights had to be pronounced and honored, because for too long it seemed as if the very existence of those groups had to be denied if one followed the Rules too closely. The Rules had structures of power embedded within them, and during the 1960s, those who had been denied power for too long felt quite comfortable challenging the Rules and demanding individual rights. And when parents tried to explain to the youth why they should respect the Rules and ignore their rights, they ended up sounding like Archie Bunker. It turned out the Rules had been hard to justify all along.[14]

As historian David Stiegerwald recently put it, many Americans in the 1960s "made radical claims for liberation from moral, social, and cultural restraints and built new social movements to secure those claims. Through collective self-assertion, they carved out emancipated zones, sometimes figurative, sometimes electronic, sometimes conventionally political, and sometimes all of the above."[15] Emancipation. Liberation. Individualism. That's what replaced the collective, structured nature of the Rules. The boundaries of acceptable public culture had been expanded, and in some realms, exploded.

Once the Rules-based society began to be replaced by a rights-based one, the other panels of the triptych did not look the same. Rational thought came under assault throughout the decade as well, as alternate faiths and psychedelic drugs promised to offer greater fulfillment than toeing the line of rational ideation. The hippies and Yippies openly flouted traditional thought. If six turned out to be nine, sang Jimi Hendrix, he wouldn't mind, because he had his own individual world to live in, and he wasn't going to live in yours. Even more powerfully, many subaltern groups began to argue that rational thought itself was simply a handmaiden to Enlightenment hierarchies that had kept them down for so long. The people who had been attacked for not following the Rules were the groups that were *always* left behind: racial minorities, the poor, women. This suggested some kind of conspiracy, or, at the very least, some prioritizing. And this prompted another deep question: if rational thought couldn't be trusted as impartial, shouldn't the very notion of progress be questioned as well? A more proper, useful way of putting the question might be: progress for whom? Deep-seated mistrust about large bureaucracies crept into the tenor of the nation. Hopes for a brighter future were replaced by dystopian stories like those of Philip K. Dick, most especially his *Do Androids Dream of Electric Sheep?* from 1968.[16] The federal government didn't help the notion that rational thought contained within bureaucracies could lead to a brighter future, with the occurrence and revelation in short succession of the Tet Offensive (1968), My Lai (1969), the Kent State massacre (1970), the Pentagon Papers (1971), and Watergate (1972–1974).

Within American public culture, what replaced the profound belief in rational thought wasn't a complete rejection of rational thought, but instead an increased sense that rational thought and progress were limited and could be deployed instrumentally. There had to be, always, various interests considered. The was no single conception of "the good," but many that required balancing. The idea of a unified America has always been something of a fiction premised on a holistic public culture, but after the 1960s, any spectacle of national unity seemed suspicious. Those doing the splitting apart were doing it gleefully, and those resisting the ruptures could harness few successful arguments. It is not an accident that historian Daniel Rodgers has called America since the 1960s "the age of fracture."[17] Once the notion that the United States government was not in fact looking out for the best interests of all its citizens, and perhaps never could have done so, increasing numbers of Americans resorted to their own group, whatever they perceived it to be. This was the era not only of black power but also of the white ethnic revival and the various attempts by the Census Bureau to diversify the way in which it categorized the nation's people. Multiculturalism in education and popular culture was on the horizon, and the American past looked more morally confusing than ever. The future looked even more uncertain. Is it possible to craft a collective national image when the intellectual underpinnings of the previous image—Enlightenment rationality—were in doubt?

As one might expect, the third arm of the triptych—a faith in friendly corporate capitalism—suffered as well. As the "do your own thing" attitude of the late 1960s and 1970s emerged, it led to rising demands for lowered income and real-estate taxes, and for decreased government regulation. While these complaints harked back to those made by business elites in the 1930s (and earlier), by the 1970s they took on a populist appeal. If the idea of the nation was proving to be a great fiction, what was the point of contributing to the common good? In the late 1960s and early 1970s, think tanks like the American Enterprise Institute emerged, advocating smaller government and less commitment to the commonweal. The National Tax Limitation Committee, meanwhile, sought constitutional limitations on federal spending in an effort to starve the beast that was now the predominant image of the federal government. In 1978, Californians declared a "taxpayer revolt" and overwhelmingly passed Proposition 13, which put limits on the rate that real estate taxes could rise in any given year. Deregulation occurred in many once-regulated industries. The results were mixed and led to numerous abuses, as well as lower costs. But the transformation reflected the sentiment within acceptable public culture: that large establishments were not to be trusted compared to individual entrepreneurs. The corporate capitalism of the postwar, pre-1960s era, with its friendly relations between business and the state, and the sense that both were doing good for the commonweal, and both would willingly pay taxes to secure that partnership, underwent significant changes in the 1970s. It was now conceivable to think of an instance where what was good for General Motors was perhaps not so good for the life of the nation. A more laissez-faire capitalism won out over the corporate capitalism of the postwar era.

And, perhaps bizarrely, this brings us back to Janis Joplin and Bobby McGee. If one is looking for a unifying theme in all these major transformation, it's clear what it is. All of the 1960s transformations were done under the guise of a single word: freedom.

In short, Americans of almost every ilk were seeking to take advantage of decent economic times in order to expand the horizons of possibility. Of course, freedom was not a new word in the American lexicon. It has a long, beautiful, terrible history, in forging freedom movements just as easily as serving as a rhetorical tool to enslave and "civilize." Who was a more articulate advocate for liberty than slave-owning Thomas Jefferson? In his 1987 book, *Contested Truths*, Daniel Rodgers argued that freedom has been the preeminent political keyword since the Second World War. "Pulled shrewdly out of the core vocabulary of the New Deal's domestic opponents," Rodgers wrote, "stretched with convenient elasticity over the deep fissures within the antifascist alliance, the word swelled with new power in the 1940s."[18] It's hard to argue with Rodgers's assessment. Freedom was indeed everywhere in American public life in postwar America. During World War II, the United States was fighting in the name of the Four Freedoms in order to secure a free Europe. It was aligned with other freedom-loving nations in order to make a free world. The postwar victory lap would take place in the form of a mobile American history museum, called the Freedom Train.

This veneration of "freedom" during the Second World War quite easily transitioned into the Cold War, as Roosevelt's 1941 image of a world rent down the middle—"divided between human slavery and human freedom"—"slipped unchanged into place as the controlling metaphor of the Cold War," as Rodgers put it.[19] The Cold War was, of course, about preserving the free world and America's cultural freedom, in defense of the free market, which was sometimes called the free enterprise system.

By the middle 1950s and definitely by the 1960s, rights talk piggybacked onto the expanding notions of freedom, and thus the word "freedom" got used and abused in the service of all sorts of rights causes, not the least of which was the civil rights movement, which had, we should not forget, Freedom Rides, Freedom Schools, Freedom Summers, a counter-Democratic Freedom Party, the March for Jobs and Freedom, and so on.

As becomes obvious, then, the word "freedom" had considerable elasticity in the postwar world. Its meaning was all over the place, used to serve numerous causes, progressive and conservative. Through the 1960s, however, the word eventually came to embody two divergent poles of thought, one prominently from the left, the other from the right. And those divergent meanings have more or less stuck, with conservatives understanding freedom to mean one thing and liberals understanding it quite differently. How you understood "freedom" helped determine how you thought about America.

This becomes evident once we explore the pantheon of conservative books in twentieth-century American intellectual life, which contain titles like F. A. Hayek's *The Road to Serfdom* and Milton Friedman's *Capitalism and Freedom*. Alongside Russell Kirk's *The Conservative Mind* and Whittaker Chambers's *Witness* sits Barry Goldwater's *Conscience of a Conservative*, which had sentences like: "The Conservative looks upon politics as the art of achieving the maximum amount of freedom for individuals that is consistent with the maintenance of the social order" and "It is impossible for one man to be free if another is able to deny him the exercise of his freedom" and "For the American Conservative, there is no difficulty in identifying the day's overriding political challenge: it is *to preserve and extend freedom*."[20]

Those on the left were equally obsessed, although their definition of freedom was less connected to fears of an overarching, domineering, freedom-denying state. It was more social and cultural. The Port Huron Statement that anchored the Students for a Democratic Society was nothing if not a long discourse on the contradictions between the language of freedom and the actions done in its name. It had foundational sentences like "We regard men as infinitely precious and possessed of unfulfilled capacities for reason, freedom, and love." Meanwhile, it suggested that Goldwater and his ilk were attempting to "seriously weaken democratic institutions and spawn movements contrary to the interests of basic freedoms and peace." The words "free" or "freedom" appeared twenty-six times in the manifesto. Michael Harrington's *The Other America*, meanwhile, talked of the poor as "those who live at a level of life beneath moral choice, who are so submerged in their poverty that one cannot begin to talk about free choice."[21]

So perhaps one way to understand the transformation in the set of assumptions within American public culture throughout the 1960s is to see it as a struggle over the meaning of the word "freedom." And in this titanic battle, both progressives and conservatives took their beatings but also claimed more than a handful of trophies. It's clear that, under the banner of extending freedom, groups like the Young American for Freedom helped usher in the increasingly laissez-faire economics that has shaped the boundaries of acceptable public culture since the 1970s. So triumphant have they been in this battle that it was a Democrat, not a Republican, who said "the era of big government is over" (President Bill Clinton, in his 1996 State of the Union Address). Only recently, with Senators Elizabeth Warren and Bernie Sanders and occasionally President Barack Obama's campaigns suggesting "you didn't build that alone" have we begun to see a direct challenge to the laissez-faire order, siding with the commonweal over the individual.

Meanwhile, if we turn our gaze to the realm of culture, the Left, not the Right, has clearly won, and has done so also in the name of freedom. The decline of the Rules and the triumph of the new sensibility to "do your own thing" were clearly a win for liberation. The resultant topsy-turvy nature of debates about the literary canon or our collective culture suggests that the welcome table has been expanded so much that it's hard to find language that allows communication, much less a coherent description of the commonweal. But it is also clear that the old cultural forms that had served as barriers to access needed to go. Dress codes are more casual, appearances more individualized, people more comfortable to tell the boss to, in the words of the 1977 country hit, take this job and shove it. The world did metaphorically split open (to use the title of Ruth Rosen's history of the women's liberation movement), and, as one leading historian of the 1990s culture wars declares, "the culture wars are over;" the Left has won.[22]

Of course, in addition to seeing the intellectual history of the 1960s as the triumph and often contradictory enactment of the rhetoric of individual freedom over that of the community, another tradition, another word, had a good run in the 1960s, too, only to ultimately lose. Love, of course, is much harder to fight for than freedom, because it typically requires a partner, someone to receive and reciprocate. It's more difficult to describe, too, and far more difficult to sustain. It is easy to say that all you need is love, but it is much harder to make happen and maintain. And, for all those reasons, perhaps, it eventually lost out as a controlling metaphor for the times. This is not to say it didn't have its advocates, perhaps the most articulate being James Baldwin. Throughout his essays from the 1950s and 1960s, Baldwin argued succinctly and powerfully that Americans had to lose their sense of "innocence," by which he meant their willful ignorance that they might be a party to hard-to-defend power relations. Of course they were, we were. Of course the assumptions of society that most Americans felt quite comfortable not investigating were helping to perpetuate a certain order of things. Baldwin was laser-focused on race relations throughout the decade, and wanted to teach white Americans what kinds of power they held just because they were white, what kinds of things they could take for granted that nonwhite folks could not. Once they became aware, once they lost their innocence, he imagined they would have to act. They could either perform a rearguard action and fight to preserve an unjustifiable order, or they could, in words from *The Fire Next Time*, fight "like lovers . . . to end the racial nightmare, and achieve our country, and change the history of the world."[23]

To Baldwin, true love was hard. "Love takes off the masks that we fear we cannot live without," he wrote, "and know we cannot live within. I use the word 'love' here not merely in the personal sense but as a state of being, or a state of grace—not in the infantile American sense of being made happy but in the tough and universal sense of quest and daring and growth."[24] It was premised on complete honesty and forgiveness of sins and abuses. It wasn't always pretty. And it consisted of a long effort to put up with one another despite everyone's flaws. No wonder it often got stymied at the level of saccharine song lyrics. When the alternative to the hard work of love is the easy if lonely road of freedom, it is clear who the winner would be, and who the winner was. Once the boundaries of acceptable public culture morphed into a deep questioning of the prevailing Rules of the culture, everything else could be questioned, including even the commonweal itself. The Right and the Left used the evident shortcomings of the postwar set of assumptions to vie for changes within the public culture, and their respective easy uses of the word "freedom" led them to the victories they won.

NOTES

1. "Me and Bobby McGee," words and music by Kris Kristofferson and Fred Foster, 1969.

2. The historiography on the 1960s is vast and rich. The best overviews include Maurice Isserman and Michael Kazin, *America Divided: The Civil War of the 1960s*, 3rd ed. (New York: Oxford University Press, 2008); Allan J. Matusow, *The Unraveling of America: A History of Liberalism in the 1960s* (1984; Athens: University of Georgia Press, 2009); David Farber, *The Age of Great Dreams: America in the 1960s* (New York: Hill & Wang, 1994); David Steigerwald, *The Sixties and the End of Modern America* (New York: St. Martin's, 1995); David Burner, *Making Peace with the Sixties* (Princeton, NJ: Princeton University Press, 1996); and Todd Gitlin, *The Sixties: Years of Hope, Days of Rage* (New York: Bantam Books, 1987). On various other aspects of the 1960s, some of the best include Ruth Rosen, *The World Split Open: How the Modern Women's Movement Changed America* (New York: Viking, 2000); Dan T. Carter, *The Politics of Rage: George Wallace, the Origins of the New Conservatism, and the Transformation of American Politics* (New York: Simon & Schuster, 1995); Matthew D. Lassiter, *The Silent Majority: Suburban Politics in the Sunbelt South* (Princeton, NJ: Princeton University Press, 2006); Timothy B. Tyson, *Radio Free Dixie: Robert F. Williams and the Roots of Black Power* (Chapel Hill: University of North Carolina Press, 1999); Christian G. Appy, *American Reckoning: The Vietnam War and Our National Identity* (New York: Viking, 2015); Christian G. Appy, *Working-Class War: American Combat Soldiers and Vietnam* (Chapel Hill: University of North Carolina Press, 1993); Bruce Watson, *Freedom Summer: The Savage Season of 1964 That Made Mississippi Burn and Made America a Democracy* (New York: Penguin, 2011); Nick Bromell, *Tomorrow Never Knows: Rock and Psychedelics in the 1960s* (Chicago: University of Chicago Press, 2000); Michael J. Kramer, *The Republic of Rock: Music and Citizenship in the Sixties' Counterculture* (New York: Oxford University Press, 2013); Peter Braunstein, *Imagine Nation: The American Counterculture of the 1960s and '70s* (New York: Routledge, 2002); Robert S. Ellwood, *The Sixties Spiritual Awakening: American Religion Moving from Modern to Postmodern* (New Brunswick, NJ: Rutgers University Press, 1994); Danielle L. McGuire, *At the Dark End of the Street: Black Women, Rape, and Resistance—a New History of the Civil Rights Movement from Rosa Parks to the Rise of Black Power* (New York: Alfred A. Knopf, 2010); and Jay Stevens, *Storming Heaven: LSD and the American Dream* (New York: Atlantic Monthly, 1987). The list could easily go on.

3. For a selection see Daniel Horowitz, *Betty Friedan and the Making of "The Feminine Mystique": The American Left, the Cold War, and Modern Feminism* (Amherst: University of Massachusetts Press, 1998); Howard Brick, *Daniel Bell and the Decline of Intellectual Radicalism: Social Theory and Political Reconciliation in the 1940s* (Madison: University of Wisconsin Press, 1986); David Milne, *America's Rasputin: Walt Rostow and the Vietnam War* (New York: Hill & Wang, 2008); David Engerman, *Modernization*

from the Other Shore: American Intellectuals and the Romance of Russian Development (Cambridge, MA: Harvard University Press, 2003); Doug Rossinow, *The Politics of Authenticity: Liberalism, Christianity, and the New Left in America* (New York: Columbia University Press, 1999); Kevin Mattson, *Intellectuals in Action: The Origins of the New Left and Radical Liberalism, 1945–1970* (University Park, PA: Penn State University Press, 2002); John David Skretney, *The Minority Rights Revolution* (Cambridge, MA: Harvard University Press, 2002); Rebecca E. Klatch, *A Generation Divided: The New Left, the New Right, and the 1960's* (Berkeley: University of California Press, 1999); David Wyatt, *When America Turned: Reckoning with 1968* (Amherst: University of Massachusetts Press, 2014); Sara M. Evans, *Journeys That Opened Up the World: Women, Student Christian Movements, and Social Justice, 1955–1975* (New Brunswick, NJ: Rutgers University Press, 2003); David Farber and Jeff Roche, eds., *The Conservative Sixties* (New York: Peter Lang, 2003); Michael W. Flamm, *Law and Order: Street Crime, Civil Unrest, and the Crisis of Liberalism in the 1960s* (New York: Columbia University Press, 2007); Nancy MacLean, *Freedom Is Not Enough: The Opening of the African American Workplace* (Cambridge, MA: Harvard University Press, 2006); and Thomas Frank, *The Conquest of Cool: Business Culture, Counterculture, and the Rise of Hip Consumerism* (Chicago: University of Chicago Press, 1997).

4. Howard Brick, *Age of Contradiction: American Thought and Culture in the 1960s* (New York: Twayne, 1998).

5. Henry F. May, *The End of American Innocence: A Study in the First Years of Our Time, 1912–1917* (New York: Columbia University Press, 1959).

6. James Baldwin, *Notes of a Native Son* (Boston: Beacon, 1955), 33. See also nearly anything Baldwin wrote during the decade, but especially *Nobody Knows My Name: More Notes of a Native Son* (New York: Dial, 1961); *The Fire Next Time* (New York: Dial, 1963); and *No Name in the Street* (New York: Dial, 1972).

7. Almost any book by Mailer can be read as such, but for the set of assumptions that defined the possibilities with American public culture, perhaps his best are *Why Are We in Vietnam?* (New York: G. P. Putnam's Sons, 1967), *Miami and the Siege of Chicago* (New York: World, 1968), and especially *Armies of the Night* (New York: New American Library, 1968).

8. This was the theme of her landmark work, *The Feminine Mystique* (New York: W. W. Norton, 1963).

9. Thomas Bender, "Wholes and Parts: The Need for Synthesis in American History," *Journal of American History* 73, no. 1 (June 1986): 127.

10. Ibid., 126.

11. I first developed this sketch of pre-1960s public culture in my 2015 book, *Buckley and Mailer: The Difficult Friendship That Shaped the Sixties* (New York: W. W. Norton, 2015).

12. Robert Moses, *Working for the People: Promise and Performance in Public Service* (New York: Harper, 1956), 2. Italics added. For more on Moses see Robert A. Caro, *The Power Broker: Robert Moses and the Fall of New York* (New York: Vintage Books, 1975).

13. Charles E. Wilson said this famous line in 1952, in a speech to the Senate Armed Services Committee.

14. Hugh Davis Graham first described, but didn't develop, the transition from rules to rights in *Collision Course: The Strange Convergence of Affirmative Action and Immigration Policy in America* (New York: Oxford University Press, 2002). It was also an unnamed theme in Skretney, *The Minority Rights Revolution*.

15. David Stiegerwald, "Marcuse in the Age of Choice," on the Society for U.S. Intellectual History's blog at http://s-usih.org/2016/06/marcuse-in-the-age-of-choice.html.

16. Philip K. Dick, *Do Androids Dream of Electric Sheep?* (New York: Doubleday, 1968).

17. Daniel T. Rodgers, *Age of Fracture* (Cambridge, MA: Belknap Press of Harvard University Press, 2011).

18. Daniel T. Rodgers, *Contested Truths: Keywords in American Politics since Independence* (New York: Basic Books, 1987), 214.

19. Ibid., 215.

20. Barry M. Goldwater, *The Conscience of a Conservative* (Shepherdsville, KY: Victor, 1960), 13, 13, and 14, respectively. Italics in original.

21. Tom Hayden and Students for a Democratic Society (US), *The Port Huron Statement: The Visionary Call of the 1960s Revolution* (1962), and Michael Harrington, *The Other America* (1962; New York: Simon & Schuster, 1997), 162.

22. Rosen, *World Split Open*; and Andrew Hartman, *A War for the Soul of America: A History of the Culture Wars* (Chicago: University of Chicago Press, 2015).

23. Baldwin, *Fire Next Time*, 105.

24. Ibid., 95.

Section II
IDEAS AND AMERICAN IDENTITIES

4
PHILOSOPHY VS. PHILOSOPHERS
A Problem in American Intellectual History

Amy Kittelstrom

When the philosopher William James (1842–1910) delivered his first lecture in the series that became *Pragmatism* (1907)—arguably the most famous and influential book in the history of American philosophy—he chose to begin with the words of a popular English writer, G. K. Chesterton. "We think that for a landlady considering a lodger it is important to know his income," Chesterton wrote, "but still more important to know his philosophy." Same for a general anticipating a battle; the size of the enemy's army is not as important as the enemy's philosophy. "We think the question is not whether the theory of the cosmos affects matters, but whether in the long run anything else affects them."[1]

James agreed with Chesterton, and American intellectual historians generally do too. Among all the intertwined causes of historical events, philosophical commitments held by historical actors lie behind every bomb dropped, every criminal sentenced, every neighborhood zoned, every business picketed, school built, and church joined or quit or ignored.[2] James did not think only professional philosophers like himself had philosophies, but everyone, "each and all of you," he told his audience. Far from being refined or elite, "the philosophy which is so important in each of us is not a technical matter; it is our more or less dumb sense of what life honestly and deeply means."[3] The trouble is that intellectual historians cannot plumb dumbness, cannot read the motivations of mute actors.

For all his populist air, however, James did not stand before his audience in order to learn about the philosophies of everyman and everywoman but to explain and defend his own pragmatism, which had developed into a significant movement among American and European philosophers, with later impact in Mexico and China as well.[4] *Pragmatism* appeared at the exact moment that philosophy, like other academic disciplines, was professionalizing by requiring faculty to hold the doctorate (which James never even tried to earn), growing organizations, and systematizing standards and subfields while separating itself from psychology.[5] James despised this development, complaining of "The Ph.D. Octopus" in a 1903 essay, but he could not entirely escape its tentacles. As early as 1905, James's wife—who had served as his secretary and interlocutor ever since marrying him for his philosophy in 1878—could no longer understand his essays. He spent the rest of his life clarifying his theories with increasingly technical parries against his critics, parsing Kant, Hume, Zeno, and more, producing such sophisticated arguments that readers not fluent in philosophical reasoning must slow way down to comprehend them.

In his last, unfinished work, intended to be his magnum opus, James explained philosophers' importance to "the progress of society." Social progress depends, he said, on individual variations from the human average:

> Among the variations, every generation of men produces some individuals exceptionally preoccupied with theory. Such men find matter for puzzle and astonishment where no one else does. Their imagination invents explanations and combines them. They store up the learning of their time, utter prophecies and warnings, and are regarded as sages. Philosophy, etymologically meaning the love of wisdom, is the work of this class of minds, regarded with an indulgent relish, if not with admiration, even by those who do not understand them or believe much in the truth which they proclaim.[6]

Philosophy is universal, but philosophers, it seems, are special. Raising two questions: So what? Who cares?

American intellectual historians have cared about philosophical reasoning—and about James in particular—since the beginning of professional American intellectual history. By popular reputation and self-identity, philosophers are the ultimate intellectuals. Controversially, intellectual history has largely entailed the study of intellectuals, who may or may not be philosophers by professional trade but who are preoccupied by theory to some degree.[7] Philosophy is both the origin of the field and its nexus with the diverse disciplinary orientations overlapping with intellectual history: literature, political science, anthropology, multicultural and queer studies, the humanities and social sciences in general. Philosophy has been central in the field of intellectual history and to this field's interface with the wider scholarly world because philosophy has functioned as both an object of study and a method for historical inquiry itself. Historians have theorized about history aplenty, using Hegel, Marx, James, and many more philosophers to guide and justify their work. The future of philosophy as an inherently important historical category, however, is probably as imperiled in American intellectual history as philosophy departments are in the American academy.

So What?

So what if there is tension between the universalist claim that everyone has a philosophy and the contention that only some people are (or have been) philosophers?

Turning back to William James begets more questions through which to probe this larger one. So what if his philosophical writing took a technical turn in the last years of his life? So what if he used the male pronoun to personify the philosopher? So what if he sprinkled German words into his arguments—an *überhaupt* here, a *grübelsucht* there—making them legible only to the educated elite? So what if the vast majority of the philosophers he took seriously were of European extraction? So what if he himself was born into extraordinary socioeconomic privilege? So what if he virtually ignored the rise of Jim Crow in his lifetime and used racial slurs occasionally in private correspondence? So what if James departed from his populism to treat philosophers as a special sort of class or human type?[8] And so what if this one philosopher wrote this or anything else?

The singular figure of James is useful for generating these questions—which need be refashioned but little to fit the vast majority of American thinkers considered "philosophers" up to now—because he is paradigmatic in powerful ways that mirror the fortunes of intellectual history over the late twentieth century and into the twenty-first.[9] A most exemplary Anglo-American elite thinker, James bridged the religious and the secular, Victorian and progressive, scientific and artistic, cosmopolitan and national and even regional in his career, producing a body of accessible work that takes stock of the European philosophical tradition, with a smattering of Hinduism and Buddhism, to produce a philosophy fashioned for modern life.[10] James was the most charming of the pragmatists, who became core figures of the American intellectual tradition and what may be called its canon; could a doctoral student in American intellectual history overlook James?[11] Like his fellow pragmatists Charles S. Peirce (1839–1914) and John Dewey (1859–1952), James engaged with democracy, science, and the fact of human diversity in works read by progressives and liberals who helped create policies and opinions in the twentieth century. Unlike Peirce and Dewey, James wrote beautifully and apparently spoke even better. And unlike Dewey, James was born to ease, a social factor that forms part of why James is such an illustrative case for the role of philosophy in intellectual history.[12]

Material ease may indeed have been an accommodating condition necessary for the temperamental flower of James's intellect to bloom. Blessed in his crib by Emerson himself, treated to transatlantic voyages and the richest cultural exposures of Europe and America, never required to do domestic labor and certainly not remunerative toil, never even expected to shoulder a share of the national military burden to fight the Confederacy, William James squirmed under the weight of his philosophical concerns alone. They were heavy enough to make suicide attractive.

In his mid-thirties—without ever having held a paying job, through a sea of depression, able to read little and write almost nothing—James finally solved these problems well enough that he could stir himself to take a position teaching anatomy at Harvard, still a rather parochial college just beginning to transform into a modern research university. Once he got married he actually became productive.

Alice Howe Gibbens James listened to her husband, reflected back what she heard, criticized and resisted his views when she disagreed, and supported his great work in every conceivable way. When he sped off to Europe or the Adirondack mountains immediately upon teaching his last class each spring, she packed up his students' examination books and sent them along. She sent the latest journals, often helpfully annotating them first, and books. Writing letters to him faithfully to ease his loneliness on those travels, she passed along quotations from her own reading and snatches of philosophic conversation. She bore five children and reared four of them, continuing to encourage James when he absconded during the early weeks after each birth, during the long illness of the son who died, and as often as he could during all the years of their upbringing. She managed the servants and staff of two households, hosted dinner parties and houseguests, packed his luggage for him, checked his train schedules, and carefully subordinated her every desire to the sacred cause of his nerves, so delicate and easily taxed, so necessary to keep in trim so that James could write.

All of this means that when the old intellectual historians—those born around the turn of the twentieth century—used James and other philosophers as jewels through which to string their historical narratives, minus any consideration of these subjects' social context, they reified the philosophers' privilege. Not only did these first professional American intellectual historians fail to consider the philosophies of millions and millions of nonelite Americans; they pretended that the ideas of such privileged philosophers somehow carried the entire national "mind."[13] Henry Steele Commager and his brethren thus laid their work bare to the charges of elitism levied by the new social historians, whose rise in the context of political activism during and after the civil rights movement is such an important part of the story of how modern intellectual history regrouped in light of their critique.[14]

The analytical category "philosophy" creates a methodological problem for intellectual historians who are ideologically committed to inclusivity and fairness across the lines of race, class, sex, gender, ethnicity, sexuality, religious commitment, physical ability, and every other conceivable identity marker. Since philosophy can be explicated only in the words of philosophers—and since popular philosophers often spill their words on back porches rather than recording them in books—the field automatically tilts toward the privileged. While a work like Lawrence Levine's *Black Culture and Black Consciousness* (1977) may be said to illuminate the philosophy of an underprivileged, nay oppressed group of people, no one is calling the slaves in his book philosophers.[15] Until the twentieth century, philosophers were some of the whitest, malest people in American history because they were the ones who had that chief prerequisite of recorded theorizing—volitional time—and were among the very few Americans so endowed.[16] When the twentieth century institutionalized professional philosophy in the academy, this demographic distortion got sealed into the highest spire of the ivory tower, while the theory-preoccupied anthropologists, artists, activists, and others diversified themselves largely outside formal "philosophy."

See, for illustration, the cover of Bruce Kuklick's *The Rise of American Philosophy: Cambridge, Massachusetts, 1860–1930* (1977). There the seven members of Harvard's philosophy department stand in front of Emerson Hall in 1929, along with three adjunct instructors and a visitor: all male, all with Anglo surnames save one, Henry Sheffer, a Jew. The picture signifies not only the demographic problem philosophy poses for intellectual history, but also the problem of professionalization. Jewish philosophers like Sheffer and the more renowned Morris R. Cohen (1880–1947) faced anti-Semitic obstacles galore, but they were allowed into the university and, once there, made contributions, shaped debates, built institutions, and fashioned research programs.[17] Barriers against all women and African-American men remained high, which actually reversed some intellectual progress that had been made in the amateur era. At the Concord Summer School of Philosophy, for example, which convened from 1879 to 1888, Elizabeth Palmer Peabody, Ednah Dow Cheney, Julia Ward Howe, and other learned women regularly appeared on the program.[18] Once philosophy became codified as an academic discipline rather than a vocational pursuit—before the turn of the twentieth century not only was the PhD not required, but many philosophers worked outside academia—being barred from the university meant being barred from the conversation. Until practically the 1970s, some "white ethnic" males could transcend their class origins thanks to academic opportunity, but they were almost the only non-WASPs who could.[19]

Even under these conditions, some exceptional female and minority students persevered in philosophy, but intellectual historians have not been interested in unearthing the obscure for the sake of their obscurity in the manner of social and cultural historians. Mary Whiton Calkins (1863–1930), for example, completed all the requirements for a doctorate in philosophy at Harvard in 1894, earning the praise, respect, and active support of James and other faculty members—Hugo Münsterberg, probably the first Jew hired there, told the president that Calkins was his "best student"—but the quality of her work made no difference: "The Corporation are not prepared to give any Harvard degree to any woman no matter how exceptional the circumstances may be." Calkins went on to publish books in philosophy and psychology that got positive reviews in the leading journals. Spending her career at Wellesley, she was elected president of the American Psychological Association in 1905 and of the Eastern Division of the American Philosophical Association in 1918. Like Ettie Stettheimer (1875–1955), who earned a PhD in philosophy at the University of Freiburg in 1908 with a dissertation criticizing James's pragmatism, Calkins still awaits the intellectual historian who will take her seriously.[20]

The white male selection bias that complicates the subject of philosophy in American intellectual history was not only born of simple prejudice, as should already be clear, but was a product of history—as prejudice itself is, but in a different way. Professionalization and the rise of the modern research university contributed to this bias, partly by covering the social conditions of American history with pretensions to objectivity. The timing of the professionalization of the professoriate was no accident. It was only one of the processes of "incorporation," bureaucratization, and modernization that followed the Civil War, which made these processes possible on a national scale and brought public schools to the American South for the first time.[21] Only once the industrializing country was fully unified—no longer trying to prevent the war that was necessary to eliminate American slavery as a political problem, not bothering to enforce truly free labor for the former slaves—could it press ahead and complete the transcontinental railroad, the subjugation of native peoples, the importation of foreign labor, and all the building and destruction necessary to manifest the great destiny this chosen nation had thought itself promised. "So may our ransomed country," orated James at the 1897 dedication of the monument depicting the Massachusetts Fifty-Fourth Colored Regiment, "like the city of the promise, lie four-square under Heaven, and the ways of all the nations be lit up by its light." (His wife had supplied him that line.)[22]

The early intellectual historians looking backward saw mostly Anglo-American philosophers because for the vast majority of American history right up until that point, such people absolutely dominated the power structures of the country, which started as a set of English colonies, after all. For most of the history visible to those historians, the overwhelming majority of the African-American population was both extremely concentrated and violently denied the chance to read, or write, or orate, or idly sit and contemplate the universe. Mexican Americans hardly existed, conceptually, disproportionately northeastern as American higher education was. Asian immigrants came relatively late and were similarly concentrated and also subjugated, as the Irish had been before them. Social segregation, together with socioeconomic hierarchy, meant that intellectual life was also segregated. Even when America's more philosophical communities developed ideas about universal moral agency—at least theoretically including slaves and their descendants—before the twentieth century they basically only managed to open their dialogue to Jews, and visitors from India.[23]

Such Americans who believed in moral agency complicate the category of philosophy in American intellectual history even more. Although it would be anachronistic to apply the term "intellectual historian" to a scholar before the modern historical profession existed, the study of the thought of the past is as old as texts. In America the first historians of thought were surely clerics—Puritans in New England, Catholics elsewhere, other denominations as they migrated and developed—which highlights the important and obvious point that religion is philosophy, too. Or was, for one of the distortions the professional lens imposes on the history of philosophy is that Anglo-American philosophy, after James, adamantly secularized, making anything supernatural anathema (even modest Jamesian overbeliefs) and emphasizing reason, logic, and increasingly arcane approaches to argumentation. Sheffer made it in the philosophy department at Harvard, just barely, because he was a brilliant logician, chief currency in the positivistic new form of the discipline. Value and meaning, so central to the thought of James, lost color under logic-chopping. As an academic specialization, philosophy became "analytical" self-consciously, proudly, and nearly exclusively.[24] While the history of philosophy done by philosophers and the intellectual history of philosophical ideas are distinct fields owing to their different disciplinary homes, scholars participating in these fields mingle often enough that the secularism and materialism of twentieth-century philosophy, especially after its Marxist phase, colored them both.

Philosophy used to be a much more expansive term, and at the same time a less freighted one, and less tightly bound; there is a reason scholars earn "doctorates of philosophy" at universities, which have always been formally devoted to the love of truth. For a long time this meant sacred, ultimate truth, of course—religious truth—and at Harvard, *veritas* signified a Reformation Christian commitment. Science used to be philosophy, too, and certainly political thought was philosophical. One reason the study of philosophy should never disappear from American history is that the role of political philosophy in the country's founding will always necessitate ongoing study. Yet although universities remain dedicated to knowledge and scholars to some notion of the truth, their lofty vocation of truth seeking became subordinated over the twentieth century to a more earthly vocational idea of the university as career building.

While this history is long and tangled, it leads back to the New Englanders of the early republic who cherished moral agency and extended it beyond their tribe. These New Englanders were liberals, self-avowedly, a label chosen to signify their openness to a further understanding of what is true and right than they already possessed, which led them to value diversity of opinion and to adore debating. "Everyone their own philosopher" might have been a slogan of the liberal way, because everyone was supposed to be their own moral agent—because the Protestant Reformation had claimed something liberals believed, which was that God granted everyone the divine right of private judgment. Moral agents should exercise their own reason and conscience rather than taking any authority's word for what the truth might be. A good number of these liberals wrote histories. Rarely history professors, such historians were also often ministers, poets, social activists, politicians, and more. And many of these were the liberals that scholars call Transcendentalists.

As Charles Capper explains, the Transcendentalists wrote their own history long before modern scholars appeared. They started by compiling biographical information on the ministers who were the movement's first prophets and leaders, for in a church that lost establishment only in 1833, men with that special human variation James was talking about—the "sages" preoccupied with "theory"—often trained in divinity and took a pulpit. Transcendentalists' historical work went far beyond this basic denominational record keeping, however. They paved the way for the modern historical profession with their attention to archives and, while Romantic and Whiggish and naively optimistic, also offered theories about their own liberal creed's recent past that have stood the test of time, according to Capper:

> Puritan and revolutionary idealism, the birth of an American culture, the tradition of religious revivalism, the contemporary surge of antinomian reform movements, the rise of European romantic literature and philosophy, the discovery of Asian literature, the spread of American democracy, the repression of the spiritual in rationalistic liberal Protestantism, the "modern" longing for an organic culture—these and other historical contexts for situating their movement, the Transcendentalists themselves articulated long before historians came along to do it for them.[25]

Philosophy and history thus grew up together in the context of an American intellectual culture largely descended from English Protestant heritage and in ongoing active dialogue with mostly European texts and thinkers who were all continuing to reckon with the implications of the Reformation, Enlightenment, and advent of the idea of universal political rights.

When professionalization came along, it created seemingly sharp distinctions between academic disciplines, which compounded the Euro-tilt of philosophy in American intellectual history even more. Consider the case of W. E. B. Du Bois (1868–1963). Born after the end of slavery, before the "New Negroes" who used everything from art to commerce to pursue full civic equality, Du Bois was called a philosopher in his *New York Times* obituary. Indeed, Du Bois had studied under James, but he did his graduate work in history, becoming, in 1895, the first African-American doctorate from Harvard. Du Bois went on to an extraordinarily varied career with a massive published oeuvre, so intellectual historians generally do not treat him as a philosopher per se, although they do now consider him important after generations of professional (white) historians egregiously ignored his scholarship. Du Bois was one of those dinner guests at the James home in Cambridge, possibly the only person of color ever to dine there, but James is also the mentor who discouraged Du Bois from continuing to pursue philosophy. James said Du Bois should devote himself to applied work, and the collection of facts, rather than the speculative inquiry of philosophy.[26] Was this the academic equivalent of African-American football players never playing quarterback? That question may be unanswerable, but there are less suspicious-minded ways of considering the role of philosophy in the career of Du Bois and other thinkers of his generation.

Du Bois said that James had encouraged him to do something more practical than philosophy, which could be read as similar to the way the math teacher of Malcolm Little (1925–1965) condescendingly discouraged him—clearly the star of the class—from aspiring to become a lawyer, directing him instead toward carpentry. This junior-high experience became a critical step on Malcolm's road toward replacing his slave name, Little, with an X.[27] But James clearly esteemed Du Bois more than that. When he advised Du Bois to master "the social sciences as the field for gathering and interpreting that body of fact which would apply to my program for the Negro," as the former student fondly recalled in his memoir, James was suggesting a specific scholarly course resonant with meaning particular to their moment at the end of the nineteenth century.[28] Du Bois already had a life purpose, and the social sciences were hot, and vital, and potent; Du Bois wanted practical applications of ideas that could live and have meaning only in action. The social sciences were where James's younger friends Pauline and Josephine Goldmark did their work, where the great Jane Addams (1860–1935), a philosophical pragmatist like Du Bois, did hers, where Anzia Yezierska (1885–1970) got her start under John Dewey, and where the antiracist Franz Boas

(1858–1942) supervised the early career of Zora Neale Hurston (1891–1960). All of these intellectuals engaged in philosophical thinking. None should probably be classified as philosophers.

The social sciences had been growing in promise and participants since the 1860s but categorically separated from philosophy only with professionalization.[29] At the same time, waves of African Americans migrating away from the racial terrorism of the South started reaching major cities in the North, the Midwest, and California. For those migrants who could afford to pursue education in their new environments—for the philosophical among them, that is—social science, the arts, and various forms of political activism made more sense than the "sterilities of scholastic philosophy," as Du Bois put it.[30]

According to the historian Mia Bay, African American thought necessarily centered on antiracism in the context of slavery and beyond.[31] Frederick Douglass (1818?–1895), to use the most prominent example, had a most powerful and penetrating intellect. All of his writings suggest him to have been one of those philosophically inclined human variants James prized; he was certainly a sage. But his moral agency was far from unfettered even after he escaped formal bondage, for Douglass devoted all his great energies toward ending slavery, first, and achieving full social and political equality, second. His works can be read philosophically, but he was not strictly a philosopher because by conscience he could never transcend the political work of persuasion related to the specific, temporal social conditions of his people in order to engage with more theoretical, technical debates. He was elected vice president of one of the leading liberal organizations, the Free Religious Association, in 1890, but he appears to have been too busy to participate in its meetings or contribute to its journal.[32] Like Du Bois, Douglass tirelessly pushed his nation to apply the philosophical principles it already claimed to believe.

Across the twentieth century and into the twenty-first, the academic discipline of philosophy has diversified but little. Cornel West (1953–) is the most prominent African-American philosopher of his generation. West's career began with a doctorate in philosophy at Princeton and soared after the publication of his first book, a reinterpretation of pragmatism, in 1989.[33] Part philosophy, part intellectual history, the book opened the doors of academia wide, enabling West to get a larger and larger audience for increasingly unorthodox, polemical, and ultimately creative work, including memoir, spoken-word albums, and acting appearances in Hollywood blockbusters. He now calls himself a "democratic intellectual" rather than a philosopher, making him consistent with other modern African-American thinkers in claiming the liberty to define himself, unique as he may be.

In *Between the World and Me* (2015), the writer Ta-Nehisi Coates describes the intellectual headiness of Howard University, which raises the question why historically black college life has not been more fully integrated into American intellectual history. Coates lists the black thinkers he devoured there: "Larry Neal, Eric Williams, George Padmore, Sonia Sanchez, Stanley Crouch, Harold Cruse, Manning Marable, Addison Gayle, Carolyn Rodgers, Etheridge Knight, Sterling Brown."[34] None of these were philosophers, but all did philosophical work.[35] How this work should be considered in relation to the formal work of academic philosophy is complicated, but unquestionably intellectual historians should be studying philosophical thinking wherever it has happened in the past, in the intellectual productions of all who have asked how things are and ought to be.

Like philosophy, American intellectual history is a practice many scholars do without necessarily identifying as intellectual historians. The final implication of the professionalization of intellectual life in America relevant to the problem of philosophy in the field is that after the rise of the new social history, a more methodologically rigorous, socially sensitive intellectual history was not the only new appearance. The social turn and the later cultural turn spawned new fields, especially interdisciplinary fields like African-American studies and women and gender studies, where scholars preoccupied with theory have done prodigious work. Just as great intellectual historians of the late twentieth century studied the theories not only of philosophers but of cultural anthropologists, literary scholars, and more—whether Robert Darnton with Clifford Geertz, David D. Hall with the French sociology of religion, or Thomas Haskell with Thomas Nagel—today's intellectual historians can continue keeping our field vital only by fertilizing it with theories and findings from outside it.[36]

So what, after all, if everyone has a philosophy worth knowing but not everyone can be considered a philosopher? So then historians need to make visible the social conditions under which philosophy has been formally produced and to explicate how they justify their own choices of inclusion and exclusion. They need to acknowledge and investigate the relationship between social privilege and intellectual privilege. The standards by which intellectual historians "objectively" evaluate philosophical works—their degree of novelty, their influence, what they reveal about their time, how they refined or challenged the arguments of others, how they fit into an enduring philosophical conversation—are not timeless, do not stand free of social circumstance. They are standards that only the few, educated elites with control over their time and access to mentors and books, as well as a Jamesian appetite for theorizing, have ever been able to achieve.

Who Cares?

Who cares about philosophy, philosophers, and American intellectual history? Mostly scholars within the professoriate, or at least trained at a research university; increasingly, historians with doctorates may not land jobs as professors themselves but continue to read, write, teach, and participate in scholarly conversation insofar as their last measure of energy allows, for they are of the theoretic bent themselves. These scholars of philosophy in intellectual history are joined by some teachers, journalists, and popular authors, some religious practitioners, some clergy and lawyers either active or retired, some activists, some political figures, and some other readers of who knows what occupation that supports their interest in learning about the philosophical past.

This is a very small and extremely threatened group, however comfortable some of them may be as individuals. Intellectual freedom, hard won as a (white male) professorial right in the early twentieth century, became compromised by market forces and political machination by the century's close. The legions of intellectual workers toiling for beans tell this tale, but so does a case of prestige and accomplishment. Among current intellectual historians with expertise in philosophy, Jennifer Ratner-Rosenhagen stands out. In order to research and write her award-winning book, *American Nietzsche* (2012), she earned multiple fellowships to study in Germany, where she mastered the language and began her archival research.[37] She spent years parsing philosophical texts in order to understand Nietzsche in the German context and the arguments he waged so that she could then analyze how his works were received and understood in the United States. On the basis of this impressive work, Ratner-Rosenhagen won appointment to a tenure-track position in the history department of the University of Wisconsin at Madison. This venerable public research institution has been distinguished in the field of American history ever since Frederick Jackson Turner (1861–1932) served there for twenty years as an embodiment of the "Wisconsin Idea," the state mission going back to the Progressive Era "to educate people and improve the human condition" and to unite around "the search for truth."[38] Moreover, Ratner-Rosenhagen holds a position named after Merle Curti (1897–1996), a Progressive intellectual historian who helped pioneer social history, which then rose up to decry intellectual history as elitist. Curti's eightieth birthday party was the occasion for the gathering at Wingspread in 1977 at which the younger generation of American intellectual historians, a single female among them, framed their methodological responses to the sense of crisis in their guild. Curti's prestige, partly owing to the "American mind"–style intellectual history he wrote as a popular paperback, ultimately rose so high that the Organization of American Historians endows not one but two book prizes in his name.[39]

Ratner-Rosenhagen is far from the only female intellectual historian of her generation, but she is distinguished because of the prominence of her position and the importance of her work. Yet despite her success, her university is not Curti's university, and her job differs vastly from his. Not only does she lack a spouse as self-sacrificial as Alice Howe Gibbens James—like most professional academics nowadays, male or female—she also lives in a Wisconsin that is a new kind of bellwether for the nation, a grim one. Ratner-Rosenhagen became Merle Curti's assistant professor in 2006, five years before the election of Scott Walker to the office of governor for the state of Wisconsin, once the nation's most progressive state. Walker has aggressively cut funding for public education from kindergarten through university, threatened the Wisconsin Idea itself, shifted power from faculty toward administrators, and weakened tenure in the state. Ratner-Rosenhagen cannot possibly look at the prospects for her graduate students with the hopefulness that Curti must have looked at his, no matter how hard she works for them, nor will her scholarship and persona have the popular reach of Curti's, no matter the excellence of what she does.

Today's historical profession is not the historical profession of Curti, either, in some very good ways and some very disturbing ones. The disturbing ways are generally not the fault of historians themselves and, alarmingly, may be beyond historians' power to change. The adjunctification of the professoriate, the quantification of impact, the rise of accountability tools, the use of technology to cheapen courses, the general monetization of postsecondary degrees, all add up to a stunningly widespread success of the assault on higher education waged by conservative politicians and activists seeking to discredit academics and defund the public sphere. The resulting squeeze suffocates scholars in every history department, but in vastly unequal ways. University administrations deny tenure, freeze lines, and follow the lead of the for-profit "universities," but well-endowed universities capable of placing their graduate students do much less of this and lavish more services on their faculty, while poorer institutions exploit graduate students to develop giant online courses, if they even have graduate students at all. If not, they push tenured faculty to take on more and more students, more and more remedial teaching, more and more administrative tasks. There are simply fewer and fewer of the kinds of jobs that can support a healthy scholarly career. In an information age when students' rapidly shrinking attention spans make it increasingly difficult to convey even the basics of American history, much less the intricacies of philosophical ideas, jobs that allow for the true intellectual freedom necessary to read German philosophy in the original and to follow historical trails where they lead—to pursue knowledge of the truth—will become ever more scarce.

Historians' collective response has been to push their graduate students to work harder, publish more, publish sooner, organize conferences, write blogs, and otherwise strive to distinguish themselves from their desperate peers. The length of a curriculum vitae has become a sorting mechanism to cut through the pile of four hundred applicants per job, which drastically compounds privilege.

The rich—the historians with research leaves, caregiving leaves, research allowances, travel budgets, research libraries, frequent speakers and workshops on their campuses—get richer. It will be increasingly difficult for very many future historians, no matter how strenuously they work or how bright they are, to follow Ratner-Rosenhagen's lead.

And there is already no room at all for temperamental hothouse intellects like William James, which may be a good thing, except that the rare and finicky can also be very fine.

NOTES

The author would like to thank Jennifer Ratner-Rosenhagen, the editors of this volume, and the participants in the symposium at IUPUI in the summer of 2016 for helpful criticism of this essay.

    1. William James, *Writings, 1902–1910*, ed. Bruce Kuklick (New York: Library of America, 1987), 487.

    2. On overdetermination and historical causality see the introduction to Peter Novick, *That Noble Dream: The Objectivity Question and the American Historical Profession* (New York: Cambridge University Press, 1988).

    3. James, *Writings, 1902–1910*, 487.

    4. Ruben Flores, *Backroads Pragmatists: Mexico's Melting Pot and Civil Rights in the United States* (Philadelphia: University of Pennsylvania Press, 2014); Jessica Ching-Sze Wang, *John Dewey in China: To Teach and to Learn* (Albany: SUNY Press, 2008).

    5. Daniel J. Wilson, *Science, Community, and the Transformation of American Philosophy* (Chicago: University of Chicago Press, 1990); Bruce Kuklick, *The Rise of American Philosophy: Cambridge, Massachusetts, 1860–1930* (New Haven, CT: Yale University Press, 1977).

    6. James, *Writings, 1902–1910*, 985.

    7. On this controversy see first David A. Hollinger, "Historians and the Discourse of Intellectuals," in *In the American Province: Studies in the History and Historiography of Ideas* (Baltimore: Johns Hopkins University Press, 1985). Although Hollinger was careful to say that anyone could participate in a community of discourse regardless of "educational level and mental capabilities" (145), his framework is contested in Daniel J. Wickberg, "Intellectual History vs. the Social History of Intellectuals," *Rethinking History* 5, no. 3 (December 2001): 383–95. Also see the forum on intellectual history in *Historically Speaking* 10, no. 4 (September 2009).

    8. My treatment of James throughout this essay draws heavily on my own research, especially for the James chapter in *The Religion of Democracy: Seven Liberals and the American Moral Tradition* (New York: Penguin, 2015).

    9. Scholars tend to pick James off the top of their heads as an exemplary elite thinker: T. J. Jackson Lears, "Against Anti-intellectualism," *Intellectual History Newsletter* 18 (1996): 21; Bruce Kuklick, "Intellectual History at Penn," ibid., 63; Wickberg, "Intellectual History," 392–93.

    10. On James as boundary crosser, the best book is also helpful for understanding the state of intellectual life before professionalization set in: Francesca Bordogna, *William James at the Boundaries: Philosophy, Science, and the Geography of Knowledge* (Chicago: University of Chicago Press, 2008).

    11. James is the only author besides Abraham Lincoln to have multiple entries in multiple categories in all seven editions of the essential sourcebook, David A. Hollinger and

Charles Capper, *The American Intellectual Tradition* (New York: Oxford University Press, 1989–2015).

12. On James's elite status and the problem this poses for historians see Amy Kittelstrom, "Against Elitism: Studying William James in the Academic Age of the Underdog," *William James Studies* 1, no. 1 (2005), http://williamjamesstudies.org/against-elitism-studying-william-james-in-the-academic-age-of-the-underdog/.

13. Perry Miller certainly falls into this category, but his *The New England Mind* (1939, 1953) treated subjects with more historicity than other monographs of the genre. On Miller see David A. Hollinger, "Perry Miller and Philosophical History," in *In the American Province*, 152–66.

14. This story is best accessed through John Higham and Paul K. Conklin, eds., *New Directions in American Intellectual History* (Baltimore: Johns Hopkins University Press, 1979). For the conception of "modern intellectual history" see the editors' preamble to the first issue of *Modern Intellectual History* 1, no. 1 (April 2004): 1–2.

15. Lawrence W. Levine, *Black Culture and Black Consciousness: Afro-American Folk Thought from Slavery to Freedom*, 30th anniversary ed. (New York: Oxford University Press, 2007).

16. See Leslie Butler's comment about her choice of intellectuals in the introduction to her *Critical Americans: Victorian Intellectuals and Transatlantic Liberal Reform* (Chapel Hill: University of North Carolina Press, 2007), 6.

17. Kuklick, *Rise of American Philosophy*, 455–58.

18. Kittelstrom, *Religion of Democracy*, 185–86.

19. David Roediger, "Whiteness and Ethnicity in the History of 'White Ethnics' in the United States," in *Towards the Abolition of Whiteness: Essays on Race, Politics, and Working Class History* (New York: Verso, 1994). This claim obscures the function of historically black colleges and universities, which provided "uplift" within segregated America.

20. On Calkins and others see Kuklick, *Rise of American Philosophy*, 590–94. Stettheimer's papers are at the Beinecke Library at Yale.

21. Alan Trachtenberg, *The Incorporation of America: Culture and Society in the Gilded Age* (New York: Hill & Wang, 1982); Robert H. Weibe, *The Search for Order: 1877–1920* (New York: Hill & Wang, 1967).

22. William James, "Robert Gould Shaw" address, quoted in Kittelstrom, *Religion of Democracy*, 196.

23. Ibid., esp. 240, 250, 270–71. I will be interested to compare my interpretation with that forthcoming from Margaret Abruzzo, "The Sins of Slaves and the Slaves of Sin: Toward a History of Moral Agency," in *The Worlds of American Intellectual History*, ed. Joel Isaac, James T. Kloppenberg, Michael O'Brien, and Jennifer Ratner-Rosenhagen (New York: Oxford University Press, 2016).

24. James T. Kloppenberg, *Uncertain Victory: Social Democracy and Progressivism in European and American Thought, 1870–1920* (New York: Oxford University Press, 1986), 162. This monograph is, among other things, a five-hundred-page illustration of the importance of philosophy to intellectual history.

25. Charles Capper, "'A Little Beyond': The Problem of the Transcendentalist Movement in American History," *Journal of American History* 85, no. 2 (September 1998): 503–4. Also see Eileen Ka-May Cheng, *The Plain and Noble Garb of Truth: Nationalism and Impartiality in American Historical Writing, 1784–1860* (Athens: University of Georgia Press, 2011).

26. James Campbell, "Du Bois and James," *Transactions of the Charles S. Peirce Society* 28, no. 3 (Summer 1992): 569–70. The tone and argument of this essay indicate how deep the problem of bias remained in the field and perhaps remains still.

27. This moment forms a critical scene in Spike Lee's film *Malcolm X* (1992) and comes from his autobiography as told to Alex Haley.

28. Campbell, "Du Bois and James," 569.

29. Thomas Haskell, *The Emergence of Professional Social Science: The American Social Science Association and the Nineteenth-Century Crisis of Authority* (Baltimore: Johns Hopkins University Press, 1977).

30. Campbell, "Du Bois and James," 569.

31. Mia Bay, *The White Image in the Black Mind: African-American Ideas about White People, 1830–1925* (New York: Oxford University Press, 2000).

32. Kittelstrom, *Religion of Democracy*, 241.

33. Cornel West, *The American Evasion of Philosophy: A Genealogy of Pragmatism* (Madison: University of Wisconsin Press, 1989). Interestingly, this book is not listed among West's works on his own website: http://www.cornelwest.com/bio.html#.V4p97I4W_hY (accessed July 16, 2016).

34. Ta-Nehisi Coates, *Between the World and Me* (New York: Spiegel & Grau, 2015), 47.

35. Keisha Blaine investigates how a historical figure qualifies as a "theorist" in her essay "Writing Black Women's Intellectual History," *Black Perspectives*, African American Intellectual History Society blog, November 21, 2016, http://www.aaihs.org/writing-black-womens-intellectual-history/.

36. Robert Darnton, *The Great Cat Massacre: And Other Episodes in French Cultural History* (New York: Basic Books, 1984); David D. Hall, *Worlds of Wonder, Days of Judgment: Popular Religious Belief in Early New England* (New York: Alfred A. Knopf, 1989); David D. Hall, ed., *Lived Religion in America: Toward a History of Practice* (Princeton, NJ: Princeton University Press, 1997), vii; Thomas L. Haskell, "Objectivity Is Not Neutrality: Rhetoric vs. Practice in Peter Novick's *That Noble Dream*," *History and Theory* 29, no. 2 (May 1990): 129–57.

37. Jennifer Ratner-Rosenhagen, *American Nietzsche: A History of an Icon and His Ideas* (Chicago: University of Chicago Press, 2012). Another important recent work in intellectual history on philosophy is Sophia Rosenfeld, *Common Sense: A Political History* (Cambridge, MA: Harvard University Press, 2011).

38. Gwen Drury, "The Wisconsin Idea: The Vision That Made Wisconsin Famous," 2011, http://ls.wisc.edu/assets/misc/documents/wi-idea-history-intro-summary-essay.pdf (accessed December 15, 2016).

39. Merle Curti, *The Growth of American Thought* (New York, London: Harper & Bros., 1943).

5

THE PRICE OF RECOGNITION
Race and the Making of the Modern University

Jonathan Holloway

In *American Slavery, American Freedom*, the historian Edmund Morgan argues that one cannot understand the history of the making of the United States without appreciating the fact that the new country's love for freedom was intertwined with its investment in slavery. So much of the American narrative in the intervening centuries has been articulated through an acknowledged and boastful love for freedom while typically ignoring histories of enslavement, racial segregation, and institutional racism. The textures of the latter phenomena have been no mystery to those who suffer from the experience of being second class; they are accustomed to the fact that so many aspects of their lives have been ignored—sometimes innocently, often willfully. But what happens when what is typically ignored, in this case the black experience broadly conceived, becomes acknowledged?

This essay pauses to reflect on the moment when that which has not been granted recognition is either uncovered or discovered. Exploring the world of ideas and its interactions with a social history of black bodies—intellectuals, students, workers—immersed in (historically white) college cultures invites an assessment about the costs associated with recognition. When we reflect upon blacks' thoughts and examine their experiences, we come to the sobering realization of how high the stakes happen to be in the making of the modern university. "Black ideas," for want of a better term, regarding recognition—the lack of it and the moment of its emergence—turn, almost inevitably, toward literal and figurative violence.[1]

Part I—The Intellectuals

I am standing puzzled, unable to decide whether the veil is really being lifted, or lowered more firmly into place; whether I am witnessing a revelation or a more efficient blinding.

—Narrator, Ralph Ellison, *The Invisible Man*

Russell Jacoby published *The Last Intellectuals: American Culture in the Age of Academe* in 1987. The book, a polemic about the failure of a new generation of scholars to replace the famed New York intellectuals of midcentury, seemed encyclopedic as it canvassed the breadth of twentieth-century American intellectual life. But the book—a clear success in the publishing world and in the world of ideas—claimed a false breadth. No black scholars, not even the ubiquitous midcentury troika of Richard Wright, James Baldwin, and Ralph Ellison, appeared in Jacoby's analysis. To his credit, Jacoby acknowledged this oversight in the 2000 edition of the book, writing admiringly about the opportunity/possibility presented by the intervening mid-1990s emergence of the "new black public intellectual":

> For the first time in many years a group of African American intellectuals has burst upon the scene—figures such as Henry Louis Gates, Gerald Early, Adolph Reed Jr., Randall Kennedy, and Cornel West. These are smart, hard-hitting, and often graceful writers who weigh into public problems of race, sports, politics, law, and culture. They have been both acclaimed as successors to the New York intellectuals and criticized as publicity hounds who ignore earlier black public intellectuals such as W. E. B. Du Bois and C. L. R. James. In no way did my book anticipate their appearance. . . . It seems to me that the new black intellectuals demonstrate that a literate, indeed hungry, public still exists.[2]

In a way, Jacoby was right: for a time in the 1990s, it really did feel like you couldn't turn a corner without running into an essay about these new public intellectuals.[3] But what was it that made them "new"? If taken literally, the newness can simply be a reflection of the fact that these figures were part of an emerging generation of thinkers who were operating in the public consciousness (and although Jacoby's brief list included only men, many of these "new" intellectuals were female). But Jacoby's original failure to recognize black scholars working throughout the twentieth century (and increasingly in white spaces as universities began to desegregate) points to a more troubling reality: for most of the century, black intellectuals' contributions simply didn't register. They did not matter to a mainstream audience.

The failure to recognize black contributions to the world of ideas had consequences. In 1968, Eldridge Cleaver, soon-to-be Black Panther Party minister of information, published *Soul on Ice*, a disturbing reflection on structural inequality, race, masculinity, violence (physical and psychological), and American culture. Cleaver criticized the "so-called molders of public opinion, the writers, politicians, [and] teachers," adding that they were "not equipped to either *feel* or *know* that a radical break, a revolutionary leap out of their sight, had taken place in the secret parts of this nation's soul."[4] For Cleaver, whites' insistent lack of recognition helped contribute to the revolutionary moment gripping the nation and the nation's campuses. Cleaver angrily assessed the risk of willful ignorance, arguing that a commitment neither to see nor to know was a commitment to extermination. The question, in Cleaver's black radical mind, was simply who was going to be wiped out first as a result of this commitment to cultural obliteration.

"Commitment" is the operative word here, since it is the systemic determination to refuse to believe in the full breadth of black humanity that has caused so much damage in the black world psychologically, phenomenologically, and literally. This is a point that bears emphasizing, because it underscores an abiding theme in black critical discourse and because for so many black intellectuals the very act of creating a critical discourse was about survival.[5] Feminist theorists like Audre Lorde made this much plain: "For women . . . poetry is not a luxury. It is a vital necessity of our existence. It forms the quality of the light within which we predicate our hopes and dreams toward survival and change, first made into language, then into idea, then into more tangible action. Poetry is the way we help give name to the nameless so it can be thought. The farthest horizons of our hopes and fears are cobbled by our poems, carved from the rock experiences of our daily lives."[6]

Other scholars and writers have written with similar urgency. For example, in the first of his two essays that make up *The Fire Next Time*, James Baldwin tells his nephew, or, rather, *prepares* his nephew for a country that was dedicated to black impossibility: "You were born into a society which spelled out with brutal clarity, and in as many ways as possible, that you were a worthless human being. You were not expected to aspire to excellence: you were expected to make peace with mediocrity."[7]

No one could claim, of course, that Baldwin was unknown on the American scene. He was, in fact, quite the opposite: the darling of talk shows, college debates, artists' salons, and the speaker circuit, generally. However, Baldwin's work revolved around his commitment to addressing what went unacknowledged in the American consciousness. This, in the end, was what he was trying to tell his nephew: the country into which he had been born could not imagine him as a fully formed human being. Ironically, Baldwin's celebrity and resulting hypervisibility allowed an admiring public to ignore the very troubles that Baldwin was pointing them toward. Admiration could feel like an acknowledgment for those bestowing the recognition, but admiration did not do anything to address the structural problems that were part and parcel of an unacknowledged existence in the first place. This caveat is important: the moment of recognition is not inexorably a move toward progress.

The failure to recognize blacks as fully human or to understand their complexity had mortal consequences. The journalist and cultural critic Ta-Nehisi Coates has delineated how the failure to recognize the full measure of blacks' humanity manifested itself in a cultural consciousness that reduced blacks to ciphers of impossibility. In his book *Between the World and Me*, Coates borrows explicitly from Baldwin's structure in *The Fire Next Time* and writes a letter to his son that is suffused with a moral and mortal urgency linked directly to the murder of one of his Howard University classmates, someone who was, to Coates, the physical embodiment of black possibility. *Between the World and Me* is a simultaneous canvassing of American history and the contemporary moment. Collectively, the past and the present are intertwined in often brutalizing and heartbreaking ways, both in service, Coates claims, to a logic of structural domination. In one of the more poignant passages, Coates connects the nation's logic of economic exploitation to its concomitant refusal to believe in an enslaved person's humanity:

> The wisdom is not unique to our people, but I think it has special meaning to those of us born out of mass rape, whose ancestors were carried off and divided into policies and stocks. I have raised you to respect every human being as singular, and you must extend that same respect into the past. Slavery is not an indefinable mass of flesh. It is a particular, specific enslaved woman, whose mind is active as your own, whose range of feeling is as vast as your own; who prefers the way the light falls in one particular spot in the woods, who enjoys fishing where the water eddies in a nearby stream, who loves her mother in her own complicated way, thinks her sister talks too loud, has a favorite cousin, a favorite season, who excels at dress-making and knows, inside herself, that she is as intelligent and capable as anyone.[8]

In a different way, Claudia Rankine identified the same phenomenon in *Citizen: An American Lyric*. Using prose, images, and poetry, Rankine captured the same moral rage we find in Coates. Here, though, there is more nuanced language that also speaks to a sorrowful mixture of resignation and resilience. Rankine understands that the battle is long and that knowing one's enemies can often mean knowing one's friends, and knowing one's friends means knowing their blindness. She writes, "You are in the dark, in the car, watching the black-tarred street being swallowed by speed; he tells you his dean is making him hire a person of color when there are so many great writers out there."[9]

Ralph Ellison prefaced Coates and Rankine. In "The World and the Jug," Ellison took umbrage with New York intellectual Irving Howe for his inability or his unwillingness to believe that there might be more than one type of "Negro writer." Blacks had a broad and complicated humanity that was no different from any others', but Howe could not see it and criticized Ellison and Baldwin for failing to follow in Richard Wright's footsteps and write "protest literature." Ellison unleashed his anger:

> I did not intend to take the stance of the "knowing Negro writer" against the "presuming white intellectual." While I am without a doubt a Negro, and a writer, I am also an *American* writer, and while I am more knowing than Howe where my own life and its influences are concerned, I took the time to question his presumptions as one responsible for contributing as much as he is capable to the clear perception of American social reality. For to think unclearly about that segment of reality in which I find my existence is to do myself violence. To allow others to go unchallenged when they distort that reality is to participate not only in that distortion but to accept, as in this instance, a violence inflicted upon the art of criticism.[10]

Cleaver. Lorde. Baldwin. Coates. Rankine. Ellison. The list goes on, and the observations compound upon one another. The chronology feels immaterial. Ideas contort with structural realities that terminate, almost inevitably, with violence. Language deflates, and compels its authors to more hard work, as it falls upon ears that will not hear or eyes that refuse to see.

This work and pain, both grounded in invisibility that is, in truth, the failure to recognize someone as fully human (or is a perverse hypervisibility that prevents careful and critical analysis because it suggests a person is superhuman) and both related to the psychological violence that springs from the fact the "black idea" can be so easily dismissed, is not unique to the black scholar and the professional maker of ideas. This work and pain are also an abiding theme among black undergraduates at historically white colleges and universities since they began to arrive on these campuses in the late 1960s in any numbers suggesting a critical mass.

Part II—Students

> Live with your head in the lion's mouth. I want you to overcome 'em with yeses, undermine 'em with grins, agree 'em to death and distraction, let 'em swoller you till they vomit or bust wide open.
>
> —Narrator's grandfather, in Ralph Ellison, *The Invisible Man*

Before he graduated from Yale in 1968, Armstead Robinson sat for an interview with the *Yale Alumni Magazine* about his experiences being black at Yale. Robinson sounded notes of dissatisfaction and anger when he spoke about the "whiteness" of a place like Yale and the absence of black history in the school's curriculum. However, when he addressed the foundational meaning of being black at Yale, Robinson sounded wise and weary beyond his years. He spoke to the role of the black individual in a virtually all-white setting and the determination to preserve a set of memories and culture that would otherwise succumb to neglect or erasure. Robinson began with a question: "The basic issue here is why were we brought to Yale in the first place?":

> I will argue that somewhere deep in the minds of the people on the admissions committee was the idea that they needed some diversity. It's sort of like when you're cooking you throw in some salt to make the food taste better. It's a fundamentally paternalistic conception, to assume that the functional utility for bringing black people here is to use them to broaden the horizons of the white students. It almost seems as if Yale said, "Let's get some Indians, a few niggers, keep the number small but have a few as spicing so you can have the whole pot taste good." I can't handle that; not very many black people can handle it either.

Robinson wanted to make it clear to the magazine's readers that his was not a defeatist attitude. He argued that black students had more to contribute to Yale than simply serving as ethnographic artifacts that would help whites feel better. Or, as he put it, "We refuse to be the spicing." Robinson continued:

> We think there's much more to blackness than simply to make whiteness a little grey. We think that blackness in and of itself is good. We refuse to come here and lose our blackness by sort of helping out the white majority. In a sense, that would be asking a black student to come here and become deculturated. That's a hell of a process. And it's not something you ask anybody else to do. The desire for positive black identification is, quite frankly, a positive assertion that I have some identity that I intend to preserve. I'm not running away saying that I can't deal with it. It's just that if you don't ask anybody *else* to do it, then don't ask *me* to do it.[11]

Robinson's insights reflect the psychological trauma of "deculturation," of being told in many ways that his and his peers' ideas weren't necessary or relevant. Their bodies, however, were required. This was the late 1960s, and Robinson's ideas were a manifestation of the processes let loose when many of the leading historically white colleges and universities started to open their doors to black students. Administrators began to concede that they had been ignoring black students and became determined to address this particular failing. Most dramatically, admissions officers moved hastily to reach into the nation's urban enclaves, hoping to identify black students who could manage the academic challenges of the traditional, rigorous liberal arts curriculum.[12]

Being on campus in still relatively small numbers made the black undergraduates hypervisible. If administrators expected that their most physically identifiable students would uniformly align themselves with their white peers and with a long-standing curriculum that revolved around the Western European canon, they were mistaken. Across the country, black students, awakened in part by the increased public profile (read: mainstream recognition) of black militants like Eldridge Cleaver, began to push aggressively for a curriculum that reflected, in part, their own lived experience. In short order, calls for black studies began to be made across the nation, beginning at San Francisco State and carrying over to Cornell, Yale, and Harvard.[13] For administrators who were paying attention, recognition meant institutional change.

In 1975, the poet and activist June Jordan was teaching at Yale. That spring, students invited her to speak at a rally protesting a talk that the Stanford scientist William Shockley was giving the next day. (Shockley was making the college rounds, calling for the sterilization of black women because of what he claimed to be blacks' genetic inferiority.)[14] Jordan was, in her words, "buoyant," and looking forward to reading a poem and making a statement when Theresa Johnson, one of her students, approached her: "She peered into my sunglasses, awkwardly, for a moment. Then she said, 'Why do they hate us, June? Why,' she asked me, 'why do they hate *me*?' I looked at the face of Theresa, at the tears on her face, and something inside me changed, irrevocably. I had conceptualized my statement as a written party to a malevolent but intellectual debate, but now I viewed it as part of a very dirty fight, which was, by its nature, apocalyptic: we could not afford to lose."[15]

Robinson and Jordan were writing, and Theresa Johnson was speaking, during an era unique unto itself. Colleges were opening their doors more widely than before, the nation was trying to come to terms with shocking rituals of violence in international theaters of war as well as on its own streets, and battles over what was defensible in the world of ideas were being waged.

This was a moment that could not be repeated. Or could it?

In 2015, citizens across the country watched—most in confusion, but many with a sympathetic awareness—as colleges and universities endured convulsions that seemed to be an echo from decades past. (Mostly) black student radicals and their allies rose up at major public institutions like the University of Missouri (Mizzou), small liberal arts schools like Amherst and Oberlin, and elite private universities like Yale and Princeton. All told, activists at over eighty schools spoke with a pain and anger that sounded achingly similar to Robinson's angry lament from forty-five years earlier in which he questioned the university's motivations for recognizing blacks as potential students.[16]

Jonathan Butler's actions and words are a case in point. Butler, a graduate student at Mizzou, rose to national prominence when he started a hunger strike to protest a range of issues, most significantly an administrative failure to acknowledge and address a campus climate hostile to black students. In a letter to Mizzou chancellor Bowen Loftin, Butler acknowledged the fact that the university leadership was finally taking some positive steps aimed at calming the roiling campus, but he criticized the administration for talking about new programs as if the administration were acting on its own accord in the absence of earlier calls to change. Butler presented a genealogy of black student activism at Mizzou that reached back to the 1930s, became amplified during the late 1960s, and then reemerged with force in recent years. The administration's failure to recognize this history of black students' struggle had contributed to the problems of the moment. Butler wrote,

> Your language that attempts to adopt strategies like diversity and inclusion training as "new strategies" without acknowledging where the ideas/strategies came from is disrespectful and false. These issues and the strategies that brave individuals have brought to the attention of administrators is not new to MU and also not new to you and your staff specifically. So to not acknowledge the protesters, organizers, students, faculty and staff who have taken of their time and energy to hold you and your administration accountable is very disrespectful and paints a false image of the work that your administration has been doing on this campus.

Butler's letter was a call for recognition and expressed the concern that the administration would not act in good faith when it came to people from marginalized backgrounds and who existed behind the scrim. Butler continued, "These 'unheard' stories are worth your time and attention; their lived experiences are worth acknowledging and their humanity worth fighting for. This constant lack of acknowledgment to the struggles of oppressed individuals reinforces the notion that administrators only react to incidents on campus that happen to people in organizations or positions of social power."[17]

Black students at Oberlin and Amherst had similar criticisms of their school's administrations. At Oberlin, the demands that students presented included a call for a more diverse faculty and changes to the curriculum—fairly standard demands across campuses in 2015 and 2016—but also went so far as to name individuals who should either be punished or promoted. The language in the demands' opening paragraph almost perfectly reflects Robinson's late 1960s' observations and also addresses the crisis that springs from an abiding failure to recognize all the school's students. While the activists observed that Oberlin was perhaps the most progressive historically white college in the country in terms of its longtime commitment to enrolling and supporting black students, they declared that these claims to an enlightened past were little more than a "public relations campaign initiated to benefit the institution and not the Africana people it was set out for." Oberlin relied on black and brown students for its publicity brochures but then erased them from day-to-day life on campus. "You profit off of our accomplishments and invisible labor," they wrote, "yet You expect us to produce personal solutions to institutional incompetencies. We as a College-defined 'high risk,' 'low income,' 'disadvantaged' community should not have to carry the burden of deconstructing the white supremacist, patriarchal, capitalist system that we took no part in creating, yet is so deeply embedded in the soil upon which this institution was built."[18] At Amherst, student organizer Mercedes MacAlpine spoke directly to the connection between the campus unrest and a sense among students that their experiences simply weren't recognized by the institution: "The turning point and why it got so large is that multiple students of all sorts of background recognized a feeling of feeling marginalized, of feeling invisible or feeling isolated in some important way."[19]

One event at Yale reaffirmed the historic phenomenon of a failure of acknowledgment and then the corresponding student anger and resentment when, in the students' minds, the university administration continued to use the students of color as window dressing and refused to address deeper, structural issues relating to quality of life and the curriculum. Roughly one week into a tense month of standoffs between the students and the administration, the Yale students held a March for Resilience. It was a transcendent moment where Yalies of all backgrounds and ranks (from undergraduates to graduate students to faculty) came together to support one another, specifically women of color who had been feeling the brunt of so much antipathy in the national press over their activism.[20] The march was led by women holding a banner. That banner declared, "We Out Here. We Been Here. We Ain't Leaving. We Are Loved." That banner and the accompanying chant were an insistence that ignoring students and their experiences was no longer a viable strategy that an ethical college administration could pursue; that people needed to know their history if they hoped to have a purchase on their future; and that if the university could not find a way to support and love its own students, then the students would do it themselves. This march may have been one calling for resilience, but it was clearly also a march about acknowledgment.

FIGURE 5.1 Photo by Alex Zhang.

Part III—Workers

> Already he's learned to repress not only his emotions but his humanity. He's invisible, a walking personification of The Negative, the most perfect achievement of your dreams, sir! The mechanical man!
>
> —Narrator, Ralph Ellison, *The Invisible Man*

Black scholars' and students' critical statements about the consequences of institutional failures of recognition are important and force a reconsideration of how universities might articulate themselves and their visions while serving all members of their communities. There is a troubling undercurrent, however, in the statements and conversations involving black intellectuals and students: too often they exist at a remove from another key constituency on college campuses—the constituency whose labor enables them to do their work.

At a place like Yale, situated in a postindustrial, black-majority urban setting, with a service workforce that is predominantly black and increasingly Latino, there is a historic and even contemporary failure to recognize that labor is itself a repetition of the same dynamic that the figures cited in this essay critique. When moments of recognition emerge, as they did in the summer of 2016, the convulsive power of the moment is laid bare, exposing other failures in a community's ability to be cohesive and underscoring the fact that these communities are typically held together by gossamer threads that could snap at any moment.

Enter Corey Menafee, a black dining hall worker at Yale, who was assigned to Calhoun College, one of the university's twelve undergraduate residential colleges. Calhoun was named for Yale alum John C. Calhoun, a nineteenth-century South Carolina political statesman, slave owner, and intellectual architect of southern secession. At the start of the 2015–2016 academic year, the name of the college had become a lightning rod for campus debates about honoring the past and acknowledging structural racism and inequality.[21] Part of the controversy was in regard to windows found in the college's public spaces that depicted representations of an idyllic South: visions of a sporting man's life, South Carolina flora and fauna, enslaved persons' quarters, a black man contentedly playing a banjo, and two enslaved individuals standing in a vast cotton field with baskets of picked cotton on their heads.

Menafee was working in the dining hall where half a dozen of these images were etched in glass fifteen feet above the floor. Menafee had been working in Calhoun for less than a year, but in early July he had had enough. He climbed atop a table and used a broom to smash the window depicting enslaved people carrying cotton. As he told reporters, "Something inside me said, you know, that thing has to come down. You know, it's a picture—it was a picture that just—you know, as soon as you look at it, it just hurts. You feel it in your heart, like, oh, man—like here in the 21st century, you know, we're in a modern era where we shouldn't have to be subjected to those primitive and degrading images."[22]

Menafee was arrested, lost his job (he was reinstated after a five-week suspension), and quickly became the rallying cause of protest marches in the city and the center of a media storm. The protests focused on the structural inequalities of the moment, declaring that a wealthy, predominantly white university with a majority-black service workforce had fired a heretofore unknown worker because he refused to abide by the university's decision to honor a nineteenth-century racist.[23] The intensity of the media attention was predictable, given the contemporary national climate regarding race and citizenship and violence, as well as the unrest on Yale's campus in the months leading up to Menafee's action. The scope and durability of the attention—this was a trending story for over a week in mainstream, national news—were equally predictable and remarkable: predictable for the reasons cited above, and remarkable for the way that they implicitly underscore Menafee's unacknowledged existence until the moment of convulsive recognition.

Menafee's actions, of course, need to be placed in their proper historical context. Black service workers from earlier eras who engaged in these kind of declarative actions knew that they would never garner sympathetic national media attention and, at best, would merely lose their jobs. These earlier workers had to know that an act of self-declaration like Menafee's would never compel an institution to acknowledge their full and complex humanity. It is safe to say that for decades, service workers' silence and invisibility were part of the code of cultural conduct that allowed Yale and similar schools to function comfortably within their own homogeneity.

One image tells this story well.

FIGURE 5.2 Student Life at Yale Photographs (RU 736). Courtesy of Manuscripts and Archives, Yale University Library.

Here, a single black worker, in this case a bartender, stands at silent attention in the middle of an idyllic 1950s scene. Dozens of older white men, a sprinkling of undergraduates (all male, all white), and a handful of older white women fill in the scene, drinks in hand. The unidentified bartender may have completed his work, but he must remain at attention, ready to pour another cocktail, ensuring that the party continues without interruption. His presence is fundamentally unrecognized, and until that glass is drained, it's safe to presume his labor also proceeds without recognition. While this image does not tell a story of convulsion like Corey Menafee's, and even though there is no record of the service worker's name or history, the composition of the image and the story that it tells is piercing. There is no way to look at this image and not see a kind of psychological violence at work.

Part IV—Compensatory Acknowledgment

Near the end of his life James Baldwin declared, "The day will come when you will trust you more than you do now, and you will trust me more than you do now. And we can trust each other. I do believe, I really do believe in the New Jerusalem, I really do believe that we can all become better than we are. I know we can. But the price is enormous, and people are not yet willing to pay it."[24] Baldwin was speaking about the "price of the ticket," an investment that everyone, black, brown, and white, needed to make in order to secure a just world.[25] Whether he was writing to his nephew in *The Fire Next Time* or to a broader readership in his other essays, novels, or plays, Baldwin was always wrestling with the high price of this ticket, and encouraging people to rise to the many challenges that got in the way of meeting that expense.

As our colleges and universities continue to pursue aspirations of supporting demographic complexity and inclusion, they would do well to listen to the histories of their own faculties, students, and workers. Recognizing those who are already members of their communities, learning their stories, and valuing their contributions will go a long way toward meeting the price of the ticket. At minimum, just a sincere acknowledgment of the full and complex humanity that makes up our nation's campuses would be a down payment worth making.

One university, however, stands out as a case study of how these institutions might do more than the minimum. In late 2015 and in a move that can be called "compensatory acknowledgment"—when an institution tries to come to figurative and literal terms with an ethically complicated past—Georgetown University began to wrestle with the cost of recognition of an earlier black workforce. That fall, the university formed the Working Group on Slavery, Memory, and Reconciliation to study the university's ties to slavery.[26] One year later, Georgetown president John DeGioia released the committee's final report. Most of the working group's six pages of recommendations revolved around the need for the university to take public steps of different types, all of which pointed toward an elusive reconciliation between the university's present values and the institution's deep ties to slavery.[27] The report raised the possibility of offering scholarships or admissions preferences to the descendants of the 272 enslaved people Georgetown's Jesuit priests sold in 1838 in order to keep the university afloat. To most observers' astonishment, DeGioia announced that these descendants would get the same preferential treatment in the admissions process as the children of

Georgetown alumni.[28] The actual price of this administrative commitment to recognition, however, is unknown.

NOTES

I extend my gratitude to my research assistant Lucy Caplan for her insightful comments and keen editor's eye. She has been a critical collaborator and interlocutor for this project.

1. The concept of recognition was developed in G. W. F. Hegel's *Phenomenology of Spirit* (1807) and has been engaged by a number of modern theorists. Notable examples include Saidiya Hartman, *Scenes of Subjection: Terror, Slavery, and Self-Making in Nineteenth-Century America* (New York: Oxford University Press, 1997), and Judith Butler, "Longing for Recognition: Commentary on the Work of Jessica Benjamin," *Studies in Gender and Sexuality* 1, no. 3 (2000).

2. Russell Jacoby, introduction to *The Last Intellectuals* (1987; New York: Basic Books, 2000), xix–xx.

3. Michael Bérubé, "Public Academy," *New Yorker*, January 9, 1995; Robert S. Boynton, "The New Intellectuals," *Atlantic Monthly*, March 1995; Adolph Reed, "What Are the Drums Saying, Booker? The Current Crisis of the Black Intellectual," *Village Voice*, April 11, 1995, 31–37.

4. Eldridge Cleaver, *Soul on Ice* (1968; New York: Delta, 1991), 223–24.

5. See Jonathan Holloway, "The Black Intellectual and the 'Crisis Canon' in the Twentieth Century," *Black Scholar* 31, no. 1 (2001).

6. Audre Lorde, *Sister Outsider* (Trumansburg, NY: Crossing, 1984), 36.

7. James Baldwin, *The Fire Next Time* (New York: Dell, 1963), 18.

8. Ta-Nehisi Coates, *Between the World and Me* (New York: Spiegel & Grau, 2015), 69–70.

9. Claudia Rankine, *Citizen* (Minneapolis: Graywolf, 2014), 10.

10. Ralph Ellison, "The World and the Jug," in *Shadow and Act* (New York: Vintage Books, 1972), 125.

11. "On Being Black at Yale," in *University Crisis Reader: Confrontation and Counterattack*, 2 vols., ed. Immanuel Wallerstein and Paul Starr (New York: Vintage Books, 1971), 2:385.

12. See Martha Biondi, *The Black Revolution on Campus* (Berkeley: University of California Press, 2012).

13. See Stefan Bradley, *Harlem vs. Columbia University: Black Student Power in the Late 1960s* (Urbana: University of Illinois Press, 2012); Biondi, *Black Revolution on Campus*; Wayne Glasker, *Black Students in the Ivory Tower: African American Activism at the University of Pennsylvania, 1867–1990* (Amherst: University of Massachusetts Press, 2002); Jonathan Holloway, *Jim Crow Wisdom* (Chapel Hill: University of North Carolina Press, 2013); Ibram X. Kendi, *The Black Campus Movement: Black Students and the Racial Reconstitution of Higher Education, 1965–1972* (New York: Palgrave Macmillan, 2012); Armstead L. Robinson, Craig C. Foster, and Donald H. Ogilvie, eds., *Black Studies in the University: A Symposium* (New Haven, CT: Yale University Press, 1969); and Joy Ann Williamson, *Black Power on Campus: The University of Illinois, 1965–75* (Urbana: University of Illinois Press, 2003).

14. Joel Shurkin, *Broken Genius: The Rise and Fall of William Shockley, Creator of the Electronic Age* (New York: Palgrave Macmillan, 2008), 235–39.

15. June Jordan, "On the Occasion of a Clear and Present Danger at Yale," in *Civil Wars: Observations from the Front Lines of America* (Boston: Beacon, 1981), 91.

16. The Demands, http://www.thedemands.org (accessed July 6, 2016).

17. Jonathan Butler, "Diversity Training Is a Good Step for MU, But It Is Not Enough," *Columbia Missourian*, October 16, 2015, https://tinyurl.com/yav8mpob.

18. https://web.archive.org/web/20160121033719/https://new.oberlin.edu/petition-jan2016.pdf.

19. Dan Glaun, "Amherst College President Biddy Martin Addresses Student Protestors during Library Sit-In," *MassLive*, November 14, 2016, http://www.masslive.com/news/index.ssf/2015/11/amherst_college_president_bidd_2.html.

20. Conor Friedersdorf, "The New Intolerance of Student Activism," *Atlantic*, November 9, 2015, http://www.theatlantic.com/politics/archive/2015/11/the-new-intolerance-of-student-activism-at-yale/414810; Jon Victor, Monica Wang, and Victor Wang, "More Than 1,000 Gather in Solidarity," *Yale Daily News*, November 10, 2015, http://yaledailynews.com/blog/2015/11/10/more-than-1000-gather-in-solidarity; Jelani Cobb, "Race and the Free-Speech Diversion," *New Yorker* online, November 10, 2015, http://www.newyorker.com/news/news-desk/race-and-the-free-speech-diversion.

21. Tyler Foggatt and Emma Platoff, "Salovey Calls for Conversation on Calhoun," *Yale Daily News*, August 29, 2015, http://yaledailynews.com/blog/2015/08/29/salovey-calls-for-conversation-on-calhoun/; "What's in a Name?" *Yale Alumni Magazine* May/June 2016, https://yalealumnimagazine.com/articles/4301-whats-in-a-name.

22. "Exclusive: Meet Yale Dishwasher Corey Menafee, Who Smashed Racist Stained-Glass Window," interview by Amy Goodman, *Democracy Now*, July 15, 2016, https://www.democracynow.org/2016/7/15/exclusive_meet_yale_dishwasher_corey_menafee. Yale University does not have a photograph of the window that Menafee destroyed that can be reproduced in high resolution. Archivists and curators continue to hope a copy surfaces.

23. See Kica Matos, "Windows on a Shameful Past," *New Haven Independent*, July 25, 2016, http://www.newhavenindependent.org/index.php/archives/entry/calhoun_glass/; Lindsey Bever, "A Yale Dishwasher Broke a 'Racist' Windowpane. Now, He's Fighting to Reclaim His Job," *Washington Post*, July 19, 2016, https://www.washingtonpost.com/news/grade-point/wp/2016/07/12/yale-dishwasher-resigns-after-smashing-racist-very-degrading-stained-glass-window/; Zoe Greenberg, "Yale Drops Case against Worker Who Smashed Window Depicting Slaves," *New York Times*, July 12, 2016, http://www.nytimes.com/2016/07/13/nyregion/yale-worker-john-c-calhoun-window-slaves.html.

24. *James Baldwin: The Price of the Ticket*, directed by Karen Thorsen (San Francisco: California Newsreel, 1989).

25. "The Price of the Ticket" is also the name of the introduction to and compilation of Baldwin's nonfiction work from 1985. James Baldwin, *The Price of the Ticket: Collected Nonfiction, 1948–1985* (New York: St. Martin's, 1985).

26. See Georgetown University: Slavery, Memory, and Reconciliation, http://slavery.georgetown.edu.

27. "Report of the Working Group on Slavery, Memory, and Reconciliation to the President of Georgetown University," Summer 2016, 41–46, http://slavery.georgetown.edu.

28. Rachel Swarns, "Georgetown University Plans Steps to Atone for Slave Past," *New York Times*, September 1, 2016, http://www.nytimes.com/2016/09/02/us/slaves-georgetown-university.html; Tressie McMillan Cottom, "Georgetown's Slavery Announcement Is Remarkable. But It's Not Reparations," *Vox*, September 2, 2016, http://www.vox.com/2016/9/2/12773110/georgetown-slavery-admission-reparations; Jaweed Kaleem, "What Georgetown's Atonement Means for the Campus Debate over Slavery," *Los Angeles Times*, September 2, 2016, http://www.latimes.com/nation/la-na-georgetown-slavery-snap-story.html.

6

THANKS, GENDER!
An Intellectual History of the Gym

Natalia Mehlman Petrzela

The woman and gender problem has persisted more tenaciously in the field of intellectual history than it has in other fields of historical inquiry. Core methodological and political commitments make overlooking women and gender untenable in realms like social history, ethnic studies, and, most obviously, women's history and its offshoots. Yet the exclusion of women thinkers and the study of gender from intellectual history can seem to make a perverse kind of sense. "Intellectual," like "scientist" or "citizen," has historically been gendered fundamentally male because of deeply embedded assumptions that rationality and uteruses cannot coexist in one body. For this reason, women were largely unwelcome in the rarefied academic and literary circles in which intellectual activity, traditionally defined, once occurred. This homogeneity of identity then meaningfully circumscribed inquiry: how could an overwhelmingly male field think to interrogate the category of gender when privilege is notoriously unseen by those who possess it?

The Possibilities of Gendered Intellectual History

The transformation of the broader historical profession—in breadth of research focus if not as dramatically in composition—due to the rights-based movements of the 1960s and '70s arguably took longer to transpire in intellectual history because of the persistence of a narrow definition of "intellectual" that provided its own tautological justification: might the number of women who qualify as intellectuals, traditionally defined, be too small to justify sustained inquiry? Yet political historians modeled an alternative way forward.[1] Politics had also been traditionally defined as white and male until African-American and women's suffrage exploded that assumption, in the process revising "politics" to comprise power relations beyond the halls of government. Scholars from marginalized groups helped bring about this shift in intellectual sensibilities and also benefited from it. Similarly, an increasingly diverse cadre of scholars has been reexamining the field's founding assumptions and their research implications for what falls under the mantle of "doing intellectual history."[2]

Crucial to this recasting has been to acknowledge the work and lives of the growing number of female and LGBTQ scientists, philosophers, and literary critics who fit the bill of "intellectual," traditionally defined, and whose experiences often reveal barriers to their full participation in the not-so-free marketplace of ideas.[3] Also urgent is charting the history of ideas *about* gender and sexuality. Dizzying shifts have made American thought about gender and sexuality especially dynamic in the past half century, and intellectual historians are uniquely trained to chart the significance of these intersecting and often contradictory trajectories.[4] These errands are often taken up by members of marginalized groups, though it is vital to remember that female/LGBTQ intellectual historians are not "naturally" drawn to such themes or topics. In *The Gender of History: Men, Women, and Historical Practice* (1998), Bonnie Smith reveals how "amateur" women have defied expectations of their irrationality and unpacks the masculinist assumptions that undergird the presumed legitimacy of historians as well as the worthiness of their subjects.[5] If the historiographical book *The History Men* that Smith identifies as emblematic of this problem was published in distant 1984, the title of the decidedly twenty-first-century history podcast *Backstory with the American History Guys* evokes a similar sensibility; the popular program, which began in 2008, added a female host (the Yale professor Joanne Freeman) to its lineup only in 2017.[6]

Change is afoot and has been gathering momentum for decades as gender has become a more meaningful category of analysis in the history of ideas. A founding mother of women's history, Gerda Lerner, is credited with teaching the first US women's history course in 1963 (which at first failed to generate sufficient student interest) while she was still an undergraduate at the New School for Social Research.[7] Soon after, Ann Firor Scott's *The Southern Lady: From Pedestal to Politics* (1970) not only added women's voices to the historical record, but also showed how different American ideas and institutions look when they are understood as gendered.[8] Ensuing scholarly generations have followed suit, revealing the limitations of ideologies like individualism, meritocracy, and citizenship, and institutions from marriage to medicine. Women and others marginalized by gender and sexuality, these accounts illuminate, have not been hapless victims of historical forces but have fought to eradicate these ideologies and institutions or to make them more just. More broadly, from the moralism of nineteenth-century reformers, to the introduction of family values as a foundation of conservative politics, to the sentimentality of an Oprahfied cultural moment, scholars have followed Ann Douglas's lead in mapping various expressions of the "feminization of American culture."[9]

Yet even these approaches can persist in excluding those who do not obviously qualify as the "Great Women"—to invoke the title of Lerner's foundational course—or more specifically, as intellectuals.[10] As the historian Mia Bay pointed out at a plenary session on women and gender at the 2016 annual meeting of the Society for US Intellectual History, working-class women of color have been unlikely to embrace or be anointed with the title "intellectual," a social fact that has served to obscure their role in the history of ideas. Yet the rise of grassroots political movements and communication technologies means those who don't conform to a traditional definition of "intellectual" are increasingly powerful sources and conduits of ideas. Contemporary "crunk" feminism is a case in point: a movement of self-described "critical homegirls" who work in haltingly more inclusive academia but who cultivated their philosophy from the decidedly extracurricular worlds of hip-hop and southern black culture and first articulated it in the blogosphere rather than in scholarly journals.[11] The aforementioned academic conference plenary itself evidenced both the magnitude of this shift and its present limits: a marquee panel composed mostly of women and people of color talking about gender and sexuality addressing an audience that, however enthusiastic, was made up mostly of white men.

The physical body—perhaps ironically, given academe is a relatively tenacious holdout of Cartesian dualism—is proving an exciting frontier in this new direction of the history of ideas.[12] In an oft-forgotten section of *Democracy and Education* (1916), John Dewey cautioned, "It would be impossible to state adequately the evil results which have flowed from this dualism of mind and body, much less to exaggerate them."[13] Dewey emphasized the urgency of meaningfully engaging one's physicality—rather than disciplining it as a gross distraction—in intellectual contexts as a prerequisite to full selfhood. While it has taken the better part of a century, historians now explore intimate bodily rituals (like makeup and dieting) and biological processes (like menstruation and breastfeeding) to illuminate shifting ideas about health, pathology, and aesthetics.[14] Dewey did not discuss gender explicitly, but his mention of "unruliness" and "mischief" obliquely refers to a contemporaneous conversation about boys, education, and savagery, as does his use of a generic male pupil.[15] Over the last century, however, the study of the body has emphasized women and others assumed to be governed by their base bodily impulses rather than cool rationality: consider the historical assumption that uteruses are the source of hysteria and that homosexuals are pathologically enslaved by the pursuit of orgasm.[16]

Troubling the category of intellectual, as Judith Butler famously demanded we do that of gender, this chapter pursues these rich new scholarly directions to take seriously the ideas cultivated in a perhaps unlikely space: the gym. In this study of "wellness"—an idea today both ubiquitous and poorly understood— I explain the emergence and power of a concept often derided as inherently anti-intellectual and hopelessly bourgeois, a slur with misogynist undertones, despite the democratic pretensions of its critics.[17] Locating important origins of contemporary wellness culture in "the gym," the site that came to take up an increasing amount of literal and figurative space in American life from the 1960s to the '80s, I contend that that the power of the wellness concept derived from a diverse range of actors buying into once-radical notions of "self-care" and of a "mind-body" connection that rejected Cartesian dualism and accepted hierarchies of expertise. Carried out through putatively physical projects pioneered largely by women and gay men, these wellness projects embraced the idea that women are essentially different from men, but challenged the value judgment usually implicit in this claim. In mainstreaming certain feminized pursuits such as tending to one's physical form, questioning medical expertise, and celebrating holism, the emergent wellness movement pushed back on the underlying gendered assumptions of inferiority even as it at times underscored difference. Notably, very few such actors—from the leotard-clad military wives who became global Jazzercise missionaries, to Big Sur yoginis, to contraception and abortion activists—defined themselves as intellectuals, even as their work brought about a revolution of ideas.

Indeed, in locker rooms and lined up before class, everyday actors have often articulated these ideas before they formed part of a simultaneously emerging canon of feminist theory and philosophy. Sandra Lee Bartky spelled out the artificiality of "feminine aesthetic difference" in the realms of slenderness and hairlessness in 1990, but at least two decades earlier countercultural yogis dispensed with the diets and ablutions considered prerequisites of proper ladyhood.[18] In 1982, Gloria Steinem theorized the sweaty, liberatory potential of the women's changing room as she observed the unabashed nakedness of female exercisers who sought community in the dance-exercise studios and spas already springing up on the coasts.[19] Before Joan Scott posited "gender as a useful category of analysis," feminist health advocates rejected a male, technocratic medical establishment as fundamentally devaluing the bodies and prerogatives of women.[20]

Regarding wellness, a gendered intellectual history illuminates the mutually constitutive realms of grass roots and grand theory and diminishes the distance between them.

Wellness and the Gym

In a 1979 clip of *60 Minutes*, a young Dan Rather intones, "Wellness, there's a word you don't hear every day." His segment profiling the Wellness Resource Center (WRC) of Marin County suggests how the term became widely used.[21] In a sun-splashed room, about thirty apparently white women and men sat cross-legged, looking surprisingly tense; on national television, the group was emphatically defending themselves against charges of being a "middle-class cult." Baffled by the allegation, these enthusiasts were united in the shared experience of suffering an ailment Western medicine failed to cure. At WRC, they found relief in techniques that emphasized the interconnectedness of their mental, emotional, and physical well-being and their own ability to take control of their healing with prevention. At best, these techniques then seemed "woo-woo"—characteristic of the flakiness of what Christopher Lasch derided as a "culture of narcissism"—and at worst, dangerously cultlike.[22]

What Is Wellness?

Two institutional definitions of the postwar era suggest the parameters of "wellness." In 1948, the World Health Organization defined the more quotidian "health" in presciently holistic terms: "a state of complete physical, mental, and social well-being and not merely the absence of disease or infirmity." The National Wellness Institute, founded in 1977, emphasized wellness explicitly as "an active process through which people become aware of, and make choices toward, a more successful existence." At spaces like the WRC, these definitions converged in concrete practices meant to achieve a higher state than the mere absence of sickness.

Broad economic, political, and cultural shifts in the postwar era enabled this moment. Briefly, the life-or-death struggles of the World Wars, Depression-era privation, or polio that had restricted earlier generations' definition of health were less urgent because of a greater—if far from evenly distributed—affluence.[23] Simultaneously, a burgeoning therapeutic culture celebrated "emotional balance" and, later, "healthy narcissism" and "self-esteem."[24] Cold warriors like president-elect John F. Kennedy idealized a physically fit and intellectually vibrant citizen, the opposite of the "soft American," a trope he introduced in the pages of *Sports*

Illustrated in 1960 and to which he frequently returned while gathering support for his Presidential Council on Youth Fitness.[25]

If affluence enabled these pursuits, it also paradoxically challenged the achievement of wellness. JFK blamed American softness on *too much* affluence—the unfortunate outcome of the "push-button" luxuries of modern convenience that bred laziness among those literally and figuratively "fittest" for citizenship. The expansion of the service economy and of sedentary desk jobs, longer journeys to work (in cars that idled on growing tangles of freeways), and many domestic labor-saving technologies fanned new fears about ill health among the largely white middle and upper classes.[26]

As these citizens were goaded into pursuing wellness more deliberately, so too did the civil rights and feminist movements galvanize people of color and women in dramatically different social positions to think intentionally about health as a political issue. As Alondra Nelson has chronicled, the Black Panthers founded health clinics to provide basic medical service and also promote African American well-being, "body and soul." Notably, Nelson points out that historians' ignorance of such activism derives from their tacit agreement with Lasch that focusing on health is antithetical to formal political engagement.[27] Yet the narrative of wellness over the past forty years is as much about the activism of the disenfranchised as about the forward march of narcissism and neoliberalism. These origins matter.

Fitness culture's similarly unexpected beginnings are related and worth recovering. Long discouraged from strenuous exercise because of concerns about its ruinous effects on reproductive potential and delicacy of character, women successfully fought for recognition as athletes as early as the nineteenth century. Title IX, the 1972 legislation that helped equalize funding for sports teams across gender, is this movement's most famous victory. The efforts to legitimize physical activity for women more generally are less glorious—midcentury slenderizing spas were attached to beauty parlors and dedicated more to fighting fat than promoting feminism. Yet a powerful and expansive recreational women's-fitness culture germinated there, later creating its own spaces in church basements and off-hours community centers rather than primarily seeking access to established realms like collegiate varsity teams.

Though best remembered for laughable leotards and leg warmers, the 1980s craze for group fitness was a turning point. Exercise studios were a "sweaty, funky, third space," the fitness pioneer Molly Fox remembers, populated mostly by women and gay men who "needed somewhere to go" and who created a subculture in places like Fox's "kind of gritty, funky downtown studio where a mix of lifestyles just came together." More rarefied establishments, such as the Lotte Berk brownstone in New York, where men were forbidden entry for more than a decade, until the early 1980s, also created opportunities to explore a more muscular and embodied femininity than widely accepted. One Lotte Berk employee recalled a client marveling at the sight of sweat beading on her body. Fox, who studied under Jane Fonda in her San Francisco studio, reminisced that Fonda's most powerful legacy was making it acceptable—even empowering—for women to exercise in public.

This history challenges the disparagement heaped on wellness and fitness "lifestyles" as evidence of a decadent society, a common characterization by the few scholars who are beginning to pay attention to wellness, if mostly to dismiss it. They generally agree that the pursuit of well-being defines our age—André Spicer and Carl Cederström's *The Wellness Syndrome* (2015) talks about the devolution of Max Weber's "Protestant work ethic" into a "workout ethic"—but also signals troubling tendencies toward social atomization, anti-intellectualism, narcissism, and a creeping technocratic neoliberalism. Even as Mark Greif's 2004 *n+1* essay, "Against Exercise," rightly echoes Lasch's critique of narcissism and explodes the reflexive what-could-be-wrong-with-wellness impulse, such studies overlook the auspicious origins of this movement, not to mention its emancipatory potential. Restoring human agency to those whose voices are marginalized in society and scholarship—writing from the bottom up—was a guiding purpose of a generation of late twentieth-century academics who pioneered the radical epistemological frameworks that critics of wellness culture employ. Yet in these new narratives, humans are either hapless victims or depersonalized villains. Indeed, Greif evokes Tom Wolfe's wealthy "social X-ray"—the quintessentially vapid gym bunny avidly pursuing her own corporeal erasure by getting thin—as a quintessential gym goer. Part of an older intellectual history model deeply skeptical of modernity, these works offer little sense of how millions of people, especially women, might have embraced wellness to make their lives more meaningful. A gendered lens on the gym and the ideas it reflects and refracts helps uncover this important past.

The Gym

One of few historians writing the "history of the gym" recently wrote that he "had not intentionally avoided any mention of women," that "knowing [he] was devoting one chapter to them allowed [him] to skip . . . the female contribution to and participation in the gymnasium from antiquity to the early twentieth century."[28] By the 1960s, such omission was no longer possible (and was arguably indefensible before as well). These new sites of communal recreation sprang up in cities and suburbs owing to a growing consensus that regular exercise was crucial to good physical, emotional, moral, and civic health. These spaces promoted mind-body holism and an ethos of self-care, philosophies that occasionally challenged the very attitudes about gender and sexuality these shiny new temples to the body beautiful most obviously promoted.

If American gym culture began in the 1930s as solidly white and male, engaging in and championing regular exercise was considered strange, if not subversive, until the 1960s and '70s.[29] Male fitness enthusiasts were often cast as sexual outsiders, their masculinity in doubt by dint of their focus on physical aesthetics.[30] Simultaneously, female exercisers were derided as hypermasculine. When fitness booster Jack LaLanne, best known for his 1950s television show, opened his first gym in Oakland, California, in 1936, he recalled the resistance from the same medical community that would irk feminist health advocates: "People thought I was a charlatan and a nut," he recalled. "The doctors were against me—they said that working out with weights would give people everything from heart attacks to hemorrhoids; that women would look like men."[31] In 1951, when he first pitched his television show (which ended up being on the air from 1953 to 1985), he had to personally purchase airtime, because no one believed exercise would command viewership. On this show, LaLanne assured the many homemakers who tuned in that they would not "ruin their figures with exercise." Yet he also interspersed his movement cues with reminders of how physical health was linked to well-being of all sorts, emotional to financial. LaLanne both introduced the radical notions of exercise for women as salutary in multiple ways *and* left intact dominant beauty ideals.

LaLanne's television personality effected broad cultural acceptance of exercise, but his less studied role in building brick-and-mortar fitness clubs is crucial to understanding the lived experience of these ideas. LaLanne operated over two hundred European Health Spas by the 1980s and joined entrepreneurs such as West Coast transplant Vic Tanny in changing the public perception and built environment of the gym as a "sweaty dungeon" populated by morally suspect male bodybuilders and weightlifters.[32] Indeed, "physique magazines" and competitions could be discreet avenues for closeted gay men to find each other in intolerant times. Although newly popular bodybuilder Arnold Schwarzenegger insisted in 1975 that he knew no homosexual bodybuilders, he acknowledged that, at his Gold's Gym in Venice Beach and at competitions, "you see them. You will find homosexuals signing up to become members of the group so they can just watch you working out . . . to them we are heaven."[33] As the book and documentary *Pumping Iron* popularized bodybuilding culture, Schwarzenegger's continued insistence that "men shouldn't feel like fags because they want to have nice-looking bodies," interspersed with over-the-top anecdotes of "gang bangs" and casual sex with women, suggested how marginalized the gym's sweaty subculture, and how precarious its attendant masculinity, really were.[34]

Operators of these newly sanitized clubs that evolved into chains strove to dispel such unseemly associations. Some, like Joe Gold, emerged from Venice Beach and built well-lit, swankier clubs that expanded beyond core bodybuilding offerings, often amid criticism about selling out to the superficial new fitness fad.[35] Most notably, Tanny and LaLanne recruited women as clients, dismissing the prevailing medical and cultural assumption that exercise would overtax ladies' delicate constitutions. But their methods arguably reproduced some normative gender assumptions about female frailty and the primacy of beauty. Some of these new clubs were sex-segregated, reflecting the notion that co-ed exercise was improper. These entrepreneurs positioned clubs as luxury "spas," assuming an affinity between poshness and femininity. Clearly drawing on the appeal of the "slenderizing spas" and "reducing salons" of the 1930s to 1960s (customarily located adjacent to beauty parlors and promoted as a luxurious accoutrement rather than as an exercise technology), such strategies solidified the assumption that female patrons were more drawn to aesthetics than athletics.[36]

Simultaneously, in vastly different spaces, more countercultural voices were also reconceptualizing the body. At the Esalen Institute, established in 1962 by two religious-studies Stanford graduates dispirited by Western approaches to religion and mental health, visitors (perhaps unwittingly) troubled gendered assumptions about spirituality and the body through their yoga programming.[37] Yoga at Esalen existed primarily as an embodied form of a marginalized spirituality—Hinduism—rather than an exercise program. Increasingly, however, yoga exceeded the theological to focus on unapologetic physicality as a form of earthly liberation. Of a piece with Esalen's nude "encounter sessions" and consumption of organic foods, yoga represented another physical practice that by the late 1960s contrasted the "natural" body and earth with the inauthenticity of the technocratic and spiritually bankrupt outside world. "Being in your body" without shame or chemical pollutants was an inherently radical act necessarily explored in secluded enclaves like Esalen. Yet signaling the incremental popularization of these practices and philosophies, especially among women, Esalen's founding yoga instructor Pamela Rainbear Portugal described how this heightened self-awareness—and physical exertion—offered the release that made bourgeois domestic life tolerable: "Punch a punching bag instead of secretly—even to you—sniping at your mate. Otherwise you might someday 'accidentally' run the family Buick over him."[38]

Core to Esalen's diverse offerings was a commitment to fostering "self-actualization, creativity, and human potentiality in general," and yoga was an important vehicle of this mind-body sensibility.[39] "As long as you use your senses, you can do whatever *YOU WANT*," Portugal wrote.[40] The ideal self was unapologetically physical but unconcerned with mainstream aesthetic ideals. She illustrated yoga poses with cartoon drawings of a woman whose lumpy waist, stringy hair, and protuberant nose figured almost as prominently as the angle of her forward bend; she wrote frankly about the need for "release" in the form of regular bowel movements.[41] This sensibility shaped Esalen's sports program; the historian Sam Binkley describes the 1973 founding of its sports center—including activities like "yoga-tennis"—in which the traditional athletic goals of competition and victory were replaced with an emphasis on collaboration, on "non-competitive organized play and deeper experiences of self-exploration, spiritual community, and transcendence." The counterculturalist Stewart Brand championed these ideas, while simultaneously questioning, along with many women, the "victory" of Title IX in enlisting women in a masculine, competitive framework for physical activity. One program organizer at Esalen commented that sports were the vehicle to universalize the retreat's guiding belief "that the body and mind are so closely related." A reporter concurred, noting that "the clout generated by Esalen" was capable of bringing about "a change in sports [comparable to] what the storming of the Bastille was to the French Revolution."[42]

Another group, motivated more by activist commitments and practical medical needs than by spiritual exploration, also championed the benefits of self-care and mind-body holism: feminist health advocates. Decrying insufficient access to contraception and the dehumanizing approach of a capitalistic, technocratic male medical establishment, some of these women articulated an expressly Marxist case for commandeering their own well-being. Quoting Herbert Marcuse, the founders of the influential Boston Women's Health Collective in 1970 excoriated the culture in which "health is defined by an elite." While men also suffered, the lot of women was especially dire: "The most obvious indication of this ideology is how doctors treat us as patients. We are considered stupid, mindless creatures, unable to follow instructions (known as orders). . . . We fare worse because women are thought to be incapable of understanding or dealing with our own situation. Health is not something that belongs to a person, but a precious something that a doctor doles out from his stores . . . and thereby controls the patient."[43] Their argument was also historical: a long-standing devaluation of women's capacity for self-knowledge and dismissal of their history as caregivers persisted even in light of policy victories such as the legalization of oral contraception (1960) and abortion (1973). Even as they remedied an immediate crisis of care, these advocates articulated a theory of health resistance.

That structural critique intersected with highly individualistic, and sometimes literal, forms of self-exploration. In 1971, Belita Cowan of the Los Angeles Feminist Women's Health Center gave an instructional public demonstration, at a feminist bookstore, on how to use a plastic speculum, flashlight, and mirror to examine her own cervix. Inspiring similar demonstrations all over the country, this act of unapologetic bodily self-knowledge, not to mention nonsexualized nudity, was itself radical. Individual acts could beget broader political activism, however, and in 1975 Cowan went on to cofound, with Barbara Seaman, the lobbying group National Women's Health Network, which exposed the collusion of the Food and Drug Administration, the medical establishment, and drug companies in hiding the adverse effects of pharmaceuticals on women.[44]

These specific concerns were linked to an underlying philosophy of preventive feminist wellness; a section of a pamphlet, distributed by one women's health center, called "Mind and Body" declared that (1) women are fundamentally different from men in their physical and psychological health needs, (2) mental and physical health are inextricably intertwined, and (3) "self-help [is essential] . . . to change women's consciousness about their own bodies" and "to provide them with skills to maintain and improve their own health."[45] That preventive emphasis defined the community built at these clinics; one advertised hypnosis and consciousness-raising groups, another "a place to just go read a book." One Atlanta clinic in the 1980s held "Healthy Love" parties, occasions where women's health treatment was presented as an opportunity to cultivate joy, rather than as clinical, transactional, or somber.[46] Feminist health advocates enabled individual women to take control of their health and resisted broader ideas and policies that pathologized their bodies.

Simultaneously, this emphasis on important but broad ideas such as joy and well-being enabled the diffusion, but sometimes dilution, of an originally radical critique. *The Joy of Sex* became a best seller in 1972 by celebrating sex, but it was devoid of political commentary and, according to some critics, disappointingly focused on male pleasure. By 1973, the Boston Women's Health Collective's *Our Bodies, Ourselves* went into commercial production with Simon & Schuster, but it was ultimately stripped of much of its structural critique. In one extreme instance, Henry Dubin, a used-car salesman whom *Newsweek* styled "Mr. Abortion" for his 1971 founding of an abortion-referral business, opened "Women Helping Women" in 1974, a center dedicated to helping "women [with their] special needs, special problems." Dubin appropriated the rhetoric of feminist health advocates, but the practices—ranging from male management to bartering breast augmentations for unpaid wages—earned the condemnation both of antiabortion pickets and of the director of the Feminist Women's Health Center of Santa Ana, which she pointed out was the "only one of its kind in the county owned by women and controlled by women."[47] Notably, the *Los Angeles Times* reported that Dubin's clinic was "jammed" with women, many more of them concerned with how "affordable care for women" translated into discount cosmetic surgery than with the incompatibility of such practices with the advertised feminist principles. Women's wellness was so capacious it began to encompass some of the very attitudes it set out to challenge.

By the 1980s, gyms were buzzing social spaces that hardly conformed to Greif's grim description that the "only truly essential pieces of equipment in modern exercise are numbers." Indeed, gyms coalesced these varied body projects and their underlying and at times contradictory sensibilities around gender. A 1983 *Rolling Stone* cover story, and *Perfect* (1985), the John Travolta and Jamie Lee Curtis film it inspired, suggested these gleaming spaces could represent a spandex-swathed arena for the "sex-charged" LA singles scene.[48] The movie's plot contained no major feminist dénouement, but a traditional cat-and-mouse courtship and the unsparing humiliation of a promiscuous character pictured spread-eagle on an adductor machine, described in the *Washington Post* "as desperate, sex-starved and tragic."[49] *Rolling Stone* described the Sports Connection, the Beverly Hills club where the film was set, as "the wailing wall of West Coast fitness religion"; an interviewee remembered it better as "the sports erection."[50] Both the spiritual and the social payoffs of working out—which found its most devoted clientele among women—were borne out as gyms became fixtures beyond coastal cities.

If fitness programs founded by men haltingly dispelled ideas about women's constitutional weakness, women in the 1970s and '80s opened independent exercise studios with more explicitly liberatory aspirations. When the Northwestern graduate and dancer Judi Sheppard Missett took a physical fitness test at her local YMCA in the 1960s and was confused by the results, she was told that the exam was geared to male physiology because so few women were interested in exercise. Jolted by this exchange and frustrated by the low participation in her dance classes because of their technical complexity and the fact that "mothers believed they should sit on the side watching their daughters rather than take part," in 1969 Missett founded the dance-exercise program that would become Jazzercise. Girls and women who were not training as dancers or athletes, Missett surmised, stood to gain from unapologetically "being in their bodies"—like the seekers visiting distant Esalen—for its own sake.

Soon after, Missett relocated to San Diego with her husband and papered supermarket bulletin boards with flyers for her classes, intended to inspire women of all ages to exercise without inhibition; she turned her students away from the mirror. Struggling to find establishments to host her program—dance studios found it too basic and gyms too unfamiliar—Missett began working with the Parks Department to hold sessions in school gymnasiums and later church basements, an arrangement that overwhelmed municipal structures when hundreds of people would line up at 6 a.m. to reserve spots for that evening. When the husbands of Missett's hard-core following of military wives faced reassignment, these heartbroken students became instructors themselves rather than abandon their favorite workout. Missett franchised her business and by 1984 counted $40 million in revenue, 350,000 students, and 2,700 instructor-franchisees (99 percent women).[51] They did not identify as entrepreneurs, activists, or intellectuals—"I was just a dancer!"—but found themselves building institutions for women, by women, on a scale previously unimaginable.

What, exactly, was Missett promoting? In her words, "the main focus here is continuing to help women understand that they can take possession of their lives by being healthy and fit." She created a "nonthreatening atmosphere," focused on "cultivating joy through music." Expanding in suburbs, Missett decisively approached women likely "intimidated" by the increasingly flashy and cosmopolitan sensibility of "big-city" clubs like Sports Connection. Thousands of letters, Missett recounts, shared that beyond physical benefits, students gained confidence to "get married or divorced or go on a safari or climb a mountain." Judith Berlin, a New Jersey schoolteacher-cum-homemaker, began teaching Jazzercise when her children entered school. She recalls flying to Chicago for her Jazzercise audition in 1989—leaving "behind three kids and husband and carpools and all that.... I was 39 and I had never lived on my own or even stayed in a hotel by myself." Berlin began teaching at a YMCA—"I didn't want to rent a church or firehouse"—and eventually opened a studio, which she was still running in 2016. To Berlin, Jazzercise has been an avenue of independence, but like Missett, she remarks on the community aspect: "It's one of the only places where women aged 20–85 come together ... to dance."[52] Deliberately or not, this new iteration of the gym shifted ideas about women's self-worth. Notably, not until the early 1990s did Missett *use* the word "wellness"; though she had been "tuned in" and influenced by mind-body formats like yoga and Pilates since the 1960s, the concept of wellness "wasn't marketable" until three decades later.

Nor did Missett and her fellow travelers at the vanguard of women's fitness necessarily see themselves as feminists in the overtly political terms adopted by her contemporaries. In our 2015 interview, she embraced the term, but quickly added: "Now that doesn't mean we were out marching in protest or anything, but we created [empowerment] in a different way and place ... in the classroom." The same year Missett founded Jazzercise, the actor Jane Fonda met an avowed feminist who remarked that Fonda's role in the sex fantasy *Barbarella* "must have done strange things to you." Fonda recalled going "absolutely blank.... I did not know she was referring to the personal cost of being turned into a sexual object. I did not even know I had been. The burgeoning new women's consciousness had not yet found its way into my mind and heart."[53] Her body ended up being the avenue for that feminist awakening; Fonda related the anecdote in the introduction of her 1981 *Workout Book*—a title that earned the largest royalties check to date from Simon & Schuster. Specifically, the aerobics she popularized in her three studios, and most explosively via VHS and mass-market books, were a vehicle for her own recovery from damaging patterns of food restriction and diet pill abuse and to "create more realistic, less anxiety-ridden standards" to support women struggling with body image.[54]

Unlike Missett in conservative San Diego County, Fonda was a creature of overtly progressive Hollywood, though her fitness pursuits have often been juxtaposed as a curiosity or outright contradiction with her activism.[55] On the contrary, the profits from her Robertson Boulevard studio (opened in 1979) funded the Campaign for Economic Democracy, her husband Tom Hayden's antipoverty nonprofit. Her own political awakening had come on a trip to India, when she was struck by the contrast to the "houses in Beverly Hills, those immaculate gardens, those neat silent streets where the rich drive their big cars and send their children to psychoanalysts and employ exploited Mexican gardeners and black servants."[56] In her follow-up book, on pregnancy, birth, and recovery through exercise, Fonda expanded beyond her Beverly Hills base to speak to an audience ranging from "women judges to women janitors."[57] The volume reflected cultural feminists' resistance to "clinical," male-dominated delivery rooms where doctors might "laugh at a poor woman's ignorance" or refuse to allow her husband or friends to participate in the birthing process or restrict "natural childbirth" and breastfeeding. The conclusion included unapologetic social commentary: "Everyone knows I'm an activist. There is no way I can write about health and leave it at urging you to make a personal commitment to nutrition and exercise.... After you read these chapters, you may want to add a little activism to your approach to health." Fonda was unique in articulating this connection between fitness and feminism, but her unparalleled platform meant she made this connection explicit to millions.

Many responded eagerly. Because "ladies weren't supposed to sweat," Fonda later remembered, unabashed exercise could lead to grander forms of self-actualization: "One woman said she was brushing her teeth one morning, saw a new bicep muscle, then went into work and told her boss to go f—himself."[58] This movement expanded beyond predictable coastal enclaves. Fonda later reflected that "women in mud huts in Guatemala" were exercising to her VHS tapes; I discovered women using them on a Soviet base in Egypt and in Colombian community centers "to find a little joy in the day." Repeatedly, interviewees shared that Fonda "made it OK for us [women] to work out in public." One interviewee added, "and for me, that changed everything." Exercise, like civic and economic participation in the preceding two centuries, became a vehicle for women to question received attitudes about femininity and to reject their relegation to the less visible, private sphere.

Unwittingly echoing Lasch's skepticism of "personal growth," one praiseful biographer described Fonda as at "the vanguard" of a broader shift among "hippies from the 60s and 70s" "turning their antiwar consciousness to self-improvement, health foods, solar energy, and nuclear disarmament."[59] Feminist scholars also looked askance at the aerobics craze—which engaged twenty-two million followers by 1986—for promoting "passive femininity," narrow aesthetic standards, and a turn to self-improvement over collective action.[60] Even aerobics star Kathy Smith agreed, acknowledging the submissive sexuality produced by the popular exercise video industry: "When I see exercise videos that have girls puckering, or arching up their backs and throwing up their fannies in contorted positions, I find it offensive."[61] Fonda declined comment, and her fellow movie-star-turned-aerobics-star Raquel Welch declared, "I resent the research." Recently, fat-studies scholars have argued that mainstream fitness contexts and especially 1980s aerobics, with its Flexatard aesthetic and emphasis on slimness and able-bodiedness as prerequisites for self-actualization, cemented the damaging assumption that fatness, disability, and laziness were mutually constitutive. Social scientists followed suit, remarking that the downside of contemporary emphasis on mind-body holism is that relentless physical cultivation has become required for full social participation.[62]

By the 1990s, the capacious meaning of "the gym" became more widely apparent. Woman-centered health was mainstream, as Eve Ensler's *Vagina Monologues*, based on the premise that "women's empowerment is ... deeply connected to our vaginas" became a critical and commercial success, its lead roles played by celebrities on HBO. Fonda appeared in *Yoga Journal*, encouraging older women to exercise strenuously and abandon the fetishization of "a younger model" in order to experience the "flowing mainstream of life" and a "self-worth and sexuality" usually reserved to men.[63] Early Esalen had left the feminist Betty Friedan unimpressed by "mountain macho men ... who kept their women barefoot and pregnant up in the mountains," even as they were "supposedly liberated hippies," but the retreat's practices began to live up to the institutional ideal that "every body" deserves enlightenment, a development the historian Jeffrey Kripal describes as "well beyond anything that ever existed in Asia or the West. This is an enlightenment that depends directly on Western history and critical theory, on Freud, Foucault, and feminism."[64] This august intellectual provenance notwithstanding, it was in the unapologetically corporeal world of the late twentieth-century gym that wellness became a widespread cultural phenomenon.

NOTES

1. Eric Foner, ed., *The New American History* (Philadelphia: Temple University Press, 1997).

2. Mia Bay, Farah J. Griffin, Martha S. Jones, and Barbara Dianne Savage, eds., *Toward an Intellectual History of Black Women* (Chapel Hill: University of North Carolina Press,

2015); Elizabeth Lunbeck, *The Americanization of Narcissism* (Cambridge, MA: Harvard University Press, 2014).

3. A few examples include Mia Bay, *To Tell the Truth Freely: The Life of Ida B. Wells* (New York: Hill & Wang, 2009); Kimberly A. Hamlin, *From Eve to Evolution: Darwin, Science, and Women's Rights in Gilded Age America* (Chicago: University of Chicago Press, 2014); Nancy Weiss Malkiel, *"Keep the Damned Women Out!": The Struggle for Coeducation* (Princeton, NJ: Princeton University Press, 2016).

4. Andrew Hartman, *A War for the Soul of America: A History of the Culture Wars* (Chicago: University of Chicago Press, 2015), chap. 5 passim.

5. Bonnie G. Smith, *The Gender of History: Men, Women, and Historical Practice* (Cambridge, MA: Harvard University Press, 1998).

6. John Philipps Kenyon, *History Men: The Historical Profession in England since the Renaissance* (Pittsburgh: University of Pittsburgh Press, 1984); "Historians Joanne Freeman and Nathan Connolly Join BackStory," Virginia Humanities, accessed January 12, 2017, http://virginiahumanities.org/2016/12/joannefreeman-nathanconnolly-join-backstory/.

7. Gerda Lerner, *The Majority Finds Its Past: Placing Women in History* (Chapel Hill: University of North Carolina Press, 1979), xviii.

8. Ann Firor Scott, *The Southern Lady: From Pedestal to Politics, 1830–1930* (Charlottesville: University of Virginia Press, 1970).

9. Ann Douglas, *The Feminization of American Culture* (New York: Alfred A. Knopf, 1977); Stacie Taranto, *Kitchen Table Politics: Conservative Women and Family Values in New York* (Philadelphia: University of Pennsylvania Press, 2017); Trystan T. Cotten and Kimberly Springer, eds., *Stories of Oprah: The Oprahfication of American Culture* (Jackson: University Press of Mississippi, 2009).

10. New School course catalog, 1962, New School University Archives.

11. Brittney C. Cooper, Susanna M. Morris, and Robin M. Boylorn, eds., *The Crunk Feminist Collection: Essays on Hip-Hop Feminism* (New York: Feminist Press, 2017).

12. Natalia Mehlman Petrzela, "When Wellness Is a Dirty Word," *Chronicle Review*, May 1, 2016.

13. "Democracy and Education, by John Dewey," 1916, accessed January 12, 2017, https://www.gutenberg.org/files/852/852-h/852-h.htm.

14. Kathy Peiss, *Hope in a Jar: The Making of America's Beauty Culture* (Philadelphia: University of Pennsylvania Press, 2011); Lara Freidenfelds, *The Modern Period: Menstruation in Twentieth-Century America* (Baltimore: Johns Hopkins University Press, 2009); Jessica Martucci, *Back to the Breast: Natural Motherhood and Breastfeeding in America* (Chicago: University of Chicago Press, 2015); Joan Jacobs Brumberg, *The Body Project: An Intimate History of American Girls* (New York: Alfred A. Knopf, 1998).

15. Gail Bederman, *Manliness and Civilization: A Cultural History of Gender and Race in the United States, 1880–1917* (Chicago: University of Chicago Press, 1995).

16. Thomas W. Laqueur, *Solitary Sex : A Cultural History of Masturbation* (New York: Zone Books, 2004).

17. André Spicer and Carl Cederström, *The Wellness Syndrome* (London: Polity, 2015).

18. Sandra Lee Bartky, *Femininity and Domination: Studies in the Phenomenology of Oppression* (New York: Routledge, 1990).

19. Gloria Steinem, "In Praise of Women's Bodies," *Ms.*, April 1982.

20. Joan W. Scott, "Gender: A Useful Category of Historical Analysis," *American Historical Review* 91, no. 5 (December 1986).

21. "Wellness Resource Center with Dan Rather," *60 Minutes*, 1979, accessed via https://www.youtube.com/watch?v=LAorj2U7PR4.

22. Christopher Lasch, *The Culture of Narcissism: American Life in an Age of Diminishing Expectations* (New York: W. W. Norton, 1979).

23. Avner Offer, *The Challenge of Affluence: Self-Control and Well-Being in the United States and Britain since 1950* (New York: Oxford University Press, 2006).

24. Eva Moskowitz, *In Therapy We Trust: America's Obsession with Self-Fulfillment* (Baltimore: Johns Hopkins University Press, 2008); Elizabeth Lunbeck, *The Americanization of Narcissism* (Cambridge, MA: Harvard University Press, 2014); *Snap Out of It! (Emotional Balance)*, Coronet Instructional Films, 1951, accessed via Archives.org, https://archive.org/details/SnapOuto1951.

25. John F. Kennedy, "The Soft American," *Sports Illustrated*, December 21, 1960.

26. Kenneth T. Jackson, *Crabgrass Frontier: The Suburbanization of the United States* (New York: Oxford University Press, 1985).

27. Alondra Nelson, *Body and Soul: The Black Panther Party and the Fight against Medical Discrimination* (Minneapolis: University of Minnesota Press, 2011).

28. Eric Chaline, *The Temple of Perfection: A History of the Gym* (London: Reaktion Books, 2015), 169.

29. Daniel Kunitz, *Lift: Fitness Culture, from Naked Greeks and Acrobats to Jazzercise and Ninja Warriors* (New York: HarperCollins, 2016).

30. Tracy D. Morgan, "Pages of Whiteness: Race, Physique Magazines, and the Emergence of Public Gay Culture," in *Queer Studies: A Lesbian, Gay, Bisexual, and Transgender Anthology* (New York: NYU Press, 1996), 280–98.

31. Bill Morem, "Fitness Guru Jack LaLanne, 96, Dies at Morro Bay Home," *San Luis Obispo (CA) Tribune*, January 23, 2011.

32. Shelly McKenzie, *Getting Physical: The Rise of Fitness Culture in America* (Lawrence: University Press of Kansas, 2013); Jonathan Black, *Making the American Body: The Remarkable Saga of the Men and Women Whose Feuds, Feats, and Passions Shaped Fitness History* (Lincoln: University of Nebraska Press, 2013).

33. Jim Stingley, "Bodybuilding: State of the Art, 1975," *Los Angeles Times*, November 16, 1975.

34. Peter Manso, "Conversation with Arnold Schwarzenegger," *Oui* magazine, August 1977.

35. Richard Tyler, *The West Coast Bodybuilding Scene: The Golden Era* (Santa Cruz, CA: On Target, 2004).

36. Natalia Mehlman Petrzela, "Slenderizing Spas, Reducing Machines, and Other Hot Fitness Crazes of 75 Years Ago," *Well+Good*, September 1, 2015.

37. Jeffrey Kripal, *Esalen: America and the Religion of No Religion* (Chicago: University of Chicago Press, 2008).

38. Pamela Rainbear Portugal, *A Place for Human Beings*, 2nd ed. (San Francisco: Homegrown Books, 1978), 95.

39. Kripal, *Esalen*, 105–6.

40. Ibid., 73.

41. Portugal, *Place for Human Beings*, 38–39.

42. Sam Binkley, *Getting Loose: Lifestyle Consumption in the 1970s* (Durham, NC: Duke University Press, 2007), 230–31.

43. Boston Women's Health Collective, *Women and Their Bodies: A Course* (Boston: Boston Women's Health Collective, 1970), 6.

44. Sandra Morgen, *Into Our Own Hands: The Women's Health Movement in the United States, 1969–1990* (New Brunswick, NJ: Rutgers University Press, 2002), 15; Marlene Cimons, "Women's Group to Sue Maker of Contraceptive," *Los Angeles Times*, January 11, 1983.

45. Stanford Women's Center, "A Guide for Stanford Women," 1972, Marjorie L. Shuer Papers, box 1, folder 11, Stanford University Special Collections.

46. Jennifer Nelson, *More Than Medicine: A History of the Women's Health Movement* (New York: NYU Press, 2015).

47. Shearlean Duke, "Clinic for Women Only Surrounded by Controversy," *Los Angeles Times*, September 15, 1974.

48. Aaron Latham, "Looking for Mister Goodbody," *Rolling Stone*, June 1983.

49. Steve Pond, "A 'Perfect' Puzzle Travolta's New Movie: How Much Is Real?," *Washington Post*, June 6, 1985.

50. Neil Karlam, "Jamie Lee Curtis Gets Serious," *Rolling Stone*, July 18, 1985; Leslie Kaminoff, oral history interview with author, 2016.

51. Judith Sheppard Missett, oral history interview with author 2015; Michael Schroeder, "Looking for a Bigger Slice," *Detroit News*, September 20, 1985.

52. Judith Berlin, oral history interview with author, 2015.

53. Jane Fonda, *Jane Fonda's Workout Book* (New York: Simon & Schuster, 1981), 18.

54. James Spada, *Fonda: Her Life in Pictures* (New York: Doubleday, 1985); Alan Citron, "No Sweat: Jane Fonda Closes Her Beverly Hills Aerobics Studio," *Los Angeles Times*, April 3, 1991.

55. Black, *Making the American Body*, 85; Margaret Morse, "Artemis Aging: Exercise and the Female Body on Video," *Discourse* 10, no. 1 (October 1987): 20–53; Nikki Finke, "Aerobics Videos Get Some People All Worked Up," *Bulletin* and *Los Angeles Times*, November 20, 1987.

56. Spada, *Fonda*, 17, 106.

57. Femmy DeLyser, *Jane Fonda's Workout Book for Pregnancy, Birth, and Recovery* (New York: Simon & Schuster, 1982), 19, 164; Spada, *Fonda*, 194.

58. Jane Fonda, "Personal Fitness: *Jane Fonda's Workout* Launched a Revolution," *Bloomberg*, December 4, 2014.

59. Spada, *Fonda*, 180.

60. Morse, "Artemis Aging"; Jenny Ellison, "Not Jane Fonda: Aerobics for Fat Women Only," in *Fat Studies Reader* (New York: NYU Press, 2009), 312–19; International Dance-Exercise Association data, 1986.

61. "All Sides Get Worked Up over Study of Aerobics Videos," *Los Angeles Times*, November 12, 1987.

62. Spicer and Cederström, *Wellness Syndrome*, 40.

63. Alice Christensen, "Easy Does It: Yoga for People over 60," *Yoga Journal*, November 1996; Jane Fonda, *Women Coming of Age* (New York: Simon & Schuster, 1984); *American Health* magazine, 1984; Spada, *Fonda*, 180, 194

64. Kripal, *Esalen*, 462–63.

7

PARALLEL EMPIRES
Transnationalism and Intellectual
History in the Western Hemisphere

Ruben Flores

In current scholarly discussion the discourse of transnationalism in the context of Mexico and the United States is overwhelmingly shaped by attention to immigration from Latin America and the intimate ties that are drawing Americans into a direct relationship with the Spanish-speaking countries of the hemisphere. Few communities in the United States have remained unaffected by Mexican labor power or the integration of laborers into the social fabric, a feature of contemporary life that we frequently experience directly in the form of new service workers in our communities or the changing demographics of our public schools. The effects of immigration have shaped our cultural history as well. Recent US Supreme Court decisions against President Obama's immigration directives have become part of jurisprudential history even as they have mirrored wider debates in our legislatures and universities about immigration and naturalization policy, while more recently, President Trump has revived reactionary discourses about immigrant criminality that have a long history in American culture. Scholars of the borderlands mirror the contemporary focus on immigration from Mexico and Central America, meanwhile, via studies of the policy structures of the US and Mexican federal governments or accounts of drug flows and migration to the Texas border with Mexico. Yet the focus on immigration in an era of globalized economics should not be mistaken for the other forms of work that transnational analysis is capable of producing for historians and other scholars of the humanistic disciplines. Mexican migration is nothing new, nor is immigration a novel category of transnational analysis, after all, and we are left with the task of considering what else transnationalism can deliver for scholars who are intent on broadening our understanding of the relationship between Mexico and the United States.[1] Here it is my intent to draw attention to the labor that intellectual history is capable of performing when transnational analysis looks beyond the usual terrain with which the term "transnationalism" is so often identified.

The payoff for thinking about transnationalism through intellectual history lies not merely in the surprising observations that it yields about the relationship of ideas and institutions in the United States to those abroad, but also to what such a relationship can teach us about the history of US civilization. It often flips the usual narrative of US domination in the hemisphere on its head, for example, insisting that parallel empires rather than a unitary one—the US by itself—were necessary for the expansion of US ideas across the Western Hemisphere. Second, it shows that the expansion of American ideas took place because foreign intellectuals engaged US ideas and voluntarily took them abroad elsewhere, a trajectory that represents a voluntary "second-order," or "indirect," transfer of ideas rather than their imperial transfer by US nationals. It also shows us a United States empire whose ideas were used by foreign nations in the hemisphere to challenge US power at the moment that the British, French, and German empires were moving toward their eclipse between the world wars. Methodologically, intellectual history as an alternative model of transnationalism transfers the balance of historical analysis away from laborers as objects of state power and toward the movement of ideas across nations as determinants of state institutions, via a micro-level analysis of historically situated discourses shared among intellectuals.[2] This alternative does not replace what labor flows can tell us about America's relationship to Mexico and other nations in the hemisphere. But its focus on frequently overlooked contingencies of history does amplify our understanding of the historical relationship between the United States and the Latin American nations of the Western Hemisphere, including Mexico.

Pragmatism in the Career of Moisés Sáenz

The analytical possibilities of transnational intellectual history for a deeper understanding of American society are well illustrated in the life of a Mexican intellectual who transferred ideas he had learned in New York to Mexico in the 1920s and then to South America in the 1930s. Moisés Sáenz was a student of John Dewey and arguably the most fervent pragmatist in Latin America during the first half of the twentieth century. For most of his career, he was committed to pragmatist institution building in Mexico as that republic rebuilt its state institutions in the wake of the devastating civil war known to Americans as the Mexican Revolution (1910–1920). Yet Sáenz had a second career as well, working as a consultant to nationalist governments in Peru and Ecuador after his career with the Mexican state ended in the early 1930s. His pragmatist commitment floated across the hemisphere to these other national communities, representing a gesture in transnationalism that can help us to think of the relationship of US society to the hemisphere in ways that we do not ordinarily do.[3]

If Sáenz's use of pragmatism was clear in his exposition of politics and state institutions in Peru and Ecuador, his transfer of Deweyan ideas also reflects the manner in which the culture of the United States became a springboard for political ideas in South America during a moment in time when liberal institution building was spreading across the hemisphere in the 1930s. His career does not reflect a narrative of American institutions being used destructively on foreigners as they arrive in the United States, moreover, a theme that is common in the immigration historiography. Rather, this is the story of a foreigner flexibly borrowing and using pragmatism voluntarily for his own nationalist ends. It is the story of ideas from the United States operating in other societies. And it is an example of how the use of intellectual history can tell us something important about the reach of American culture when we pay careful attention to foreign intellectuals who adapted ideas of American culture for their own ends.

Moisés Sáenz was one of the handful of academically educated social scientists who have been credited with building Mexico's modern twentieth-century state. The Mexican Revolution had proven to be a costly civil war despite the resounding success it had achieved in overthrowing the dictator Porfirio Díaz and eliminating British, French, and US control of the Mexican economy. Nearly one million persons were killed out of a population base of sixteen million people, a percentage of death twice that suffered by the United States during the American Civil War (1861–1865). The federal government had ceased to function with regularity amid war debts that had to be financed by creditors and investors. The transportation infrastructure had to be rebuilt, as did public schools, universities, energy plants, and the commodities infrastructure of the nation.

Among the state builders, Sáenz was a chief architect of Mexico's new public school system. He had long been interested in Mexico's social diversity, especially the relationship between Indians and whites and that between Catholic and Protestant Christians, a feature of his intellect that mirrored John Dewey's own questions about pluralism and diversity. Beginning in 1919, he traveled abroad from his native Monterrey, Mexico, and studied with Dewey at Columbia University, where he adopted the tenets of Dewey's pragmatism to develop an institutional system of schools in 1920s Mexico that was responsive to the postrevolutionary republic's wide social diversity. The labor was a massive undertaking that is little recognized among Americanists. It consisted of establishing more than twenty thousand new public schools between 1920 and 1940, developing a federal system of teacher training and inspection, and establishing the bureaucracies needed to send federal resources out of Mexico City to the overwhelmingly rural provinces of the nation at a moment when the future of the state was being debated by Mexican intellectuals.

I have told a history of Sáenz's career with the Mexican state elsewhere, but here I want to focus my attention on Sáenz's second career, after he had left the employment of the Mexican state in 1931 and gone to work as a consulting social scientist to the federal governments of Peru and Ecuador.[4] Already he had credited Dewey with some of the most important insights with which he had approached the Mexican public school project, and he had become a leading authority in North America on pragmatism in the specific contexts of rural and Native American education. What followed in Peru and Ecuador after 1931 was a second attempt at pragmatist-inspired school building, this time at the behest of federal agencies in Lima and Quito that had tracked the success of Mexico's revolutionary new schools with attention. Mexico had begun to redevelop its government infrastructure in the wake of its revolution, and the use of pragmatism in the public schools there had become a model for national governments in South America that juxtaposed white and Indian diversity in their societies to Mexico's own. Sáenz's pragmatism in Peru and Ecuador displayed itself in three ways in the decade following his departure from the Mexican federal government.[5]

In the first, Sáenz underscored over and over again the importance of practice to the reconfiguration of institutions rather than the importance of theory alone, an argument that Dewey had captured in his 1920 *Reconstruction in Philosophy*.[6] In Ecuador, for example, Sáenz noted that sufficient legal codes had been established to ensure the protection of Native Americans before the national community, but he underscored in the pragmatist-inflected reports that he subsequently wrote that what was still missing was "a public opinion that calls for and is willing to apply existing laws." The problem was one of "institutions directed at translating into practical action the thoughts of the legislature and the will of the citizens," he argued.[7] He poked fun at the Catholic Church, noting that missionaries in the past had looked with sympathy on Native Americans in Ecuador, yet pulled no punches in commenting that the fundamental weakness of the church was its claim on the logic of metaphysical reward rather than terrestrial action. "The ultimate aim of the Church is to produce citizens of Heaven, and for that reason, it is not the institution most fit for the formation of citizens of the nation of Ecuador, or for any other nation," he argued.[8]

Second, Sáenz forcefully repeated the importance of diversity and pluralism to the national community, something he had already done in the case of Mexico during the 1920s but now continued to repeat for the multiethnic societies of

South America. "This book presents the Indian as a living force, not a person who exists merely in the skewed manner that politicians want to see him. The Indian is a vibrant element of the nation, desiring, restless, dissatisfied. My book does not present him as a dead Indian, but as a living one, not like something that existed in the past, but like someone who is alive today and will be alive tomorrow."[9] The living, breathing Indian was central to recognize, Sáenz argued, because diversity was an organizing feature of the nation in Peru that officials had to accommodate themselves to. "If we understand the school in this manner, then we make room for multiple and various components," he argued with respect to public education. Such a school "diffuses the full range of thoughts, information, and culture, and the intellectual integration and the sympathetic understanding of all of the inhabitants of the nation," he argued.[10]

A third tenet was Sáenz's repetition of Dewey's dictum that the primary failure of the public schools had not been questions of method and programming, but the failure to rethink what the purposes of the school had been in the first place. What were the ends of the schools that one had in mind, and why? Sáenz asked. This reflected Sáenz's functionalist analysis, one that drew on his training and continuing engagement with the middle Dewey. Schools were important only insofar as they matched the needs of the local communities, and not because their goals were self-evident or because they matched the goals prescribed by state officials from afar. "The Indian is more interested in plants than in the alphabet, but more than anything else, he is interested in his own way of life, the conservation of his land, and the welfare of his children," he wrote in Ecuador.[11] For that reason, any schools claiming to represent the nation had to be faithful to the vernacular traditions of the peoples of the nation and not to ideals that were extraneous to the communities they served.

As an installment in the genealogy of ideas, Sáenz's use of Dewey in South America reflected the international dimensions of pragmatism as a philosophy of action at the moment when pragmatism and New Deal liberalism were in the cycle of ascendance that would climax in the post–World War II decades. US ideas have been charted abroad in the Western Hemisphere for small intervals of time corresponding to widely different moments in US cultural and political history. Franz Boas's functionalist anthropology has received some attention for the period of early American modernism, for example, and the transmission of free market ideas from the University of Chicago to Pinochet's Chile in the 1970s has been traced for a post–World War II period that followed some sixty years later. But a focus on intellectual history for international thinkers like Sáenz helps to close the wide gaps that continue to exist in our understanding of the history of American ideas abroad and gives us a fuller view of the effects of US civilization on other nations, even as it helps us to better understand the dimensions of pragmatism and New Deal liberalism both as philosophies of action and as structures of politics in more specific ways.

The Parallel Empires

The connections between Sáenz and his mentor John Dewey reflected in the history of the state in Ecuador and Peru deserve more space that I can provide. Moreover, I have presented a very truncated version of the middle Dewey here, and even then I have not drawn the genealogy from the US to Mexico, and then to Peru and Ecuador, of the strands of Deweyan thought that I have attributed to Sáenz's second career. I have also not traced the history of Dewey's ideas in South America beyond Sáenz himself, to the Peruvians and Ecuadorians who took up pragmatism in light of Sáenz's time in Lima and Quito. What transformations to *Democracy and Education* or *Reconstruction in Philosophy* these other intellectuals may have made is not clear.[12] Nor have I discussed the institutionalization of the public schools in either country, or how it reflected practice as Dewey understood it rather than the theory of education alone. But we need not answer these questions fully here in order to outline the contributions that intellectual history as transnationalism is capable of producing for our understanding of the history of US society.

One such contribution is reflected in two features of Sáenz's career. The first feature is that the influence of American pragmatism in Peru and Ecuador was "second order," in the sense that pragmatism came through the work of Moisés Sáenz rather than that of an American. Moisés Sáenz was Mexican-born, had lived the entirety of his life in Mexico, and except for his time in New York studying with Dewey, had not lived in the United States. His work with pragmatism took place entirely within the bureaus of the Mexican federal state and its satellite institutions in the rural provinces of Mexico after 1921. For a period of ten years, until 1931, he worked for the agencies of the Mexican state as they were being reconstructed in the aftermath of the devastating Mexican Revolution. When he went to Peru and Ecuador in the 1930s, he did so as a Mexican citizen rather than an American one, as a representative of the Mexican state, not the US government, and as a social scientist well-known in North America for his deep attachment to the reconstituted Republic of Mexico.

The second feature is that the influence of American ideas in South America owed as much to the institutional work that American pragmatism had performed outside the borders of the United States as it had within. If the expansion of pragmatism in the Western Hemisphere depended on foreign thinkers who had studied in the United States and not Americans who had traveled abroad, it also depended on the experiments those foreign thinkers had created within their own nations, had accommodated to their own nation-building projects, then had subsequently exported to South America after others had noted the work of American ideas in the context of Latin America. Such a flow of ideas across multiple national traditions was important in its own right, showing the extent to which pragmatism was a highly flexible set of ideas relevant to multiple societies as each wrestled with industrialization, migration, and ethnic difference in the context of the twentieth century. It was flexible enough to absorb the nationalistic leanings of the foreign thinkers who came to the United States, and flexible enough thereafter to accommodate the unique nationalist projects that they first fashioned in Mexico and then beyond it.

But taken together, these dual features of Sáenz's career are important because they help to define a postcolonial moment in which ideas from the United States were used by foreign intellectuals to deflect US influence in the hemisphere despite the rise of twentieth-century America to global power. Contrary to any exceptionalist assertion that the flexibility of pragmatism was the product of the unilateral imperialism of American culture in the early decades of what would become known as the American century, Saénz's career with pragmatism in Peru and Ecuador reflected, in fact, the simultaneous rise of multiple nations to power in the hemisphere rather than the United States alone. Consider that as an intellectual, Moisés Sáenz made it a point in his writings on Peru and Ecuador to underscore the successful history of pragmatist projects conducted in postrevolutionary Mexico rather than the success of pragmatist projects in the United States, commentary that was made possible only because of the successful rise of the Mexican nation after 1920. His study of the Indians of Ecuador and Peru had been partially commissioned by Mexico's Secretariat of Public Education, a cabinet-level department of the Mexican government that had quickly established itself across the hemisphere for the breadth of its public school projects. Sáenz was able to study abroad at the request of his federal state precisely because Mexico had been more than modestly successful as an independent nation-state in the decade following the end of the Mexican Revolution. Already, the Mexican Republic had begun the process of nationalizing its subsoil rights via the new Constitution of 1917, which had resulted in the expropriation of the subsoil rights of US corporations like Asarco and Phelps Dodge. Within ten years of Sáenz's trip to Peru and Ecuador, Mexico would also strip away from John D. Rockefeller the petroleum rights throughout the Mexican territory that Porfirio Díaz had conceded to the American oil tycoon at the end of the nineteenth century. Not since 1916, furthermore, when General John Pershing had invaded Mexico while chasing General Pancho Villa, had the US military threatened Mexico.

For Americanists who are thus used to reading about Mexico as a "failed" state or as a "failed" society, Sáenz's career does not reflect a hapless political history of the Republic of Mexico at a moment when the US was rising to superpower status. Instead, the flow of pragmatist ideas southward in the hemisphere took place because of Mexico's strength rather than its perceived weakness. Sáenz's history in Peru and Ecuador was not a tale of one-sided American ingenuity and intellectual culture, then. The rise of American ideas in South America that Sáenz's pragmatist work represented was made possible not by the unilateral rise of the American Empire alone, but by the rise of the Mexican Empire that took place simultaneously. It was the tale of the rise of multiple empires that took place in the Western Hemisphere at the same moment that the European empires were going into worldwide decline. Already England, Germany, and France had destroyed one another during the Great War, and it would be only a short matter of time before they would once again collide in a second world war, an episode in combat that would destroy their nineteenth-century empires for good. In the middle of the destruction of the European empires, Mexico and the United States were both rising in the power vacuum and in response to the changing global order.

This challenge to notions of US exceptionalism and colonialism reflected in Sáenz's career is deepened by the fact that Sáenz was not possessed of overwhelming confidence as he worked in South America. For Sáenz, ideas birthed in the caldron of American culture were not preordained instruments for predetermined efforts in social engineering in the hemisphere, but hesitant possibilities fraught with danger that intellectuals raised in quite distinct historical traditions found amenable for their own nationalist and internationalist projects.[13] The tendency given America's often colonialist and militarist history in the Western Hemisphere is to assume that any usage of American ideas, manpower, and resources has been a unidirectional flow of US civilization for the benefit of the US and none for Latin America. But if ideas flowed through thinkers like Sáenz, then we are in need of a model of idea transfer that accounts for the reasons why independent thinkers like Sáenz found hope in American ideas even as they recognized that adapting such ideas to Mexico and South America was not an instantaneous panacea for the ills of those societies. At the very least, to borrow an older model from economic history in the 1970s, it suggests that thinkers were not "dependents" of American ideas, but that they were free actors who considered the cost and benefits of models constructed in the unique laboratory of the United States before finding them worthy of application in the unique laboratories of Mexico, Peru, and Ecuador.[14]

Sáenz's career also contributes to a renewed understanding of the way that anticolonialism in this larger, more hemispheric sense depended on the use of

American science as Dewey defined it as an instrument that was used to counter the power of ecclesiastical authority in South America. The Mexican Revolution was well known for its attack on the Catholic Church, representing a Latin American Kulturkampf that witnessed the bloody Cristero Revolt of the late 1920s, resulted in the banishment of the church from performing educational functions in Mexico, and established a federal state that sought to eliminate the influences that flowed from the church's landed wealth. The use of pragmatism in Peru and Ecuador saw a similar dynamic in the 1930s, as it was fielded across sections of South America in the effort to curb the power of Catholic bishops and other clerics in Peruvian and Ecuadorian societies. Again, this was a voluntary effort by Latin American intellectuals, not American ones, but it reflects how the attempts by American philosophers at the end of the nineteenth century to destroy the metaphysical foundations of religious-based truth at home reverberated in the fight against hierarchy in other countries of the Western Hemisphere as the US was rising to empire status by the time of World War II.

Thinking about Sáenz and the rise of Mexico as a historical process in the twentieth century through transnational intellectual history also contributes to a renewed understanding of US-Mexico relations that otherwise has become stale and overdetermined in much contemporary commentary. The challenges faced by the Mexican state as it transformed its economy amid the rise of the US has resulted in a narrative of transnationalism that emphasizes US power alone rather than focuses our attention on the historical distinctiveness of power relations at particular moments in the past. But such focused attention on a single interpretation obscures others. We cannot see Mexico's contribution to the hardening of the US-Mexico border between 1910 and 1950, when the postrevolutionary republic sought to reimagine itself as a collectivity of people oriented toward the overthrow of US imperialism. It prevents us from deep readings of some of the canonical works of Mexican cultural and intellectual history, like the philosophy of Luis Villoro and poetry of Jorge Cuesta, both of which, like the work of Moisés Sáenz, were deeply inflected with excavating the meaning of Mexico at the moment of the US rise to global power. In short, thinking about Moisés Sáenz complicates a usual narrative of history that emphasizes US power alone and instead trains our analysis on the historical distinctiveness of discrete moments in the twentieth-century past.

Transnational intellectual history helps us to see that imperialism was not a unidirectional American process, but a negotiated one that moved in bilateral directions rather than a north-to-south axis alone. Such an approach trains us to look to the processes of state administration that are central to any history of the US and Mexico but that get dissolved when we do not look beyond the northward flow of labor power or the immigrant as the carrier of transnationalism.

Last, it suggests that we are in need of a model of national power that adjusts for the power balance between the United States and the countries of the Western Hemisphere. Already I have noted that the Mexican Empire was a necessary condition of Sáenz's work in Peru and Ecuador, rather than the unilateral rise of the United States. But Sáenz was using pragmatism to rebuild the internal institutions of Peru and Ecuador as well, a model that suggests that power relationships were being redeveloped within nations as much as they were being rebuilt across nations. The rise of American ideas was not, in other words, merely registered in the rise of the US and Mexico, but in the internal changes to national hierarchies that followed as those societies put pragmatism to work in the service of the imagined community. Transnational history makes it possible to see power relations between nations as a transactional relationship in which power rises and falls as national communities change over time. This is not a top-down, anti-historicist view of American society, but one that is more porous to the changing significance of US and Mexican civilizations over time.

Contrasting Methodologies

While I have tried to show how transnational intellectual history raises new questions about America's relationship to the Western Hemisphere and helps us to think with more subtlety about American history, it is also useful to say a few words about the configuration of its methodology. These methodological distinctions are not applicable to every case of transnational scholarship, of course. Rather, they are heuristic generalizations made for the purpose of underscoring the significant differences that exist in the organizing principles among the various forms of transnationalist scholarship. The various forms are all concerned with ideas and people across nations on some level, of course, yet they reflect significant differences in their approaches to the crossing of national lines in the Western Hemisphere.

First, transnational intellectual history pays careful attention to the circulation of seminal works of intellectual history like *Democracy and Education* and *Reconstruction in Philosophy* across national lines, and follows the application of the ideas those texts contain within nationalist traditions different from our own. This is an essential first step, since the foreign actors who moved in and out of the United States and into the nations of the Western Hemisphere were activated to politics by their engagement with nationalist problems at home that they refracted through canonical works of social science that were produced in the context of the United States. The analysis of these texts and their Spanish translations cannot be completed as a literary exercise alone, by which I mean a formalist analysis that does not place the text within its greater social context. Rather, we must inquire about the social and political history that allowed foreign intellectuals like Moisés Sáenz to target specific philosophical works and specific philosophical traditions if we are to understand why foreigners and Americans came into a single conversation given the historical differences between their societies. I do not subscribe to the idea that paying attention to the circulation of these texts is tantamount to elite history, or to history that is counter to social history, as is often common in critiques of intellectual history. Many of the intellectuals who traveled to other nations came from modest origins and identified with working-class men and women, not cohorts of the wealthy or the political classes. Quite the contrary. Their close affiliation to the popular classes magnified the discontents of war, labor strife, dispossession, and despotism that led them in the direction of university study, a process that brought them into contact with intellectuals like John Dewey. Such episodes of strife were the lived experiences that brought them into conversation with episodes of strife in the United States implicitly conveyed in works like *Democracy and Education*.

Second, transnationalism insists that intellectuals engage with others across the hemisphere in distinct clusters of thinkers whose ideas are chronologically and spatially bounded. By chronologically bounded, I mean to draw attention to an analysis of the narrow windows of time when intellectuals find common cause with one another across their national differences, via explicitly framed questions and answers to precise social problems, in order to excavate the reasons and moments when their intellectual alliances appear and disappear. Such attention to moments of agreement contrasts with a historiography that often assumes that intellectuals necessarily clash with each other by virtue of their status as citizens of different nations. Tracking the common cause that intellectuals make with one another across nations implies paying careful attention to clusters of thinkers that are smaller than the wide and expansive set of actors that transnationalism often situates as the carriers of cultural practices. This is partially a function of the need to track arguments carefully, which necessarily limits one's view, but it is also a form of analysis that is rooted in the attempt to understand the precise historical motors that caused people to enter into conversation with one another. Such precision allows us to better understand why intellectuals from distinct nations can sometimes find common cause with one another in alliances that are tighter than those formed between intellectuals who come from the same national traditions.

The distinct attention to the historicity of the state is a significant characteristic of the practice of intellectual history as well, and may be fairly described as "prior to the state." That is, among its chief concerns in the context of war, revolution, and economic conflict in the United States, Mexico, and South America is an abiding discussion of the normative role of the state in social conflict in an era when federal statecraft was exceedingly small. The expansion of the state was a deep question to which it pays attention, including the terms under which the state could be financed, resourced, and politically supported. By contrast, much historiography of transnationalism in the Western Hemisphere is a history of the late twentieth-century federal state, especially for the post-NAFTA years overwhelmingly represented by the literature. In such a chronological context, the state is generally critiqued as an obstacle to reform and an immoral participant in policies that prevent the movement of laborers across nations in an era of globalization, and one that often remains static and under-analyzed. This is true for the case of Mexican laborers, for example, who overwhelmingly represent the bulk of immigration to the United States since 1990. In their case, the federal state represents an obstacle to family reunion, an enforcer of unjust labor policies, and a vehicle of economic control by elites. The state in this latter example is generally seen as a paralyzed, post-liberal institution, by which I mean an institution directly counter to the tenets of New Deal liberalism and the redistributionist state that characterized US society from 1930 to 1980.

Together, these characteristics of intellectual history as a method suggest that transnationalism is less a category of historical inquiry than a lens of interpretation through which historians can use the study of ideas as a way of deepening our historical understanding of the US and its relationship to the other nations of the hemisphere. Certainly the requirement that historians must use foreign-language sources implies a culturally specific approach to historical analysis that can be formidable. But transnational intellectual history as I have sketched it here does not vary significantly from a purely domestic approach to the nation. It varies in its breadth and reach of evidence, but that is less a category of analysis than it is the application of a familiar tool kit to the case of hemispheric relationships. We can use a useful contrast here between pragmatism as a philosophy and transnationalism as a lens of interpretation. Pragmatism is sui generis, a site-specific and self-contained critique of Western thought that is a category unto itself by virtue of its unique matrix of ideas, relationship to idealism and Marxism, and specific attention to its dialogue with psychology and the fields of philosophical inquiry like epistemology, metaphysics, and ethics. For these reasons, it requires careful analysis and systemic reflection from within the traditions of German, Russian, and American philosophy. By contrast, transnationalism in ideas does not require specialized tools beyond the important power of observation and contextualization. The same tools used to analyze pragmatism in the United States suffice to analyze pragmatism in Mexico, and the result for historical analysis comes from a juxtaposition of the two and the attempt to draw inferences about their relationships to one another. Drawing such a contrast does not mean that transnationalist analysis is any easier to accomplish. Like any form of historical analysis, its success lies in the extent to which it can convince the reader of the utility of its interpretative approach. But its approachability does suggest that more historians could profit from intellectual history at a moment when the economic and political links between nations have not only intensified, but magnified the presence of international links between nations at moments in the past as well. In a globalized world, such utility can help us to better understand our own society in the United States, and those of the nations with which it has historically interacted.

NOTES

1. The analysis of immigration as a transnational phenomenon that requires the study of both the sending and receiving countries was forcefully described by Rudolph J. Vecoli, "*Contadini* in Chicago: A Critique of *The Uprooted*," *Journal of American History* 51 (December 1964): 404–17.

2. Here I draw attention to David A. Hollinger's frequently cited definition of the discourse of intellectuals, as he defined it in "Historians and the Discourse of Intellectuals," in his *In the American Province: Studies in the History and Historiography of Ideas* (Baltimore: Johns Hopkins University Press, 1989), 130–51. The contrast is to analysis that identifies ideas without considering their sociological genealogy across space and time based on questions shared in common.

3. My current work attempts to better understand why Moisés Sáenz studied with John Dewey in the first place and what such a relationship tells us about the history of democracy in the twentieth-century Western Hemisphere.

4. For a look at Sáenz's career with the Mexican state see John Britton, "Moisés Sáenz: Nacionalista mexicano," *Historia Mexicana* 22 (1972). For my own interpretation of his career see Ruben Flores, *Backroads Pragmatists: Mexico's Melting Pot and Civil Rights in the United States* (Philadelphia: University of Pennsylvania Press, 2014).

5. Sáenz continued his work in Peru and Ecuador though 1941. He died in Lima in 1941 while working on the school and universities there.

6. John Dewey, *Reconstruction in Philosophy* (New York: Henry Holt, 1920).

7. Móises Sáenz, *Sobre el indio ecuatoriano y su incorporación al medio nacional* (Mexico City: Secretaría de Educación Pública, 1933), 182. All translations from the original Spanish sources are by the author.

8. Ibid., 185.

9. Móises Sáenz, *Sobre el indio peruano y su incorporación al medio nacional* (Mexico City: Secretaría de Educación Pública, 1933), xv.

10. Ibid., 265.

11. Sáenz, *El indio ecuatoriano*, 183.

12. John Dewey, *Democracy and Education* (New York: Macmillan, 1916).

13. Sáenz's sensibility was closer to that of Franz Boas in *The Mind of Primitive Man* (New York: Macmillan, 1911). Boas there noted the rise and fall of political orders throughout history without any sense of necessary progress or a teleology of triumph.

14. Dependency theory proved tautological and overdetermined in its insistence that the economies of poor nations were solely determined by decisions in wealthier ones. For one account of its rise and fall see Omar Sánchez, "The Rise and Fall of the Dependency Movement: Does It Inform Underdevelopment Today?," *Estudios Interdisciplinarios de América Latina y el Caribe* 14, no. 2 (2003).

Section III
DANGEROUS IDEAS

8

TOWARD A NEW, OLD LIBERAL IMAGINATION
From Obama to Niebuhr and Back Again

Kevin Mattson

I want to recall one of the weirder experiences I had in following contemporary American politics (no slim pickings there). I was watching, being the good citizen I am, the presidential primary debates between Hillary Clinton and Bernie Sanders. I had a clear desire to watch Bernie Sanders "win," however that would be determined. After all, my politics lean toward the robust liberalism of FDR (the American politician whom Sanders mentioned the most as a predecessor to his own ideas, when he wasn't talking about socialism), and I thought Clinton—along with her husband—had helped push the Democrats in a direction that was too centrist, too based upon the principles of the Democratic Leadership Council, too conciliatory toward a Republican Party that had tacked way too far to the right. So there I was rooting for my side when a weird thing happened. . . .

I started to dislike Bernie Sanders. That's not to say that I fell into the arms of Hillary Clinton, because I didn't. And it wasn't Sanders's supposed "mansplaining," that grotesque term created in our current political idiom. There were certainly big differences between him and Hillary that had nothing to do with her being born a woman. Some of what I disliked was his overpromising: Every time I heard him touting free college tuition and national health care, all the while promising to stop climate change while generating more economic growth, I saw the dour face of Mitch McConnell and then thought how all my millennial students would feel the burn (pardon me) when they found out that none of those promises would be easy to obtain within the confines of the American political system. He bordered on concocting his own version of the "imperial presidency" if he was to get the things he wanted, the darker side of FDR as a model president. There was also something about his tone, that barking tendency he honed on stump speeches, the jutting of the finger, the raising of the vocal chords, the fulmination (maybe he was trying to channel Eugene Debs?). But really, what I think it came down to was that I faced not just a socialist belief system—which differed from my own liberal worldview—but also a historical materialism that drove so many of Sanders's arguments. There was a reductionism in his thinking and public rhetoric, a reductionism that stemmed from the ideas he held to.

When Black Lives Matter (BLM) protested Sanders's rallies, some, including close friends of mine, were surprised. I wasn't. I remember the factionalized politics of the American Left throughout the twentieth century—you know, the sort of pick-an-argument-with-someone-you're-close-to-rather-than-keep-your-attention-on-the-real-opponent. But I didn't think that factionalism drove the BLM protests against Sanders. What drove those activists, as I saw it, was Sanders's idea—widely shared on the left—about economic populism. Like the original populists back in the late nineteenth century, the whole thing hinged on the idea that race diverted the poor from understanding the *economic* nature of their oppression. *You are kept separate so you can be separately fleeced* went the logic of southern populist leaders like Tom Watson (who, it should be noted, became a rabid racist after the populists lost and fused with the Democrats). BLM picked up on this, I think, and drove the idea into reverse. The notion that if people put class before race, a unified movement could then tackle both problems at once ignored that racial discrimination had its own determining power unto itself. Race prejudice could not be reduced merely to materialistic interests, the way economic populists in the past and present wished.

Here I think Sanders, knowingly or not, was channeling the voice of numerous left-leaning intellectuals during the 1990s and early 2000s, those heightened years of what some call the culture wars. Think Todd Gitlin, Michael Tomasky, and Tom Frank. I'll admit that during the 1990s, I found their arguments fairly persuasive, but they were growing thin for me by the 2010s. Excuse my gross oversimplification here, but all these thinkers made the case that race (and other "cultural" divides) got in the way of focusing on socioeconomic inequality. For someone like a Tom Frank, the idea was that ideas and beliefs—including some of the zany ideas of the wing-nut Right in 2004—never had their own autonomy from the material structures that shaped them. It's what in sociology is called materialist reductionism. I don't know if Sanders read Gitlin, Tomasky, or Frank, but I think that my reaction against his own variant of economic populism had a lot to do with watching the reality of living in the 2010s (and the long history before!) and seeing young black men facing down the prospects of police guns and imprisonment and very little else. Economic populism wasn't up to tackling that problem. As Trump was rising on the other side of the aisle, it became especially difficult to believe that the white working class would be won over to a cross-racial politics grounded in some sort of economic vision (let alone that "the people," the core of right- and left-leaning populism, deserved the mantle of virtue). Trump was clearly articulating some sort of white nationalism and winning the white working-class vote by all we could tell. So talking about economic issues just wasn't going to help us confront some rather important issues—including the question of racial equality. Or to put it another way, I was rediscovering the principle of pluralism, an idea so central to the intellectual history of postwar liberalism (more on that later). Power doesn't operate purely on a socioeconomic axis. There are, quite simply, other axes, including race and gender.

There was one real jaw-dropper during the debates. It was Sanders at his most left-leaning and mechanistic-reasoning, driven by his economic materialism. "Climate change is directly related to the growth of terrorism," he insisted on November 14, 2016, having made a variant of that argument earlier and being asked for clarification. I'm pretty sure television viewers scratched their heads on this one. But really the bold statement simply reflected Sanders's materialism, right? For sure, I'm certain that there's a relation of some sort, as resources grow thinner and thinner across the planet, people look to apocalyptic variants of political action. OK, maybe. But they also tend to survive as refugees, seeking protection from a world come unglued largely by ideas. What Sanders's comment suggested was that terrorism could not be driven by an autonomous idea or belief system grounded in religion or ideology; no, it was the materialistic—and scientifically proven, for sure—heating of the planet that created the Osama bin Ladens and 9/11 hijackers of the world (certainly a step up from Donald Trump's stupid claim that Obama actually formed ISIS). Obviously, the fact checkers went into overdrive on this one and mostly panned Sanders's statement. But for me, it was no surprise to hear the line being played out: a materialist on race becomes a materialist on explaining terrorism. There's always just one axis of power operating: the material axis, be it class position in structure or the changing material world around us. I remember hearing Sanders's quip during the debate and asking myself, Does this man *think*, does he have any sense of suppleness about explaining how the world operates? Or does he reduce and see the world through goggled lenses? Or reduce all the problems in the world to one prima facie principle?

So, Sanders sounded, well, rigid to me, like he could talk about only one axial plane. I started to cringe when I heard the repeated phase "one percent" offered over and over and over. Sanders never sounded complex or like he was really thinking about what he was saying, but rather spouting, scoring his points against an opponent shriveled by her own tendency to play it safe, generating a "line" of thought rather than thinking. I was reminded of Daniel Bell's quip that an ideologue was like a machine you cranked to hear the same thing over and over again. I remembered those activists I met on the left during the 1980s, the sort that hawked newspapers with the word "Workers" always prominent somewhere in their title. They would approach me and say they had something important to talk about. And then a stupid debate would ensue between me and my Trotskyist, Stalinist, Luxemburgian, revolutionary, democratic, or whatever opponent. I remembered always thinking that these guys thought in slogans, wanting to convince me of what they would call their "line." And I always remembered the takeaway I had from these conversations: that these people didn't listen to a word I said, they only barked back their "line," seeing me as someone to bulldoze into their camp.

I know, I know, it's unfair to make the comparison between those on the hard Left and Bernie Sanders, the democratic socialist. But my mind flashed to that when I watched Bernie debate and heard his tone. And it started me on what so many other Americans thought about when faced with the battle between Bernie and Hillary. Many of us were starting to realize that we were missing Obama (when he appeared on the stump for Hillary, sometimes the crowds would chant "Four More Years"). Yes, this for sure, Bernie Sanders had made me miss Obama. And that's remarkable. Because in many ways, I, like a whole litany of liberal intellectuals, was frustrated by Obama's presidency in terms of how much he seemed guilty of allowing the drift to the right in politics go even further, much like Hillary and Bill Clinton had done.

But as I watched Bernie versus Hillary, I have to admit that my mind just kept drifting back to 2008, sometimes out of nostalgia, but I think more because I was so *not* enjoying the politics of 2016. A voice had disappeared from the debate. All of which, believe it or not, brings me to the idea of liberal virtues, both in terms of facing the realities of race, as opposed to the economic populists of today, but also the ethics of complexity, pluralism, and a rejection of deterministic arguments. Those things now suggest why liberals believe in a certain public discourse and play of mind that require explanation and defense. Power doesn't operate on just one axis, and things are never simple; that's likely the most important takeaway from my experience here. My frowning at Sanders and my unwillingness to celebrate the candidacy of Hillary Clinton (even though I would vote for her in the general election) led me down memory lane, to understand how liberalism can graft a public philosophy that can work to reach "the people"—not a category of fetish or celebration—without pandering or overpromising or mechanistic reduction.

I still remember the candidate I supported from the get-go back in 2008, because of numerous biographical details I had gleaned about him. I knew he was well-read in Tocqueville and all the other things that James Kloppenberg would later cite in his book, *Reading Obama*. I had read his memoir and thought it surprisingly honest, not the sort of book you would expect from someone about to enter politics. I knew his background in community organizing, having done some of that myself. But it was one act in particular that now in 2016 made me see how Obama wasn't Hillary Clinton and wasn't Bernie Sanders. It wasn't the man's slogans of "Hope" and "Change" that sounded dangerously overpromising (and as we learned later, those slogans actually made Obama cringe at the time). The thing that swayed numerous voters was Obama's make-or-break speech. Looking back, it was a speech I couldn't imagine Bernie Sanders giving. That's not just because Bernie Sanders is white top to bottom, and the speech had to do with race. The real reason that Bernie Sanders couldn't give this speech is that it combined different values held in balance with one another, and it projected a vision of complexity and pluralism rather than just hard exertion. It was not a speech of slogans. And being that, I believe, gets us to understanding liberalism as a philosophy of sorts, and how necessary it is. It was a speech of a man thinking out loud, showing the virtues of balance and complexity and suppleness. Let me deal with the speech and then try my best to place Barack Obama in the context of postwar liberalism, where he belongs.

The "A More Perfect Union" speech grew out of a crisis during the 2008 primary. The media was tape looping images of Obama's friend and mentor, the Reverend Jeremiah Wright, screaming out to his brethren, "God Damn America!" Obama had to clarify, and using a skill that sadly diminished once he assumed the presidency, he used his speech to explore some key liberal principles, and even to prod some naive liberals to see the world in a more complex manner.

Then candidate Obama explained why he could not "disown" Jeremiah Wright for what sounded like incendiary rhetoric. This comes at the heart of the speech, and it seemed something a lot of listeners took away from it, because Obama brought big ideas down into the mundane everyday life of families (all of us have some crazy uncle or aunt, right?). "I can no more disown him than I can disown the black community. I can no more disown him than I can my white grandmother—a woman who helped raise me, a woman who sacrificed again and again for me, a woman who once confessed her fear of black men who passed by her on the street, and who on more than one occasion has uttered racial or ethnic stereotypes that made me cringe." (Conservatives actually complained with that line that Obama had betrayed his own family by throwing his grandmother under the bus.) Obama explained that Reverend Wright's incendiary rhetoric was no doubt tied to growing up black in America during the 1950s and 1960s, "when segregation was the law of the land and opportunity was systematically constricted," making it clear that he could not let his fellow Americans just ignore the dark realities of their history even as he called for a "more perfect union." What Obama did, in both the case of Wright and his grandmother, was refuse to reduce people to their worst moments, to say that he could hold on to people who were contradictory, that he could deal with the complexity of being indebted to others but also being autonomous enough to make adult judgments about human beings' weaknesses and strengths. It was resisting the tendency to turn real people into cartoon images; it was a rejection of romanticizing people or seeing them as either devils or saints.[1]

And then Obama set out his view of a "more perfect union," *not*, it should be noted, of a "*perfect* union," an impossibility, given the pitfalls of human nature. "In the end, then, what is called for is nothing more, and nothing less, than what all the world's great religions demand—that we do unto others as we have them do unto us." That line sounded like a synthesis of Jesus and John Rawls, with a little bit of Immanuel Kant sprinkled in. And he called for a politics that echoed FDR's: "to give health care to the sick, . . . jobs to the jobless, . . . education to our children" so as to create a more rigorous national community bound together with egalitarian values. It was a fine statement of postwar liberalism.

I want to emphasize what Obama did along the way of making this case. He chided fellow liberals. As he pointed out, some "wide-eyed liberals" wanted to "purchase racial reconciliation on the cheap" by suggesting that if he won the presidency, *zap*, racism would vanish. "I have never been so naive as to believe that we can get beyond our racial divisions in a single election cycle." Now, because I am arguing that Obama's message of complexity and balance go to the heart of liberalism, I probably should say something about this in-house criticism of fellow liberals. I'm pretty sure that in these passages Obama was channeling one of the greatest liberal political thinkers since World War II, the theologian Reinhold Niebuhr. I can't say for sure, but I think Obama's "wide-eyed liberals" were targets in Niebuhr's sights earlier, especially during the late 1940s and early 1950s (including those "fellow travelers" who were soft on communists who certainly had a teleological understanding of history as progress). "Wide-eyed liberals" sound an awful lot like Niebuhr's "children of light" (more later). These types of liberals were the sort of people who had a naive faith in "progress," refusing to understand that humankind was just too full of self-love and self-interest to glide magically into a utopia free of conflict and hatred. Giving up on a naive view of the world, though, didn't entail passivity, it just counseled humility and an ethical sense of realism.

The speech worked, literally and figuratively, because it relied on a certain sophistication in its listeners. This was not pandering, this was walking through the murky world most people inhabit, where no one is perfect, where good people do bad things, where we overlook family members' weaknesses, where we often have to put aside our internal rage against stupidity in order to go on with our lives.

Not only did Obama's speech set out an ideal of complexity; it set out a style of public rhetoric that he became associated with ever since giving it: cool and calm (hence the nickname No Drama Obama). It was, it has to be said, a highly *intellectual* style. Some compared him to John F. Kennedy, who in his own time was often considered an intellectual, especially in contrast with Eisenhower (Kennedy at least had a book with his name on it, *Profiles in Courage*, though we now know it was ghostwritten). Even Norman Mailer, usually a man with a bit more critical acumen, saw JFK as an intellectual (and a hipster existentialist).[2] Obama was actually a writer before becoming a politician (there's no evidence, though I'm sure some right-wing nutcase has tried, to argue that Obama didn't write his memoir, *Dreams of My Father*), and he, of course, had a very good liberal arts education from Occidental College and Columbia University and a strong legal education from Haaaaarvard, as it should be remembered. In essence, he made JFK look like a hayseed. Obama even did things like write his girlfriend about T. S. Eliot's poetry and its tenuous relationship with conservatism and would read books even as he entered the White House (something that George W. Bush, his predecessor, would never be caught doing).[3]

Here can be found the unspoken rejection of Sanders's and the American Left's populism on the part of Obama (and other liberals). Populism always celebrates the people as they are; commoners are virtuous, elites evil. And don't get started on educated intellectuals. . . . Indeed, one of the most recent blasts of left-leaning populism came in 2008 when Hillary Clinton—oh, the ironies!—tried to say how into hunting she was as a child and how Obama sounded like he wanted to take guns away from hardworking Americans (Hillary was getting a lot of bad advice from Mark Penn, who wrote memos about how she should portray Obama, owing to his Kenyan father and childhood in Hawaii, as somehow out of contact with "American" values).[4] Clinton was jumping onto a boat that had already left the docks and was about to head straight for the right, namely for Sarah Palin's vice presidential run of craziness and right into the person that Hillary lost to—Donald Trump. That populism is now so tied to white nationalism and an abject celebration of ignorance—to the art of believing conspiracy theories and mindlessly touting the virtues of the white working class against the evil people who inhabit the federal bureaucracy—that it makes it impossible for any liberal to imagine it as anything more than a bloated, dead corpse as a political concept.

That doesn't mean economic inequality is something that liberals shouldn't talk about, of course. It's just not going to be solved by sloganizing about the "one percent" or "making America great again." It will have to require, as Obama famously explained to Joe the Plumber, some "spreading" of wealth across the board; it will have to require raising the minimum wage; it will have to require getting rid of tax loopholes that benefit the wealthiest in this country, as it will have to hope against hope that labor organizing can become more effective than it has in the last number of years (or perhaps have the labor movement be displaced by minimum-wage laws at the state and city levels). But it also has to balance those things with a respect for free markets and the wealth disparity that markets create. That's because liberalism stands for equality but also for "freedom," the value that the Right trumpets but is better associated with liberalism. In other words, liberals need to articulate not a socialist system but rather a system that balances more equity with markets staying in place. Liberals, like socialists, believe government has a role to play; but unlike socialists, liberals recognize the need to check governmental power. Again, the liberal project is about balance, complexity, and championing intelligence over its more brutish possibilities. It's about holding tensions within a vision of social justice. If Hillary Clinton had been on her best when she debated Bernie Sanders, she would have engaged this difference in political philosophy (and in fact, at one point in the primary, Chris Matthews tried to get Debbie Wasserman Schultz to spell out this distinction between liberalism and socialism, and she, as expected, dropped the ball).

So, I've mentioned Reinhold Niebuhr already in the chapter. There are two good reasons why. First, his thought had a profound impact on Barack Obama. The not-so-liberal journalist David Brooks had interviewed Obama in 2007 and asked him if he had ever read Niebuhr. Obama lit up and said, "I love him. He's one of my favorite philosophers." This brings us to the second reason to focus on Niebuhr: He was much more than one of Obama's favorite philosophers; he was the godfather or granddaddy of postwar American liberalism's ideas and cast of mind. For sure, there were other writers who helped fuel the postwar tradition of American liberalism: Arthur Schlesinger Jr. (whose seminal book *The Vital Center* was deeply indebted to Niebuhr—especially, in Schlesinger's own words, the idea that "the plight of the self is that it cannot do the good it intends"), John Kenneth Galbraith, Richard Hofstadter, C. Vann Woodward, James Wechsler, Bernard DeVoto.[5] But if any of these intellectuals were asked, they would have admitted that Niebuhr was the man who framed a public philosophy that could help correct major problems in the liberal (and progressive) tradition in America—especially a penchant for optimism and a faith in progress. Niebuhr was less the man who set out concrete policies—he was a theologian, activist, political theorist, and public philosopher more than anything—and more the man who articulated a worldview that helped liberals (what today might be called progressives) make sense of their role in history, providing a vision of cautious orientation to a world inevitable to disappoint.

There's a reason why Niebuhr deserves such high status in the intellectual history of American liberalism, especially in light of trying to tease out distinctions between liberalism and socialism. Importantly, Niebuhr started out, after his academic training, as a Socialist; so he was a rethinker as much as a thinker. He ran for Congress on the Socialist Party ticket in 1930 (two years before he published one of his most famous books, *Moral Man and Immoral Society*) and voted for Norman Thomas, the presidential candidate of the Socialist Party, throughout the 1930s, rejecting FDR's New Deal as paltry fare. His break with the Socialist Party was, at first, over its pacifism, a dangerous and naive reaction to the spread of fascism abroad, Niebuhr argued. Socialists seemed to cling to their purity rather than react realistically to a violent threat bent on destroying democratic ideals. From this position, Niebuhr carved out his liberal and realist philosophy against the sentimentalism that fueled too much liberal reform. Some intellectual historians would be tempted to place Niebuhr in the traditional narrative arc of once-radical thinkers during the 1930s becoming more conservative and shifting to the center by the 1940s and 1950s.[6] But I take the move as one that was guided by a purposeful search not for intellectual comfort or quietism but a critique of socialism that is still important to listen to today and for a liberalism Niebuhr hoped could guide American politics into the future and that could provide intellectual ballast against communism, fascism, and traditional conservatism.

Niebuhr's realism—his critique of pacifism—pressed him to discount both the conservative idea of a free market unhampered by the state and the doctrine of communism (and revolutionary socialism). What these intellectual enemies of Niebuhr posited was a utopian and unrealistic assessment of humankind's progress in the future. Drawing upon his own reading of the Bible and thinking about human nature, Niebuhr believed that free marketers and communists suffered from a feeble and naive view of human nature. "Liberal democrats dreamed of a simple social harmony" made up self-seeking actors operating in unfettered markets. On the other hand, "Marxism was the social creed and the social cry of those classes who knew by their miseries that the creed of the liberal optimists was a snare and a delusion." Niebuhr went on, "Marxism was also convinced that after the triumph of the lower classes of society, a new society would emerge in which exactly that kind of harmony between all social forces would be established, which Adam Smith had regarded as a possibility."[7] Niebuhr believed in a liberal potential that rejected its own doctrine of optimism and understood that the impulses of self-love and conflict could never be completely eradicated in some future utopia. "Bourgeois property theory has no safeguard against the power of individual property; and Marxist theory has no protection against the excessive power of those who manipulate a socialized economic process."[8] Only a "mixed economy" and a pluralistic civil society could resist the faults of bourgeois liberalism or Marxian utopianism. A pluralistic society with conflicts of power allowed for individuals to seek self-interest yet recognize their own limits by the power of the state protecting communal goods. Those who wanted to reform the American economy to become more just had to face the limits of their own sentimentalism and grandiose faith in their own goodness. In seeking power and influence, even what Niebuhr called "the children of light"—those guided by a naive optimism about progress and improvement—could do harm, could become consumed by their own power. "Man is, despite his increasing freedom, a finite creature."[9] But that didn't mitigate the need to act on behalf of justice; it heightened awareness of the idea that good intentions could cause misery and tragedy, as witnessed in Stalinism.

Following these ideas, it's interesting to note what Obama said he took from Niebuhr when given the chance to explain his ideas to Brooks sixty-three or so years after Niebuhr made the remarks I quote from here. "I take away," Obama explained, "the compelling idea that there's serious evil in the world, and hardship and pain. And we should be humble and modest in our belief we can eliminate those things." He countered that with, "But we shouldn't use that as an excuse for cynicism and inaction." Niebuhr's thought for him pushed back against both "naive idealism" and "bitter realism." Which in my own mind is a fine definition of the central principle of postwar liberalism that we should resuscitate today. Again, this is not a policy formulation but rather seeking a cast of mind, a way of holding your ideas about political change and social justice.[10]

Which brings me to the final chapter in this last election, Hillary Clinton's loss to Donald Trump. If Sanders had played the role of the perfectionist and idealist, Trump played up the role of authoritarian bully and crass realist, one who lacked all the virtues that Niebuhr and Obama had articulated (and that the liberal literary critic Lionel Trilling once called, following a term used by a professor at Columbia named John Erskine, "the moral obligation to be intelligent").[11] As much as he ran against "crooked Hillary," Trump also ran against Obama, against his health care reform policy, against his deliberativeness, and especially against a sense that Obama was a weak leader (in contrast, Trump often asserted, to Vladimir Putin).

In the context of the election, many people started remembering a confrontation between Trump and Obama. It took place at the 2011 White House Correspondents' Dinner—you know, that place where the "lamestream" media elites gather to conspire against conservatives (a forum that Trump recently skipped as president). Also in attendance that day was none other than Donald Trump.

Then, Trump was a major "birther" exponent, arguing that Obama couldn't provide a birth certificate because he was hiding the fact that he was born overseas. Well, Obama had just released his birth certificate that showed him being born in the States and was just about to take out Osama bin Laden, which added a weird tension to the evening's performance by the president. Obama—with the wit of a liberal who has a populist enemy in sight—let it rip, smiling a big smile all the while mocking the hell out of a man now known less for real estate deals and more for his adventures in reality television. Here's what Obama said:

> Now, I know that he's taken some flak lately, but no one is happier, no one is prouder to put this birth certificate matter to rest than The Donald. And that's because he can finally get back to focusing on the issues that matter—like, did we fake the moon landing? What really happened in Roswell? And where are Biggie and Tupac? But all kidding aside, obviously, we all know about your credentials and breadth of experience. For example—no, seriously, just recently, in an episode of "Celebrity Apprentice"—at the steakhouse, the men's cooking team did not impress the judges from Omaha Steaks. And there was a lot of blame to go around. But you, Mr. Trump, recognized that the real problem was a lack of leadership. And so ultimately, you didn't blame Lil Jon or Meatloaf. You fired Gary Busey. And these are the kind of decisions that would keep me up at night. Well handled, sir. Well handled.[12]

It was a strike of liberal humor, aimed right for a man who symbolizes right-wing populism and the postmodern desire to live in a world where facts and knowledge no longer matter. But it was also, I would argue, a celebration of postwar liberalism's virtues. Obama's performance, for lack of a better word, reminded me of the writings of the liberal historian Richard Hofstadter, who himself was supposedly a marvelous mimic in everyday life and who was notorious for having a good sense of humor, besides being the author of the ever-relevant book, *Anti-intellectualism in American Life* (discussed by one of the participants in this book). Writing about Adlai Stevenson—the two-time beautiful loser for the presidency during the 1950s who also admired Niebuhr's thinking—Hofstadter gleaned Stevenson's "wit." Hofstadter wrote: "Wit is humor intellectualized; it is sharper; it has associations with style and sophistication, overtones of aristocracy."[13] Minus the aristocracy term (a misuse, I think, since in actuality this sort of humor can often be radically democratic), this statement symbolizes what many liberal intellectuals saw in Obama, the same thing that Hofstadter saw in Stevenson.

It also reminds me of what drives a large number of people crazy about Trump. It's not just his policies, which seem hastily written and ill-defined. Rather, it's his,

Hey folks, we're going to build a wall and get the Mexicans to pay for it style. Meaning it's his pandering, overpromising style. It's his calling Obama the founder of ISIS and then saying he was just being sarcastic. It's his buffoonery, his right-wing populist bluster. And it's his belief that he can simply wave his arms and get the things he wants done done, that executing a reality television plot is like governing in the universe the rest of us call reality. Call it a liberal's disdain for the political philosophy of bullyism and authoritarianism and overreach of executive power.

I think that Obama's takedown of Trump back in 2011 highlights what I hope liberalism can still offer us: A politics of humility that struggles against a politics of bullying assertiveness. A politics that doesn't disgrace itself into pandering. A politics that worries about the state of our civic debate as much as getting policies formulated and passed. Against the sinful desire (in the Niebuhrian sense of that term) to think we live in a world where grandiose transformations can be made by a simple wave of the arm, liberalism emphasizes complexity and deliberation, recognizing the messy world of real people like Jeremiah Wright and Obama's own grandmother. Some people reject liberalism precisely for that reason (you could hear it in the complaints that Obama didn't get enough done, that he was too deliberative to be president). They dream of strong leaders who make "bold" moves and transformative decisions, who build walls in a stroke of the pen (or who hope to) or who bring socialism overnight to a country whose underlying mythos at the very least highlights the creed of individualism. They celebrate "outsiders" against those who have knowledge about the complexities of American government. The sort of liberal vision that I think must combat such abstract visions of transformation would be one that sees our better (not perfect) selves confronting complexities and admits that there are no perfect solutions, that we can never acquire the "*perfect* union," that we will never find a utopian alternative that will eradicate all conflicts and the self-love of human nature. Liberals have to proceed with caution as well as ideals. They have to see limits as much as possibilities. It's not an *easy* philosophy, and that's exactly what makes it so crucial today.

NOTES

1. I rely here upon T. Denean Sharpley-Whiting, ed., *The Speech: Race and Barack Obama's "A More Perfect Union"* (New York: Bloomsbury, 2009). The speech itself is reprinted there. See also Thomas Sugrue, *Not Even Past: Barack Obama and the Burden of Race* (Princeton, NJ: Princeton University Press, 2010).

2. See Norman Mailer, "Superman Comes to the Supermarket," in *The Time of Our Time* (New York: Modern Library, 1999), 345–56.

3. See here Michael Tomasky, "Barack Obama and the Intellectual as President," *Democracy Journal*, January 6, 2016, http://democracyjournal.org/alcove/barack-obama-and-the-intellectual-as-president/; see also my more favorable argument, "The Intellectual

as President," *Chronicle of Higher Education*, September 25, 2016, http://www.chronicle.com/article/The-Intellectual-as-President/237860.

4. See my piece on Penn, titled "Micro Man," originally posted at the *Guardian* on April 11, 2008: https://www.theguardian.com/commentisfree/2008/apr/11/microman.

5. Arthur Schlesinger Jr., *A Life in the Twentieth Century* (New York: Houghton Mifflin, 2000), 511.

6. This is of course the story told by Richard Pells in his now classic work of intellectual history, *The Liberal Mind in a Conservative Age* (Hanover, NH: University Press of New England, for Wesleyan University Press, 1985).

7. Reinhold Niebuhr, *The Children of Light and the Children of Darkness* (1944; New York: Scribner's, 1972), 31.

8. Ibid., 113.

9. Ibid., 187.

10. All quotes of Obama in conversation with Brooks come from a *New York Times* story in 2007 that can be found at http://www.nytimes.com/2007/04/26/opinion/26brooks.html.

11. See Leon Wieseltier, ed., *The Moral Obligation to Be Intelligent* (New York: FSG, 2000).

12. See Adam Gopnik, "Trump and Obama: A Night to Remember," *New Yorker*, September 12, 2015, http://www.newyorker.com/news/daily-comment/trump-and-obama-a-night-to-remember.

13. Richard Hofstadter, *Anti-intellectualism in American Life* (New York: Vintage Books, 1963), 225.

9

AGAINST THE LIBERAL TRADITION
An Intellectual History of the American Left

Andrew Hartman

If anyone personifies the American Left, that person is Eugene Victor Debs. Debs led the American Railway Union in the violent 1894 Pullman strike, cofounded the International Workers of the World (the Wobblies) in 1905, and led the Socialist Party of America during its early twentieth-century heyday. As the five-time Socialist Party nominee for president, Debs won millions of votes, yet this was the same man who went to prison for opposing American entry into World War I, and the same man who in 1919 proclaimed, "From the crown of my head to the soles of my feet I am Bolshevik, and proud of it."[1]

Debs was not always a fire-breathing class warrior. Prior to serving a six-month sentence at Woodstock Prison in 1895 for his role in the notorious Pullman strike, he often promoted the republican idea of a "grand cooperative scheme" that would allow people to "work together in harmony in every branch of industry." Rather than calling for a working-class struggle to wrest control of the means of production from the capitalists—rather than building a socialist party to capture the bourgeois political system—Debs had called for the creation of utopian colonies. The future of socialism, for the early Debs, lay in the vision of the Welsh reformer Robert Owen, who founded the short-lived New Harmony, Indiana, utopian colony in 1825, and in the dreams of Edward Bellamy, who imagined a utopian socialist future in his 1888 novel, *Looking Backward*. Debs's biographer Nick Salvatore writes that by "invoking the model of utopian community, the beacon light upon a hill demanding society return to its true values, Debs drew on the most basic American archetypes." Debs believed that a rapacious form of capitalism had betrayed the spirit of brotherhood that had animated Americans from the revolutionaries to the abolitionists and beyond, and that the moral example set by the utopian community would help persuade Americans to live up to their highest ideals.²

But to a growing number of hard-boiled Gilded Age radicals fluent in the theories of Karl Marx and Friedrich Engels, utopian socialism was a naive approach to fighting capitalism. Marx and Engels wrote in the 1848 *Communist Manifesto* that utopian socialists like Owen fantasized that "historical action is to yield to their personal inventive action." Engels developed this idea further in his 1880 pamphlet, *Socialism: Utopian and Scientific*, where he conceded that utopian socialists had indeed sought to solve the problem of class antagonism that the bourgeois revolutions of the eighteenth century had failed to address. But because history had not yet revealed to early nineteenth-century utopian socialists the inevitable development of the proletariat as a revolutionary class— had not yet shown them that the bourgeoisie "produces, above all, its own grave-diggers"—they were incapable of correctly seeing that utopian communities were doomed to failure. Latter-day utopians had no such excuse. They lived in a time when more and more people were subjected to a capitalist labor market— when millions of proles manned the machines of capitalism—a historical fact readily apparent to anyone with eyes to see it.³

Despite Debs's steadfast republican instincts, which prioritized labor independence of the type that predated corporate capitalism, he came to agree with Marx and Engels. Debs underwent an ideological conversion from the utopianism that had inspired past American radicals to a European brand of socialism that emphasized capitalism as a system and class as an antagonism at the heart of that system. He came to believe that the nation's salvation was dependent on waging a class war against capitalism. This was a belief that Debs first discovered during his Woodstock Prison stint, which he spent reading socialist texts like *Das Kapital*, "the very first," in his words, "to set the wires humming in my system."⁴

Debs was also won over to Marxism by the persuasive Milwaukee-based German socialist Victor Berger, the person responsible for placing *Das Kapital* in Debs's hands. Berger insulted utopians by calling them "hazy reformers." The utopians, for their part, smeared Berger and his foreign-born comrades as "un-American." This divide between immigrant Marxists and Yankee radicals roiled the 1898 convention of the Social Democracy, an organizational forerunner to the Socialist Party. Would the Social Democracy go the utopian route, and build a model socialist colony in some remote locale, such as rural Tennessee? Or would it focus on class struggle, and work in concert with the growing labor movement?⁵

Both sides in the battle for the Social Democracy sought the support of Debs. He was, after all, a certified working-class hero. Before the convention closed, Debs hesitantly affiliated with Berger. By joining the Marxists, Debs hammered the last nail in the coffin of utopian socialism in the United States. With the utopians gone, the new, more focused organization renamed itself the Social Democratic Party in America. (In 1901 it merged with disaffected members of the Socialist Labor Party to form the Socialist Party of America.) The inaugural platform of the Social Democratic Party, largely written by Berger, declared that "two distinct classes with conflicting interests" had emerged under capitalism: "the small possessing class of capitalists" and "the ever-increasing large dispossessed class of wageworkers." And with that, the American Left was born.[6]

This chapter argues that the American Left came into existence after it took up Marxism in the early twentieth century. It is common knowledge that the idea of a left-right political spectrum originated during the French Revolution, when the monarchists on the National Assembly sat to the right of the president while the revolutionaries sat to his left. But an *American* Left came into being only after modern capitalism had rapidly transformed American life beyond anything antebellum Americans would have recognized, thus creating an intellectual vacuum that old explanatory schemes such as republicanism had difficulty reckoning with.

To suggest that Marxism made the American Left is not to imply that the Left sprouted from foreign soil. Why were more and more Americans from a multitude of ethnic, racial, and national backgrounds forced to sell their labor to survive, much less prosper? Why were fewer and fewer Americans able to build sustainable and rewarding lives by working the land? What should be done? Marxism offered persuasive answers to these perplexing questions. American radicalism, broadly conceived, dates back at least as far Tom Paine's incendiary Revolution-era writings. As such, it played a prominent role in several nineteenth-century movements, including abolitionism and Populism. But American radicalism became the American *Left* only after it redefined its program as anticapitalist. The historian John Patrick Diggins put it this way: "In drastically transforming the character of modern society, capitalists did more than anyone else to give birth to the left."[7]

In *The Rise and Fall of the American Left*, Diggins contends that it took longer for a Left to gain traction in the United States than in Europe, because the European Left developed in opposition to a feudal aristocracy that never really existed in North America. Europe had a weak liberal tradition, which explains why European liberals, too fragile to stand on their own, sided with the reactionary monarchs who crushed the 1848 revolutions. It also clarifies why the European Left had a special claim on concepts like democracy and liberty. In contrast, the United States had a strong liberal tradition, which explains why Americans from most political persuasions, slavers aside, had a stake in terms like democracy and liberty.[8]

By contrasting American and European political traditions in a way that implied American exceptionalism, Diggins built on ideas first elaborated by political scientist Louis Hartz in his forceful 1955 book, *The Liberal Tradition in America*. For Hartz, any analysis of American political thought had to begin with what he termed the "storybook truth about American history," that is, the United States had no feudal past. This truth helped explain why the United States, unlike Europe, lacked both "a genuine revolutionary tradition" and "a tradition of reaction." The philosopher who embodied American political thought was not Marx, nor Burke, but rather Locke. Neither class struggle nor aristocratic distinction shaped American political sensibilities. Rather, the idea that animated American politics was Locke's theory that government was socially contracted to protect the natural rights of the individual, and that property was one such right. Hartz recognized that there were historical exceptions to this American rule, most glaringly the political philosophy of the slave South, which Hartz called "an alien child in a liberal family." But over time, the liberal tradition crushed all that stood in its way. Whereas both the apologist of American slavery George Fitzhugh and the early Marxist theorist Daniel De Leon were, in Hartz's words, "crucified by the American general will," liberals like John Marshall and John Dewey "flourished in consequence of their crucifixion."[9]

Hartz was a friendly but critical student of American liberalism. For although Hartz believed liberalism a superior political philosophy to its challengers on the left and the right, and that the United States was exceptional in its dedication to it, he recognized that the American liberal tradition displayed "a vast and almost charming innocence of mind." Because American liberalism lacked the "class passion" that animated European politics—the passion that gave life to revolutionary and reactionary forces—it was premised on the assumption that moral questions about the good life had been settled. And when ethics are taken for granted, Hartz argued, "all problems emerge as problems of technique." This technocratic disposition explained the "unusual power of the Supreme Court and the cult of constitution worship" in American political life. Americans had replaced political speculation with legal tinkering. The American liberal tradition, in this way, was less a political philosophy than an anti-philosophy. Or so it seemed.[10]

Other Cold War liberals defined liberalism in more assenting ways. Lionel Trilling described it as a "political position which affirmed the value of individual existence in all its variousness, complexity, and difficulty." Diggins defined liberalism as a political philosophy "committed to a pluralistic balance of power, an equilibrium of class interests, an ethic of opportunity and achievement, and a realistic vision of human limitations." These definitions are useful. But they are normative rather than historical. They confuse description with prescription.[11]

Such muddled analysis led consensus thinkers to overstate the case for liberal hegemony. In doing so they often characterized non-liberal ideologies as atavistic and beyond the pale of psychological health. At a time of relative liberal dominance, it was perhaps understandable that liberal intellectuals had trouble seeing rival political ideologies. Trilling's claim that conservatism expressed itself not in ideas but rather "in irritable mental gestures which seek to resemble ideas" lacked prescience. But it was a somewhat reasonable statement to make in 1950. Hartz was wrong to discount the hold that reaction had on the American imagination. He was wrong to assume that slavery and its ideological residues were aberrational. But he could not have foreseen the waves of reaction that have swept the land since he wrote *The Liberal Tradition in America* in 1955—the most recent such wave personified by Donald Trump. Conversely, in the wake of left-leaning Henry Wallace's ignominious 1948 electoral failure—Wallace and the Progressive Party ticket captured a paltry 2 percent of the popular vote, as Cold War liberal Harry Truman sailed to victory—Hartz, Trilling, and the rest can perhaps be forgiven for discounting the role of the Left in American political life. But even during the early Cold War, the Left had an American history, as well as an American future.[12]

Despite their narrow views of American political development, Cold War liberals were largely correct that the basic political freedoms Americans came to enjoy by the early twentieth century were byproducts of the liberal tradition that ran deep in American political culture. Unlike in Europe, the American Left cannot take credit for the freedoms guaranteed by political democracy, at least as such freedoms stood as the nineteenth century turned into the twentieth. But by then the capitalist economy had revealed the limits to such freedoms to a growing number of Americans attuned to the historical transformations wrought by capitalism. "Liberalism may have succeeded in democratizing political institutions and expanding suffrage," Diggins wrote, "but the Left recognized that the masses would remain without effective power as long as work, wages, and welfare were controlled by those who owned the means of production." The Left's mission—the reason for its existence—was to expand the idea of political freedom, which was limited and went by the name of liberalism, to include economic freedom, a broadened conception that went by the name of socialism. The route to such freedom was class struggle.[13]

Precisely because the United States had such a robust liberal tradition, the American Left developed in tension with American liberalism, in a dialectical dance of sorts. It is no easy task to separate these two political strains. Political categories are notoriously difficult to pin down. They are ceaselessly malleable and highly specific to time and place. Hard-and-fast distinctions between leftism and liberalism often fall apart when examined across divergent contexts. For example, pragmatism, that classically twentieth-century American philosophy, emerged as perhaps the best philosophical representation of social democracy. In this way, pragmatism might be thought of as a left-wing project, or as James Kloppenberg defines it, a liberal-socialist fusion. But William James and John Dewey, the two most renowned pragmatic thinkers, are remembered as giants of American liberalism, not socialism. Moreover, when limited to its philosophical underpinnings, pragmatism seems more consistent with the liberal tradition than with Marxism.

Pragmatism accentuated the notion that humans have freedom of voluntary action, which, as Kloppenberg writes, "revealed that freedom is an irreducible part of immediate experience that neither science nor metaphysics can challenge or explain away." Not even capitalism could erase human agency. Pragmatism extended one of the primary aspects of the classic liberal project—the search for individual freedom—into a new era of capitalism in a way that challenged alternative political theories, including Marxism. Where Marxists maintained that corporate capitalism had destroyed working-class autonomy, pragmatists argued that conceptions of the individual had changed but that the individual remained intact and potentially powerful. Marxists envisioned freedom in a socialist future, pragmatists in the capitalist present. Put another way, even the intellectual history that serves as the most serious challenge to my argument that the Left should be defined in its opposition to liberalism—*even* pragmatism—reveals the Left-liberal divide's usefulness in clarifying an intellectual history of the American Left.[14]

Fleshing out a genealogy of the American Left requires a dive backward into the second half of the nineteenth century, because many historians of the American Left locate its origins in the movement to abolish slavery. Perhaps more than any other radical movement in American history, abolitionism went from the fringes of American political culture—from religious fanatics, eccentric nonconformists, and maroon communities of runaway slaves—to the center, with the Union army transformed into an army of slave liberation. This rare but powerful moment of radicalism's ascendance made unlikely allies. As James Oakes has written, it brought together the "radical" Frederick Douglass with the "republican" Abraham Lincoln. Perhaps it also explains the unlikely convergence between Lincoln, who championed the capitalistic free labor system under development in the North and the northwest United States, and Marx, the world's most famous critic of capitalism, who also became the Union's most influential supporter among European radicals.[15]

At the outset of the Civil War, many European radicals were hesitant to criticize the rebellious Southern states since they believed in national self-determination and, more to the point, because they were confused about the reasons for Southern secession. But Marx convinced the members of the International

Workingmen's Association (IWA)—the First International—that the Civil War was about slavery, and that defeating the Confederacy would be a blow to transatlantic slavery, and thus an important step toward working-class emancipation. Union victory, Marx believed, would create conditions more favorable to organizing the working class, since a free labor system would no longer have to compete with slavery. It was through this lens that Marx viewed Lincoln. "The workingmen of Europe," Marx wrote in a letter to Lincoln on behalf of the International, "consider it an earnest of the epoch to come, that it fell to the lot of Abraham Lincoln, the single-minded son of the working class, to lead his country through matchless struggle for the rescue of an enchained race and the reconstruction of the social world."[16]

Marx's letter to Lincoln heralded a hopeful future for many would-be leftists. Perhaps the international Left that Marx had helped cultivate across Europe would take root in the United States. Perhaps the radicalism of the abolitionist movement would carry over into a militant, class-based movement of the sort that Marx and his comrades idealized. Indeed, many abolitionists, not satisfied with ending race-based chattel slavery, turned their righteous anger against a labor system they termed wage slavery. The abolitionist Wendell Phillips declared in response to the 1871 Paris Commune: "There is no hope for France but in the Reds." His fellow abolitionist Theodore Tilton said: "The same logic and sympathy—the same conviction and ardor—which made us an Abolitionist twenty years ago, makes us a Communist now."[17]

Such a left-wing future was not to be, at least not in nineteenth-century America. When the London-based IWA opened shop in the United States in 1866, its membership was a combustible mix of Yankee radicalism and European Marxism. Almost from the outset, the American IWA was divided over its reason for existence. Yankee radicals like Victoria Woodhull, groomed in the radical republicanism that had informed abolitionism and utopian socialism, and newly enamored with liberalism's focus on individual rights, promoted a vigorous program of reform intended to make individual lives more dignified. Humans had inalienable rights, and these rights, which had been extended to former slaves, were also to be extended to workers, women, and other marginalized Americans. Individual dignity had become a prerequisite of the beloved republican community that Yankee radicals hoped to build. In contrast, immigrant socialists like Marx's friend Friedrich Sorge wanted the American IWA to singularly focus on advancing one cause and one cause only: lifting up the proletariat as the vanguard of global communist revolution.[18]

The Marxists ultimately won the battle for the IWA, thanks in no small part to the ruthless machinations of Marx and his allies. At the time, nobody could have foreseen the meaning of this seemingly insignificant sectarian squabble. But in retrospect, the battle for the IWA anticipated the battle for the Social Democracy a few decades later, also won by Marxists. The Yankee radicals of the IWA, as with the early Debs who followed in their footsteps, had an idealistic view of what America ought to be, and believed that such a society could be achieved through moral persuasion, democratic action, and utopian example. In this, the Yankee radical vision of the world was firmly planted in the liberal tradition. The later Debs broke with Yankee radicalism, and the liberal tradition, by turning to Marxism and its laser-hot form of anticapitalism. Marxism won the war for the soul of Eugene V. Debs, and with it, the soul of the American Left across the twentieth century and beyond.

American intellectual history is full of compelling people whose thought illuminates the ways in which Marxism distinguished the American Left from the liberal tradition. Consider John Reed, author of *Ten Days That Shook the World*, a celebratory, firsthand account of the Russian Revolution that has since been hailed as an American classic. The qualities that made Reed's "slice of intensified history" a masterpiece are the same qualities that engendered efforts to censor it. Reed's unreconstructed Marxism, which allowed him proximity to Lenin and the Bolsheviks, provided *Ten Days* its unique outside-inside vantage point. But it also alienated the widely circulated publications that had previously published the globetrotting journalist's electrifying essays—publications that included the *American Magazine*, *Collier's*, the *Saturday Evening Post*, and *Metropolitan Magazine*. Whereas *Ten Days* earned Reed burial at the Kremlin Wall Necropolis, one of only two Americans to receive that honor, Reed's adoring take on the Russian Revolution also merited him the scorn of the liberal American publishing world. Reed's glowing evaluation of the "great Lenin," "loved and revered as perhaps few leaders in history have been," was held in high contempt by a liberal intellectual culture that had once embraced the intrepid reporter.[19]

Reed came to the Left, and Marxism, through the experience of reporting on labor conflict. While covering the 1913 silk strike in Paterson, New Jersey, Reed grew outraged by the weavers' meager wages, poor working conditions, long workdays, and the brutal treatment they received at the hands of the police. He joined their picket line and was promptly thrown in jail for four days. While behind bars, Reed became engrossed by the life stories told to him by the striking silk workers, engendering a sympathy for the working class that remained steadfast the rest of his life. Such a pro-labor position notwithstanding, Reed's reporting was not yet Marxist. He did not yet connect the exploitation he saw in Paterson to larger systems. In short, capitalism was not yet Reed's enemy, and Reed was not yet persona non grata in the publishing world. Rather, at that point in his journalism career he had a reputation as a first-rate reporter fearlessly willing to go wherever a good story took him. This reputation was further bolstered by his reporting from the front lines of the Mexican Revolution, where he lived with and fought for Pancho Villa's forces for several months.[20]

Reed's political education continued while reporting on the coal miners' strike in Ludlow, Colorado, where state militia forces massacred two dozen women and children. This tragedy—and the otherwise awful media coverage of it—pushed Reed to conduct research that allowed him to make broader connections between the state repression of impoverished immigrant workers and their families and the larger political economy of mining. Although Reed's lengthy story was full of the drama befitting the Great Colorado Coal War, it also included sharp analysis of how the inexorable profit motive was responsible for the skimpy wages and horrid work conditions that precipitated the strike. In the words of his biographer, his Ludlow efforts "marked his growth as a class-conscious writer not easily satisfied with recording his impressions but who must dig deeper into the play of forces behind them." In short, Reed had become a Marxist, which began to put him at odds with his liberal publishers. But being cut off from liberal intellectual culture freed Reed to write *Ten Days* his own way.[21]

Reed concluded *Ten Days* in memorable fashion: "I suddenly realized that the devout Russian people no longer needed priests to pray them into heaven. On earth they were building a kingdom more bright than any heaven had to offer, and for which it was a glory to die." That passage made Reed a prophet of sorts. Not for forecasting the course of the Soviet Union—on that he was enormously and tragically wrong. Rather, Reed unknowingly anticipated that he would pay the ultimate price for his devotion to the Russian Revolution. After illegally returning to Russia in 1919 with sedition charges hanging over his head in the United States, and then after the US government prevented him from returning home to face those charges, Reed fell ill with typhus. Because of a blockade imposed by the Western nations waging war against the fledgling Communist state, he was unable to receive proper medical treatment. Reed died an untimely death in Moscow on October 17, 1920, five days shy of thirty-three. Becoming a leftist meant the evaporation of Reed's mainstream bylines. But far worse yet, it led to his death in exile.[22]

W. E. B. Du Bois, like Reed, died in a foreign land partly for his leftist beliefs. He also, again like Reed, wrote a work of genius—*Black Reconstruction in America* (1935)—that was great precisely for its Marxism. Notwithstanding these left-wing credentials, Du Bois is mostly famous as a giant in the pantheon of American liberalism. This is no surprise, given that in 1909 he helped found the National Association for the Advancement of Colored People (NAACP), which has ever since worked for the liberal goal of securing rights for blacks within the American system. Remembering Du Bois as a liberal also makes sense, given that he is the author of an earlier work of liberal virtuosity, *The Souls of Black Folk* (1903), which forwarded his utopian theory about a "talented tenth" of African

Americans who would lead blacks to racial equality by the example they set. With that context in mind, it is less well known that Du Bois is one of the most innovative readers of Marx in American history. *Black Reconstruction*, which Du Bois wrote while running a *Capital* seminar for his graduate students at Atlanta University, used a Marxist framework against the grain of Jim Crow America, and in the process anticipated a revolution in American historiography.[23]

In his effort to transform how people thought about the Civil War and Reconstruction—in telling his story "as though Negroes were ordinary human beings"—Du Bois ran headlong into a legion of white historians who worked in lockstep with the Dunning school. According to Columbia University historian William Archibald Dunning and his followers, including Woodrow Wilson, Reconstruction was the most calamitous and corrupt period in the nation's history because imperialistic Radical Republicans empowered riotous, subhuman blacks to rule over the respectable white South. This racist interpretation, popularized by *The Birth of a Nation*, the 1915 silent film that rekindled the Ku Klux Klan, doubled as a rationale for stripping southern blacks of citizenship. Progressive historians like Charles and Mary Beard, who in other ways had helped advance new liberal interpretations of American history that accounted for the dignity of many ordinary, non-elite Americans, held the Dunning-style view that blacks were to blame for not improving their condition.[24]

Those liberals who took racism seriously as an impediment to black progress argued that racism would recede if the nation heeded its own liberal ideals. The sad fact that racial inequality existed in a nation with such a strong liberal tradition was what Gunnar Myrdal called the "American dilemma," the title of the Swedish economist's 1944 book. In contrast, *Black Reconstruction* interpreted racism as a labor problem. By 1935, Du Bois had eschewed liberalism and had instead embraced Marxism as a weapon in his battle against white and liberal historiography.[25]

Du Bois built on Marx's argument that the American Civil War was a revolutionary opening for the international working class by contending that the Civil War was a proletarian revolution within a bourgeois republic. To this, Du Bois added an important revision to the particular historical context of the Civil War: as opposed to the white working class of the orthodox Marxist imagination, black slaves represented the proletariat. Du Bois labeled black resistance during the Civil War a "general strike," thus equating it to the militant labor actions making headlines during the time he was writing *Black Reconstruction*, such as the West Coast waterfront strike of 1934. By resisting work on Confederate plantations, and by swamping approaching Union lines, black slaves were responsible for winning the Civil War and emancipating themselves. Black slaves had created the revolutionary opening that Marx had envisioned.[26]

But class struggle went both ways. Building on his interpretation of the Civil War, Du Bois showed that Reconstruction was "America's unfinished revolution," as Eric Foner later termed it. When black labor came under white control once again—when the Union armies of liberation deserted the South in 1877—the revolution was smashed. Reconstruction was brought to an end not only because the nation was unwilling to live up to its liberal ideals, but also because it needed a chastened black labor force. In sum, the fact that Du Bois wrote his masterpiece with Marx on his mind—that, as an avowed leftist, he conceptualized it through a Marxist framework—was more than merely incidental. Du Bois's use of Marx was constructive. Eventually—decades later—many more American historians would catch up to Du Bois in his understanding of the Civil War, in his use of Marx, and in his leftism. The American Left failed to transform American political life, but leftist thought has done a lot to reshape American intellectual life, especially in the academy.[27]

American intellectual life was electrified by left-wing thought in the 1960s—at a time when left-wing thought was galvanized by its confrontation with liberalism. Take for example the writings of the Frankfurt School refugee Herbert Marcuse, who became known as the "philosopher of the New Left" for helping renew leftist thought, especially Marxism, in an age of affluence. This, of course, was the primary task of New Left intellectuals. More than a Westernized Marxism that heeded Stalin's wreckage, New Left intellectuals sought an Americanized Marxism attuned to the particularities of American economic development. Against the grain of Marx's expectations about the immiseration of the proletariat—expectations that energized earlier leftists like Debs—the American working class had become wealthier.[28]

Such a perspective made New Left intellectuals skeptical that conditions were ripe for socialist revolution. Unlike Marx's proletariat—the embodiment of revolutionary immanence—no revolutionary class existed in postwar America. Left-wing intellectuals thus believed their theoretical task was to go beyond Marx in ways that accounted for the fact that nothing about contemporary class relations revealed the contradictions in the capitalist system. Gabriel Kolko argued in 1966 that Marx's teleology did not equip leftists with the tools necessary to grapple with the corporate organization of the modern capitalist economy. Moreover, Kolko contended that Marxists had misinterpreted the economic interventions of the liberal state as having been on behalf of socialism instead of corporate capitalism. "Nothing in socialist theory," Kolko wrote, "prepared socialists for the possibility that a class-oriented integration of the state and the economy in many key areas would rationalize and strengthen capitalism." It was time to rethink leftist thought in light of a corporate liberalism that Marx and other earlier leftists could not have foreseen.[29]

Into this breach stepped Marcuse with the book that made him famous: *One-Dimensional Man: Studies in the Ideology of Advanced Industrial Society*, published in 1964. At its most basic level, *One-Dimensional Man* proposed a theory of false consciousness. An affluent American society had purchased the loyalties of the working class, making it ill prepared to fulfill its historic revolutionary role. By the 1960s, it had become clear that capital and labor sought the same basic goals: maintenance of the status quo. The contradictions so transparent to Marx—contradictions that would usher in communist revolution—no longer appeared self-evident in an era of affluence and total administrative control. Ironically, in this way Marcuse presupposed a consensus, like many of his liberal contemporaries, including Hartz. There was no outside to the system, whether that system was called the "liberal tradition" or "corporate liberalism." But unlike his liberal contemporaries, consensus for Marcuse and the New Left was a Kafkaesque nightmare. "A comfortable, smooth, reasonable, democratic unfreedom prevails in advanced industrial civilization, a token of technical progress."[30]

The New Left is best known for its efforts to end the Vietnam War. But its most lasting legacy is cultural liberation. Marcuse's criticisms of cultural repression help explain the popularity of *One-Dimensional Man*. He argued that repression—sexual and otherwise—was a product of capitalism. Or as Andrew Hacker put it in a review of Marcuse's work: "The frustrations and repressions of their elders can be ascribed—with no little truth—to the restricting roles forced on them by their employment and environment." So when Marcuse opened a 1967 speech he gave to a group of students in Berlin by summoning "flower power," he truly meant it as a call to revolution.[31]

In expanding its concerns to include sexual freedom, countercultural expression, feminism, gay rights, ethnic and racial identity, and more, the New Left fostered an unprecedented radicalization of the culture. A thousand liberating flowers bloomed. But the reason this fight for cultural liberation was so successful was that, much like the earlier Yankee radicalism of someone like Victoria Woodhull, it aligned with the liberal tradition. Ironically, the New Left compelled the nation to live up to the ideals of its liberal tradition. But in the process, the Left gave up on its own tradition. The Left seemingly forgot its anticapitalist roots.

In the wake of Richard Nixon's two electoral victories, Ronald Reagan's right-wing counterrevolution, and Bill Clinton's corporate centrism, the Left retreated and began to take its cues from the likes of Subcomandante Marcos, the masked voice of the Zapatista rebels in Chiapas, Mexico: "Marcos is gay in San Francisco, black in South Africa, Asian in Europe, Chicano in San Isidro, Anarchist in Spain, Palestinian in Israel." The Marcos approach is what counts as left-wing solidarity in the age of neoliberal identity politics. This is a whack-a-mole Left: protest a lumber company here, a trade organization there, police brutality here, Israeli settlements there. Meanwhile capitalism does what it does—mostly unabated—and inequality once again becomes the scourge of the times.[32]

Identity politics submerge class and focus instead on creating opportunities for individual ascent by previously excluded peoples. In this way identity politics go hand in glove with the neoliberal dismantling of a social welfare state, since individual achievement is privileged over the social good. Hillary Clinton shatters glass ceilings (not the ultimate one, alas), but millions of women remain in poverty. Blacks can now sit at the front of the bus, but the buses rarely come, and they cost too much. People have witnessed the expansion of individual rights (a liberal victory) alongside the shrinking of the collective good (a left-wing defeat).[33]

In the face of this defeat, more and more people on the Left are once again recognizing that liberalism and capitalism are not necessarily mutually exclusive. Such recognition signifies the Left becoming reacquainted with its long-standing Marxist tradition, and rediscovering the necessity of positioning itself against the liberal tradition. This is where the future of the Left, if there is to be such a future, lies.

NOTES

1. Nick Salvatore, *Eugene V. Debs: Citizen and Socialist*, 2nd ed. (1982; Urbana: University of Illinois Press, 2007), 291.

2. Ibid., 162.

3. Karl Marx and Friedrich Engels, *Manifesto of the Communist Party* (1848), and Friedrich Engels, "Socialism: Utopian and Scientific," in *The Marx-Engels Reader*, 2nd ed., ed. Robert C. Tucker (New York: W. W. Norton, 1978), 683–715.

4. Salvatore, *Eugene V. Debs*, 150.

5. Ibid., 165.

6. Ibid., 167.

7. John P. Diggins, *The Rise and Fall of the American Left* (New York: W. W. Norton, 1992), 28.

8. Ibid., 27–48.

9. Louis Hartz, *The Liberal Tradition in America: An Interpretation of American Political Thought since the Revolution* (New York: Harcourt, Brace & World, 1955), 3, 10.

10. Ibid., 9.

11. Trilling wrote that much-repeated definition in a 1974 foreword to his 1950 book *Liberal Imagination*, as quoted in Nathan Glick, "The Last Great Critic," *Atlantic*, July 2000; Diggins, *Rise and Fall*, 40.

12. Lionel Trilling, *Liberal Imagination: Essays on Literature and Society* (New York: Viking Press, 1950), 5.

13. Diggins, *Rise and Fall*, 34.

14. Corey Robin offers a model study of how opposing political ideologies are forged in combat with one another—in his case how conservatism is a reaction against revolutionary leftism: *The Reactionary Mind: Conservatism from Edmund Burke to Sarah Palin* (London: Oxford University Press, 2011). James Kloppenberg, *Uncertain Victory: Social Democracy and Progressivism in European and American Thought, 1870–1920* (New York: Oxford University Press, 1986), 412.

15. Two examples that locate the original history of the Left in abolitionism, or the "movement of movements," are Michael Kazin, *American Dreamers: How the Left Changed a Nation* (New York: Vintage Books, 2012); and Howard Brick and Christopher Phelps, *Radicals in America: The U.S. Left since the Second World War* (New York: Cambridge University Press, 2015). James Oakes, *The Radical and the Republican: Frederick Douglass, Abraham Lincoln, and the Triumph of Antislavery Politics* (New York: W. W. Norton, 2008); Robin Blackburn, *The Unfinished Revolution: Karl Marx and Abraham Lincoln* (London: Verso, 2011).

16. Blackburn, *Unfinished Revolution*, 48.

17. Brick and Phelps, *Radicals in America*, 11.

18. See Timothy Messer-Kruse, *The Yankee International: Marxism and the American Reform Tradition, 1848–1876* (Chapel Hill: University of North Carolina Press, 1998).

19. John Reed, *Ten Days That Shook the World* (New York: Boni & Liveright, 1919), 77; John Stuart, *The Education of John Reed* (New York: International, 1955), 31.

20. Stuart, *Education of John Reed*, 17–19.

21. Ibid., 21.

22. Reed, *Ten Days*, 143. Stuart, *Education of John Reed*, 30–38.

23. David Levering Lewis, *W. E. B. Du Bois: The Fight for Equality and the American Century, 1919–1963* (New York: Henry Holt, 2000), 352–73; W. E. B. Du Bois, *The Souls of Black Folks* (1903); W. E. B. Du Bois, *Black Reconstruction in America: An Essay toward a History of the Part Which Black Folk Played in the Attempt to Reconstruct Democracy in America, 1860–1880* (1935; Cleveland: Meridian Books, 1964).

24. Lewis, *W. E. B. Du Bois*, 350–60.

25. Gunnar Myrdal, *An American Dilemma: The Negro Problem and Modern Democracy* (New York: Harper and Bros., 1944).

26. Du Bois, *Black Reconstruction in America*, 57.

27. Eric Foner, *Reconstruction: America's Unfinished Revolution, 1863–1877* (New York: HarperCollins, 1988).

28. Andrew Hacker, "Philosopher of the New Left," *New York Times*, March 10, 1968, 1, 33–34.

29. Gabriel Kolko, "The Decline of American Radicalism in the Twentieth Century," *Studies on the Left* 6, no. 5 (September–October 1966), in *For a New America: Essays in History and Politics from "Studies on the Left," 1959–1967*, ed. James Weinstein and David Eakins (New York: Random House, 1970), and the quotes are from that book, 203.

30. Herbert Marcuse, *One-Dimensional Man: Studies in the Ideology of Advanced Industrial Society* (Boston: Beacon, 1964), 1.

31. Hacker, "Philosopher of the New Left," 1.

32. Brick and Phelps, *Radicals in America*, 275; Perry Anderson, "Renewals," *New Left Review*, January–February 2000.

33. Brick and Phelps, *Radicals in America*, 315.

10

FROM "TALL IDEAS DANCING" TO TRUMP'S TWITTER RANTING

Reckoning the Intellectual History of Conservatism

Lisa Szefel

For a long time, the tools of intellectual history seemed particularly well suited to studies of conservatism. Since George Nash's seminal volume, *The Conservative Intellectual Movement in America since 1945*, intellectual historians have centered on high ideas. This decades-long gossamer focus makes sense, given the midcentury existential and epistemological dilemma of the movement's founders, which demanded engagement with acute questions about human nature, good and evil, power and authority. Just as religion had riven Europe in the Thirty Years' War of the seventeenth century, ideology inveigled nations to violence on a global scale during what some call the second Thirty Years' War between 1914 and 1945.

Examining the frayed nerves of citizens and shredded landscapes of countries unraveled by world war, concentration camps, and atomic peril, postwar conservatives gathered scraps from the wreckage to create a usable past on which to build and move forward. Picking up remnants from the Enlightenment and Counter-Enlightenment, transhistorical discourses about civilization, along with transatlantic cultural artifacts, they strove to disentangle the Western heritage from the warp of political debility that enabled Axis strength and the weft of statist approaches that thinned the batting of democracy. The first to discern the way those patterns fastened into a whole cloth, Nash tied together the strands of traditionalism, anticommunism, and libertarianism that composed conservatism in the early Cold War.

In this midcentury endeavor, the project of literary modernism offered inspiration because, as Russell Berman has explained, it involved "any attempt by modern men and women to become subjects as well as objects of modernization, to get a grip on the modern world and make themselves at home in it."[1] Beginning in the 1910s, modernist poets stripped away adjectives, imprecision, sentimentality, and sermonizing in order to render the experience of living in a feral financial and industrial capitalist world with more fidelity. Self-described "classical in literature, royalist in politics, and Anglo-Catholic in religion" T. S. Eliot led the way. For over three decades, he probed the need for originality to arise from within a tradition and elucidated the "structural emotions" of poetry and drama: instead of performing an overt social function, they fastened "floating feelings" into "a new art emotion." Cultural texts offered not a release of emotions but an "escape from personality."[2] Eliot called on literary critics to craft the right kind of feeling or "sensibility" of readers so they could pivot from close analysis of intricate texts to a complex understanding of contemporary life. Not all sentiments were equal; some elevated, while others summoned chaos. The only sure method was "to be very intelligent."[3] A flourishing democracy, after all, demanded greater discernment from citizens. And in Eliot's verse, most notably *The Waste Land*, with its elaborate stitching of allusions, the poet tendered a landscape ravaged by materialism and technology that could be repelled only by the sustaining force of canonical texts, connection, and spirituality: "These fragments I have shored against my ruin."

A cohort of academic scholars known as the New Critics answered Eliot's call for developing critical thinking skills. They diagnosed the "spiritual disorder of modern life" and prescribed limited government, an aristocracy of talent, and resistance to the siren call of acquisition. Donald Davidson summed up their contempt for the imaginary conjured by the "terrifying expansion" of consumer credit: "It will be to corrupt the public life ... by persuading people to believe that life is made up of material satisfactions only, and that there are no satisfactions that cannot be purchased." "Financial chaos" and "a degraded citizenry" prone to overspending awaited.[4]

Following the defeat of fascism, amid implacable communism, New Critical questions took on greater heft, particularly their concern about the best way to express and manage personal freedom through aesthetic representation. In best-selling textbooks, they instructed readers to appreciate the knotty nature of composition (and life) and that the final result, far from a definitive statement, delineated a "process" of searching "for meanings and exploration of meanings."[5] They allied with the urban, northern, and liberal New York intellectuals out of a shared conviction that literature required protection from the corrosive effects of middlebrow mediocrity in a mass consumer society. Showcasing works of the imagination also demonstrated the superiority of American individualism and freedom in contrast to oppressive Soviet interference with artists.

Indeed, across the political spectrum—from Lionel Trilling's *Liberal Imagination* to Arthur Schlesinger Jr.'s *Vital Center*, *Witness* by Whittaker Chambers and academic reports—came appeals for cultivating the imagination through the liberal arts. Even national security experts heeded this counsel. The many English majors with Ivy League degrees in the Congress of Cultural Freedom and CIA were referred to as "Ransom's Boys" (after New Critic John Crowe Ransom). They published poems, academic articles, and translations of Eliot's writings. As Richard Elman averred: "The CIA not only engaged in a cultural cold war ... they had a very definite aesthetic: they stood for High Culture."[6]

The founding texts of modern American conservatism drew from this cultural vein. A student of Ransom's at Vanderbilt University and advisee of Cleanth Brooks and Robert Penn Warren at Louisiana State University, Richard Weaver injected New Critical prescriptions into discussions of politics and society. His doctoral dissertation idealistically (and mistakenly) lauded the Old South as "the last non-materialist civilization in the Western world," and his book *Ideas Have Consequences* (1948) espoused what became known as "traditionalist" conservatism: private property symbolized independence; the rule of law brought order; and a reverence for immutable truths acted as a bulwark against utopian excess. Just as New Critics with their advanced degrees basked atop an intellectual pecking order, traditionalists declared that democracy's safety demanded distinction because "Modern man," Weaver wrote, "has become a moral idiot."[7] If bad ideas had sown an evil reality, then good ideas—those grafted with a full grasp of man's fallen nature, the naturalness of hierarchies, and saving grace of transcendental ideas—if replanted by those who curated values through cultivating knowledge, could reap harvests not of sorrow but of joy.

Russell Kirk recruited Weaver to contribute to the inaugural issue of *Modern Age*, which he founded in 1957 as "a dignified forum for reflective traditionalist conservatism."[8] Kirk shared with the author a conviction that culture, not just economics and national security, should underpin political life. In *The Conservative Mind* (1953), Kirk traced a respectable genealogy from Edmund Burke to modern-day New Humanist Paul Elmer More. This pedigree stood as an alternative to an ancestral chart of illicit liberalism, which began with Rousseau and his spawn, the French Revolution, and culminated in the twentieth-century disasters wrought by communism and fascism. Kirk counterpoised their respective family credos as well. Those on the left believed in human perfectibility, abjured tradition, and promoted economic and political leveling, while those on the right insist upon original sin and looked to the church, community, and customs to tamp down deep-rooted evil.

Whereas Eliot had advocated correct "feeling," Kirk called for proper thinking: "Principle is right reason expressed in permanent form; abstraction is its corruption."[9] Instead of a system or ideology, conservatism involved an outlook and temperament. The book's title, *The Conservative Mind*, consecrated not politics but a cognitive orientation. Combining Burke's "moral imagination" and Eliot's "permanent things," conservative minds strengthened through a deep engagement with the liberal arts could support republican civic virtues while combating the allure of fanaticism.

Whereas Kirk's books helped to legitimize conservatism in an era that labeled it an "impulse" characterized by "irritable mental gestures" of angry paranoids, William F. Buckley Jr. did much to channel its energies into a political powerhouse. Determined since his undergraduate years at Yale to challenge the primacy of liberalism, Buckley founded the *National Review* in 1955. An elitist, libertarian, and Catholic, Buckley made the publication the movement's epicenter for the next half century. Along with senior editor Frank S. Meyer, who articulated a policy of "fusionism," Buckley did this in part by welcoming into the fold traditionalists who, albeit anti-collectivist conservers of the Judeo-Christian tradition, held ideas that were incompatible at best and antagonistic at worst with libertarians—increasingly prominent with the infusion of academic émigrés who joined with anti–New Deal Republicans in crusading for limited government and free-market capitalism. Testifying to the horrors of planned economies, these economists, social theorists, and political philosophers extolled private enterprise as (to use the Austrian American economist Joseph Schumpeter's phrasing) the "perennial gale of creative destruction."

How could denizens of disruption consort with conservatives determined to preserve? Meyer's accord divvied out responsibility, assigning to government the task of protecting freedom and fostering an environment ripe for entrepreneurship, while designating individuals the job of pursuing virtue. So, while traditionalists agonized with Polish émigré Czesław Miłosz over captive minds, libertarians strategized with Friedrich Hayek about redirecting roads to serfdom onto superhighways of capitalist innovation. In the years to come, the two sides would find more common ground on the issues of homeschooling and school choice, private charity instead of public largesse, voluntary associations and limited government, private property and a prosperity gospel that divined virtue via financial success.

Print media and radio soon propelled conservatism from philosophy and periodicals into the more pragmatic realm of political power. Brent Bozell, Buckley's teammate on the champion Yale Debate Team, brother-in-law, and the magazine's senior editor, was commissioned by John Birch member Frank Brophy to ghostwrite Barry Goldwater's *The Conscience of a Conservative* (1960). The slim 120-page book denounced welfare and taxes as gateway drugs to collectivism, the foreign policy of containment as "treason," liberals as "swindled," and translated conservative principles that had been swirling around for the previous decade and a half into an actionable political agenda. Pat Buchanan attested: "It contained the core beliefs of our political faith, it told us why we had failed, what we must do. We read it, memorized it, quoted it.... For those of us wandering in the arid desert of Eisenhower Republicanism, it hit like a rifle shot."[10]

This newfound acclaim, combined with the founding of conservative organizations, publishers, bookstores, reading groups, and radio programs, along with the cross-country barnstorming of the redoubtable Republican organizer F. Clifton White, nudged Goldwater to run for the presidential nomination in 1964. However, because some of his policy prescriptions abutted those of the John Birch Society, Goldwater solicited help in distancing himself from the radical group.[11] Buckley attempted to do so in a way that did not offend the many Bircher loyalists, by calling out Birch founder Robert W. Welch Jr. for creating "confusion." Yet, at the Republican National Convention, where Senator Mark Hatfield of Oregon and Governor Nelson Rockefeller of New York condemned the Birch Society, Goldwater flabbergasted some audience members. Instead of making a case for party unity, the Arizona senator invoked the extreme phrasings and doctrines of the Birchers. In the months that followed, moderate Republicans publicly positioned themselves away from their nominee. After the disastrous loss that November and Welch's public opposition to the Vietnam War, Buckley decisively closed ranks to inoculate the movement against the disease of "Birchitis."[12]

The sixteen years that followed, filled as they were with rights movements and race riots, the Vietnam War and Watergate, along with Communist advances in Angola, Nicaragua, and Afghanistan, upended American liberalism and became a breeding ground for conservatism. For nine seasons, from 1971 to 1979, on *All in the Family*, "lovable bigot" Archie Bunker voiced what many in the Silent Majority dared not say out loud about hippies and affirmative action, welfare programs and women's libbers, forced busing and lenient judges. By the decade's end, stagflation, the Iran hostage crisis, and another oil shock further pushed blue-collar workers like Archie in their exodus away from the New Deal coalition.

Conservative pitches about work and responsibility, law and order, struck a chord. Waiting in the wings since his electrifying 1964 Republican National Convention speech, "A Time for Choosing," catapulted him to national prominence, was Ronald Reagan. As governor of California from 1966 to 1974, "the Gipper" appealed to the Archie Bunker constituency. Reagan likened hippies to someone who "looks like Tarzan, walks like Jane, and smells like Cheetah," unhesitatingly called out the California Highway Patrol and National Guard to quell Berkeley protests, and referred to those on public assistance as "welfare bums."

Landslide elections in 1980 and 1984 gave the Great Communicator a mandate to effect sweeping policy changes, inaugurating a conservative era of dominance to rival that of liberalism from the Great Depression to the Great Society. Reagan held in equipoise the conflicting credos of conservatism. Libertarians received deregulation, anticommunists collected a bonanza of military funding and a rollback policy that saw American engagements in Africa, Central America, and the Middle East. The Christian Right, an increasingly formidable political player, particularly since the Christian Broadcasting Network's founding in 1977, got a vocal opponent of abortion and proponent of school prayer.

Religious Right influence can be gauged in Reagan's handling of the public health emergency, HIV/AIDS. Although he had opposed the Briggs Initiative in 1978, which would have outlawed gay individuals and their supporters from teaching in California's public schools, Reagan, as president, deferred to the religious Right on key domestic issues. Jerry Falwell, the leader of the "Moral Majority," articulated the dominant convictions of Reagan's White House when he declared "AIDS is not just God's punishment for homosexuals; it is God's punishment for the society that tolerates homosexuals." In 1985, despite 15,527 known cases and 12,529 deaths, Reagan had yet to provide substantial research funding or information campaigns about the deadly disease, nor did he publicly utter the word "AIDS" until asked a question by a reporter on September 15 of that year. A public health crisis that could have been contained was allowed to fan into a global pandemic.[13]

Reagan showed more leadership resolve in foreign policy. A year after he left office, the Berlin Wall came down, and two years later the Soviet Union officially dissolved. Between 1991 and 9/11, as Russian oligarchs and former Soviet bloc billionaires sought safe havens for their money, US banks surged with investment funds. The Internet boom, the rise of the Nasdaq, and the lack of a viable option to the free market lent ballast to a triumphalist form of capitalism, rejuvenating the libertarian cause. Pundits predicted an end of history, with democratic capitalism sprouting across the world. The appearance of former Soviet premier Mikhail Gorbachev in a 1998 Pizza Hut commercial drove home the lesson that the conflict between the empire of freedom (USA) and the empire of justice (USSR) had been decisively won by America.[14] Likewise, the idea of cosmopolitanism, as an ethic and inclination, experienced a heyday, with scholars from across a wide range of disciplines heralding its imminent realization. In 1989, as the Berlin Wall came down, an English translation of Jürgen Habermas's *The Structural Transformation of the Public Sphere* (originally published in German in 1962) appeared, depicting a universally accessible, idealized demos where educated, rational individuals hashed out differences through critical discourses in a post-national world. In a widely hailed 1994 article, "Patriotism and

Cosmopolitanism," Martha Nussbaum, a scholar of the Stoics who originated the concept of cosmopolitanism, advocated a universal community of world citizens united by a commitment to shared values and reason.

Neoliberal globalists aggressively pursued such supranational and transnational economic arrangements, transforming societies the world over. Supply-side economics and shareholder prerogatives, trade deals and tax codes, high tech and low wages, combined to put into high gear the "Great U-turn" as fiscal and monetary policies engineered to stall the widening of the gap between rich and poor slipped into reverse, exacerbating rather than ameliorating income equality. Confounded at the polls, Democrats, such as Bill Clinton, practiced a "third way" centrism. Whereas Congress previously pursued a bipartisan foreign policy against communism, representatives now practiced a bipartisan economic policy that legislated commerce-friendly policies and unleashed new financial instruments.

It was only after a dozen years of a Republican-controlled White House, the historic GOP takeover of Congress after forty years of Democratic control, and the election of another Republican in 2000 that scholars turned their attention to the history of conservatism in significant numbers. Largely, the literature further developed the narrative laid out by George Nash thirty-five years earlier, then expanded on the original design to include women, African Americans, culture and canon wars, institutions including the Federalist Society and think tanks, and some of the more current iterations of "compassionate conservatives," Tea Party protesters, and "crunchy cons." Other authors investigated the transformation of populism on the right from anti–big business in the 1890s to antigovernment a century later. Accounts of the reconciliation between socially conservative evangelical Christians and fiscally conservative free-market capitalists featured the poor meekly serving while the wealth of the rich purportedly reflected Calvinist-like election.

Yet the history of conservatism is not only a tale of ascension; it also comprises a declension narrative about liberalism. Books that uncovered the internal schisms, missteps, and misdeeds on the left deconstructed the downfall of Democrats, including the internecine warfare and hubris in the union halls of organized labor during the disco decade, and blue-state denizens who ditched their century-long commitment to "the social question" in favor of a laissez-faire, allegedly meritocratic, playing field. Liberals received their comeuppance for redirecting their focus on have-nots to cheering on the entrepreneurial classes.[15]

While this historiography has portrayed an amazing technicolor dreamcoat of modern American conservatism, it has failed to perceive the living, breathing individuals who don this garment and elected Donald Trump for president in 2016. To be sure, not all Republicans are conservative. A number of prominent figures formed a #NeverTrump contingent. Even the *National Review* ran a "Conservatives against Trump" feature. The Republican Party, nonetheless, has served as the vehicle for conservatives for the last half century, and the real estate mogul receives support from "West Coast Straussians" in the *Claremont Review of Books* and from those who espouse "radical #Trumpism" at the website "American Greatness." After November 8, 2016, conservative standard bearers fell into line and lined up at Trump Tower to audition for cabinet positions. Across the country, Republicans gained, since 2008, 919 state legislative seats, with a majority in sixty-seven of ninety-eight chambers, and trifectas (Republican-controlled legislatures and governorships) in twenty-four states. The surprise election of Trump and GOP supremacy sparked questions about the motivations and morals, concerns and critiques animating huge swaths of the American population.

Until recently, scholars have largely focused on racism, rage, and resentment as key drivers of the rightward shift of rural and working-class voters, contending that Republicans successfully stripped away hodgepodge elements—white ethnics, lower-middle-class Jews, and southerners—from the New Deal coalition with the solvents of bigotry. Those constituencies formed a new demographic known as "Middle Americans," then switched allegiance after Johnson's signing of the Civil Rights Act of 1964 and Voting Rights Act of 1965. In significant numbers, they began to pull the lever for Republican candidates in the 1966 midterm elections and continued until the South and Midwest changed out blue for solid red. These "disprivileged whites," the story goes, launched a civil rights campaign of their own, protesting taxes and "reverse discrimination." Northern working-class voters brought out their pitchforks to join southern evangelicals in a populist revanche.[16]

Less reductionist explanations that treated with validity the values shared by blue-collar and blue-blood citizens appeared in the field of political history. In *The Silent Majority* (2007), Matthew Lassiter moved beyond simplistic arguments about "white backlash" or Nixon's "Southern Strategy" to analyze the effects of large corporations and white-collar suburbs at the neighborhood level, where a language of color-blind conservatism and middle-class entitlement supplanted the prejudiced patois of racism. As Andrew Wiese demonstrated, middle-class black families also moved to the suburbs in search of space and security.[17] In *There Goes My Everything* (2007), Joseph Sokol explored the genuine cognitive dissonance experienced by white southerners of all stripes during the age of civil rights. They had to square what their white family, neighbors, schools, and churches had taught them about African Americans with the words and actions of black activists themselves. This time-consuming imaginative work, as much perhaps as reluctance or malice, determined the pace of integration.

Whether economics or culture drove the country's rightward shift is the question that looms over treatments of modern American conservatism. On the economics side of the ledger, working-class positions that afforded good wages, health care, and pensions vanished. Faced with dead-end service jobs and dashed American dreams, whites without a college degree succumbed to despondency, drugs, and premature deaths.[18] On the cultural side of the ledger, social and religious issues supplanted pocketbook politics. In the most famous take on this debate, *What's the Matter with Kansas?* (2004), Thomas Frank made the case that Republicans duped the poor and working class into voting against their economic interests by a kind of rhetorical legerdemain: while placing front and center issues of guns, gays, and God, politicians on the right actually went behind their backs to rig the economic system in favor of the haves. In essence, Frank argued that the non-rich who voted for the historic party of bankers, Brahmins, and business elites did so out of false consciousness. The book represented standard historical fare: conservatism was so obviously craven, cruel, and corrupt that alert citizens could see through it. Liberals came off without much critique at all.

A series of best-selling books deployed ethnographies to address this lacuna and get a more granular view. Whether hillbillies in Appalachia scarred by a "dignity gap" or left-behind rural poor in Louisiana finding salve in the Tea Party, residents in terrains pockmarked by underemployment lived a kind of Moynihan Report redux; only this time whites suffered the tropes that supposedly dogged blackness: absent dads, derelict schools and subdivisions, drug addiction, and general dysfunction.[19] Not only did the wages of whiteness stop paying dividends; automation, robotics, and 3-D printing liquidated pride. From Ross Perot's warning that NAFTA augured a "giant sucking sound" as jobs migrated to Mexico, to the bankrolling of the *Citizens United* decision by dark-money billionaires, the top 1 percent siphoned more and more of the nation's wealth.[20] In the hollowed-out heartland, financial straits eviscerated opportunities and escalated cynicism.

Structural changes in the economy have been ongoing since the 1960s. What made turn-of-the-twenty-first-century struggles different was the emergence of social and alternative media, which transmogrified frustration into an incendiary force. As a speechwriter for press-beleaguered Richard Nixon, Pat Buchanan remembered, "With Nixon we had nobody."[21] By the time Reagan left office, a cadre of conservative entrepreneurs had staked claims in formerly uncharted broadcasting territory. Partnered with Roger Ailes, pioneering Rush Limbaugh struck gold with a media empire that included radio, TV, and books. In recognition of Limbaugh's influence, Reagan wrote: "Now that I've retired from active politics, I don't mind that you've become the number one voice for conservatism in our country." Rupert Murdoch, fresh from hiring Ailes to run Fox News, went on to create Clear Channel, which by 2001 assumed ownership of one-tenth of all radio stations in the country.[22]

The tone of conservatism consequently changed dramatically. Across the airwaves and aisles, diatribes designed to entertain and win ratings, or wear down and discredit, replaced well-mannered erudition. George Packer likened Capitol Hill at the end of the twentieth century to total war, crediting Newt Gingrich for marshaling the troops. The House Speaker stormed the trenches of politesse to win battles on welfare, taxes, and federal spending: "Whether he ever truly believed his own rhetoric, the generation he brought to power truly did. He gave them mustard gas and they used it on every conceivable enemy."[23]

Pat Buchanan likewise shed rules of decorum during his three campaigns for the presidency as he forged a path to the far right. After honing debate skills on the television show *Crossfire*, Buchanan roused crowds with improvisational speeches denouncing the UN, the IRS, federal agencies, immigrants, NAFTA, and limousine liberals. Into the breech created by the Cold War's end, Buchanan stepped in and pitched a new battlefront: "a cultural war for the soul of America." Instead of communists, Buchanan set his sights on abortion, public school curricula, gay rights, and Hollywood: "While we were off aiding the Contras, a Fifth Column inside our own country was capturing the culture."[24] In contrast to neocons who wanted the US to continue in the role as global police, stepping in no matter the cost, paleocon Buchanan preached against intervention. After a series of primary wins against Bob Dole in 1996, Buchanan beamed: "They are frightened. They hear ... the shouts of the peasants from over the hill. You watch the Establishment, all the knights and barons will be riding into the castle, pulling up the drawbridge in a minute. And they're comin'! All the peasants are comin' with pitchforks after them!"[25]

Buchanan helped to construct the parameters and style of conservatism for the next generation. Donald Trump capitalized on this populist brand. From William F. Buckley's *Firing Line* to *The O'Reilly Factor* to *Celebrity Apprentice*, norms that cable condoned were no longer cordoned off in modern American politics. Trump entered the political fray with a speech at the Conservative Political Action Conference in February 2011, then followed the next month with morning show appearances suggesting President Obama might be a secret Muslim. During the 2012 election, when the *Apprentice* protagonist considered throwing his hat in the ring for the Republican presidential nomination, he pressed birther claims via Twitter, his preferred method of communication. When he did run for the presidency in 2016, Trump decried expensive, ill-conceived, destabilizing wars in the Middle East, trade and federal deficits, infractions on civil liberties by governmental overreach, and the betrayal of middle-class Americans by global market neoliberals. He beat out other contenders for the nomination through a combination of insult and innuendo, with a showman's panache that resembled a reality show rather than a political debate. With Americans watching an average of five hours of television each day, this presented a huge advantage. One commentator noted: "Trump understands how Americans actually think. . . . They think entertainment. We are a TV-based culture."[26] Reagan, too, had benefited from his unconventional background. When asked about his experience as an actor to fill a role usually manned by lawyers and generals, he responded, "I don't understand how anybody could do this job without having been an actor."[27] In 2016, television viewing habits turned out to be better predictors than polls. Districts with high ratings for *Duck Dynasty*, *16 and Pregnant*, and *Pawn Stars* went to Trump. Regions where viewers tuned into *Modern Family*, *Love and Hip Hop*, and *The Simpsons* went to Clinton.[28]

Although Trump's opponent Hillary Clinton ran on an impressive record of helping children, blue-collar workers, and the marginalized, and issued detailed plans to assist the working class and address economic inequality, she still lost in cities and towns across the former manufacturing belt (just over seventy-seven thousand votes in Wisconsin, Michigan, and Pennsylvania would have swung the election). Clinton's alleged lack of charisma, past support of NAFTA and other trade deals, problematic e-mail server, and long history in politics suggest reasons for the loss, particularly among those looking for a change agent. Billionaire Trump picked up many of those Rust Belt ballots, speaking in Manichean terms as he promised to build walls and bring back factory jobs. At a campaign rally in Iowa, he bragged, "I could stand in the middle of Fifth Avenue and shoot somebody and I wouldn't lose voters."[29] This boast bespeaks the fervor, blind loyalty, ideology, and tribalism (or teammate dynamics) among his admirers. Misogynistic statements and threats were also at play. Yet despite the release of an audiotape where he crowed about sexually assaulting women, questionably treasonous appeals to Russia to hack into his opponent's e-mails, and a long cavalcade of bigoted statements, Trump won the Electoral College vote. At a victory rally, the president-elect complimented his supporters' virulence: "You people were vicious, violent, screaming, 'Where's the wall? . . . Prison! Prison! Lock her up!' I mean you were going crazy. I mean, you were nasty and mean and vicious."

In his appointments, Trump united the Right and Far Right by filling his cabinet and other high-level positions with Republican Party stalwarts alongside more radical activists, including Steve Bannon, who, as head of Breitbart News, provided a forum for the anti-Semitic, white supremacist "alt right" (also known as "alt Reich" for their similarity to Nazis). From his Blackberry, Trump spread analogous truth-eliding, conspiracy-theory-peddling, and xenophobic propaganda directly to his seventeen million Twitter followers. Delegitimizing mainstream media and claiming for himself the mantle of truth sayer, Trump speaks in the vernacular, invoking emotion, not evidence, true believers, not fact checkers, personality, not composure. A spokesperson, Scottie Nell Hughes, even insisted, "There are no such thing, unfortunately, anymore, as facts." Veracity's depreciation prompted the Oxford Dictionaries to name "post-truth" the 2016 word of the year, defining the term as "relating to or denoting circumstances in which objective facts are less influential in shaping public opinion than appeals to emotion and personal belief."

What does the election of a president who trucks in abhorrent ideals portend for intellectual historians, who traffic in ideas? In a "post-truth" society where fake news drowns out accuracy and flouts need for proof, of what use are the methodological tools of our discipline? A line of inquiry gaining traction attempts to move beyond rise-and-fall narratives to examine conservatism not merely as an ideology, a grassroots social movement, or a party, but as a sensibility, temperament, and mentality. Casting conservatism as an orientation brings into relief values shared by the Left and Right. The insurgency against globalization that Trump instantiated also appeared in the primary challenge of Democratic Socialist Bernie Sanders. Political scientists refer to a "horseshoe theory": instead of plotting left and right on a straight line, they position them on a dual curve with the extreme ends almost touching. A disposition toward localism, community, and connection to land crosses party affiliation and, in the intellectual history of conservatism, unites such disparate thinkers as Christopher Lasch, Charles Taylor, Wendell Berry, Eugene Genovese, and Michael Oakeshott.[30] Their midcentury precursors—Weaver, Ransom, and Kirk—offered a vision of human nature and habits, order and community that consequently deserves reexamination.

Indeed, the current existential and epistemological predicaments bring the field full circle to the immediate post–World War II originary moment when the constitutive ideas of modern American conservatism emerged. Then, scholars across disciplines raised alarms about the fate of reason, the scientific method, cosmopolitanism, human dignity, and liberty.[31] Intellectuals and writers today share this consternation. "Enlightenment humanism and rationalism," Michael Ignatieff laments, "can't explain the world we're living in."[32] A number of recent titles on conservatism evoke midcentury anxieties about thinking: Corey Robin's *The Reactionary Mind* (2011), Jonathan Haidt's *The Righteous Mind* (2012), Mark Lilla's *The Shipwrecked Mind* (2016). This makes sense, given that the slogan for *Infowars*, run by Trump's favorite conspiracy theorist, Alex Jones, reads: "There is a war on for your mind!" Lilla's explanation for the rise of reaction recalls the struggles inherent in modernism that Russell Berman diagnosed: "to live a modern life anywhere in the world today, subject to perpetual social and technological changes, is to experience the psychological equivalent of permanent revolution."³³ Rod Dreher acknowledges this state of affairs by referencing the term "liquid modernity" to decry the deliquescing effects of capitalism and technology on the foundations of social institutions.³⁴

Fred Koch, father of brothers Charles and David who funded the Tea Party, was a founding member of the John Birch Society. The reappearance of the Professor Watchlist picks up where Joseph McCarthy left off. Roy Cohn, one of McCarthy's assistants, served as a key mentor to young Donald Trump. The spirit of Orwell's *1984* hovers over postelection fears about censorship, surveillance, fake news, and cult of personality. Hannah Arendt is in the midst of a revival for uncovering the toxic cocktail of credulity and cynicism that led unmoored masses to latch on to the lies of totalitarian leaders. Echoes of Arendt also appear in documentary filmmaker Michael Moore's refutation of Trumpism as populism (rule by ordinary people) on the grounds that, consigned to impotence, average citizens resort to voting as sabotage. Explanations for the election results that draw on studies of psychology likewise bear a resemblance to the early Cold War "Age of Anxiety." Adorno's *The Authoritarian Personality* (1950) has been cited in light of Brexit and Trump's election.

The resurrection of "America First" isolationism, United Nations–bashing, and immigration intolerance harks back to another concern among intellectual historians in the years following the defeat of the Axis powers in 1945. The president of the American Historical Association that year was Carlton J. H. Hayes, the preeminent scholar of nationalism. After the Great War, as empires calved, and newly formed nation-states committed genocide and expelled minorities, Hayes, in 1926, deemed nationalism "the most significant emotional factor in public life today." Because nationalism insidiously pervaded all kinds of prejudice and subsumed other identities, he advocated knowledge of psychology, philosophy, and anthropology in order to comprehend the phenomenon.³⁵ Almost two decades later, as the Allies demolished Hitler's Third Reich and decolonization incubated across Asia and Africa, Hans Kohn delineated benevolent and malevolent forms of nationalism. A "civic Western" strand appeared before the rise of nation-states and bound citizens together in a common good through a legal system and responsive government. The "Eastern ethnic" variant that developed in Central and Eastern Europe (as well as Spain and Ireland) had coalesced in opposition to Napoleon's occupying forces. Consequently, in these areas ridden with a weak middle class and few civic institutions, a nationalism infused with culture and chauvinism, myth and blood, took the place of covenants and constitutions, contracts and plebiscites.³⁶ Despite the reductionist schema found in these early studies, worries about nationalism's impact on the fate of democracy appear in contemporary probes of "tribal epistemology."³⁷

Emotions (what Hume calls "passions"), from love to hatred, anger and jealousy, can also inform the intellectual history of conservatism. From behavioral economics to economic psychology, other disciplines have extended analyses beyond rational, autonomous, self-interested individuals to elucidate the affective perceptions (such as the role of prejudice and irrationality in decision making) to unveil the neglected, often hidden, injuries inflicted on the working class. Yet, separating out emotions from the ideas that undergird them presents challenges. Since the publication of Anthony Damasio's *Descartes' Error: Emotion, Reason, and the Human Brain* (1994), neurologists cast doubt on the mind-body dualism. Instead of antipodes, cognitive and noncognitive mental processes may exist as a helix, a spiral chain of emotion and reason. Conservative columnist David Brooks harnessed such findings to shed light on the unconscious mind as a key composter of experience, one that fertilizes conscious choices and moral positions.[38] The Founding Fathers recognized this interconnection. Leery of majoritarian tyranny, they constructed a series of checks and balances to create a federal republic fortified by separate branches of government, laws, and civil rights, as well as informal associations that fostered a democratic culture.

Finally, a reexamination of midcentury traditionalist conservatives offers the opportunity to rediscover the "First Conservative" Peter Viereck, whose work wrangled with ideologues and demagogues of all stripes.[39] His doctoral dissertation, published as *Metapolitics: Roots of the Nazi Mind* (1941), disinterred the utopian thinking of nationalism, racism, and romanticism that gave rise to Hitler. After the war, Viereck trained his scholarly lens on the American political scene to make a case for conservatism as "a complex mixture between politics, temperament, ethics, and even aesthetics."[40]

Disavowing extremes and holding dear individual dignity allowed Viereck to dodge the noxious dogmas of peers. While libertarians railed against the New Deal as socialism, Viereck praised its capitalist-saving measures. Standing between two strands of materialism—capitalism and Marxism—Viereck's centripetal conservatism calibrated obligation and responsibility. Just as unbridled capitalism ignored the ethic of "decent compassion," unlimited state subsidies enervated drive.[41] Unions, far from foes, worked within the system of capitalism to create better living standards. They fashioned informal networks that provided community and empowered workers. While the crowd around *National Review* rallied to the side of Joseph McCarthy (Buckley and Bozell even wrote a book defending him), Viereck publicly criticized the senator's red-baiting and lambasted conservatives for "appeasing the forces of the hysterical right." This was, he sensed in 2005, "the original sin of the conservative moment, and we are all suffering from it."[42] Viereck likewise incurred the wrath of those on the

National Review masthead for his support of the *Brown v. Board of Education* decision, which they opposed, along with the Voting Rights Act of 1965.[43]

In the poverty of culture or culture of poverty debates, Viereck split the difference: Great Books and governmental aid. As he said in a lecture at UCLA: "Dostoyevsky alone would never give us housing for the old; you need both." Viereck eschewed the rigidity of ideology or "-isms" of any kind. Flexibility mattered more than being *en pointe*, which accounts for Viereck's incantation "ideas, ideas, the tall ideas dancing."[44] He set a high bar, demanding a nonconforming, somewhat contrarian, always-striving stance. Not everyone could be a constantly calibrating, freethinking, staunchly individualistic but community-oriented lover of beauty. Condemned by mainstreaming conservatives, Viereck eventually retreated (or strategically redeployed) to a college campus where he turned away from politics to teaching. Education imposed a premium but, Viereck maintained, provided indemnity against naiveté.

Intellectual historians of conservatism would do well to examine individuals such as Viereck who transcended dichotomies of left and right, and to avoid the error of New Critics who, after World War II, remained intent on trying to save "fragments from the ruin." Along with their traditionalist conservative compatriots, they did not recognize, as the literary scholar Patrick Pritchett has argued, that the ruins actually constituted the new landscape.[45] To avoid this fate, Richard Rorty's call to institute programs in "unemployed studies, homeless studies, or trailer-park studies" deserves heeding.[46] Rather than seeing the rural poor and working class through the lens of midcentury mob theory or as creatures of emotion besotted by a billionaire, the task of the intellectual historian going forward is to acknowledge agency, gauge affect, and identify cultural norms that act as push and pull factors. Lopping off the suffix "ism" to examine instead conservative tenets and tempers, ethics and aesthetics, bares the reality that *My 600-lb. Life*, *Dance Moms*, and *Pitbulls and Parolees* reveals as much as do *God and Man at Yale*, *Atlas Shrugged*, and *Witness*.

NOTES

1. Russell Berman, *All That Is Solid Melts into Air: The Experience of Modernity* (Simon & Schuster, 1985), 5.

2. T. S. Eliot, "Tradition and the Individual Talent," in *Selected Essays* (London: Faber & Faber, 1932), 19–22.

3. T. S. Eliot, *The Sacred Wood: Essays on Poetry and Criticism* (London: Methuen, 1920), 10.

4. Quoted in *The Superfluous Men: Conservative Critics of American Culture, 1900–1945*, ed. Robert Crunden (Wilmington, DE: ISI Books, 1999), 120.

5. Cleanth Brooks and Robert Penn Warren, "Postscript," in *Understanding Poetry* (New York: Henry Holt, 1938), xxii–xxiv.

6. Frances Saunders, *The Cultural Cold War: The CIA and the World of Arts and Letters* (New York: W. W. Norton, 1999), 234, 239.

7. Richard Weaver, *Ideas Have Consequences* (1948; Chicago: University of Chicago Press, 1984), 1–2.

8. Russell Kirk, "Apology for a New Review," *Modern Age* 1 (Summer 1957), in *Modern Age, the First Twenty-Five Years: A Selection*, ed. George Panichas (New York: Liberty, 1988), 5.

9. Russell Kirk, *The Conservative Mind: From Burke to Eliot*, (1953; Washington, D.C.: Gateway Edition, 2016), 40, 31.

10. Quoted in Patrick Allitt, *The Conservatives: Ideas and Personalities throughout American History* (New Haven, CT: Yale University Press, 2009), 188.

11. See Carl T. Bogus's discussion in *Buckley: William F. Buckley Jr. and the Rise of American Conservatism* (New York: Bloomsbury, 2011), 174–98.

12. Ibid., 195, 8.

13. See Jennifer Brier, *Infectious Ideas: U.S. Political Responses to the AIDS Crisis* (Chapel Hill: University of North Carolina Press, 2011).

14. The terms "empire of justice" and "empire of freedom" come from Odd Arne Wested in *The Global Cold War: Third World Interventions and the Making of Our Times* (Cambridge: Cambridge University Press, 2007).

15. See Jefferson Cowie, *Stayin' Alive: The 1970s and the Last Days of the Working Class* (New York: New Press, 2010); Thomas Frank, *Listen, Liberal: Or What Ever Happened to the Party of the People?* (New York: Metropolitan Books, 2016); and Lily Geismer, *Don't Blame Us: Suburban Liberals and the Transformation of the Democratic Party* (Princeton, NJ: Princeton University Press, 2014).

16. Thomas Byrne and Mary Edsall, *Chain Reaction: The Impact of Race, Rights, and Taxes on American Politics* (New York: W. W. Norton, 1991); Dan Carter, *The Politics of Rage: George Wallace, the Origins of the New Conservatism, and the Transformation of American Politics* (New York: Simon & Schuster, 1995).

17. Andrew Wiese, *African American Suburbanization in the Twentieth Century* (Chicago: University of Chicago Press, 2004).

18. Annie Lowery, "Income Gap, Meet the Longevity Gap," *New York Times*, March 15, 2014.

19. J. D. Vance, *Hillbilly Elegy: A Memoir of a Family and Culture in Crisis* (New York: HarperCollins, 2016); Arlie Hochschild, *Strangers in Their Own Land: Anger and Mourning on the American Right* (New York: New Press, 2016).

20. Jane Mayer, *Dark Money: The Hidden History of the Billionaires behind the Rise of the Radical Right* (New York: Doubleday, 2016).

21. Eleanor Clift, "Pat Buchanan Celebrates Donald Trump's Win, Has the Last Laugh," *Daily Beast*, December 6, 2016.

22. Nicole Hemmer, *Messengers of the Right: Conservative Media and the Transformation of American Politics* (Philadelphia: University of Pennsylvania Press, 2016).

23. George Packer, *The Unwinding: An Inner History of the New America* (New York: Farrar, Straus and Giroux, 2013), 24.

24. See Andrew Hartman, *A War for the Soul of America: A History of the Culture Wars* (Chicago: University of Chicago Press, 2015).

25. Joel Achenbach, "Outsiders: Trump, Bernie, Ted Cruz and the Peasants with Pitchforks," *Washington Post*, August 13, 2015.

26. Michael Rosenblum, "Donald Trump Is Going to Be Elected," *Huffington Post*, August 20, 2016.

27. Quoted in Lou Cannon, *President Reagan: The Role of a Lifetime* (New York: Perseus Books, 1991), 32.

28. Josh Katz, "'Duck Dynasty' vs. 'Modern Family': 50 Maps of the U.S. Cultural Divide," *New York Times*, December 27, 2016. Throughout the 2016 campaign, two Uni-

versity of Rochester graduate students deployed data mining tools to analyze candidates' Twitter usage to predict accurately the victor. "Twitter Researchers Offer Clues for Why Trump Won," *Newscenter*, February 20, 2017.

29. Jeremy Diamond, "Donald Trump 'Could Shoot Somebody' and Not Lose Voters," CNN, January 24, 2016.

30. My thanks to Daniel Wickberg for reminding me of the relevance of these authors.

31. Lisa Szefel, "Critical Thinking as Cold War Weapon: Anxiety, Terror, and the Fate of Democracy in Postwar America," *Journal of American Culture*, Spring 2017. Also see Mark Greif, *The Age of the Crisis of Man: Thought and Fiction in America, 1933–1973* (Princeton, NJ: Princeton University Press, 2015).

32. Quoted in Pankaj Mishra, *Age of Anger: A History of the Present* (New York: Farrar, Straus and Giroux, 2017), 39.

33. Marl Lilla, *The Shipwrecked Mind: On Political Reaction* (New York: New York Review of Books, 2016), 3.

34. The term derives from Marxist sociologist Zygmunt Bauman. Quoted in Joshua Rothman, "Rod Dreher's Monastic Vision," *New Yorker*, May 1, 2017.

35. Carlton J. H. Hayes, *Essays on Nationalism* (New York: Macmillan, 1926), 1–3, 5.

36. Hans Kohn, *The Idea of Nationalism: A Study in Its Origin and Background* (1944; New York: Routledge, 2005), 351.

37. David Roberts, "Donald Trump and the Rise of Tribal Epistemology," *Vox*, May 17, 2017.

38. David Brooks, *The Social Animal: The Hidden Sources of Love, Character, and Achievement* (New York: Random House, 2011).

39. Tom Reiss, "The First Conservative," *New Yorker*, October 24, 2005.

40. Peter Viereck, *Conservative Thinkers: From John Adams to Winston Churchill* (1956; Piscataway, NJ: Transaction, 2006), 185.

41. Peter Viereck, "New Conservatism," *Antioch Review*, Summer 1955, 220.

42. Quoted in Reiss, "First Conservative."

43. Kevin Schultz discusses Buckley's views on race in *Buckley and Mailer: The Difficult Friendship That Shaped the Sixties* (New York: W. W. Norton, 2015), 116–17, 123–28, 265–81.

44. Viereck, "Incantations," in *Terror and Decorum* (1948; Westport, CT: Greenwood, 1973), 83.

45. Patrick Pritchett makes this argument about modernism in "Writing the Disasters: The Messianic Turn in Postwar American Poetry," PhD diss., University of Colorado–Boulder, 2011.

46. Richard Rorty, *Achieving Our Country: Leftist Thought in Twentieth-Century America* (Cambridge, MA: Harvard University Press, 1998), 80.

11

THE REINVENTION OF ENTREPRENEURSHIP

Angus Burgin

In the midst of the binary rhetoric of the 2016 presidential campaign, an article posted on *Tech Crunch* drew attention to a dependable source of common ground. During an "otherwise contentious" campaign season, Aaron Chatterjee and David Robinson observed, there was "one issue on which both candidates can agree: entrepreneurship is good."[1] As they turned their attention to the general election, Hillary Clinton and Donald Trump joined with down-ballot candidates across parties in emphasizing that their policies would foster entrepreneurial activities. Even as Trump fielded questions about his Trump Entrepreneur Initiative (previously known as Trump University), Clinton emphasized that her approach to student loans would make it "easier for young people to become entrepreneurs."[2] In extolling entrepreneurship, they joined a bipartisan tradition: in 2012, Mitt Romney announced that he wanted to make America "the most attractive place in the world for entrepreneurs"; in 2008, John McCain's tax plan proclaimed that entrepreneurs created "the ultimate job security" and were "at the heart of American innovation and growth"; in 2004, John Kerry highlighted his role as ranking member of the Senate Small Business and Entrepreneurship Committee; following his defeat in 2000, Al Gore taught entrepreneurship at Stanford.[3] As his own presidency drew to a close, Barack Obama dropped hints of a post-presidential career in venture capital.[4] Entrepreneurs, it seems, had become the least controversial figures in American politics.

The universality of the political embrace of the entrepreneur is all the more striking for its novelty. A simple Google NGram reveals that references to

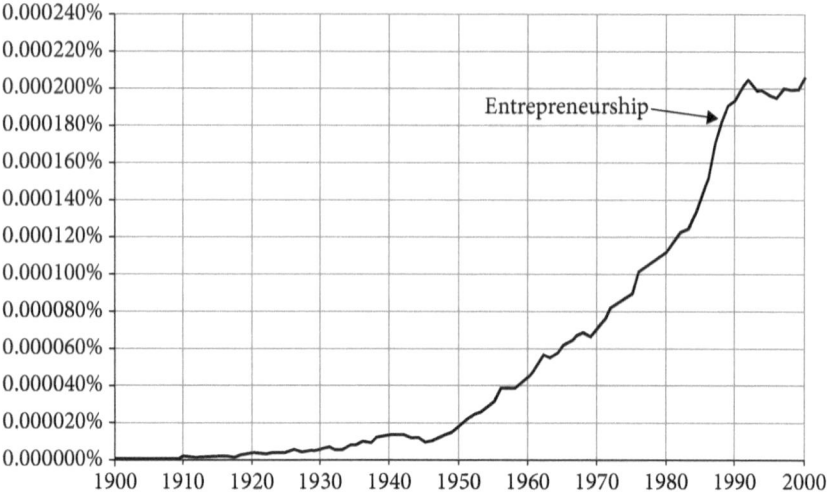

FIGURE 11.1 The vertical axis shows the percentage of references to the term "entrepreneurship" among printed words in Google's English-language corpus. "Entrepreneurship," Google NGram viewer, http://books.google.com/ngrams, accessed June 2016.

"entrepreneurship" grew exponentially over the middle decades of the twentieth century: a term that languished in obscurity until the 1940s had entered into common parlance decades later (see figure 11.1).

Such a chart raises an obvious question: What led a recondite concept to gain traction over the second half of the twentieth century? How did abstract debates among a small community of academics become a bipartisan staple of contemporary political discourse?

The history of entrepreneurship has generated a robust literature from certain corners of the academy. Ever since the founding of the Harvard Research Center in Entrepreneurial History in the late 1940s, economic historians have been investigating the degree to which various societies throughout human history have fostered or foreclosed entrepreneurship.[5] Several economists since the 1950s have explored changes in the role accorded to entrepreneurship by leading economic theorists.[6] Researchers in business schools have written extensively on the origins and institutional development of entrepreneurial studies.[7] While all of these literatures have informed my inquiries, none of them explain how conceptions of entrepreneurship shifted in the middle decades of the twentieth century, or why references to the term propagated so rapidly thereafter.

My hope is that such an investigation might help to demonstrate the unique role intellectual historians can play in addressing some central questions about the transformation of economic life since the late nineteenth century. The past 150 years have been marked by an extraordinarily rapid pace of technological change, which has unmoored societies from long-standing social traditions, reshaped the nature and experience of work, and made the future seem ever more uncertain. This can be (and has been) told in part as a story about social practices, cultural norms, political praxis, or the transformation of the state. But it is also, crucially, a story about ideas: how changing circumstances led people to understand their economic lives in new ways, and how those novel understandings, in turn, affected their actions and political identities. As Daniel Rodgers wrote in *The Work Ethic in Industrial America*, which remains (nearly forty years later) an exemplary text in this mode, such histories are focused where "intellectual history becomes most vital—on the meeting of fact and value."[8] Exploring the interplay between ideas and circumstances helps us to recognize the contingency of current assumptions about political economy, and to understand how and why some beliefs persisted long after the contexts that produced them were "all but obliterated."[9] Contemporary approaches to political economy were born in the moral struggles of prior generations. Recovering those struggles, and the conditions that produced them, can imbue the constrained economic debates of recent years with depth and dissonance.[10]

Many recent works on the intellectual history of political economy have explored the feedback loops between economic circumstances and academic theory. Perhaps the most striking example is the growing body of work on the invention of the idea of "the economy," as statistical indicators allowed theorists to model, and broader populations to naturalize, a concept that was barely invoked before the twentieth century.[11] The changing patterns of economic life called forth a novel theoretical literature, which itself provided an analytical framework that people and politicians have drawn upon to explain and interpret their economic lives ever since.

This chapter will pursue a similar genealogy of the concept of "entrepreneurship" as it migrated from the periphery to the center of popular discussions of political economy. Michel Foucault, in his *Birth of Biopolitics* (1978–1979), argues that a distinctive aspect of "American neo-liberalism" is the universalization of entrepreneurship, such that every individual could be considered an "entrepreneur of himself."[12] This is Foucault's way of framing the distinctive logic of rational choice, in which each individual adopts the planning faculties of a firm based on a reductive fiscal calculus analogous to the maximization of shareholder value. But Foucault's story also provokes crucial questions about the conceptual history of entrepreneurship. When and why did theorists begin arguing that "entrepreneurs" were common, rather than exceptional? How might we draw connections between such novel understandings of the concept and the increasing frequency of its use?

In the immediate postwar period, the meaning of entrepreneurship underwent a fundamental shift. Between the late nineteenth century and the 1940s, most theorists argued that entrepreneurship was rare because of the appetite for uncertainty or the cost of capital it required; and many worried that the growth of large corporations was marginalizing the role of entrepreneurship in the economy by routinizing innovation and creating increasingly rigid barriers between ownership and management, and management and technical work. In the early 1950s, a growing number of scholars began to emphasize, in contrast, that entrepreneurship was broadly accessible: anyone, whether working within a large organization or as a sole proprietor, could display and should try to cultivate entrepreneurial role behavior, and learning such behaviors should be a fundamental part of business education for the masses.

This transformation was in large part precipitated by shifting understandings of the implications of technological change. Over the course of the 1950s and early 1960s the idea of automation inspired an enormous popular literature, in which social theorists wrestled with the expectation that machines would eventually replace most workers who performed repetitive tasks.[13] Some responded to this prospect by expressing concerns about the potential growth in inequality and unemployment, and anxieties about the social problems such deep uncertainties might cause.[14] But others adopted the ebullient tones of the era's futurists, envisioning the many ways in which new technologies would help to bypass long-standing sources of friction and strife.[15] The leading theorists of entrepreneurship in the 1950s and 1960s were exemplars of this second approach. They became convinced that technological innovations were eliminating the pathological routines of repetitive labor and opening new opportunities for those who possessed impressive capacities but little capital. They argued that the incipient growth of the service economy was a harbinger of a new age of "knowledge work," in which even employees of large corporations could draw on the capital of their accumulated education and experience to act as proto-entrepreneurs. Whereas the preeminent figures of the preceding generation wrote encomia to a vanishing "age of enterprise," this new generations of scholars suggested that they heyday of entrepreneurship had only just begun.

The concept of entrepreneurship is always slippery and never unitary: recently two economists listed no fewer than twelve separate definitions that have been associated with it.[16] That slipperiness led most economists in the late nineteenth and twentieth centuries to ignore it altogether. When Joseph Schumpeter argued for its crucial importance to economic theory in *The Theory of Economic Development*, first published in German in 1912, he was a dramatic outlier in the profession.[17] Although that book didn't appear in English until 1934, it had a decisive impact on Frank H. Knight's 1922 book *Risk, Uncertainty, and Profit*—which made an influential distinction between risks that could (theoretically) be insured and uncertainties that could not, and identified the entrepreneur as a person who tried to profit from that uncertainty. In the wake of Schumpeter and Knight, more economists began to wade into discussions of the significance of entrepreneurship, albeit often in tentative and desultory terms.

Observers in the 1920s, 1930s, and 1940s were troubled by several developments that seemed to be eroding the role that Knight prescribed for the entrepreneur. One was the growing separation of management from ownership. Knight argued that the entrepreneur was almost always at least a "part owner" of an enterprise, as that ensured a direct personal stake in the attempt to exploit opportunities made possible by uncertainty.[18] But as the Columbia economist John M. Clark observed in 1942, "the coming of the large corporation means a splitting-up of the entrepreneur function until it merges indistinguishably into investment and management."[19] The Harvard Business School scholar Arthur Cole wrote in more vivid terms that "entrepreneurial power" was "more like an uneven fringe than a neat clear line," as "the diffusion of authority" had become "so great that sovereignty may be no less difficult to locate than in the British form of government."[20] The corporate form was making it more difficult to associate entrepreneurship with any single individual.

Second, these corporations were working hard to minimize the very uncertainties that made entrepreneurship possible. Knight himself had written of this phenomenon, observing that people tried to "club" uncertainties by creating large-scale organizations with elaborate research departments. In subsequent decades, a number of theorists wondered if such efforts were reaching a degree of scale and sophistication that rendered entrepreneurship irrelevant. New products emerged from research departments that required more technical knowledge than business executives could cultivate. As Thorstein Veblen argued in *Absentee Ownership*, "the function of the entrepreneur, the captain of industry, gradually fell apart in a two-fold division of labor, between the business manager and the office work on the one side and the technician and industrial work on the other side."[21] Over time such institutions developed a different character from the smaller and more freewheeling and holistic business structures of an earlier era. In 1933 the German historical economist Werner Sombart suggested that societies were therefore witnessing a "rationalization of entrepreneurship," in which a growth in size led enterprises to "attain the character of administrations, their leaders, the character of bureaucrats."[22] The following decade an American historian, Thomas Cochran, made the transition from entrepreneurship to bureaucracy a centerpiece of his synthetic economic history, *The Age of Enterprise*. The "age of individual enterprise, its fables, folklore and mythology, was finished," he wrote, as businesses had become "much more cooperative than competitive, much more social than individualistic." Barriers to entry had become insuperable for nearly everyone, apart from those who had "access to large amounts of investment capital."[23] Even the growth of theoretical interest in entrepreneurship after the publication of Knight's book struck some as a sign of its diminishing importance in everyday economic life. After all, the émigré historian of entrepreneurship Fritz Redlich reminded his readers in 1942, the owl of Minerva flies only at dusk.[24]

Cole, Cochran, and Redlich were each associated with the Research Center in Entrepreneurial History at Harvard, which was founded to explore the use of Schumpeter's idea of entrepreneurship for historical research. It should therefore be no surprise that they derived this pessimistic perspective in large part from Schumpeter himself. In the emerging "'trustified' capitalism," Schumpeter had written in 1928, "innovation . . . goes on . . . largely independently of individual persons. It meets with much less friction, as failure in any particular case loses its dangers, and tends to be carried out as a matter of course on the advice of specialists." "Progress becomes 'automatised,'" leading capitalism to create "a mentality and a style of life incompatible with its own fundamental conditions."[25] These anxieties formed the foundation for his analysis in *Capitalism, Socialism, and Democracy*, in which "technological progress" became "the business of teams of trained specialists," destroying "the romance of earlier commercial adventure" and the source of all economic dynamism.[26]

Thus, by the mid-1940s, most of the leading writers on entrepreneurship saw it as a contested concept that was becoming diffuse and diminished amid the rise of the modern corporation. Even after the writings of Schumpeter and the early publications of the Harvard Research Center, there were few clues that entrepreneurship would become a dominant rubric for describing and defending the patterns of American economic life in the second half of the twentieth century.

In the early 1950s, one prominent theorist began to position himself against this wave of scholarship, arguing instead that changing business conditions were leading entrepreneurship to become *more* central to contemporary economic life: Peter Drucker. Remarkably little has been written about Drucker, and still less about his writings after *The Concept of the Corporation*.[27] Much could be written about Drucker's role in the midcentury evolution of advisory literature for corporate executives, but my focus here will be on the transformation of his social criticism, and what it illuminates about the dramatic shift in attitudes toward entrepreneurship in the decades that followed.

Drucker was an early example of a phenomenon that has become omnipresent in the late twentieth century: the business school scholar who makes grand pronouncements about innovation, entrepreneurship, and the right and wrong ways to structure corporate organizations, while writing mass-market books and moonlighting as a lucrative consultant. At the same time, his childhood in interwar Vienna, his wide reading in the history of philosophy, and his unlikely friendships with figures including Karl Polanyi, Buckminster Fuller, and Marshall McLuhan make him an unusually cosmopolitan intellect in the sometimes cloistered firmament of management theory. And management theory itself is remarkably understudied, perhaps because it is too abstract and ethereal for business and social historians, and too practice-oriented to attract the prolonged interest of many intellectual historians.[28] It is precisely the bastard nature of that discipline—evident in its attempts to address deep problems of social, economic, and political organization through reorganizations of the corporate form—that makes it a fascinating subject of inquiry. Its practitioners, to return to Daniel Rodgers's phrase, earn their livelihoods by traversing the uneasy divide between "fact and value."

A close analysis of Drucker's writings will reveal that he was not a static figure who espoused a common set of precepts over the extended course of his career. Rather, he underwent a dramatic transformation, with deep implications for the practical advice he provided to businesspeople and the social vision he expounded. Most of what has been written about Drucker, including two admiring biographies and frequent mentions in business reviews, distills his arguments into a limited series of aphoristic tenets derived largely from *The Practice of Management*—the importance of "management by objectives," the idea that the nature of a "business is not determined by the producer but by the consumer," the insight that too many businesses, in order "to obtain profit today ... tend to undermine the future," or the conviction that (in Drucker's dauntlessly extravagant prose) "managing managers is the central concern of every manager."[29] Two intellectual historians, Nils Gilman and Daniel Immerwahr, have written illuminating essays on the early Drucker and his engagements with both Kierkegaard and Karl Polanyi, but they leave his writings after 1950 mostly unaddressed.[30] If we look at Drucker's career longitudinally, this hard shell of aphorisms and carefully cultivated aura of constancy begins to break apart, and we can see him as a figure whose social theories were deeply conditioned by the changes in the surrounding social and technological environment.

The story of Drucker's transformation can help to illuminate a broader shift in the ways people spoke about markets in the decades following the Second World War. Historians have produced an enormous amount of work in recent years on the postwar evolution of "conservatism," addressing topics that range from the politics of evangelical Christianity, to the social engagements of business enterprises, to the language of postwar economics, to the social politics of property in

American cities.³¹ But only rarely do intellectual historians turn their attention to the underlying technological transformations that in some cases drove and in some cases significantly reshaped the emerging political configurations of the time.³² A brief journey through Drucker's writings will help reveal how powerful aspects of conservative discourse about markets in the postwar era emerged in response to changes in the experience of work precipitated by the transition from an industrial to a postindustrial age.

In his diagnostic work from *The Future of Industrial Man* in 1942 to *The New Society* in 1950, Drucker argued that a disharmony had emerged between social values and institutional contexts. As he wrote in *The Future of Industrial Man*, many of the patterns of twentieth-century social and cultural life remained at least to some extent preindustrial. However, the foundations of that social order had collapsed: the managerial revolution had challenged the belief that property was the basis of legitimate power in social and economic life, the emergence of mass production and the increasing specialization of labor had diminished the sense of independence and fulfillment individuals could derive from the work they produced, and the rise of the factory system had created an indelible dividing line between family life and productive work. The factory or plant had become "the basic social unit" of many communities, but failed to play the social or political role that such an identity required.³³

The experience of work, Drucker argued, had become "automatic and mechanical," as the qualities associated with craftsmanship—"understanding of the process, knowledge of all its phases, initiative, the personal touch"—became perceived as "obstacles to efficiency and productivity."³⁴ Instead, productive labor had become "that of the man on the assembly line who, standing rigidly all day, holds in his outstretched hand a paint brush which automatically draws a red line on the flanks of slowly passing automobile bodies. He neither understands how an automobile works nor does he possess any skill which could not be acquired by everyone within a few days. He is not a human being in society, but a freely replaceable cog in an inhumanly efficient machine."³⁵ Drucker's critique of these working conditions reached beyond the monotonous and repetitive nature of the work itself to rebuke the resulting political dynamics of the workplace. As he explained in *The Concept of the Corporation*, "it is not the character of the work which determines satisfaction but the importance attached to the worker. It is not routine and monotony which produce dissatisfaction but the absence of recognition, of meaning, of relation of one's own work to society. . . . In many unskilled jobs in modern mass-production industry those workers who have ability and who are willing to take initiative and responsibility, have little or no opportunity to assert themselves. . . . the worker has not enough relation to his work to find satisfaction in it."³⁶ The specialization induced by mass production had led workers to lose a holistic understanding of the goods they were producing or a clear sense of investment in and control over the political conditions of their employment.

But Drucker married this robust critique of the stultifying nature of industrial labor with a suspicion of its capacity to be effectively redressed by the state. Instead, he argued that the problems with the workplace experience were rooted in the social and institutional structure of the modern corporations and could best be remedied by both managers and the plant communities they oversaw. In Drucker's view, previous theories of workplace management had failed in their attempts to resolve these fundamental antinomies. For example, scientific management—in separating the planning function from the actions themselves—embodied precisely the separation of the part from the whole that he sought to overcome. Human relations theory recognized the pathologies of industrial organization but sought to address them through interpersonal relations rather than structural reform. Drucker's goal was to create a new management theory that would overcome these limitations and provide a blueprint for those who sought to resolve the basic problems of industrial society through the vehicle of the corporation itself. He believed that this restructuring of the corporate form, rather than the management of the business cycle or the pursuit of economic growth, would be the most important social issue in the decade to come. As he wrote in an essay on Henry Ford in 1947, "The chief economic problem of our time—the prevention of depressions—should be solvable by basically mechanical means: by adapting our employment, fiscal, and budgeting practices to the time span of industrial production—that is, to the business cycle. Much more baffling, and more basic, is the political and social problem with which twentieth-century industrialism confronts us: the problem of developing order and citizenship within the plant, of building a free, self-governing industrial society."[37]

It is possible to read Drucker in this period as a business-friendly conservative in his reluctance to invoke the state as a solution to the problems he observed.[38] But acknowledging Drucker's suspicion of the state should not mask the seriousness of his critique of industrial society and the radicalism of the corporate reforms he envisioned. He was persistently and robustly skeptical of the capacity of the competitive market to provide an ordering structure for economic life. "We have learned that freedom and justice cannot be realized in and through the economic sphere," he wrote. "We have learned that a functioning society can no longer be organized in and through the market."[39] In contrast he emphasized the need for "drastic changes in our existing institutions" and called for "an entirely new concept of the government in economic life, that is neither 'laissez-faire' nor collectivism, but one of joint responsibility."[40] His proposed reforms included income and employment protections, profit sharing, a depression policy that would redress "the deep feeling of insecurity under which the worker today lives," and a reorganization of the corporate form under the "principle of federalism."[41] Most importantly, he called for the creation of a "plant community," in which workers would take sole control of transportation, meals, recreation, education, vacation schedules, and shift assignments, and joint control of safety and health matters, promotion, wage differentials, job descriptions, even new hires.[42] Drucker was unequivocal in emphasizing the radicalism of these proposals. "*An industrial society is beyond Capitalism and Socialism,*" he wrote. "*It is a new society transcending both.*"[43]

What happened to this early Drucker, who was so deeply concerned with the social pathologies of industrial civilization and eager to implement radical transformations in workplace organization to address them? What led him to become the more familiar Drucker of later years, who focused on innovation and the "systematic management of change" as the primary concern of the manager, and stopped talking of full employment schemes, plant community, and the catastrophic failings of free enterprise and the market society?

The answer lies in the early pages of his 1954 book *The Principles of Management*, the compendium of his management philosophy that worked its way into corporate offices across America through the late 1950s and 1960s. In the first substantive chapter of that volume, he begins talking about something that went unmentioned in his previous books, and had only just been processed in a few articles since his arrival at the NYU School of Commerce, Accounts, and Finance in 1950: automation. According to Drucker, its gradual but inexorable arrival heralded the transformation of the workplace experience. "Automation derives its efficiency and productivity mainly from the substitution of highly trained, high-grade human work for poorly trained or semi-skilled human work," he wrote. "It is a qualitative change requiring people to move from work that is labor-intensive to work that is brain-intensive."[44] Thus "the unskilled laborer of yesterday who contributed only animal strength has become the semi-skilled machine operator of today who has to exercise judgment."[45] Machines take over the "repetitive," "routine," and specialized tasks that were at the heart of his anxieties about industrial man.[46] This was the moment when human societies would begin moving away from industrial labor and toward what he famously termed later in the decade "knowledge work."[47]

The implications of automation now percolated through Drucker's writings, transforming his political sensibility at nearly every turn. The problems of social and industrial organization that had preoccupied the first phase of his career now seemed irrelevant: over time, he believed, the ongoing development of novel technologies would do more to solve them than industrial organization ever could.

The first effect of automation was a transformation of human interactions with machines. Whereas the mass-production technologies of the early twentieth century had forced people into ever more specialized tasks, new machines would perform those tasks themselves, freeing people to take on roles as creators and managers rather than subjects of machine technology. Drawing on the tropes of the contemporary literature on cybernetics and the early writings of Lewis Mumford, Drucker wrote that automation "might, with considerable over-simplification, be called an 'organic' philosophy—if only to distinguish it from the strictly mechanistic approach on which Henry Ford's concept of mass production was based." Its foundation in "*self-regulating control*" enabled it to respond to economic activity as a dynamic "process" based on "*pattern, order, or form*" rather than as a static event. To reduce automation to "gadgeteering" or "engineering" was therefore to miss its fundamental insight and contribution: "it is a concept of the structure and order of economic life, the design of its basic patterns integrated into a harmonious, balanced, and organic whole."[48] Control technologies enabled machines to become reactive, dynamic, and newly capable of integrating themselves into complex systems. This language is strikingly similar to the concluding chapter on automation in Marshall McLuhan's later book *Understanding Media*, and the close consonances between their views make their longtime friendship unsurprising.[49] Both perceived that new technologies mimicked the activities of animals and nervous systems, providing a supple and reactive connective tissue that responded to complex stimuli in sophisticated ways. The arrival of automation heralded a new era when technology would become an extension of rather than an obstacle to the human personality, and managers no longer needed to worry about devising radical social and institutional solutions to the stultifying effects of industrial labor.

Even as automation solved what Drucker had previously perceived as the basic problem of labor-management relations and industrial organization, it was symptomatic of a novel set of challenges that Drucker now reoriented himself around. "Innovation," a word that went unmentioned in *The Concept of the Corporation* and received only one disparaging reference in *The Future of Industrial Man*, suddenly appeared in *The Principles of Management* as one of the three central concerns of the executive, extending "across all parts of the business, all functions, all activities."[50] Drucker granted innovation such primacy because of a belief that the United States had entered "the technological revolution of the second half of the twentieth century," with implications as far-reaching as the onset of mass production.[51] "Throughout most of history change was considered catastrophe, and immutability the goal of organized human efforts," he wrote in 1957. "By contrast we today no longer even understand the question whether change is by itself bad or good. We start out with the axiom that it is the norm."[52]

Executives would therefore need to manage businesses with a heightened sense of the uncertainty of the future, and a disciplined capacity to steer their organizations toward the deliberate practice of "innovation," or "purposeful, directed, organized change."[53] The idea of "systematic innovation"—or, as Drucker later termed it, "organiz[ing] for entrepreneurship"—became the centerpiece of his message to executives in the decades that followed.[54]

The changing nature of his work captures a powerful but often latent political dimension of the discourse on automation and postindustrialism that flourished from the 1950s through the early 1970s. New technologies could be invoked to argue that long-standing radical critiques of the nature of industrial labor no longer applied to an age marked by the rise of the service sector and the growing centrality of knowledge work. Unshackled from the routine, repetitive, and highly specialized tasks of industrial labor, people would be freed to adopt an "entrepreneurial" approach to their workplace challenges, and organizations could focus on harnessing technological changes for profit without worrying about their social and cultural effects. Schumpeter's chiliastic vision thereby began to evolve into the relentlessly optimistic discourse of entrepreneurship that has pervaded business education ever since.

In the years following Drucker's transformation, two leading centers of free-market discourse adopted a similar emphasis on the rise of "knowledge work" and the capacity of most people to behave as "entrepreneurs." One was the economics department at the University of Chicago, where—in terms strikingly similar to Drucker's—Ted Schultz drew on the successes of postwar Germany and Japan to argue that "skills and knowledge are a form of capital," and that their rapid "growth may well be the most distinctive feature of the economic system."[55] In Schultz's representation, anyone who leveraged his or her human capital to reallocate effort in the face of uncertainty—whether a laborer, or a housewife, or a student—should be seen as an entrepreneur. It is easy to see here how Schultz's expansive understanding of "human capital" paved the way for the universalization of the entrepreneurial function in Gary Becker's book on the subject in 1964. "Persons investing in human capital can be considered 'firms' that combine such capital perhaps with other resources to produce earning power," Becker wrote.[56] In contrast to the prior generation's anxieties about the disappearance of the entrepreneur, in Becker's analysis *everyone* became an entrepreneurial firm, investing in his or her own human capital in the face of an uncertain future.

Austrian economists differed from their Chicago counterparts in many ways, but they too drew attention to the capacity of individuals to acquire unique knowledge and derive economic advantages from it. Israel Kirzner argued that all people could be entrepreneurs if they could merely determine "where to look for knowledge" and thereby see opportunities that others had missed—a capacity open to "*anyone*," since it presupposed "no special initial good fortune in the form of valuable assets."[57]

During the late 1950s and early 1960s a proliferation of works adopted a similarly broad understanding of the scope of entrepreneurship. The psychologist David McClelland's *The Achieving Society* became a landmark in the field, in part owing to its argument that even those who were not labeled by society with the status of entrepreneurs could nonetheless display entrepreneurial "role behavior." Thus one could see (and celebrate) politicians, or physicians, or ditch diggers, or even university professors behaving in an entrepreneurial manner.[58] Edith Penrose's classic text *The Theory of the Growth of the Firm* (1959) described a segment of the corporation as providing "entrepreneurial services," following Drucker's inference that entrepreneurial activities could fall within the mandate of salaried employees.[59] In a telling phrase, *The Enterprising Man* (1964) divided entrepreneurship into two categories, one of which was exemplified by the "bureaucratic entrepreneur."[60] The propagation of such a paradoxical term served as a testament to the broadening of the concept of entrepreneurship in the emerging age of knowledge work.

The shift toward a more expansive understanding of "entrepreneurship"—as a set of qualities that could be embraced by all, rather than an economic function reserved for a dwindling few—emerged only shortly before the study of entrepreneurship began receiving an extraordinary influx of money and attention. A review of courses on the topic, beginning with Drucker's 1953 offering at NYU, reveals an acceleration almost without parallel in late twentieth-century postsecondary education.[61] By the 1990s more than one hundred institutions had established separate entrepreneurship centers.[62] Entrepreneurship became a major subject in flagship business publications, after having previously been almost entirely ignored (see figure 11.2). And the number of endowed positions

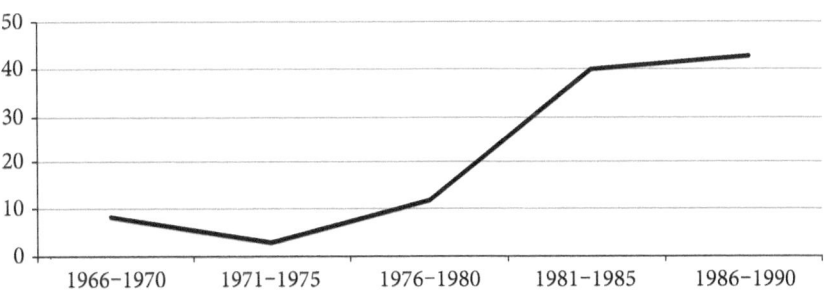

FIGURE 11.2 Number of mentions of the word "entrepreneurship" per issue, aggregated from the *Harvard Business Review*.

in the field grew rapidly: after the first was created in 1963, the number grew to 11 by 1980, 102 by 1991, and 208 by 1998.[63] Financial support for the study of entrepreneurship was at first provided by the Small Business Administration, which itself was created in 1953; later the field received major support from donors including the Coleman Foundation, the Price Foundation, the NFIB Foundation, and—adding a massive new influx of funds in the early 1990s—the Kauffman Foundation.[64] This was all paralleled by the rise of an entirely new journal literature, ranging from a wide array of academic journals (nearly all founded in the 1980s or thereafter) to a variety of more popular publications.[65] For a field that was still granting hardly any PhD degrees as late as the 1990s, the establishment of such a robust research and teaching apparatus was remarkable. This entailed the creation of an entirely new academic subfield, based not on questions emerging from within academic disciplines, but rather on the conjunction of financial support and perceived student demand.

The conceptual history of entrepreneurship cannot be reduced to any single causal chain: it was not driven solely by theoretical debates about the role of the entrepreneur in economic development, or the influence of foundation financing on a previously nonexistent field, or the romance of the tech entrepreneur in the age of Silicon Valley. Instead, a dynamic approach to its intellectual history reveals feedback loops at every turn, some detailed here and some beyond the scope of this chapter. Technological transformations inspired new understandings of entrepreneurial behavior, which were taught in business schools with growing foundation support and seemed to be further validated by the diminishing costs of capital in the Internet age. Only by following such circuitous pathways can intellectual historians begin to understand the origins of the upside-down rhetoric of the twenty-first-century service economy, in which change seems the only constancy, humans are the most important form of capital, and even bureaucrats can describe themselves as entrepreneurs.

NOTES

I would like to thank Nic Johnson for research assistance in the early stages of work on this article.

    1. Aaron Chatterji and David Robinson, "The Golden Age of American Entrepreneurship," *Tech Crunch*, June 30, 2016, https://techcrunch.com/2016/06/30/the-golden-age-of-american-entrepreneurship.

    2. Jillian Berman, "Hillary Clinton Wants to Help Young Entrepreneurs with Their Student Loans," *Market Watch*, June 28, 2016, https://www.marketwatch.com/story/clinton-wants-to-help-young-entrepreneurs-with-their-student-loans-2016-06-28.

    3. Elaine Pofeldt, "The Hidden Winner of the Debate: Entrepreneurs," *Forbes*, October 18, 2012, http://www.forbes.com/sites/elainepofeldt/2012/10/18/the-hidden-winner-of-the-debate-entrepreneurs/#65d318c35257; Donald Lambro, "Joe Exposes Candidates'

Sharp Divisions," *Washington Times*, October 17, 2008, http://www.washingtontimes.com/news/2008/oct/17/joe-exposes-candidates-sharp-divisions; Elizabeth Olson, "Courting the Small-Business Owner," *New York Times*, September 23, 2004, http://www.nytimes.com/2004/09/23/business/courting-the-smallbusiness-owner.html; Ellen McGirt, "Al Gore's $100 Million Makeover," *Fast Company*, July/August 2007, http://www.fastcompany.com/60067/al-gores-100-million-makeover.

4. Jessica Stillman, "Silicon Valley VCs to President Obama: We're Hiring," *Inc.*, June 29, 2016, http://www.inc.com/jessica-stillman/obama-the-vc.html.

5. On the early history of the Harvard Research Center see Eduardo Canedo, "Entrepreneurial Economics: Arthur Harrison Cole's Challenge to the New Orthodoxy in Economics, 1946–1959" (unpublished essay). For a recent broad-gauged history of entrepreneurship see David Landes, Joel Mokyr, and William Baumol, eds., *The Invention of Enterprise: Entrepreneurship from Ancient Mesopotamia to Modern Times* (Princeton, NJ: Princeton University Press, 2010). Recently R. Daniel Wadhwani and Christina Lubinski have called for historians to return to the Harvard Research Center's commitment to research on entrepreneurial history, without falling into the "structural and normative" approaches that scholars in the field later pursued. See "Reinventing Entrepreneurial History," *Business History Review* 91 (Winter 2017): 767–99.

6. Bert Hoselitz, "Entrepreneurship and Economic Growth," *American Journal of Economics and Sociology* 12, no. 1 (October 1952): 97–110; Mark Blaug, "Entrepreneurship before and after Schumpeter," in *Economic History and the History of Economics* (New York: NYU Press, 1986); Robert Hébert and Albert Link, "Historical Perspectives on the Entrepreneur," *Foundations and Trends in Entrepreneurship* 2, no. 4 (2006): 261–408.

7. Arnold C. Cooper, "Entrepreneurship: The Past, the Present, the Future," in *Handbook of Entrepreneurship Research*, ed. Z. J. Acs and D. B. Audretsch (Dordrecht, Netherlands: Kluwer, 2003), 21–34; Jerome Katz, "The Chronology and Intellectual Trajectory of American Entrepreneurship Education," *Journal of Business Venturing* 18 (2003): 283–300; Jerome Katz, "Endowed Positions: Entrepreneurship and Related Fields," *Entrepreneurship: Theory and Practice*, Spring 1991: 53–67; Jerome Katz, "The Growth of Endowments, Chairs, and Programs in Entrepreneurship on the College Campus," in *The Art & Science of Entrepreneurship Education*, ed. Frank Hoy, Thomas Monroy, and Jay Reichert (Project for Excellence in Entrepreneurship Education, 1994); Jerome Katz, "The Institution and Infrastructure of Entrepreneurship," *Entrepreneurship: Theory and Practice*, Spring 1991: 85–102; W. Ed McMullan and Wayne A. Long, "Entrepreneurship Education in the Nineties," *Journal of Business Venturing* 2 (1987): 261–75; Peter Robinson and Max Haynes, "Entrepreneurship Education in America's Major Universities," *Entrepreneurship: Theory and Practice*, Spring 1991: 41–52; William Sandberg and Elizabeth Gatewood, "A Profile of Entrepreneurship Research Centers: Orientations, Interests, Activities, and Resources," *Entrepreneurship: Theory and Practice*, Spring 1991: 11–24; Karl Vesper and William Gartner, "Measuring Progress in Entrepreneurship Education," *Journal of Business Venturing* 12 (1997): 403–42.

8. Daniel Rodgers, *The Work Ethic in Industrial America, 1850–1920* (Chicago: University of Chicago Press, 1978), xii.

9. Ibid., xiii.

10. Howard Brick makes a similar case for the intellectual history of political economy in the midcentury United States in *Transcending Capitalism: Visions of a New Society in Modern American Thought* (Ithaca, NY: Cornell University Press, 2006).

11. Adam Tooze, *Statistics and the German State, 1900–1945: The Making of Modern Economic Knowledge* (New York: Cambridge University Press, 2001); Timothy Mitchell, *Carbon Democracy: Political Power in the Age of Oil* (New York: Verso, 2011); Timothy Shenk, "Inventing the American Economy," PhD diss., Columbia University, 2016.

12. Michel Foucault, *The Birth of Biopolitics: Lectures at the Collège de France, 1978–1979*, trans. Graham Burchell, ed. Michel Senellart (New York: Palgrave Macmillan, 2008), 219, 226.

13. For a discussion of automation in the context of long-standing debates about technological unemployment see Amy Sue Bix, *Inventing Ourselves out of Jobs? America's Debate over Technological Unemployment, 1929–1981* (Baltimore: Johns Hopkins University Press, 2000).

14. For examples see Frederick Pollock, *The Economic and Social Consequences of Automation*, trans. W. O. Henderson and W. H. Chaloner (Oxford: Basil Blackwell, 1957); Ben B. Seligman, *Most Notorious Victory: Man in an Age of Automation* (New York: Free Press, 1966); Ad Hoc Committee on the Triple Revolution, *The Triple Revolution* (Santa Barbara, CA: Students for a Democratic Society, 1964).

15. John Diebold, *Automation: The Advent of the Automatic Factory* (New York: Van Nostrand, 1952).

16. The definitions include (1) The person who assumes the risk associated with uncertainty; (2) The person who supplies financial capital; (3) An innovator; (4) A decision maker; (5) An industrial leader; (6) A manager or superintendent; (7) An organizer and coordinator of economic resources; (8) The owner of an enterprise; (9) An employer of factors of production; (10) A contractor; (11) An arbitrageur; (12) An allocator of resources among alternative uses. See Hébert and Link, "Historical Perspectives on the Entrepreneur," 264.

17. Joseph Schumpeter, *The Theory of Economic Development: An Inquiry into Profits, Capital, Credit, Interest, and the Business Cycle*, trans. Redvers Opie (New York: Oxford University Press, 1934).

18. Frank H. Knight, *Risk, Uncertainty, and Profit* (Boston: Houghton Mifflin, 1921), 290.

19. J. M. Clark, "Relations of History and Theory," *Journal of Economic History* 2, S1 (1942): 139.

20. Arthur Cole, "An Approach to the Study of Entrepreneurship: A Tribute to Edwin F. Gay," *Journal of Economic History* 6, S1 (1946): 5.

21. Thorstein Veblen, *Absentee Ownership and Business Enterprise in Recent Times* (Boston: Beacon, 1967), 106.

22. Werner Sombart, *Die Zukunft des Kapitalismus* (Berlin, 1932), 8–9, as translated and cited in Bert Hoselitz, "Entrepreneurship and Economic Growth," *American Journal of Economics and Sociology* 12, no. 1 (1952): 101.

23. Thomas Cochran and William Miller, *The Age of Enterprise: A Social History of Industrial America* (New York: Macmillan, 1942), 326, 355.

24. Fritz Redlich, *History of American Business Leaders: A Series of Studies*, vol. 1 (Ann Arbor, MI: Edwards Bros., 1940), 1.

25. Joseph Schumpeter, "The Instability of Capitalism," *Economic Journal* 38, no. 151 (1928): 384–86.

26. Joseph Schumpeter, *Capitalism, Socialism, and Democracy* (New York: Harper Collins, 1976), 132.

27. For an admiring biography of Drucker see John Flaherty, *Peter Drucker: Shaping the Managerial Mind* (San Francisco: Jossey-Bass, 1999).

28. On the midcentury evolution of management theory see Christopher McKenna, *The World's Newest Profession: Management Consulting in the Twentieth Century* (New York: Cambridge University Press, 2006); Rakesh Khurana, *From Higher Aims to Hired Hands: The Social Transformation of American Business Schools and the Unfulfilled Promise of Management as a Profession* (Princeton, NJ: Princeton University Press, 2007).

29. Peter Drucker, *The Practice of Management* (New York: Harper & Bros., 1954), 50, 62, 112.

30. Nils Gilman, "The Prophet of Post-Fordism: Peter Drucker and the Legitimation of the Corporation," in *American Capitalism: Social Thought and Political Economy in the Twentieth* Century, ed. Nelson Lichtenstein (Philadelphia: University of Pennsylvania Press, 2006), 109–31; Daniel Immerwahr, "Polanyi in the United States: Peter Drucker, Karl Polanyi, and the Midcentury Critique of Economic Society," *Journal of the History of Ideas* 70, no. 3 (2009): 445–66.

31. Darren Dochuk, *From Bible Belt to Sun Belt: Plain-Folk Religion, Grassroots Politics, and the Rise of Evangelical Conservatism* (New York: W. W. Norton, 2011); Bethany Moreton, *To Serve God and Wal-Mart: The Making of Christian Free Enterprise* (Cambridge, MA: Harvard University Press, 2009); Kevin Kruse, *One Nation under God: How Corporate America Invented Christian America* (New York: Basic Books, 2015); Kim Phillips-Fein, *Invisible Hands: The Making of the Conservative Movement from the New Deal to Reagan* (New York: W. W. Norton, 2009); Matthew Lassiter, *The Silent Majority: Suburban Politics in the Sunbelt South* (Princeton, NJ: Princeton University Press, 2006); Joseph Crespino, *In Search of Another Country: Mississippi and the Conservative Counterrevolution* (Princeton, NJ: Princeton University Press, 2007).

32. Two notable exceptions include Fred Turner, *From Counterculture to Cyberculture: Stewart Brand, the Whole Earth Network, and the Rise of Digital Utopianism* (Chicago: University of Chicago Press, 2006), and Brick, *Transcending Capitalism*.

33. Peter Drucker, *The Future of Industrial Man: A Conservative Approach* (New York: John Day, 1942), 297.

34. Ibid., 102–3.

35. Ibid., 112.

36. Peter Drucker, *The Concept of the Corporation* (New Brunswick, NJ: Transaction, 2005), 157–58.

37. Peter Drucker, "Henry Ford" (1947), in *Men, Ideas and Politics* (New York: Harper & Row, 1971), 171–72.

38. Gilman, "Prophet of Post-Fordism," 125.

39. Drucker, *Future of Industrial Man*, 280.

40. Ibid., 283; Peter Drucker, *The New Society: The Anatomy of Industrial Order* (New Brunswick, NJ: Transaction, 2006), 10.

41. Drucker, *New Society*, 232, 281.

42. Ibid., 283–85.

43. Ibid., 351. Emphasis Drucker's.

44. Drucker, *Practice of Management*, 256.

45. Ibid., 255.

46. Ibid., 286.

47. Peter Drucker, "The Next Decade in Management," *Dun's Review*, December 1959, 52.

48. Peter Drucker, "The Promise of Automation" (1955), in *America's Next Twenty Years* (New York: Harper & Bros., 1957), 24–25, 34. Emphasis Drucker's.

49. Marshall McLuhan, "Automation: Learning a Living," in *Understanding Media: The Extensions of Man* (New York: McGraw-Hill, 1964), 346–59.

50. Drucker, *Practice of Management*, 40.

51. Drucker, "Promise of Automation," 18.

52. Peter Drucker, *Landmarks of Tomorrow* (New York: Harper & Bros., 1957), 21–22.

53. Ibid., 18.

54. Ibid., 62; Peter Drucker, *Preparing Tomorrow's Business Leaders Today* (Englewood Cliffs, NJ: Prentice-Hall, 1969), 280.

55. Theodore W. Schultz, "Investment in Human Capital," *American Economic Review* 51, no. 1 (1961): 1.

56. Gary Becker, *Human Capital: A Theoretical and Empirical Analysis with Special Reference to Education* (Chicago: University of Chicago Press, 1964), 115–16.

57. Israel Kirzner, *Competition and Entrepreneurship* (Chicago: University of Chicago Press, 1973), 16, 68. Emphasis Kirzner's.

58. David C. McClelland, *The Achieving Society* (Princeton, NJ: Van Nostrand, 1961), 207.

59. Edith Tilton Penrose, *The Theory of the Growth of the Firm* (Oxford: Blackwell, 1959), 31n1.

60. Orvis F. Collins, *The Enterprising Man* (East Lansing: Bureau of Business Administration, Michigan State University, 1964), 19.

61. The number rose from two courses (in 1953) to well over two hundred by the mid-1980s. See K. H. Vesper, *Entrepreneurship Education: 1993* (Los Angeles: Entrepreneurial Studies Center, 1993).

62. Jerome Katz, "The Chronology and Intellectual Trajectory of American Entrepreneurship Education, 1876–1999," *Journal of Business Venturing* 18 (2003): 283–300.

63. Ibid.

64. Jerome Katz, "The Institution and Infrastructure of Entrepreneurship," *Entrepreneurship: Theory & Practice*, Spring 1991, 94; Cooper, "Entrepreneurship: The Past, the Present, the Future," 21–34.

65. Katz, "Institution and Infrastructure of Entrepreneurship," 96.

Section IV
CONTESTED IDEAS

12

WAR AND AMERICAN THOUGHT
Finding a Nation through Killing and Dying

Raymond Haberski Jr.

"I believe in your story . . . and I believe in the good it can do for our country. It's a story of courage, hope, optimism, love of freedom, all the convictions that motivated you young men to do what you did, and I think this film will go a long way toward reinvigorating our commitment to the war."[1] So gushes a character named Norm Oglesby in Ben Fountain's award-winning novel about contemporary American war culture, *Billy Lynn's Long Halftime Walk* (2012). Oglesby is the fictional owner of the Dallas Cowboys and has invited a group of American soldiers from Bravo Company to the traditional Thanksgiving Day game at Texas Stadium. The event is the last stop on a national tour before these men return to fighting, killing, and dying in Iraq; it is also an opportunity for Oglesby to get the movie rights to a story that made these men heroes. Feted by Oglesby as combination cash cows and patriotic saviors, the men of Bravo Company become known properties because of a firefight captured by a Fox News team imbedded with the American military—keeping with media conventions, their skirmish even earned a marquee-appropriate title, "the battle of Al-Ansakar Canal."

In the novel, Oglesby's character shows how easy it is to turn wars and the soldiers who fight them into consumer products and marketing strategies. Whereas Bravo Company exists in one reality—as confused, heroic, real, violent, and drunk—Oglesby creates another reality—through his wealth, power, the movies, and ultimately interpretation. But the contrast between the soldiers and the salesman also captures a deeper intellectual dualism of war—war is nasty and violent, but also romantic and vital; people die without ceremony, but nations celebrate those who give their lives in war; no people want to admit that they are a product of war, yet war undoubtedly shapes the identity of a people, including (or perhaps especially) Americans. Oglesby shows his solidarity with Billy Lynn and his fellow soldiers by explaining that he too has a patriotic duty in times of war, a cause to which his wealth and single-minded ambition can be deployed like real weapons. In his theater of action, the home front, his mission is to sell the war: "They forget why we went there in the first place—why are we fighting?" Oglesby laments about his fellow Americans. "They forget some things are actually worth fighting for, and that's where your story comes in, the Bravo story. And if the Hollywood crowd won't step up to the plate, well, I'm happy to pinch-hit, more than happy. This is an obligation I willingly assume."[2]

Fountain dwells on an irony central to so many war stories—wars don't belong to those who fight them; they barely belong to those who die in them.[3] Oglesby's pitch, then, to turn tragedy into a feel-good movie reflects a dangerous truth about war: transforming war into an idea is often more important than the consequences of fighting, killing, and dying. "This is about a lot more than just money," Oglesby says in response to the skepticism and cynicism of the soldiers of Bravo Company. "Our country *needs* this movie, needs it badly," he pleads. "I really don't think you want to be the guys who keep this movie from being made, not with so much at stake. I sure wouldn't want to be that guy."[4]

Oglesby plays with the universal "we" in narratives about war: we need war, we see war as a narrative, we find war significant to understanding our identity as a people. As a national, trans-generational narrative, war functions like the other blanket ideas, such as religion and democracy: America is a Christian nation, and Americans are a free people. In war, Americans fight, kill, and die for good reasons. Even when a war fails, such as the Confederacy's war against the United States or the American war in Vietnam (and perhaps Iraq and Afghanistan), the nation does not, has not, reimagined the standard narrative about war. We have told ourselves a simple story about war since Puritans decimated the Wampanoags, Narragansetts, and other native peoples in the seventeenth century's King Philip's War. But the ubiquity of the tale has also made it a target for criticism, and Fountain's book fits into a tradition of critiquing the story we tell ourselves about war. This interplay between a dominant narrative about war and the often eloquent, biting challenges to it reveals the significance of American thought about war in ways similar to how Americans like to debate national assumptions about religion and freedom. Broadly speaking, the American story of war has three acts.

In the first act, the nation was made sacred through war. Americans from the Puritans to Progressives told themselves that people kill and die for reasons that go beyond the immediate circumstances of violence and death. The American Civil War serves as the pivot for this section of the story, conflating God and war to affirm the meaning of the nation. Mark Twain challenged this interpretation: while he did not deny the pivotal role played by the Civil War, he parodied the way it made possible the sanctification of all wars in American history.

In the second act, the power of the state is remade through two world wars and the Cold War. During the First World War, Randolph Bourne, a former student of John Dewey's and a prolific pragmatist intellectual, bemoaned the attraction many American intellectuals had to the power of war. So where Twain pointed out the irony of using war to sanctify the nation, Bourne identified the irony of intellectuals using war to reform the state.

The final act starts in the wake of the Vietnam War, in a time when the critiques of Twain and Bourne had seemingly been confirmed by the tragedy of that war. End of the story, right? Not quite. The failure of Vietnam as a war did not undermine the meaning of war as an idea in America. In the wake of Vietnam, "just war" theory rose to prominence as a way to address a very basic question: when is war moral? Thus, just war theory added a sense of moral evaluation, offering a way to determine what kind of wars were right and good. Into an atmosphere of anxiety about the nation's moral health created by the moral disaster of Vietnam, the political theorist Michael Walzer emerged as a contrarian advocate for a moral defense of war, arguing that just war theory made war a universal action, not an expression of American exceptionalism. Walzer's twist shares similarities to those of Twain and Bourne—he contended that soldiers in war, no matter what side they fought for, share essential elements that unite them personally, politically, and culturally. In this sense, war is indeed an idea, but not one safe for popular consumption.

It might seem odd to use critics of American wars to talk about significant strands of American thought about war, but it is through such criticism that I think we see these traditions most clearly. In short, Twain, Bourne, and Walzer wouldn't have written about the power of narratives about war if they didn't find those stories significant and perhaps even dangerous to their nation.

The Power of War

From the first European settlers to the present day, stories of war—and the remaking of war into an idea—have played a crucial role in the formation of America. What gives the idea of war such power? First, sacrifices made in war create tremendous momentum for interpretation. People kill and die for reasons that the living hope will go beyond the immediate circumstances of violence and death. Second, comprehending such sacrifices produces another aspect of war's power: unlike almost any other human action, war galvanizes people who would otherwise have little reason to unify. And finally, the stories of unity generated by war produce narratives that operate with universal appeal—so universal that they can cut across generations, faiths, genders, and ethnicities, and become useful tools for those who run the nation. In the American experience it is not too much to say that without war, America as we know it today would not exist. War helped give the nation purpose, it provided a narrative that helped the state galvanize the allegiance of the people, and it offered a seamless interpretation of heroic action that stretched back to the origins of the nation and forward to imperial projects of the modern day.

In American letters, no other statement about war in American life is more profound and more often cited than the address President Abraham Lincoln gave at the Gettysburg battlefield. In his historically brief speech, Lincoln made plain how war could transcend its immediate context (beyond Confederate and Union war aims and war dead), to become timeless and nation defining. It was the abstract quality of the speech that made the difference, allowing interpretations that served an endless variety of needs. Indeed, the abstract nature of the speech established it as the dominant interpretation of war in American thought. Michael Sherry observes that the Civil War capped a particular kind of American history with war: "A nation born in war, threatened by invasion, expanded through conquest, and finally reconceived in civil war, owed much to Mars."[5]

In his address at the Gettysburg Cemetery, Lincoln offered a moral reckoning for the carnage of the Civil War. Looking out at the freshly dug graves of thousands of soldiers from both sides of the war, Lincoln proposed that the only suitable testament to such sacrifice was to make a solemn pledge: "It is rather for us, the living to be dedicated to the great task remaining before us—that, from these honored dead we take increased devotion to that cause for which they here, gave the last full measure of devotion—that we here highly resolve these dead shall not have died in vain; that the nation, shall have a new birth of freedom, and that government of the people by the people for the people, shall not perish from the earth."[6] The war was not an end in itself; Lincoln wanted his audience and future generations to accept that the tragedy of his war and perhaps any war could be redeemed if Americans rededicated themselves to the founding principles of their nation. However, Lincoln's intellectual reckoning carried a terrible dilemma, that the nation might use war to find redemption for its political failings.

For that reason, the Gettysburg Address remains among the most significant statements about the nation made by any president. For President Lincoln and his successors, the tragedy of war carries within it the founding promise of their nation. Practically speaking, the Civil War forced Lincoln to confront a paradox that all presidents face when they send Americans into war: that his nation, though pledged to peace, found its identity through death. The fact that Lincoln's interpretation of the Civil War did not require squaring this obvious contradiction fed the power of war as an idea in American history. Historian and president of Harvard University Drew Gilpin Faust relates how the scale of death gave Lincoln and his political heirs a powerful intellectual tool: "In the address the dead themselves become the agents of political meaning and devotion; they act even in their silence and anonymity." While similar views of war had resounded earlier in American history, Lincoln's interpretation of the Civil War consolidated what had yet to become a tradition. Faust asserts that it was the Civil War that provided "narratives of patriotic sacrifice that imbued war deaths with transcendent meaning."[7] The drift of history as well as the shock of the moment made it possible for Lincoln's address to reveal how much Americans needed war to know themselves. He told Americans then and for all time what they already wanted to believe.[8]

Lincoln's address offered both a rhetorical and intellectual script, one that literally could be adapted to any war that demanded sacrifice, and one that was useful to justify sacrifices made for the nation. A mark of a rich idea is that it travels well, and Lincoln developed an idea about war and the nation that has proved to be context-resistant—his argument has consistently appeared from his time to ours. The historian Jared Peatman writes in *The Long Shadow of Lincoln's Gettysburg Address*, "From 1914 to 1918 and 1939 to 1945, the Gettysburg Address was invoked more often and for greater purposes than ever before."[9] Its effect continues into the twenty-first century: in an editorial for the *Washington Post* in 2013, Admiral Mike Mullen, a former chairman of the Joint Chiefs of Staff under both George W. Bush and Barack Obama, spoke about drawing inspiration from Lincoln's address when meeting the families of fallen soldiers. When they ask "Was it worth it? Did his death mean anything?" Mullen tells them "It mattered. . . . Regardless of the terms of the treaty, the surrender, the withdrawal, the defeat or the victory, no American who sheds blood to preserve that which his ancestors fought to establish can ever be said to have made that sacrifice without meaning. No one who dies in the service of country dies in vain."[10] Mullen has it about right—at its core, the Gettysburg Address abstracted the particularities of battle to create a singular, unified notion about a nation at war.[11]

Perhaps less obvious, though, is the physical manifestation of Lincoln's address—how the abstraction of war was made tangible and visible in front of Lincoln. The historian Mark S. Schantz reminds us that the Gettysburg Address was most immediately a dedication ceremony to a new cemetery. He explains that William Saunders, its architect, designed the layout of the graves to impose a certain kind of intellectual order on those buried there. "The dead at Gettysburg belonged fully to the American nation," Schantz states, "not to their families, not to their friends, and not even, in the end, to themselves."[12] In death, the soldiers of Gettysburg became equal and equally abstract. The structure of the cemetery was, Schantz points out, "relentlessly egalitarian.... There would be no discrimination in ... [the] cemetery or distinctions made among individuals. Families of wealth and taste would be powerless to adorn individual graves or to embellish them with tombs or crypts or more extensive monuments. By insisting on the regularity and the uniformity of the graves, Saunders's design simultaneously sent a strong message of national unity."[13] And Lincoln heartily endorsed that message through his address.

The Gettysburg Address was far from the only statement of its kind, but it resonated with special force because, better than all others, it expressed an American theology that joined the aspirations of the nation with massive sacrifice made in the war. The use of religion to understand war has deep roots in American history, but it was the Civil War, as many historians have reminded us, that made manifest a particular kind of American faith. Religious historian Harry Stout contends: "Only as causalities rose to unimaginable levels did it dawn on some people that something mystically religious was taking place, a sort of massive sacrifice on the national altar. The Civil War taught Americans that they were a Union, and it absolutely required a baptism of blood to unveil transcendent dimensions of that union."[14] The Civil War with Lincoln's interpretation became an apotheosis of the intellectual power of war to shape American identity—war as the expression of *E Pluribus Unum*.

A Dangerous Theology of War

The historian John Bodnar reminds us that even though war serves as an organizing force in American history, "there were always those who could never forget the suffering war had brought, who were never completely comforted by patriotic rhetoric, and who resented the fact that they had to relinquish some of their most basic rights to liberty and life."[15] Mark Twain was one such critic. A generation after the end of the Civil War, the United States inaugurated new ways to affirm its identity through a war for an empire overseas. Few observers of the Spanish-American War felt brazen enough to point out the irony of America using this conflict, which was hopelessly tangled up in racism, imperialism, and violence, as an exercise in national affirmation; even fewer though were willing to criticize the nationalist theology that pervaded popular support for the soldiers sent to kill and die in the Caribbean and far across the Pacific. Twain joined other anti-imperialists in opposing American adventurism, but he distinguished himself even among that group by attacking the sanctification of the troops.

While Twain understood like many men of his generation that no other experience forged a union between people and their nation better than war, the historian Edward Blum notes that the writer "had long opposed American cultural and military imperialism [and] particularly fumed at the notion that the Christian God was an imperialist."[16] Indeed, if American wars were sacred, Twain embraced sacrilege. The best expression of Twain's heresy was an essay titled "The War-Prayer." "Turn[ing] his 'weapons of satire' against religiously legitimated imperialism," Twain eviscerated the powerful mixture of piety, violence, and patriotism that, as Blum points out, "could have taken place at any white Protestant church."[17]

Twain's story unfolds in a small town, where celebrations, speeches, pageants, and church services prepare the people for the war to come. "In the churches the pastors preached devotion to flag and country," Twain writes, "and invoked the God of Battles, beseeching His aid in our good cause in outpourings of fervid eloquence which moved every listener." Twain wrote, "It was indeed a glad and gracious time." In a passage worth dwelling on, Twain observed that "the half dozen rash spirits that ventured to disapprove of the war and cast doubt upon its righteousness straightaway got such a stern and angry warning that for their personal safety's sake they quickly shrank out of sight and offended no more in that way." In his typescript, Twain excised the article "the" from the phrase "to disapprove of the war." He did so, perhaps, to emphasize the universality of war—he knew it was heresy to mock those who idolized war. While such dissent might exist and even have the freedom to exist, it was still a transgression punishable, as Twain sardonically suggested, by more violence.[18]

The heart of his story is a church service at which, Twain writes, "volunteers sat [with] their dear ones, proud, happy, and envied by the neighbors and friends who had no sons and brothers to send forth to the field of honor, there to win for the flag, or failing, die the noblest of noble deaths." The congregation sang their militarism, and the preacher made his long prayer over the uniformed soldiers. Praising them and the violent work they would undertake for God and America, he concluded, "Bless our arms, grant us the victory, O Lord our God, Father and Protector of our land and flag!"

At this moment in the tale, a stranger enters the church and joins the preacher in front of the congregation. "I come from the Throne," he says, "bearing a message from Almighty God!" The preacher gives way so that his uninvited guest can have his say: "You have heard your servant's prayer," the stranger tells the congregation. "I am commissioned of God to put into words the other part of it—that part which the pastor—and also you in your hearts—fervently prayed silently. And ignorantly and unthinkingly? When you have prayed for victory you have prayed for many unmentioned results which follow victory—*must* follow it, cannot help but follow it," intones the stranger. Of course, what has gone unsaid in the first prayer is asking God to destroy the enemy. And so the stranger completes the prayer: "blast their hopes, blight their lives, protract their bitter pilgrimage, make heavy their steps, water their way with their tears, stain the white snow with the blood of their wounded feet! We ask it," Twain's messenger bellows, "in the spirit of love, of Him Who is the Source of Love, and Who is the ever-faithful refuge and friend of all that are sore beset and seek His aid with humble and contrite hearts. Amen."

Not surprisingly, Twain could not get this piece published during his lifetime—it was simply too caustic, too brutally honest about the vainglorious contract Americans had made to wage war. A Christian preacher declared at the time: "The present crisis of this Nation . . . is in harmony with Christian teachings. . . . This contest is a holy uprising in God's name for the uplifting of a wronged and downtrodden people."[19] While many anti-imperialists voiced profound skepticism about such a mission, it was Twain who most directly eviscerated the theology of war that Americans had adopted as the legacy of the Civil War. Twain simply could not tolerate the tendency, the intellectual historian Jackson Lears writes, "to wrap the pointless slaughter of war in the robes of righteous heroism."[20] But, of course, like his messenger, Twain's sensibility was lost on his audience. "It was believed afterwards," Twain concluded his essay, "the man was a lunatic, because there was no sense in what he said."

War and the State

A generation later and in the midst of a war unlike anything anybody had seen before, Randolph Bourne identified a new kind of madness—"War in the interest of democracy!" Bourne opposed American intervention in the First World War for reasons that other Americans also did: war aims seemed fatuous, allies acted little different from enemies, patriotism had grown dangerous to outliers, and, as he stated in his first essay on American intervention, many intellectuals had accepted far too easily the government's rationale for this war. As a self-conscious member of the intellectual class, Bourne seemed especially sensitive to the self-referential, self-aggrandizing tendencies of his world. "The intellect craves certitude," he wrote. "It takes effort to keep it supple and pliable. In a time of danger and disaster we jump desperately for some dogma to cling to."[21] To the intellectual historian John Patrick Diggins, this was a devastating insight: "Bourne became the first writer, as far as I know, to discern in pragmatic philosophy a tendency to equate authority with power and to look to force as a solution to problems."[22] And while Bourne clearly believed he had gotten the better of fellow intellectuals, especially his mentor John Dewey, in debates over this particular war, Bourne's more general sense of intellectual helplessness in the face of war had a much more profound effect. The idea of war ultimately defeated Bourne's critique of it.

Throughout a series of essays on American intervention in the war and the changes wrought by popular acceptance of war, Bourne suggested how such mythology grew into an operational technique for the state—he saw how an intellectual vision merged with a bureaucratic process. In an essay titled "The State," unfinished before his death, Bourne observed: "War—or at least modern war waged by a democratic republic against a powerful enemy—seems to achieve for a nation almost all that the most inflamed political idealist could desire. Citizens are no longer indifferent to their Government, but each cell of the body politic is brimming with life and activity. We are at last on the way to full realization of that collective community in which each individual somehow contains the virtue of the whole. In a nation at war, every citizen identifies himself with the whole, and feels immensely strengthened in that identification."[23] The tone of Bourne's analysis went beyond the battle over ideas, demonstrating that what he argued was, effectively, an end to ideas. For Bourne, ideas were messy and cultivated conflict. What he saw in war was the dying of intellectual life, not its ascension to power or fulfillment through the state. "The allure of the martial in war," he contended, "has passed only to be succeeded by the allure of the technical." War became a state of nature for the United States that required a system—policies, analysts, a state—to carry it out.[24]

So what was the alternative? "Once the war is on," Bourne wrote with obvious exasperation, "the conviction spreads that individual thought is helpless, that the only way one can count is as a cog in the great wheel. There is no good holding back.... Not only is everyone forced into line, but the new certitude becomes idealized. It is a noble realism," he concluded, "which opposes itself to futile obstruction and the cowardly refusal to face facts."[25] More to the point, the keeper of truth was no longer a reality one might experience but simply and emphatically one the state manufactured.

In an essay about a friend who opposed the war, Bourne wrote: "He still feels himself inextricably a part of this blundering, wistful, crass civilization we call America. All he asks is not to be identified with it for warlike ends." Fat chance. In a statement that echoed Twain's ironic judgment on religious support for war, Bourne declared,

> The moment war is declared ... the mass of people, through some spiritual alchemy, become convinced that they have willed and executed the deed themselves. Then they with the exception of a few malcontents, proceed to allow themselves to be regimented, coerced, deranged in all the environments of their lives.... The citizen throws off his contempt and indifference to Government, identifies himself with its purposes, revives all his military memories and symbols, and the State once more

walks, an august presence through the imaginations of men. Patriotism becomes the dominant feeling, and produces immediately that intense and hopeless confusion between the relations which the individual bears and should bear towards society of which he is a part.[26]

The political theorist Leslie Vaughan asserts: "No other critic linked American liberal politics to military absolutism. And no other writer recognized that something new had happened in the technical organization and management of modern war that made the collaboration of intellectuals crucial to its success." Bourne responded to the universalizing force of American war. "War was not a moral obligation," Vaughan noted, "but the state's raison d'etre."[27]

Like the Gettysburg Address and "The War-Prayer," Bourne's description of war grew more influential as Americans experienced more war. The Second World War demonstrated the extraordinary power the US government possessed to mobilize the nation, its military, and its mythology. From war bonds to the atomic bomb, and from FDR to the Greatest Generation, World War II fostered a popular awe in the nation's war-making capacity. Remarkably, Bourne's critique of the attraction American intellectuals had to the power of war held up throughout the post-1945 era, as politics became deeply intertwined in the warfare state. And so, if war provided a narrative of national rebirth in nineteenth-century America, the world wars and Cold War of the twentieth century produced a narrative of national realization. Except for the persistence of a small antiwar and pacifist tradition, Bourne's analysis of the war complex sounded anachronistic. For almost a century of constant war, Americans became inured to a "war technique" or the promise of war to create profound change that rarely materializes. "War determines its own ends," Bourne cautioned his compatriots while they waited for the slaughter in Europe "to make the world safe for democracy."[28] What Bourne did not imagine was how a war technique might operate in a world in which war has no end.

Just War and Endless War

The decades following the Second World War are often referred to as postwar—a euphemism that we should regard as misbegotten hope of an earlier generation. The implications of our reality, according to the legal historian Mary Dudziak, are that even though "military conflict has been ongoing for decades, [our] public policy rests on the false assumption that it is an aberration.... Wartime," she states bluntly, "has become normal time in America.... Wartime has become the only kind of time we have, and therefore is a time within which American politics must function."²⁹ Thus as Americans grew more comfortable with war, they needed a language with which to speak about their martial reality, one that acknowledged how war provided moral affirmation for the nation and popular support to the state. The vocabulary that has helped make sense of this time is in Latin, and the story it tells is that American wars are just wars.

Just war theory has long offered a moral language for describing why people need to kill and die. The theory comprises three basic categories—*jus ad bellum* (or having a just cause to fight), *jus in bello* (or conducting a just war), and (a more recent edition) *jus post bellum* (or creating a just peace)—and together they promise to contextualize experiences of war within universal principles of violence. Just war also has an advantage of sounding neutral—it moves among religious interpretations and patriotic rationalizations without appearing to come from the preachers or politicians. While just war has been claimed by Catholic theologians, one can find discussion and application of just war theory in the American experience from the beginning of violent conflict between Europeans and indigenous peoples to the present day. In short, just war theory fits into the narrative Americans have developed over generations about war. All the better, as the theologian Stanley Hauerwas points out, because obedience to just war principles have never prevented the United States from going to war.³⁰

Indeed, just war made a determined reappearance following the Vietnam War when scholars and the public alike sought to reorient themselves in debates over America as a moral place. The apparent irony in the rediscovery of just war theory in the wake of arguably the most unjust war in American history illuminates the strength of the American narrative about war. The capacity of just war theory to act in a moral register with neutral language enabled it to serve all sides in a debate over the wars that followed America's failure in Vietnam.

Published in 1977, Michael Walzer's book *Just and Unjust Wars* helped crystallize this American interest in just war theory. In a recent edition of his book, Walzer observed: "Vietnam is the major reason for the surge in interest [in just war theory], but interest has been sustained by America's subsequent wars, which have been greater in number and longer in duration than anyone expected."³¹ When Walzer's book first appeared, as Thomas Pangle pointed out at the time, it had "a compelling seriousness because it [arose] from vivid accounts of actual political leaders, citizens, and soldiers, rather than from clever but naïve examples spun out of professors' imaginations."³² Walzer explained that when he first approached writing about just war, "the greater part by far of my reading [for the book] was not in theory at all but in military history ... and then in memoir literature produced by soldiers of different ranks. I read many of the novels and poems that deal with the experience of fighting and the company of soldiers." In the realities of war, rather than the abstractions of moral theory, Walzer looked for ways to describe why and how we fight. Never having experienced war as a combatant, he delved deeply into "histories, memoirs, essays, novels, and poems because," he said, "I wanted the moral arguments of my book to ring true to their authors—and to the men and women about whom they were writing."[33] In short, Walzer needed to understand the world that war creates before imagining he could write about laws that might govern that world. Yet, just as often just war has existed as an idea that, in keeping with American tradition, has been employed to justify rather than challenge American actions.

In a postscript to another edition of his book, Walzer addressed the misunderstanding that often accompanies interpretations of just war theory. He argued that rather than bicker over just causes, or endlessly debate the alternatives to war, just war focuses attention on the world that war creates. Looking at war from the inside out, from those who fight it rather than those who write about it, redirects the meaning away from the abstract debates about the nation toward the harsh reality of soldiering. Accordingly, Walzer hoped to make those who fight war more than fodder for a battle of ideas.[34]

American wars are no different from those fought by other people, and American enemies fight for reasons similar to Americans themselves. In other words, the way Americans make heroes out of their warriors has its corollary on the other side. Even those who critique the resort to war should take heed: "Patriotism and loyalty are, no doubt, often misguided, but they shouldn't be incomprehensible," Walzer observed. "Collectives like the state (or the army of the state) are indeed instrumental: they have no intrinsic value. But they make possible, and they defend, another collective, a community whose existence is of centrally important value to . . . its members."[35] At his best, Walzer uses just war theory to rescue the historical experience of war from its abstract forms. Like Twain's messenger, Walzer wants to remind us that soldiers might be characters in stories we tell about ourselves, but we shouldn't pretend that those stories are about anything other than death and killing.

A passage from Ben Fountain's book makes this point better than most debates about war in America. In a scene in which Billy Lynn speaks directly to the national liturgy of war, Fountain forces his readers to consider our popular consumption of tragedy. Just before they hit the field for the halftime show, Billy gets peppered with questions about the day he became a hero, which also happens to be the worst day of his young life, because despite killing many insurgents, he could not prevent the death of his friend and mentor. In a perfect expression of American pious patriotism, Billy is asked if he'll think about his friend "during the playing of the national anthem." "He says yes just to keep it upbeat and on track," Fountain writes:

> Yes, I sure will, which sounds obscene to his ears, and he wonders by what process virtually any discussion about the war seems to profane these ultimate matters of life and death. As if to talk of such things properly we need a mode of speech near the equal of prayer, otherwise just shut, shut your yap and sit on it, silence being truer to the experience than the star-spangled spasm, the bittersweet sob, the redeeming hug, or whatever this ... closure is that everybody's always talking about. They want it to be easy and it's just not going to be.[36]

Fountain captures the lunacy of perhaps the most popular idea about war, that we can use war—manipulate it like a movie—for a particular end. In David Finkel's book *The Good Soldiers*, about a specific battalion (the 2–16, the Rangers), that fought in the middle of "the surge" in Iraq in 2007, he recounts a discordant moment between President George W. Bush and the wife of a severely injured soldier. Bush came to visit the hospital where Maria Emory's husband lay a severely injured soldier. She remembers Bush saying, "Thank you for your husband's service to his country" and that "he was sorry for what our family was going through." Emory thanked the president for visiting but wanted to say something else. "I mean, when I saw him, I was angry I started crying, and he saw me and came to me and gave me a hug and said, 'Everything's going to be okay.'" Like Billy Lynn, Emory knew that nothing would be "okay." In fact, war and its effects are the opposite of okay. Finkel notes, Bush "had no idea that [Maria's tears] were because of anger, and he had no idea they were because of him. And nothing was okay, she said, so he was wrong about that too. Her husband was ruined."[37]

In an era of war without end, we have witnessed a curious development captured by Finkel's snapshot: wars are being fought without grand causes and understood at an almost granular level. Americans—from their presidents to the people—expect to wrap familiar narratives around wars of the twenty-first century and the people who fight them, but these wars are about fewer and fewer people because fewer and fewer Americans actually fight in them. In fact, as drones replace soldiers in the seemingly endless war on terror, the idea of the battlefield has shifted to the sphere of media, where battles over meaning rage across movie screens, flat-screen televisions, social media sites, and, of course, in novels and nonfiction books. The idea of war as a unifying, nation-defining, policy-making force falters when Americans can't imagine a world without war, and therefore are forced to confront war through the few individuals fighting them. Americans have a tradition of thought that makes war seem useful and even therapeutic, but as Billy Lynn tells himself (and us), "they want it to be easy and it's just not going to be."

NOTES

1. Ben Fountain, *Billy Lynn's Long Halftime Walk* (New York: HarperCollins, 2012), 274.

2. Ibid.

3. John Keegan, *The Face of Battle: A Study of Agincourt, Waterloo, and the Somme* (New York: Penguin, 1983), 1–13; Elaine Scarry, *The Body in Pain: The Making and Unmaking of the World* (New York: Oxford University Press, 1987), 63; Jill Lepore, *In the Name of War: King Philip's War and the Origins of American Identity* (New York: Vintage Books, 1999), xi.

4. Fountain, *Billy Lynn's Long Halftime Walk*, 278.

5. Michael Sherry, *In the Shadow of War: The United States since the 1930s* (New Haven, CT: Yale University Press, 1997), 1.

6. Abraham Lincoln, draft of the Gettysburg Address, Nicolay copy, transcribed and annotated by the Lincoln Studies Center, Knox College, Galesburg, IL. Available at Abraham Lincoln Papers at the Library of Congress, Manuscript Division (Washington, DC: American Memory Project, 2000–2002), https://www.ourdocuments.gov/doc.php?doc=36&page=transcript.

7. Drew Gilpin Faust, *The Republic of Suffering: Death and the American Civil War* (New York: Alfred A. Knopf, 2008), 119.

8. Sherry, *In the Shadow of War*, 3.

9. Jared Peatman, *The Long Shadow of Lincoln's Gettysburg Address* (Carbondale: Southern Illinois University Press, 2013), 115.

10. Mike Mullen, "At Gettysburg and Today, No One Who Dies in Service Dies in Vain," *Washington Post*, November 18, 2013, https://www.washingtonpost.com/opinions/at-gettysburg-and-today-no-one-who-dies-in-service-dies-in-vain/2013/11/18/bbe5b8b6-5073-11e3-9fe0-fd2ca728e67c_story.html?utm_term=.33dbb946f3bc.

11. Peatman, *Long Shadow*, 115–16.

12. Mark S. Schantz, "Death and the Gettysburg Address," in *The Gettysburg Address: Perspectives on Lincoln's Greatest Speech*, ed. Sean Conant (New York: Oxford University Press, 2015), 107.

13. Ibid., 113–14.

14. Harry S. Stout, *Upon the Altar of the Nation: A Moral History of the Civil War* (New York: Viking, 2006), xxi.

15. John Bodnar, *The "Good War" in American Memory* (Baltimore: Johns Hopkins University Press, 2011), 2–3.

16. Edward Blum, "God's Imperialism: Mark Twain and the Religious War between Imperialists and Anti-Imperialists," *Transnational American Studies* 1, no. 1 (2009): 35.

17. Ibid., 36.

18. Mark Twain, typescript of "The War-Prayer," *Journal of Transnational American Studies* 1, no. 1 (2009): 1.

19. As quoted in Blum, "God's Imperialism," 36.

20. Jackson Lears, *Rebirth of a Nation: The Making of Modern American, 1877–1920* (New York: HarperCollins, 2009), 218.

21. Randolph Bourne, "The War and the Intellectuals," in Carl Resek, *War and the Intellectuals: Essays, 1915–1919* (New York: Harper & Row, 1964), 12.

22. John Diggins, "John Dewey in Peace and War," *American Scholar*, 50, no. 2 (Spring 1981), 215.

23. Randolph Bourne, "The State," in Resek, *War and the Intellectuals*, 71.
24. Randolph Bourne, "Twilight of Idols," in Resek, *War and the Intellectuals*, 63.
25. Bourne, "Twilight of Idols," 12.
26. Ibid., 13.
27. Leslie Vaughan, *Randolph Bourne and the Politics of Cultural Radicalism* (Lawrence: University Press of Kansas, 1997), 87.
28. Bourne, "A War Diary," *Seven Arts* 2 (September 1917), http://fair-use.org/seven-arts/1917/09/a-war-diary.
29. Mary Dudziak, *War-Time: An Idea, Its History, Its Consequences* (New York: Oxford University Press, 2012), 13.
30. Stanley Hauerwas, *War and the American Difference: Theological Reflections on Violence and National Identity* (Grand Rapids, MI: Baker Academic, 2011), 33.
31. Michael Walzer, *Just and Unjust Wars: A Moral Argument with Historical Illustrations* (New York: Basic Book, 2015, Fifth Edition), xiii–xiv.
32. Thomas Pangle, review of *Just and Unjust Wars: A Moral Argument with Historical Illustrations*, by Michael Walzer, *American Political Science Review* 72, no. 4 (December 1978): 1394.
33. Walzer, *Just and Unjust Wars*, 336.
34. Ibid., 346.
35. Ibid., 340.
36. Fountain, *Billy Lynn's Long Halftime Walk*, 137, Kindle.
37. David Finkel, *The Good Soldiers* (New York: Picador, 2009), 82.

13

UNITED STATES IN THE WORLD
The Significance of an Isolationist Tradition

Christopher McKnight Nichols

Once dismissed derisively as simply the study of "what one clerk said to another clerk," the field of "diplomatic history" has undergone a transformation in recent years, expanding its scope and methods to encompass everything from hard power and formal political processes to soft power and nongovernmental organizations.[1] Now called "United States in the World," this field owes its current renaissance in part to intellectual history, as it has reached beyond traditional methodologies and incorporated new techniques from cultural history and innovative transnational approaches.[2] In roughly the past decade, many "US in the World" scholars have explicitly placed ideas, ideology, intellectuals, discourse analysis, and key texts at the heart of their work, whether on human rights, development, self-determination, law, or religion.[3] No longer (usually) limited to state actors, this new range of scholarship spans transnational exchanges of every kind, by sailors, sex workers, and missionaries, activists and intellectuals, and even the transfer and transformation of ideas as they cross borders. With this broadened focus, the new diplomatic history has also begun to contextualize nationalist US narratives, delimiting their scope and reconfiguring the received wisdom about the role that the United States has played in the world.

Intellectual history deepens our understanding of policy precedents and tradition in foreign-policy worldviews. On the one hand, the relations of the United States with other nations and peoples have been determined by specific stances based on ideology espoused largely by the nation's elite class. Yet, because American traditions in foreign relations encompassed beliefs and behaviors, in addition to explicit policy initiatives, the scope of scholarship must expand beyond that. Historians of foreign affairs must enlarge their study to include commercial, scientific, and religious activities, as well as the patterns of migration and transit that link peoples and groups in profound ways. Only through the amalgamation of these varied perspectives can we begin to understand the intellectual history of American foreign policy.

An exploration of the contested role of "isolationism" can help make sense of the wide array of principles at work in the shaping of US foreign policy. Approaching the isolationist tradition as an intellectual history reveals that isolationism represents a significant and driving US foreign-policy tradition, in spite of the fact that some scholars view it as a historical anachronism confined to a very small and undistinguished group of American thinkers and irrelevant to the contemporary world. Focusing primarily on the constitutive ideas of isolationism, as well as their historical expressions and the breadth of the isolationist tradition, reveals a long history that has been missed by many more conventional diplomatic-history narratives and transnational analyses alike.

Though the term "isolationism" came to prominence only in the 1920s, and burgeoned in the 1930s, a longer, broader intellectual view demonstrates that isolationism as a concept predates that particular vintage. Moreover, this new perspective clarifies that isolationism should be understood not in the singular, but in the plural. In the place of a monolithic or systematic isolationist tradition, it suggests that isolationism represents a cluster of ideas gathered around a central opposition to US alliances or intervention in conflicts outside the Western Hemisphere, particularly in Europe, and an antipathy to most forms of binding politico-military alliances.[4] These ideas can be divided into two main types—political isolationism and protectionist isolationism—with distinct points of emphasis undergirding them. Distinguished primarily by their relationship to economic determinants, both political and protectionist isolationism opposed forms of internationalism that would oblige or compel the United States to enter permanent commercial or military alliances.[5]

Traditionally, Americans who opposed restrictions on national sovereignty—that is, any limits imposed by entering into global agreements, permanent alliances, and interventions in foreign conflicts—have advocated for *political* isolationism. Often aligned with liberal market-oriented economic views, political isolationism considered free economic exchanges to be independent of politics. Because they maintained that economic ties did not entail political entanglements and did not erode American autonomy, political isolationists viewed such ties as permissible and even essential to national progress. Indeed, one group of political isolationists aggressively advocated free trade. Today, libertarians frequently have taken up this particular politically isolationist position.

Critics of foreign economic ties, on the other hand, argued that these forms of commercial exchange eroded national autonomy and self-sufficiency, especially as they shored up the processes and policies of globalization. Historically, as the US increasingly integrated into the world economy, these critics confronted the realities of global exchange, interchange, and interdependence by advocating *protectionist* isolationism. Unlike political isolationists, protectionist isolationists viewed economic exchanges as essentially political acts. They insisted that economic ties eroded American autonomy, enhanced the strength of foreign powers and their capacity to damage US standing, and increased the likelihood that the US would be dragged into endless foreign conflicts. Although political isolationism customarily monopolized the isolationist tradition, protectionist isolationism has come roaring back in recent years, and with particular virulence during the 2016 presidential election. Protectionist isolationism characterized Donald Trump's antipathy to globalization and immigration as well as his transactional and unilateral approach to international trade, including the introduction of new tariffs, and, to a lesser extent, it inflected Bernie Sanders's critical positions on trade policy, globalization, and international economic regimes.

These twenty-first-century figures constructed their arguments for a modern, contemporary isolationism on the basis of historical isolationist claims. From the 1770s onward, American thinkers and policy makers sought to build on a tradition of autonomy-based isolation in an effort to protect the world's first large-scale democracy from what they perceived as a world of corrupt monarchies. With the making of potential enemies within and without (enslaved people, indigenous peoples, European empires), the United States negotiated a tenuous position. Weakness, not strength, defined the majority of American history and therefore determined how American policy makers, thinkers, activists, military leaders, and citizens tended to understand their nation's "traditional" place in the world. Through the late nineteenth century and, for many, well into the twentieth century, US leaders and citizens alike tended to prefer foreign policy and military and diplomatic strategies that shielded the country's autonomy, avoided expending scarce power abroad, and fended off European, especially British, encroachment.

New variations on isolationist political and protectionist points of emphasis borrowed from and updated old traditions. Focused on non-entanglement and unilateralism, these historical isolationist arguments emphasized neutrality, self-sufficiency, hemispherism or continentalism, the temporary (ad hoc) nature of alliances and treaties, and American exceptionalism, as well as specific invocations of America's domestic and global mission, shadings of laissez-faire economics, and an aim to minimize war (whether doctrinally pacifist or conditionally antiwar). These isolationist points of emphasis appeared in vastly different contexts—in addition to the more narrowly defined diplomatic terms, military strategies, or specific foreign policy proposals—supporting progressive and racial reform at home, for example, or underpinning evangelical missionary efforts abroad. In the isolationism that emerged in the so-called "interwar" period, when the term "isolationism" itself came into usage, unilateralism, neutrality, and non-entanglement remained central, but the different strains and variations that had proliferated in prior decades informed the specific methods, directions, institutions, and articulations that interwar isolationists pursued.

If we follow Daniel Rodgers's methodological injunction to emphasize the "agenda-setting role of ideas," we can better appreciate how these variations had political consequences on "new world(s) of social experience and appropriable policy models."[6] In his 1936 work *Peace or War*, for example, the historian Merle Curti observed that the isolationist tradition could not be understood outside the context of American history. As Curti argued, "What Americans did to limit or to uproot the war system was at every point affected by the traditions and ideals of American life which were dominant in varying degrees at different times."[7] American policy makers and citizens alike, from the early years of the republic through the First World War, were informed by immigration, technological and social changes, the frontier, European ideas, religion, and "above all the rise of nationalism." Because Americans had tended to equate international engagement with the "war system" (and especially European intrigues), Curti explained, they habitually defaulted to an uncompromising policy of neutrality and nonintervention, rejecting the pacifist potential of cooperative internationalism. In other words, the isolationist perspective set the agenda for US foreign policy, restricting the available models for US foreign relations and molding the competing visions of the US role in the world.

This chapter builds on such insights to analyze the intellectual foundations of American isolationism and the ways in which it intersected with notions of interventionism, war, and peace. In so doing, it draws two lessons from the history of US foreign policy: first, that isolationism amounts to an intellectual tradition that has shaped foreign policy thought since the 1790s; and, second, that isolationist arguments cannot be understood without considering their domestic and transnational contexts. Just as isolationism shaped US domestic and foreign politics and policies, those politics and policies shaped the development and application of later isolationist arguments.[8]

"Creedal" Nation's Foreign Policy Precedents

Because the United States began as a revolutionary republic, its leaders and activists often had to invent the concepts and practices of a democracy's foreign policy. As a result, the US comprises an odd amalgam of affinities, particularly in foreign relations, among which relative isolation from foreign entanglements has served as a fundamental foreign policy precedent. In part, this position stemmed from the geographic and historical conditions in which the country developed. From first contact, the colonies and colonials themselves were linked by a shared geographical separation and by varied ideological separations from the Old World, whether they came to the colonies to escape political repression, religious oppression, or economic adversity, or to search for success via exploration and adventure.[9] Yet their sense of ideological and geographic isolation never fully reflected the material reality of their situation. The continent's indigenous peoples lived side by side with newcomers to the English colonies, not to mention the other European empires operating in their under-defined spheres of colonial interest, putting the lie to any vision of complete isolation. The separation from Europe, or from the rest of the world, was never anywhere near complete.

Given that the nation developed partially because of the international and domestic slave trade, as well as through a systematic settler-colonial advance against indigenous peoples, the fantasy of "isolation" represented a self-serving assertion of power (real, imagined, and aspirational) that tacitly acknowledged the illusory nature of its control. Ideas about isolation emerged from and coexisted with profound contradictions about the meaning of freedom and conditions of security, in light of the challenges from the French, Spanish, and British empires, as well as from enslaved people and Native Americans. No wonder that so many people in the fledgling democracy felt everything could change in an instant.[10] Ultimately, their attempt to establish a firm footing in foreign policy through tradition and precedent—linking foreign policy initiatives to iconic founders and key moments—was influenced by the widespread concerns about the temporality of the US project.

In the archival record, Americans frame an exceptionalist sense of US history from the nation's origins, proclaiming its destiny as both singularly precarious and messianic. Though other nations evolved through different stages before their current political configurations, Stanley Cavell contends, the United States project was that of a "creedal" nation—a nation founded on a shared idea or set of ideals rather than via a common material history. As a result, according to Cavell, "before there was Russia, there was Russia; before there was France and England, there was France and England; but before there was America there was no America. America was discovered, and what was discovered was not a place, one among others, but a setting, the backdrop of a destiny."[11] This account does not represent an accurate description of the material processes involved in "discovery," of course. Rather, it reflects the shared beliefs that fundamentally informed many Americans' sense of their country's inherent fragility. In this sense, as Cavell argued, the country's present is "continuously ridiculed by the fantastic promise of its origin and its possibility." To the extent that Americans framed their nation as elect, therefore, they inherently premised its exceptionalist mission on the possibility of failure and dissolution. Unlike the governing classes of France or Russia, Cavell observed, the founders and framers of the United States wished "proof not merely of [their country's] continuance but of its existence, a fact it has never been able to take for granted."[12] Although this orientation has never been monolithic, and often has led to contentious debate and discord related to the proper course of the US at home and abroad, this tangible sense of America's ephemerality unquestionably shaped its foreign policy.

Even if they never achieved complete "isolation," the vast majority of those American colonists and, later, US citizens, fixated on steering clear from "foreign" conflict. In this context, they developed new ideas, new behaviors, and new mechanisms of interaction in relation to these other groups and peoples in their midst (and across the Atlantic). These habits of mind and general principles ultimately underpinned the new nation's foreign relations. Over time, US foreign policy ideologies—not always clearly articulated, often hotly contested, and frequently updated to meet new conditions and circumstances—constituted sets of beliefs and values that made US relations with the world not only intelligible, but also possible.[13] Intellectual history provides insights into how these perspectives fit together and how they have structured the United States' relations with the world.

Three Policy Pillars: Washington, Jefferson, and Monroe

For a nation premised on a break with the traditions of the Old World, the foreign relations of the United States have been strikingly tradition oriented. If Walter McDougall correctly characterized American foreign relations when he suggested that "confusion and discord have been the norm," it is not because the US has lacked principles as a guide, but rather because "[Americans] have canonized so many diplomatic principles since 1776 that we are pulled every which way."[14] Nonetheless, three policy pillars articulated during the early days of the republic formed the basis for American foreign relations thereafter: neutrality, unilateralism, and nonintervention. Emanating from the presidencies of Washington, Jefferson, and Monroe, these pillars provided the guidelines for the proper role of the United States in the world, particularly on issues of when, where, and how to deploy US military and diplomatic power, as well as options beyond the formal exercise of power. As a foundational pronouncement, each policy pillar coupled what scholars now term "cautious realism" with the imperative of isolation, seeking to keep the US out of power politics, foreign wars, and binding international treaties.

Washington's 1796 Farewell Address laid the foundation for American neutrality on one firm principle with a range of applications: "to steer clear of permanent alliances with any portion of the foreign world." Even before that speech, Washington had established the nation's neutrality as a formal policy with the Proclamation of Neutrality (1793) and the Neutrality Act (1794), both of which contravened the Revolutionary-era alliance with France. Officially, these declarations asserted the guiding position that America would pursue "a conduct friendly and impartial towards the Belligerent powers" during the French Revolution, distancing the US from allies and enemies alike. In his Farewell Address (partly written by Alexander Hamilton and James Madison and read in Congress almost every year until recently), George Washington set an explicitly isolationist tone. He did not advocate a walled-and-bounded nation, as the dominant but flawed understanding of isolationism suggests, but, rather, he emphasized the limits of US power in light of the young nation's commercial, cultural, and intellectual interests in the world.[15] In short, Washington's address aimed to nurture the safety of the state during its early development.

Accounting for the fragility of American power and the nation's precarious place in the world, Washington's address recognized that geographical distance from Europe permitted the nation's "isolation," and it framed this "isolation" as both the key to the nation's strategic separation and a brake on its potential involvement in Europe's hazardous political turmoil.[16] Building on the notion of the United States as a neutral and impartial nation, with inherently limited power, Washington constructed the classic formulation of American foreign policy:

> The great rule of conduct for us, in regard to foreign nations, is in extending our commercial relations, to have with them as little political connection as possible.... Europe has a set of primary interests, which to us have none, or a very remote relation. Hence she must be engaged in frequent controversies the causes of which are essentially foreign to our concern.... Therefore, it must be unwise in us to implicate ourselves, by artificial ties, in the ordinary vicissitudes of her politics, or the ordinary combinations and collisions of her friendships or enmities.[17]

As many scholars have noted, Washington's statement projected a form of realism in foreign policy, arguing for a cautious place in the global order. These principles did not turn the nation away from the world, but instead advocated for flexibility in choosing, as Washington put it, "war or peace, as our interest, guided by justice, shall counsel." In making American neutrality the cornerstone of formal policy, the address established an Old World–New World divide, affirmed US interests and ideals as discrete from those of other countries, and prioritized commerce over the vicissitudes of international politics. This speech provided the basis for virtually all subsequent invocations of a "tradition" in American foreign relations.[18]

Because the French did not formally invoke the terms of the 1778 treaty in the 1790s or thereafter, no one challenged the new US stance at the outset. Thomas Jefferson confirmed his commitment to Washington's precedent in his 1801 inaugural address, succinctly framing his own version as "peace, commerce, and honest friendship with all nations, entangling alliances with none." During his presidency, Jefferson fought to harmonize this delimited foreign policy perspective with his more "continental" understanding of America's potential and his desire to emphasize agriculture in building a "republican empire." While Jefferson's inaugural stressed the practicality of avoiding alliances and conflicts with the Old World, he still pursued the Louisiana Purchase in 1803, which resulted in a treaty with France that doubled the nation's territory. When Jefferson came under fire for acquiring the Louisiana Territory, he insisted that it remained consistent with Washington's unilateralist vision of isolation as protecting national sovereignty because it limited the amount of North American land that European powers could claim. In addition to Jefferson's interest in balancing empires, economic incentives motivated him to make the purchase. Besides opening up hundreds of thousands of square miles of arable land to American settlers, it secured the port of New Orleans for American markets and, through it, established a bulwark against foreign interference.

Nonetheless, the purchase also pushed an "empire for liberty" upon the native peoples and others residents who occupied large swaths of the newly acquired land, and arguably increased the long-term likelihood that the US would come into conflict with one or another of the empires on its borders, whether colonial or native.[19] Furthermore, the economic opportunities offered by the new land simultaneously enmeshed the US in imperial economic networks that further implicated it in international affairs and politics. In their foreign policy formulations, both Washington and Jefferson treated foreign economic and political concerns discretely, as if they could be neatly divided, but that was never the case. Economic interests were never a neutral force, and defense of them dragged the US into foreign conflicts almost as soon as Washington took office.[20]

Just over twenty years later, President James Monroe rearticulated this circumspect view of American power in what came to be known as the Monroe Doctrine. Largely the vision and grand strategy of Secretary of State John Quincy Adams, the Monroe Doctrine offered an ambitious expression of American hemispheric power. Though not particularly momentous when introduced, this Monroevian position evolved to become a guiding view and near-constant referent for later foreign policy advocates of both intervention and isolation. It reaffirmed Washington and Jefferson's unilateralist aversion to foreign involvement in US affairs, while also expanding the geographical territory that official US policy would consider as part of those affairs. "With the movements in this hemisphere we are of necessity more immediately connected," Monroe declared; therefore, "we should consider any attempt on their [European powers'] part to extend their system to any portion of this hemisphere as dangerous to our peace and safety."[21] In the process of extending Washington's doctrine of nonintervention to the entire North and South American continents, Monroe established a precedent that later politicians would use to justify expansion, occupation, and colonization across the Western Hemisphere. Further, the Monroe Doctrine expressed an early iteration of the doctrine of what can properly be understood as popular sovereignty, in which newly independent governments determined their own political systems without outside interference (so long as those governments remained friendly to US interests). Nominally democratic, the doctrine took on a paternalistic bent in its application. For many of its later proponents, the doctrine authorized unilateral involvement across the Americas, while reinforcing the proscription against foreign entanglements beyond the Western Hemisphere, and, especially, Washington's warning to avoid the corruptions of Old World political intrigues.

In three audacious strokes, Washington, Jefferson, and Monroe laid out the isolationist mode of thinking, an intellectual framework for American foreign relations that continues to frame US foreign policy. As later politicians, thinkers, and citizens built their own cases for engagement abroad, they had to confront these benchmarks. In this way, an isolationist orientation factored into the worldviews of policy makers, even in the negative space. Regardless of whether they rejected these three policy pillars in light of changing geopolitical conditions, policy makers still had to justify their positions in reference to this tradition.[22] This is ever-evolving; Washingtonion, Jeffersonian, and Monroevian notions continue to be updated to underpin a range of perspectives on the US's "proper" role in the world from across the political spectrum. These policy pillars can be seen in contemporary politics, including forms of nativism and anti-immigrant rhetoric, liberal anti-interventionism, and skepticism about collective security.[23]

In spite of the fact that the United States engaged with foreign powers through treaties, wars, and land purchases—and everyone from missionaries to merchants regularly interacted with foreign governments—"isolation" persisted as the default setting for American policy makers and citizens alike through much of the nineteenth century. So long as US power, particularly its naval capacity, remained modest, statesmen purported that the limits of American democracy came "at water's edge." For most of this period, the Atlantic and Pacific Oceans enabled the US to enjoy a kind of "free security," as C. Vann Woodward termed it, keeping it largely detached from Old World conflicts (even if it was pulled, at least tangentially, into every confrontation that impacted the Atlantic). As the Whig Henry Clay noted when the Hungarian revolutionary Louis Kossuth solicited American aid for his cause in 1852, the US entertained the "liveliest sympathies in every struggle for liberty in Hungary," but they would not intercede with material aid. The United States had "done more for the cause of liberty in the world" in its exemplary role, Clay explained, than force of arms could accomplish. "Far better is it for ourselves, for Hungary, and for the cause of liberty," Clay concluded, "that, adhering to our wise, pacific system, and avoiding the distant wars of Europe, we should keep our lamp burning brightly on this western shore as a light for all nations, than to hazard its utter extinction amid the ruins of fallen and falling republics in Europe." Indeed, the US lacked the money, the manpower, and the means to intervene overseas in this period, making it all the easier to maintain the "policy [of nonintervention] to which we have adhered since the days of Washington."[24]

Although European policy makers recognized that the US posed a long-term economic threat, it posed virtually no military threat to the major European powers. Besides its physical distance from Europe, the country's minuscule military and relative industrial and institutional weakness presented little for Europe to worry about in the short term. As a result, US policy makers enjoyed significant latitude in fashioning the nation's foreign affairs, employing what would later be called "soft power" politics that eschewed military alliances and commitments while fostering commercial, cultural, and religious international exchanges.[25] In this way, the US developed along the lines that William Appleman Williams termed "imperial anticolonialism," a process by which the US expanded to gain new lands and markets—whether through public governmental channels or the informal commercial and social activities of individual citizens and groups—as its primary means of engaging with foreign powers, solving domestic problems, and fulfilling its national promise.[26]

This brand of isolationism, highly selective in its application, supported nonintervention in behalf of strategically advantageous and democratically inclined hemispheric companions, but failed to extend to regions and peoples whose geographic, economic, and sociopolitical subjugation served the "national" interest. In the antebellum period, both major political parties expressed variations of this hybrid isolationist-expansionist orientation, which authorized a set of policies that avoided overseas intervention, while exploiting hemispheric neighbors (following the core conceit of the Monroe Doctrine) and advancing the avaricious interests of American slaveholders. In general, the Whigs pursued treaties with European governments, but opposed territorial acquisition, liberal immigration policies, and expansionist military engagements. On the other side, the Democrats uniformly voted against foreign treaties while promoting geographic expansion and endorsing the resulting wars. In their schema, proponents of American imperial adventurism insisted, neither the annexation of Texas in 1845 nor the massive land-grab following the Mexican-American War in 1848 violated Washington's injunction against overseas entanglements or their country's unofficial commitment to unilateralist neutrality.[27] Why? Because these foreign policy maneuvers were fundamentally "continental," unilateral, or could be cast as "defensive."

Meanwhile, as the southern and northern states came into conflict over the new territories and their transition into (slave or free) states, they laid out the basic arguments for "nonintervention" and "self-determination" that would come to play such a large role in twentieth-century foreign policy. Of course, in the case most southern politicians, they advocated specifically for "nonintervention" of the federal government into slave-state affairs and "self-determination" for states to establish the institution of slavery if they chose. When it served their interests, southern and northern politicians alike sought to expand territorially, intervene abroad, or meddle in the affairs of other peoples. Throughout this period, for example, Congress debated purchasing Cuba from Spain, with US pro-slavery groups vacillating over whether they wanted it or not, based on where Cuba's slave-politics stood. Similarly, what counted as nonintervention and neutrality depended on a combination of opportunism, geopolitical conditions, and domestic dynamics. In case after case, however, from Hungary to Haiti, US policy makers stepped back from defending the interests of fellow democrats around the world, opting instead to protect the nation's own interests at home and on its borders. This habitual choice solidified the isolationist position—both as tradition and as policy.

After the Civil War demonstrated the fragility of the American project, the US turned inward, pursuing a defensive and isolationist foreign policy centered on the idea that domestic reform at home would obviate the need to engage politically abroad. In his first State of the Union message, Andrew Johnson reiterated that the country remained "singularly independent of the varying policy of foreign powers," protected by its size, climate, and geography from the "temptation to entangling alliances," in Jefferson's turn of phrase.[28] With all of its wants supplied by its own soil, the US could focus its attention on the "re-establishment of harmony, and the strength that comes from harmony," which would be the country's "best security" against "nations who feel power and forget right," Johnson argued, alluding to Jefferson's first inaugural. As the nation engaged in domestic reconstruction, Johnson refused outside help on the grounds that it violated Washington's injunction against foreign interference. In the late 1860s, when Great Britain volunteered to oversee a joint commission to settle US war damages, Johnson declined, claiming that joint arbitration violated US neutrality, distracted US politicians and citizens from peacefully settling their own domestic affairs, and set a dangerous precedent in international law. Johnson's stance established a precedent for reform-focused isolationism, where US leaders would respond to international crises and instability by fixating on internal reform.

As the world grew more interconnected toward the end of the nineteenth century, the US cycles of economic boom and bust resulted in a rising imperative to reform domestic society that reinforced essential ideas about isolation. As Johnson had, Grover Cleveland invoked America's isolationist tradition to justify his inwardly focused plan for reform in his first inaugural address. "The genius of our institutions, the needs of our people in their home life, and the attention which is demanded for the settlement and development of the resources of our vast territory," Cleveland intoned, all "dictate the scrupulous avoidance of any departure from that foreign policy commended by the history, the traditions, and the prosperity of our Republic." Rejecting pressures to project US power abroad through naval buildup or territorial acquisition, Cleveland adhered to what he saw as the country's bedrock policy of "neutrality," continuously "rejecting any share in foreign broils and ambitions upon other continents and repelling their intrusions here."[29] While in office, he followed through with these commitments, immediately shutting down the Frelinghuysen-Zavala Treaty between the US and Nicaragua during his first term, which would have authorized an isthmus canal, and resisting the urge to annex Hawaii during his second administration. Keeping in line with the distinction that Washington and Jefferson had made between foreign economic and political entanglements, Cleveland pushed trade and cultural exchange but maintained a defensive foreign policy, interceding on behalf of American material interests as a last resort and only to enforce prior commitments (e.g., in Panama and Samoa).

The US took an increasingly visible role in world affairs at the turn of the twentieth century, making the isolationist position seem increasingly untenable. In particular, politicians, intellectuals, activists, and policy makers all struggled to justify the unprecedented annexation of territory *outside* the continental US with the country's nominal commitment to neutrality, unilateralism, and nonintervention. To square extra-continental extension directly involving European nations, the Monroe Doctrine took on a new global-hemispheric dimension. In 1895–1896, for example, the Massachusetts Republican senator Henry Cabot Lodge insinuated the United States into a boundary dispute between Venezuela and Great Britain over a resource-rich area being claimed by British Guiana. In this case, Lodge invoked the Monroe Doctrine as long-standing US policy, giving the British cover to accept US arbitration, the conditions of which overwhelmingly favored US cognizance. Lodge's newly expansive doctrine deployed a view of unilateral coercion that granted the US authority to subordinate the interests of foreign governments to its own. Lodge returned to this updated form of isolationist imperialism in 1898, making the case that the US had both the right and the imperative to annex Puerto Rico, Hawaii, the Philippines, and other territories unilaterally because, from his perspective, US material needs outweighed these places' claims to sovereignty or inchoate autonomy. In addition to strategic coaling stations, naval bases, and harbors to help project US power and protect its interests, Lodge noted, the US needed new markets to help grow its economy.

This interpretation set the stage in international law and diplomacy for other countries to adapt the Monroe Doctrine to their own ends. In the early twentieth century, imperialist powers justified their own local-regional hegemony as spheres of influence according to the precedent established by US doctrine. The British made such claims for India and Australia; the Japanese in Southeast Asia; and Russia, Germany, and others followed suit. For many historians analyzing the Monroe Doctrine, such as William Appleman Williams, Dexter Perkins, and, more recently, Jay Sexton, these later invocations underscore the implicitly imperialist nature of the Monroe Doctrine. As the history of the Monroe Doctrine and the historiography of its adaptations underscore, the development and application of isolationist arguments in US foreign policy and politics can be best understood in their transnational context. In turn, this context clarifies the complexity of the isolationist tradition in both its imperialist and anticolonial iterations.[30]

For example, in the 1910s, the antiwar cultural critic Randolph Bourne generated an alternative to this type of belligerent, imperialist nationalism in a theory of transnationalism that fused a soft type of isolationism to a pluralistic ideal.[31] His self-described "below the battle" politics were neither a retreat nor a position taken outside the fray, but rather a "third way" formula for creating an alternative politics.[32] Bourne's program for a "transnational America" combined fierce pluralistic and progressive reform at home, avid pacifistic internationalism abroad, and passionate advocacy for a noninterventionist American role in the world. Composed "of a freely mingling society of peoples of very different racial and cultural antecedents," Bourne's "transnational" Americans would share "a common political allegiance and common social ends but with free and distinctive cultural allegiances which may be placed anywhere in the world they like."[33] In this hybrid cosmopolitanism, Bourne imagined a "wholly novel international nation" woven "out of our chaotic America" that would "liberate and harmonize the creative power of all these peoples and give them the new spiritual citizenship, as so many individuals have already been given, of a world." In the context of World War I, Bourne's work adapted the tradition of American isolationist foreign policy to the irrevocably interconnected twentieth-century global order. In spite of its geographic and political isolation, he noted, the United States could no longer stand aloof from the world, but its historical separation from European affairs and the reality of its cultural hybridity had generated an unprecedented platform on which the US could build this new kind of transnational consciousness. Indeed, he argued, the "traditional isolation" of the US, combined with its "unique liberty of opportunity," made it the "only" country that could "lead this cosmopolitan enterprise."[34]

In spite of Bourne's generous reading of the idealistic potential of US isolationist foreign policy, most isolationists continued to stress the unilateralist components of their tradition. In this way we see some clear connections from the World War I era to the present and near past. Bourne and Bernie Sanders's anticapitalist and anti-imperialist critiques echo each other. Similarly, post–World War I partial retrenchment, anti–League of Nations, anti–World Court, and anti-immigration positions bear significant resemblance to Pat Buchanan's 1991–1992 "America First" presidential campaign against international collective security organizations, trade regimes, and multilateral accords, as well as immigration. Strikingly similar, too, are the resonances with the Trumpist/Bannonist visions of ethno-nationalist self-determination in which the same phrase—"America First"—is used to promote a view of American isolation that separates the country from the corrupting elements of an impure or undeserving world, yet secures the best from international exchange unilaterally while limiting exposure to multilateralism or judgments and ties from abroad (e.g., foreclosure of the proposed Trans Pacific Partnership, withdrawal from the Paris Climate Accords). When Bourne criticized what was to become the nationalist (and vindictive postwar) basis for the League of Nations, he did so not because he distrusted foreign alliances or leagues a priori, but because he did not trust the particular nations in the League to repudiate their own militarism and parochialism unconditionally. In contrast, when Lodge and his fellow "Reservationists" stood against the League in Congress, joining with the anti-imperialist Idaho Republican William Borah and his "Irreconcilables," they did so on the grounds that it violated both the strategic and unilateralist intent of the Monroe Doctrine, as well as the traditional Washingtonian injunction against entangling alliances. As chairman of the Senate Committee on Foreign Relations, Lodge summarized the unilateralist interpretation of the Monroe Doctrine in its most direct formulation. "The real essence of [the Monroe] doctrine is that American questions shall be settled by Americans alone," Lodge claimed. He took a hard line against European interference that separated "American freedom and order" from, for example, "Russian anarchy and destruction."[35]

Similarly, in his writings against the League, the publisher George Harvey singled out its "attack" on the Monroe Doctrine as its most "insidious" and "dangerous" feature. In attempting to define the doctrine, Harvey contended, the Covenant of the League of Nations took an unprecedented step, abrogating the exclusive authority of the US to interpret and apply the doctrine as it saw fit, as the proprietary expression of its national policy.[36] In a 1923 speech, Harvey, then serving as the US ambassador to Great Britain, reiterated that the doctrine sustained a "purely American principle," "of American origin exclusively and absolutely," "unchanged and unchangeable by any President, any Congress, or any Court, for the simple reason that it is implanted in the will of the American people, who alone in the United States possess sovereign powers." Still, like Bourne, Harvey recognized the need to update the doctrine to meet the transformation in world affairs since its original expression. The "living part of the Monroe Doctrine which confronts us today" fused the political independence of the US with a "practical idealism" that left it the liberty and the leverage to come to the strategic aid of "men" in "need." In this way, Harvey alleged, it "continues to be, in all its phases, the cornerstone of our national policy," which the United States "is fully warranted in considering and upholding . . . as a part of the modern international code of the civilized world."[37]

This capsule history reveals some of the ways in which progressive—or organic—self-government ultimately served an isolationist (or at least a non-interventionist) position in American foreign policy. In this test case, isolationist ideas operate counterintuitively to the assumptions many critics have of US foreign policy; these critics have tended to portray the idea, or set of ideas and related principles regarding isolationism, in grossly simplified and negativistic ways. The varied visions of US foreign policy represented here demonstrate the malleability of ideological choices arising from long-standing tradition, especially when linked to a progressive narrative of democratic government, localism, and other notions of self-government.[38] Thus, an intellectual history of an isolationism "tradition" provides a counternarrative of sorts to the more common view of American belligerency.

Narratives and New Lenses of Analysis

This brief history of isolationism as a counternarrative dovetails with current work on grand strategy, which offers fresh ways of conceptualizing the role of ideas and intellectuals in foreign policy making. Traditionally, grand strategy has been located in more formal studies of strategic thought and action directly related to war and great-power politics. In recent years, however, scholars have extended their approach to grand strategy beyond strictly military analyses to other fields of study, such as history, security studies, and political science. The expanded understanding of grand strategy emerging in this new scholarship is better understood as an epistemology—that is, a theory of knowledge about international relations that organizes outcomes around methods, means, and desired ends. By examining grand strategy as an epistemology, scholars can explore the process by which experts and policy makers arrive at specific foreign policy solutions and configure those solutions as the particular expression of larger presuppositions, shared foundations and processes, the joint production of knowledge, and the extent, validity, and scope of their outcomes. This epistemological approach becomes especially relevant for twenty- and twenty-first-century formulations of US grand strategy, as foreign policy increasingly became the purview of experts institutionalized at a handful of scholastic centers for international affairs.[39]

According to the historian Perry Anderson, the early twentieth century marked the beginning of an imperialist-intellectual intersection in US foreign policy—when a door (subsequently revolving) opened between academia and government. Anderson argued that the intersection of ideas and interests clinches the historical case for material drivers. Generally, his grand strategists were bent on making the US a world power, or hegemon. Although Anderson's economic determinism takes ideas and thinkers seriously, materialism ultimately shapes the history he chronicles in his "Imperium." In what might be termed a "reverse-exceptionalist" case, Anderson largely confirms the thesis put forward by William Appleman Williams and the Wisconsin school at midcentury—that an economic engine propelled the American ship of state as the nation rose in military and commercial power. In "Consilium," the second segment of Anderson's influential analysis, he grounds these insights in their intellectual foundations. He eviscerates the American "grand strategists," who "axiomatically" believed in the country's global leadership. In Anderson's telling, their historical-intellectual interpretations led to an exceptionalist hubris that united them across diverse political positions (including neoconservatives and liberal internationalists, realists and idealists) in their shared belief in the power of US hegemony "to serve both the particular interests of the nation and the universal interests of humanity."[40]

As David Milne has rightly pointed out, this unanimity conveys a great deal, as well, about scholastic disciplines and intellectual training. Virtually all these grand strategists were also grand "scientists," political scientists and international relations scholars trained in the methods of foreign affairs at "Paul Nitze's SAIS [School of Advanced International Studies] and its emulators: the Wilson, Kennedy, Fletcher, and Walsh Schools."[41] Having been trained by the same group of people, in a relatively uniform cluster of methods and ideas, these foreign policy experts then consistently advocated a scientistic interventionism on strategic and moral grounds. Over time, Milne demonstrates, they transformed the United States' "traditional quest for liberty" into a policy of intervention, at odds with traditional foreign policy ideas that sought to avoid foreign entanglements and warned against going abroad in search of monsters to destroy. In *The Limits of Power: The End of American Exceptionalism*, Andrew Bacevich reached a similar conclusion. Whether or not the US ever lived up to its isolationist ideals, Bacevich identifies the Vietnam era as the historical moment when the country firmly rejected them. This had been the crucible moment when Americans and their leaders, faced with the choice of "curb[ing] their appetites and learn[ing] to live within their means," or deploying "United States power in hopes of obliging others to accommodate," chose to overreach.[42] For Bacevich, the Iraq War serves as the ultimate confirmation of this historical trajectory.

A grand strategy epistemology expands our historical reach and perspective to move beyond historical accounts that tend toward (over)emphasis on military means or state actors. Such an analysis cannot ignore high-level figures, groups, or power, and yet must also include "the range of cultural conditions which shape the perceptions strategists have of material conditions" as well as the outcomes they seek.[43] Grand strategic internationalism as an epistemological model might usefully refer to an idea or set of ideas, a movement, or an association or cultural internationalist institution. In its epistemological formulation, grand strategic internationalism logically flows from the isolationist tradition for which the three policy pillars served as a structuring idea-system, which established a set of vital interests, delimited policy options, and provided a check on nonstrategic interference in foreign affairs.[44] Or, to borrow the terms of Charles Edel's and Hal Brands's recent work, the concept and practice of grand strategy can be used to examine the "intellectual architecture that lends structure" to foreign policy. This expanded view also lends structure and direction to relations beyond the scope of the conventional nation-state.[45]

I have argued for the significance of an isolationist tradition and, specifically, for scholars to take seriously the three policy pillars that form the foundations for debating, adapting, or rejecting US foreign policies. Still, before concluding, I must address a concern that has vexed scholars of foreign relations, in particular—and intellectual historians, in general—and that sits at the heart of debates over the constituent parts of any given grand strategy: causality and the role of ideas. If we take ideas seriously, then how should we understand the "role of ideas" and of intellectuals in constructing US foreign policy? And, further, who counts as a foreign policy intellectual? These interlocking questions are deceptively simple, but their answers hold important implications for our project as intellectual historians.[46] The "role of" implies causality, for example, and yet the exact relationship of cause and effect is often elusive in the historical record. Locating causality is arguably even more tenuous, and subtle, in the historical record regarding ideas and ideologies. Perry Anderson's materialistic (Marxist) understanding of ideas helps shed some light on this conundrum; he takes ideas seriously only insofar as they channeled material (economic) drivers. In contrast to Anderson, I have aimed to show that ideas have more power than as (mere) reflections of materialistic developments. The constellation of ideas developed, updated, applied, and debated about the advantages and disadvantages of forms of isolation reveals the significance and shaping effects of an isolationist intellectual tradition. From Washington, Jefferson, and Monroe in the early republic, to the imperialists, irreconcilables, and legal internationalists of the interwar years, to the most recent politics of immigration restriction, anti-NATO and anti-UN sentiment, tariffs and protectionism, along with opposition to trade accords such as NAFTA and the Trans-Pacific Partnership, isolationist ideas and their attendant "tradition" have played a crucial "agenda-setting" role in US foreign policy, often hotly debated or used in the negative as an epithet intended to spur a rejection of such notions and related actions.[47]

NOTES

The author would like to thank the editors of this volume, Raymond Haberski and Andrew Hartman, and the participants in this project for their generous reading and comments. Special thanks are due to David Milne for his reading of the chapter and to Danielle Holtz for her research and editing assistance. Work on this chapter was supported by an Andrew Carnegie fellowship from the Carnegie Corporation of New York. This chapter presents some of the key arguments that will be forthcoming in the Carnegie-supported American Isolationism project. Aspects of this chapter draw on and adapt ideas and sections from my previous publications, including *Promise and Peril: America at the Dawn of a Global Age* (Cambridge, MA: Harvard University Press, 2011); "The Enduring Power of Isolationism: An Historical Perspective," *Orbis: A Journal of World Affairs* 57, no. 3 (Summer 2013): 390–407; and "Rethinking Randolph Bourne's Trans-National America: How World War I Created an Isolationist Antiwar Pluralism," *Journal of the Gilded Age and Progressive Era* 8, no. 2 (April 2009): 217–57. This analysis is indebted to close readings of a wide array of archival sources, most notably scores of presidential and political speeches and correspondence and foreign policy documents, from the collections of the Library of Congress and the *Foreign Relations of the United States* series.

This chapter derives its subtitle from the title of Frederick Jackson Turner's famous paper, given at the annual meeting of the American Historical Association in 1893, and also adapts one of his central ideas about the new institutional tradition the US developed to shape its policies and expansion. "Behind institutions, behind constitutional forms and modifications, lie the vital forces that call these organs into life and shape them to meet changing conditions," wrote Turner in 1893. In articulating the "significance of the frontier to American history" Turner argued that an essential peculiarity of the historical development of American institutions is the fact that they have been compelled to adapt themselves to a wide variety of changes and challenges in foreign as well as domestic arenas, and yet have tended to be reliant on forms of tradition (even recent ones befitting a young nation) to help guide them. We see much the same in US foreign policy thought and practice, thus my argument for the significance of an isolationist tradition. Frederick Jackson Turner, "The Significance of the Frontier in American History," paper read at the meeting of the American Historical Association in Chicago, July 12, 1893; Turner, *The Frontier in American History* (New York: Henry Holt, 1921), 1.

1. The statements of the historian G. M. Young epitomize this sort of dismissal. While there was an element of truth in his assessment, in all fairness, the bulk of the best older diplomatic history hardly deserved this critique any more than the newer cultural and transnational work does.

2. Some of the recent groundbreaking works include Mary Dudziak, *War Time: An Idea, Its History, Its Consequences* (New York: Oxford University Press, 2012); David Milne, *Worldmaking: The Art and Science of American Diplomacy* (New York: Farrar, Straus and Giroux, 2015); David Engerman, *Know Your Enemy: The Rise and Fall of America's Soviet Experts* (New York: Oxford University Press, 2011); Eliga Gould, *Among the Powers of the Earth: The American Revolution and the Making of a New World Empire* (Cambridge, MA: Harvard University Press, 2012); Michaela Hoenicke-Moore, *Know Your Enemy: The American Debate on Nazism, 1933–1945* (Cambridge: Cambridge University Press, 2009); Elizabeth Borgwardt, *A New Deal for the World: America's Vision for Human Rights* (Cambridge, MA: Belknap Press of Harvard University Press, 2005); Paul Kramer, *The Blood of Government: Race, Empire, the United States, and the Philippines* (Chapel Hill: University of North Carolina Press, 2006); Erez Manela, *The Wilsonian Moment: Self-Determination and the International Origins of Anticolonial Nationalism* (New York: Oxford University Press, 2007); Brooke Blower, *Becoming Americans in Paris: Transatlantic Politics and Culture between the World Wars* (New York: Oxford University Press, 2011); Andrew Preston, *Sword of the Spirit, Shield of Faith: Religion in American War and Diplomacy* (New York: Alfred A. Knopf, 2012); Daniel Immerwahr, *Thinking Small: The United States and the Lure of Community Development* (Cambridge, MA: Harvard University Press, 2015); Daniel Bessner, *Democracy in Exile: Hans Speier and the Rise of the Defense Intellectual* (Ithaca, NY: Cornell University Press, forthcoming).

3. Emily Rosenberg's superb edited collection *A World Connecting, 1870–1945* (Cambridge, MA: Belknap Press of Harvard University Press, 2012), which traces intensifying networks of globalization from the 1870s to 1945, epitomizes the current direction of this scholarship, as does similar work emphasizing "connectedness" by scholars including Ian Tyrrell, Thomas Bender, Daniel Rodgers, and Carl Guarneri. These works situate the US within a global historical perspective. Other recent works that reflect the breadth of this new common project include the following topics: an intellectual-legal analysis of the concept of wartime; the rise of Sovietology in the US; the art and science of diplomatic "world making," nation making, and treaty-worthiness in the Revolutionary era; Wilsonian ideas about self-determination and the international origins of anticolonial nationalism; the political discourse of Nazism before World War II; and the rise of the defense "intellectual." These studies reveal some of the dynamic, expansive approaches to US foreign relations topics in which ideas and intellectuals play central roles. See Daniel Rodgers, *Atlantic Crossings: Social Politics in a Progressive Age* (Cambridge, MA: Belknap Press of Harvard University Press, 1998); Thomas Bender, ed., *Rethinking American History in a Global Age* (Berkeley: University of California Press, 2002) and his *Nation among Nations*; Ian Tyrrell, *Transnational Nation: United States History in Global Perspective since 1789* (New York: Palgrave Macmillan, 2011) and his *Reforming the World: The Creation of America's Moral Empire* (Princeton: Princeton University Press, 2010); Carl Guarneri, *America in the World: United States History in Global Context* (New York: McGraw Hill, 2007) and his textbooks entitled *America Compared: American History in International Perspective* (Boston: Wadsworth, 2005). On icons and iconic texts see Brooke Blower and Mark P. Bradley, eds., *The Familiar Made Strange: American Icons and Artifacts after the Transnational Turn* (Ithaca, NY: Cornell University Press, 2015). Religion has been a particularly productive lens of analysis to explore an expanded view of the history of the US in the world; see Preston, *Sword of the Spirit*; Gene Zubovich, "The Global Gospel: Protestant Internationalism and American Liberalism in the Twentieth Century," a talk for the

Department of American Studies, St. Louis University, March 31, 2017; and Ian Tyrrell's work. Particularly exceptional recent examples of this work include Michael Thompson, *For God and Globe: Christian Internationalism in the United States between the Great War and the Cold War* (Ithaca, NY: Cornell University Press, 2015) and Emily Conroy-Krutz, *Christian Imperialism: Converting the World in the Early American Republic* (Ithaca, NY: Cornell University Press, 2015).

4. On the main typologies of isolationism see "Strains of Isolationism" in Nichols, *Promise and Peril*, 347–52.

5. These definitions are elaborated in my *Promise and Peril* (2011) and in several of my essays and articles, including an article in *Orbis* (2013).

6. Rodgers, *Atlantic Crossings*, 6. Citing John Kingdon, Rodgers notes that "ideas and problems, solutions and potential crises, circulate remarkably independently through the political stream. Generated from myriad sources, their futures depend on their finding one another. Just as a political idea becomes politically viable only when it is successfully attached to a sense of need and urgency, no less do problems become politically significant only when they become attached to politically imaginable solutions."

7. Merle Curti, *Peace or War: The American Struggle, 1636–1936* (New York: W. W. Norton, 1936), 14.

8. Some of what follows builds on my *Promise and Peril*. This chapter also represents a first analysis of this tradition as part of my new study of isolationist ideas from the founders to the present.

9. Even though colonial residents of European extraction tended to see themselves as nationals of their sovereign (largely as English subjects), their writings and actions reveal that they understood that their distance in space and time dictated a difference in kind for their politics and their relations with the world. This seemingly fundamental state of being and its core contradiction—both of and not of Europe—have been at the heart of US relations with Europe and with the world.

10. On the often religious character and conditions of these debates and predictions see Charles Mathewes and Christopher McKnight Nichols, eds. *Prophesies of Godlessness: Predictions of America's Imminent Secularization from the Puritans to the Present Day* (New York: Oxford University Press, 2008).

11. Stanley Cavell, "The Avoidance of Love: A Reading of King Lear," in *Must We Mean What We Say? A Book of Essays* (Cambridge: Cambridge University Press, 1976), 344–45.

12. Ibid.

13. In my view, intellectual history matters deeply to the "US in the World," in part because it can illuminate the ideas and mind-sets—as well as the widest range of intellectual actors—in terms of what Michael Hunt refers to as the "interrelated set of convictions or assumptions that reduces the complexities of a particular slice of reality to easily comprehensible terms and suggests appropriate ways of dealing with that reality." Michael Hunt, *Ideology and U.S. Foreign Policy* (New Haven, CT: Yale University Press, 1987); Michael Hunt, "Nationalism as an Umbrella Ideology," in *Explaining the History of American Foreign Relations*, 3rd ed., ed. Frank Costigliola and Michael Hogan (New York: Cambridge University Press, 2016), 217.

14. Walter McDougall, *Promised Land, Crusader State: The American Encounter with the World since 1776* (Boston: Houghton Mifflin, 1997), 4.

15. George Washington, *Farewell Address* (New York: Bedford, rept. 2002, original printing in 1796), 29–30. I am indebted to conversations with Peter Onuf in helping me to develop some of these ideas and this interpretation.

16. The word "isolation" appears in a political and foreign policy sense in some of the political writing and numerous speeches, public documents, and personal letters during America's early republic era and, more so, in terms of the attendant ideas related to

establishing the new foreign policy tradition; however, the first recorded appearance of the word "isolationist" came in 1862, during the Civil War. Prominent and repeated uses of the term "isolationist" had to wait more than thirty years, when they became more common during the Spanish-American War in 1898–1899 in debates over American intervention and imperialism. Naval expansionist and avowed imperialist Captain Alfred Thayer Mahan helped coin the nominal-epithet form of the word, describing his anti-imperial opponents—critics of the war, such as Andrew Carnegie and Mark Twain—as "isolationists." The British political context during the 1890s also served to heighten the profile and broaden the usage of the term and closely related ideas. In the 1880s and 1890s there was much talk (often ironic) of England's global power and dominion over its colonies as being supported by a policy of "splendid isolation." But it was not until the early 1920s that a conceptually thick ideological form of the word—"isolationism"—came into widespread and accepted use, on both sides of the Atlantic, to describe the irreconcilable "isolationism" espoused by those who rejected American ratification of the Treaty of Versailles, entry into the League of Nations, and other binding alliances. The outspoken senators William Borah and Robert La Follette best embodied such a position. As a relatively coherent political ideology, "isolationism" then found prominent use and meaning in the 1930s, in light of the challenges of the Depression and roiling global turmoil, as characterizing a foreign policy premised on avoiding politico-military commitments and alliances with foreign nations (particularly in Europe), following a strict path of neutrality, non-entanglement, and unilateralism, with a number of domestic policy corollaries. (Many making such arguments preferred to associate isolationist ideas and policy prescriptions with less charged labels such as hemispherism, continentalism, Americanism, and, of course, America First.) Another way to consider the etymological underpinnings of isolationism is explained by the *Oxford English Dictionary* (*OED*), which codified the Mahanian meaning of the term while advancing a less pejorative definition just after the turn into the twentieth century. The 1901 *OED* edition characterized an isolationist as "one who favors or advocates isolation. In U.S. politics one who thinks the Republic ought to pursue a policy of political isolation." Still, despite defining the term in a modern political manner, the article the *OED* cites as originating the term in the *Philadelphia Press* in March 1899 used the word in a medical context (i.e., to be "isolationist" by separating and quarantining individuals during a smallpox epidemic): see *Oxford English Dictionary* (Oxford: Oxford University Press, 1901 and 1922); see also Ronald Powaski, *Toward an Entangling Alliance* (New York: Greenwood, 1991), ix. For a more overtly conservative contemporary (quasi)isolationist political view of the term and its historical meaning (and in light of his 1991–1992 "America First" campaign) see Patrick Buchanan, *A Republic, Not an Empire* (Washington, DC: Regnery, 1999), esp. 161. For more on the term, its etymology, as well as how it has been mangled and maligned over time, see Manfred Jonas's superb brief overview on "isolationism" in the *Encyclopedia of American Foreign Policy: Studies of the Principal Movements and Ideas*, ed. Alexander DeConde (New York: Charles Scribner and Sons, 1978), 2:496–506. See Nichols, "Strains of Isolationism," in *Promise and Peril*, 347–52; Justus D. Doenecke and Christopher McKnight Nichols, "Isolationism," in *The Oxford Encyclopedia of American Military and Diplomatic History* (New York: Oxford University Press, 2013), 560–63.

17. Washington, *Farewell Address*, 30.

18. Considering that the 1778 military alliance with France helped to win the Revolution, the key precepts here are remarkable. It is incumbent on scholars to recognize, in addition to the French alliance—which Washington discarded when it was no longer self-serving—the other treaties that Washington's message elided, particularly the alliances forged with indigenous peoples. To that end, historians of the US in the world should attend to the superb work being done on American–Native American relations as US

foreign relations, which conceptualizes these relationships as part of the intellectual and ideological makeup of American foreign policy. For example, see Brian DeLay's *War of a Thousand Deserts: Indian Raids and the U.S.-Mexican War* (New Haven, CT: Yale University Press, 2008); Alexandra Harmon's *The Power of Promises: Rethinking Indian Treaties in the Pacific Northwest* (Seattle: University of Washington Press, 2008), as well as her essay "From Dispossessed Wards to Citizen Activists: American Indians Survive the Assimilation Policy Era" in *A Companion to the Gilded Age and Progressive Era*, ed. Christopher McKnight Nichols and Nancy C. Unger (Malden, MA: Wiley Blackwell, 2017), 124–36; Andrew Lipman's *The Saltwater Frontier: Indians and the Contest for the American Coast* (New Haven, CT: Yale University Press, 2015); Daniel Richter's *Facing East from Indian Country: A Native History of Early America* (Cambridge, MA: Harvard University Press, 2001); and Ned Blackhawk's *Violence over the Land: Indians and Empires in the Early American West* (Cambridge, MA: Harvard University Press, 2006). See also Matthew Kruer's PhD dissertation, which won the 2016 Allan Nevins Prize, "'Our Time of Anarchy': Bacon's Rebellion and the Wars of the Susquehannocks, 1675–1682," University of Pennsylvania, 2015.

19. Peter Onuf, *Jefferson's Empire: The Language of American Nationhood* (Charlottesville: University of Virginia Press, 2000). See also Thomas Jefferson, *Writings: Autobiography / Notes on the State of Virginia / Public and Private Papers / Addresses / Letters* (New York: Library of America, 1984). On Franklin, see Benjamin Franklin to Lord Kames, January 3, 1760, in *The Papers of Benjamin Franklin*, ed. Leonard W. Labaree (New Haven, CT: Yale University Press, 1966), 9:7. On British debates about expansion and America's "empire" see Felix Gilbert, *To the Farewell Address: Ideas of Early American Foreign Policy* (Princeton, NJ: Princeton University Press, 1961), 33–35. Also, Gerald Stourzh, *Benjamin Franklin and American Foreign Policy*, 2nd ed. (Chicago: University of Chicago Press, 1969), Franklin quote on 120.

20. Here I include, of course, the Cherokee wars and the Northwest Indian wars, as well as the Quasi-War with France and the long run-up to the War of 1812. This overarching logic endured and deepened. It can be seen in sharpest relief in the ultimately flawed rationale of neutral trade with belligerents—"neutral in mind and deed," according to Woodrow Wilson—which became America's foreign policy stance from the outbreak of World War I in August 1914 through US entry in the war in April 1917. Likewise, the Roosevelt administration maintained commercial neutrality as its default foreign policy position in the 1930s leading up to US entry into the world war in December 1941.

21. James Monroe, Annual Address to Congress on December 2, 1823. For the Monroe Doctrine's ideological development in later narratives of American empire see Gretchen Murphy, *Hemispheric Imaginings: The Monroe Doctrine and Narratives of U.S. Empire* (Durham, NC: Duke University Press, 2005).

22. Elizabeth Borgwardt, *A New Deal for the World* (Cambridge, MA: Belknap Press of Harvard University Press, 2005).

23. In the process, they carried out a crucial transmission of a shared set of beliefs from generation to generation about what precepts of foreign policy had been laid out at the founding and had been most successful. See Nichols, "Enduring Power of Isolationism," 390–407.

24. Henry Clay to Louis Kossuth, January 9, 1852, excerpted in John C. Chalberg, ed., *Isolationism: Opposing Viewpoints* (San Diego: Greenhaven, 1995), 26.

25. On Franklin see Benjamin Franklin to Lord Kames, January 3, 1760, in Labaree, *Papers of Benjamin Franklin*, 9:7. On British debates about expansion and America's "empire" see Felix Gilbert, *To the Farewell Address: Ideas of Early American Foreign Policy* (Princeton, NJ: Princeton University Press, 1961), 33–35. Also, Stourzh, *Benjamin Franklin and American Foreign Policy*, Franklin quote on 120.

26. William Appleman Williams, *The Tragedy of American Diplomacy* (1959; New York: W. W. Norton, rept. 1972), chap. 1, "Imperial Anticolonialism," 18–57.

27. Along these lines it is illuminating to compare the interpretations of the "manifest destinies" that propelled US hemispheric expansionism and could be understood as part of a white-supremacist schema. See, for example, Robert Kagan, *Dangerous Nation: America's Foreign Policy from Its Earliest Days to the Dawn of the Twentieth Century* (New York: Alfred A. Knopf, 2006); Amy Greenberg, *A Wicked War: Polk, Clay, Lincoln, and the 1846 U.S. Invasion of Mexico* (New York: Alfred A. Knopf, 2012) and *Manifest Manhood and the Antebellum American Empire* (New York: Cambridge University Press, 2005); and Matthew Karp, *This Vast Southern Empire: Slaveholders at the Helm of American Foreign Policy* (Cambridge, MA: Harvard University Press, 2016).

28. Andrew Johnson, from James D. Richardson, ed., *A Compilation of the Messages and Papers of the Presidents, 1789–1902* (Washington, DC: Bureau of National Literature and Art, 1903), 6:366.

29. Grover Cleveland in Richardson, *Compilation*, 8:301.

30. This draws on *Promise and Peril*, chaps. 1–6; see also Jay Sexton, *Monroe Doctrine: Empire and Nation in Nineteenth Century America* (New York: Hill & Wang, 2011); Juan Pablo Scarfi, "In the Name of the Americas: The Pan-American Redefinition of the Monroe Doctrine and the Emerging Language of American International Law in the Western Hemisphere, 1898–1933," *Diplomatic History* 40, no. 2 (2016): 189–218; and Christopher McKnight Nichols, "Making the Monroe Doctrine Global," paper presented at the annual meeting of the Organization of American Historians (San Francisco, 2013), draft in author's possession.

31. On American pluralism see David A. Hollinger, *Postethnic America: Beyond Multiculturalism* (New York: Basic Books, 1995); John Higham, "Multiculturalism and Universalism: A History and Critique," *American Quarterly* 45 (June 1993): 195–219; Philip Gleason, *Speaking of Diversity: Language and Ethnicity in Twentieth-Century America* (Baltimore: Johns Hopkins University Press, 1992); Nathan Glazer, *We Are All Multiculturalists Now* (Cambridge, MA: Harvard University Press, 1997); Everett Helmut Akam, *Transnational America: Cultural Pluralist Thought in the Twentieth Century* (Lanham, MD: Rowman & Littlefield, 2002). For an excellent overview see Philip Gleason's entry, "Americanization and American Identity," in the *Harvard Encyclopedia of American Ethnic Groups* (Cambridge, MA: Harvard University Press, 1980).

32. A selection of the best historical scholarship on Bourne includes Casey Blake, *Beloved Community: The Cultural Criticism of Randolph Bourne, Van Wyck Brooks, Waldo Frank, and Lewis Mumford* (Chapel Hill: University of North Carolina Press, 1990); Bruce Clayton, *Forgotten Prophet: The Life of Randolph Bourne* (Baton Rouge: LSU Press, 1984); John Adam Moreau, *Randolph Bourne: Legend and Reality* (Washington, DC: Public Affairs, 1966); and James R. Vitelli, *Randolph Bourne* (Boston: Twayne, 1981), 155, 158. Also, Casey Blake, "Randolph Bourne," in *A Companion to American Thought*, ed. Richard Wightman Fox and James T. Kloppenberg (Oxford: Oxford University Press, 1998), 85–87; and Leslie J. Vaughan, *Randolph Bourne and the Politics of Cultural Radicalism* (Lawrence: University Press of Kansas, 1997), 5–6.

33. Randolph Bourne, "The Jew and Trans-National America," *Menorah Journal* 2 (December 1915): 277–84, reprinted in *War and the Intellectuals: Essays by Randolph S. Bourne, 1915–1919*, ed. Carl Resek (New York: Harper and Row, 1964), 130.

34. Randolph S. Bourne, "Trans-national America," *Atlantic*, July 1916, https://www.theatlantic.com/magazine/archive/1916/07/trans-national-america/304838/.

35. Brian C. Rathbun, *Trust in International Cooperation: International Security Institutions, Domestic Politics and American Multilateralism* (New York: Cambridge University Press, 2011), 77.

36. George Harvey, "The Monroe Doctrine Again," *Weekly* 2, no. 1 (January 4, 1919): 4.

37. "A Correction," *North American Review* 220, no. 824 (1924): 10–17. Many of these ideas became embedded in legalist internationalist positions in this era, as explained by Benjamin Allen Coates, *Legalist Empire: International Law and American Foreign Relations in the Early Twentieth Century* (New York: Oxford University Press, 2016).

38. But what are those ideas and how have they developed to impact relations to and with the world? What is more, how does the American democratic system of government and liberal tradition influence formal as well as informal relations and interactions? And what should we make of these varied, seemingly conflicting statements about the character and conditions of US foreign relations? What do they tell us about the broader contours of the relationship of the US with the world? At stake in these debates is nothing less than the meaning of America. Scholars and scholarship grappling with these questions and that have informed this work included Norman Graebner, *Ideas and Diplomacy: Readings in the Intellectual Tradition of American Foreign Policy* (New York: Oxford University Press, 1964); Michael Hunt, *Ideology and U.S. Foreign Policy* (New Haven, CT: Yale University Press, 1987); Wayne Cole, An Interpretive History of American Foreign Relations (Homewood, IL: Dorsey, 1974); George Herring, *From Colony to Superpower: U.S. Foreign Relations since 1776* (New York: Oxford University Press, 2008); Thomas Bender, ed., *Rethinking American History in a Global Age* (Berkeley: University of California Press, 2002); David Armitage, *Foundations of Modern International Thought* (Cambridge: Cambridge University Press, 2013); Samuel Moyn and Andrew Sartori, eds., *Global Intellectual History* (New York: Columbia University Press, 2013); Perry Anderson, "American Foreign Policy and Its Thinkers," *New Left Review*, September/October 2013. See also Akira Iriye, *Global and Transnational History: The Past, Present, and Future* (New York: Palgrave Macmillan, 2013). Still, Moyn, Sartori, and others rightly find much to criticize about the "global" framing of global intellectual history.

39. The use of "grand strategy" as a way of viewing and studying international relations and in the application of a science of foreign relations to contemporary issues also has its own history. The origins of the Council on Foreign Relations in the United States and the UK's Chatham House in the post–World War I era stemmed in large part from the disappointments of the group of elite policy thinkers known as "the Inquiry," who advised President Wilson in shaping the postwar order. With the emergence of international relations as a discrete discipline came more of the same sort of systemizing of thought about foreign policy and a search for capacious doctrines to establish and guide policy (rendered legible institutionally in the founding of programs of study, aimed in part at impacting policy, such as what would become the School of Advanced International Studies in 1943). See Christopher McKnight Nichols, Elizabeth Borgwardt, and Andrew Preston, eds., *Rethinking Grand Strategy* (New York: Oxford University Press, forthcoming).

40. Perry Anderson, *American Foreign Policy and Its Thinkers* (New York: Verso, 2015), 163.

41. Ibid.; David Milne, "The Dangers of Scientism," *Diplomatic History* 39, no. 2 (April 1, 2015): 391–95. See also Milne, *Worldmaking*.

42. Andrew Bacevich, *The Limits of Power: The End of American Exceptionalism* (New York: Henry Holt, 2008), 30.

43. Alastair Johnston, "Thinking about Strategic Culture," *International Security* 19, no. 4 (Spring 1995): 32–64; Darryl Howlett, "Strategic Culture: Reviewing Recent Literature," *Strategic Insights* 4 (October 2005).

44. Such ideas, movements, or initiatives, matching of means and ends, might fit with Akira Iriye's conception of cultural internationalism as it "seeks to reformulate the nature of relations among nations through cross-national cooperation and interchange" or to transcend nation-states altogether. See Akira Iriye, *Cultural Internationalism and World Order* (Baltimore: Johns Hopkins University Press, 1997), 2–3. See also Glenda Sluga,

Internationalism in the Age of Nationalism (Philadelphia: University of Pennsylvania Press, 2013).

45. Charles Edel, *Nation Builder: John Quincy Adams and the Grand Strategy of the Republic* (Cambridge, MA: Harvard University Press, 2014); Hal Brands, *What Good Is Grand Strategy? Power and Purpose in American Statecraft from Harry S. Truman to George W. Bush* (Ithaca, NY: Cornell University Press, 2014), 1. My view of grand strategy as being best understood as epistemology—that is, as a structure and study of knowledge and justified belief set in action—is derived from philosophy, political science, and historical theory. My argument is particularly informed by Bertrand Russell's distinctions about knowledge types, and Michael Polanyi's argument for structuring knowledge to achieve particular ends ("knowledge how, that"), as well as ideas about skepticism. On the numerous kinds of epistemology and schools of thought (and not yet grand strategy) see the useful essays by Matthias Steup, "Epistemology," *The Stanford Encyclopedia of Philosophy* (Spring 2014 ed.), ed. Edward N. Zalta, http://plato.stanford.edu/archives/spr2014/entries/epistemology/. For more on my definition of an expanded understanding of "grand strategy," as well as my take on the intersection of intellectual history, the US role in the world, and scholarship on grand strategy, see my chapter and the introduction to the volume that I coedited and coauthored, *Rethinking Grand Strategy* (Oxford, forthcoming).

46. These questions were central to some of the conversations that gave rise to this volume. Indeed, when I revisited *New Directions in American Intellectual History*, produced from the 1977 conference at Wingspread in Racine, Wisconsin, I was surprised to find almost nothing about foreign relations, diplomacy, or direct international action. A great many of the essays in the volume, however, discussed the transmission of ideas across borders, hotly debated concepts and keywords, and the influence of intellectuals and their thought in what can be seen as an international context. So, why did not a single foreign policy thinker, tradition, or debate appear in the book? Virtually no recent volume on historiography devotes even a chapter to the intellectual history of the US role in the world. Charles Capper and David Hollinger's canonical two-volume compendium on *The American Intellectual Tradition* is typical; it gives scant attention to foreign policy thinkers and ideologies, prompting the question: what qualifies as intellectual history in the arena of foreign relations? See John Higham and Paul Conkin, eds., *New Directions in American Intellectual History* (Baltimore: Johns Hopkins University Press, 1979).

47. Here I adapt the "agenda-setting" conception of ideas in intellectual history advanced by Daniel Rodgers, cited above, to clinch my point about the power and shaping effects of ideas in foreign relations. See also, regarding the philosophy of history, cause and effect, and intellectual historical methods, Higham and Conkin, *New Directions in American Intellectual History*, Paul Conkin's afterword, esp. 231.

14

REINSCRIBING RELIGIOUS AUTHENTICITY

Religion, Secularism, and the Perspectival Character of Intellectual History

K. Healan Gaston

In the 1950s, attendance at American churches and synagogues soared. The revivalist Billy Graham packed stadiums and arenas, even in cosmopolitan Manhattan. Professions of faith appeared throughout American culture and politics. President Eisenhower repeatedly invoked the divine origins of democracy. The Supreme Court called Americans "a religious people whose institutions presuppose a Divine being." Congress added invocations of God to currency and the Pledge of Allegiance. Drive-in churches and film treatments of Moses reinforced the message.

This portrait of the 1950s is well known. But what exactly was going on? What categories apply to that phenomenon? And what motives lay behind it? A sharp interpretative divergence emerged at the time, one that scholars continue to reproduce even today. For some, the surge in attendance at religious institutions and the newfound prominence of religious themes in American culture represented a dyed-in-the-wool "religious revival." Others saw something much more secular at work. "The Unreal Revival," *Time* famously labeled the religious upswing, as commentators of every stripe, from journalists to academics, vigorously debated its authenticity. Then, as now, views of the postwar burst of public piety reflected competing understandings of what counts as genuine religion. Those commentators who identified the business-friendly theologies of Graham and the positive-thinking guru Norman Vincent Peale as genuine expressions of religious faith saw a full-fledged religious revival in postwar America. Those who considered Graham and Peale charlatans saw the postwar resurgence of religious enthusiasm as a sham: a crass, consumer-driven, conformity-seeking wave of American triumphalism and business-worship at their worst. Indeed, many postwar critics interpreted the alleged revival as a dramatic acceleration of the secularization of American public life. In their view, secularism had entered the churches and synagogues, cloaking itself in religious symbols and corrupting religion from within.[1]

Such debates continue today, as a capitalist icon—himself one of Peale's best-known conservative disciples—occupies the Oval Office. Even the most professedly disinterested historians take sides in the battle over the postwar revival's contours and authenticity, simply by applying the term "religion" (and its linguistic opposite, "secularism") to some viewpoints but not others. In important respects, this tendency is inescapable, insofar as we craft our narratives and arguments in ordinary, emotionally resonant language. But it is here that we can clearly see intellectual history's great interpretive promise, as well as its inevitably perspectival character. Intellectual historians specialize in carefully parsing the contested linguistic meanings that shaped past arguments. At the same time, the intrinsically normative quality of language causes historians to enlist in these arguments themselves. Still, this process of simultaneously dissecting and reifying can be undertaken with greater or lesser sensitivity. And intellectual history itself, by revealing the perspectival character of all human thought, can alert us to the importance of looking past simple assertions and familiar phrases to the deeper layers of meaning behind them, even if we never entirely transcend our own cultural and historical contexts.

Religious Perspectives

What was going on? What categories apply to it? What motives lay behind it? These questions, applicable to all historical cases, become especially pressing—and especially vexing—in the field of religious history. In that highly contested terrain, one must either analyze the operations of subtle, inner motives or write off such intangible factors as mere epiphenomena of something more concrete and observable. Either way, the central category of religion is everywhere and always up for grabs, with a host of competing definitions vying for supremacy. And most historians partake in this interpretive struggle much less self-consciously than do, say, sociologists of religion. Indeed, although historians routinely confront questions about the religious and the secular in their work, they often uncritically reproduce naturalized definitions of those categories. Sometimes these definitions even cut against the grain of their own evidence, closing off promising interpretive paths. Attending more closely to the deeply perspectival nature of historical interpretation can help us think in new ways about the category of religion as a narrative tool for scholars.

It can also help us think about the field of religious history itself, especially in its guise as a form of intellectual history. In 2006, Robert Orsi suggested that "American religious history, as it is practiced in the universities today, is insistently committed, consciously or not, to Niebuhrian neo-orthodoxy as its moral vision. . . . We celebrate those aspects of American religious history that are admirable from the neo-orthodox perspective." Lifting the Niebuhrian veil, Orsi proposed, might lead us to take more seriously figures such as Peale and his Gilded Age predecessor Henry Ward Beecher.[2] And it remains true that historians of religion have generally viewed the postwar revival with the jaundiced eye of the mid-twentieth-century Protestant theologians Reinhold and H. Richard Niebuhr and so many of their liberal Protestant counterparts. Following the Methodist minister and radio preacher Ralph E. Sockman, who dismissed the revival as a series of "attempts to sell religion as a means to health, happiness and prosperity," many contemporary interpreters remain skeptical of the revival's authenticity.[3] Most historians assume that Eisenhower's crusading approach to the Cold War was driven by political opportunism rather than a sincere personal faith (let alone a compelling state interest), and many harbor similar doubts about Graham and his followers. The journalist William Lee Miller's quip that Eisenhower was "a very fervent believer in a very vague religion" remains widely quoted to this day.[4]

Others, however, have argued that a vague religion is still a religion, not secularism in disguise, or insisted that Eisenhower's faith was not that vague at all. Although the postwar surge of piety faced many confirmed doubters, it also had outspoken advocates. One was President Eisenhower's pastor, the Reverend Edward Elson of Washington's National Presbyterian Church. Elson questioned the "rash of articles and public utterances denouncing or at least minimizing" what he ceremoniously termed "the religious renaissance of our times." He charged that the revival's critics systematically discounted key features of postwar religiosity: "emotionalism in religious experience"; the idea that religion should provide "self-confidence and inner assurance"; and the prospect that social pressure might compel people to "commit themselves to the church in the same manner and for the same purposes they join a cultural organization or a service club." To Elson, in short, Peale and Graham offered genuine religious resources. "One does not have to agree precisely in theology nor in the methods," he argued, "to find spiritual exaltation" when encountering souls "redeemed and renewed through the ministries of these men." "Can it be," Elson asked pointedly, "that the lamentation of some critics is so boisterous because the religious awakening does not emerge from their particular theological school, their academic cult, or their personally approved techniques and methods?" He concluded, "Men do not have to get religion in the same way, nor serve Christ in the same office, to have the marks of authentic Christianity."[5]

The Jewish thinker Will Herberg split the difference between lamentation and celebration, carving out a middle-ground position on the revival's authenticity. Herberg's 1955 blockbuster *Protestant-Catholic-Jew* set out to explain "the paradox of pervasive secularism amid mounting religiosity" in 1950s America. Like many other skeptics, Herberg had been influenced by Niebuhr, whose penchant for paradox and distrust of figures such as Graham inspired a 1952 description of America as both "the most religious and the most secular of nations." Historians frequently identify Herberg's book as a simple celebration of the "tri-faith," Judeo-Christian character of much postwar piety. Other interpreters have emphasized that Herberg attacked the 1950s religious revival for consecrating "the American Way of Life" as a national religion. Yet Herberg's position on the revival was actually more complex than either account suggests. Borrowing Niebuhr's image of a nation at once pious and secular, Herberg portrayed a paradoxical revival that intertwined authentic elements with inauthentic ones. "Within the general framework of a secularized religion embracing the great mass of American people," Herberg detected "signs of deeper and more authentic stirrings of faith." With a hopeful eye to the future, Herberg argued that no one could predict what those "deeper stirrings of faith" might ultimately produce.[6]

Herberg thus posited a two-tiered revival that included portents of both secularization and redemption. Even as he recounted the demise of true religion, he left the door open to a rebirth of genuine faith in a world he found desperate for it. Herberg believed that the vacuous Christian nationalism touted by President Eisenhower could be redeemed and worked to inject what he saw as Niebuhr's saving insights about democracy and human nature into the revival: first into the circles around Eisenhower, through Herberg's involvement with the anti-communist Foundation for Religious Action in the Social and Civil Order, and later into the new postwar conservatism during his tenure as the first religion editor of William F. Buckley Jr.'s *National Review*.[7]

As these examples suggest, the judgments of postwar American commentators on the authenticity of the 1950s revival reflected widely divergent views of what genuine religion was and which paths could lead individuals to it. Indeed, they show that one person's "secularism" may literally be another's "true religion," and vice versa. It is this fact that makes the writing of religious history so intensely perspectival.

Historical Perspectives

Given the potential for such massive disparities in meaning, how should the historian proceed, if merely using the term "religion" enlists us in the debates we describe? At the very least, the tools of intellectual history can enable us to recognize that claims about the revival were contested and highly politicized, rather than representing simple descriptions of reality, to be taken at face value. Even the term "revival" involves normative implications, as Niebuhr's close ally Paul Tillich recognized. (He urged interpreters to speak instead of a "resurgence of interest in religion.") Intellectual history also draws our attention to the discursive contexts in which accounts such as Herberg's and Tillich's—and our own—operate.

This point holds well beyond the particular case of 1950s American piety. Anxieties about religious authenticity are a ubiquitous feature of secularization narratives, and secularization narratives circulate freely in the historiography on American religion. But there are linguistic alternatives that might help clarify the stakes, even if they do not free us from the imperative to make linguistic choices with normative implications. For example, in a 2001 essay, David Hollinger pondered how substituting "de-Christianization" for "secularization" in the American case might change our views of twentieth-century history. The term "secularization," he argued, is not sufficiently specific to account for what actually happened in this particular case. Hollinger's terminological move makes us immediately aware of the deeply Christian assumptions that have long shaped secularization narratives. By replacing "secularization" with a less familiar term, Hollinger asks us to reconsider the usual grand narrative from a non-Christian standpoint. Like the term it replaces, however, "de-Christianization" both lumps and splits, albeit in a different manner. Hollinger's category yokes together non-Christians and Christian dissenters and posits a fundamental affinity between them, based on a particular understanding of religious authenticity, and thus of religion itself.[8]

Hollinger's proposal highlights the deeply perspectival nature of religious history and reminds us of the inevitability of conflict in a diverse democracy where no lumping-and-splitting strategy—and thus no single term—will do equal justice to all perspectives. I would argue, in fact, that when we look closely at the local level, narratives of secularization and religious pluralism always rest upon assumptions about the nature of religious authenticity: assumptions about what proper or normative religion is and how it ought to be cultivated.[9]

We need not apply Hollinger's specific lens of de-Christianization to the postwar period in order to accept his broader claim that "secularization" is often too blunt a term to describe what is actually happening on the ground. As an interpretive category, secularization tends to evacuate conflict from our narratives, including both conflict between religious groups and conflict within those groups. Too often scholars portray secularization as a zero-sum game wherein the fortunes of all religious groups and subgroups rise or fall together, like so many boats lifted or lowered by the tide. Narratives of secularization pit religion in general against science, technology, capitalism, or simply modernity, as if these forces impacted all religions in exactly the same manner.

By contrast, redefining secularization as de-Christianization acknowledges the obvious fact that dismantling a quasi-official Protestant establishment affected Jews and Protestants differently. And it affected Catholics in still different ways, to say nothing of Muslims, Buddhists, and others outside the Judeo-Christian fold. Moreover, this process affected various subgroups differently as well: some kinds of Protestants fared better than others under the new regime, whereas others had fared better under the old one. Here, as elsewhere, intellectual history proves uniquely helpful in teasing out clues about the positionality of individuals and groups and the specific ends that language and ideas have served. As we see in the cases of the 1950s religious revival and secularization narratives more broadly, the methods of intellectual history enable us to historicize claims from our sources that we might otherwise reify through uncritical repetition.

Yet there remains the problem of our own need to use categories such as "religion" in our historical analyses. How do our constructions of religious authenticity influence our narrative choices? And how do the methods of intellectual history help us address the fact that our own perspectives shape our interpretations of the past? After all, we are forever enmeshed in history, even as we seek vantage points apart from the fray—or at the very least, new lenses that will expose valuable insights missing from our current perspectives on the past. Every imaginable portrait of the past falls short of the complexity of lived experience, and every confident assertion about the causes of historical change must bow in the face of that complexity. We trade not in truths but in questions and hypotheses, woven into constructed pasts that capture aspects of historical reality but never the whole story or the only story.

This feature of historical interpretation contradicts the objectivity claims that arose with the professionalization of history as a discipline in the nineteenth century. The twentieth century brought a gradual retreat from the strong objectivity rhetoric associated with the modernist project and a corresponding expansion of our sense of the range of perspectives at work in the world. This shift has been particularly acute since the 1960s and 1970s, when activists and scholars came to stress the depths of human diversity and the immense range of interpretive perspectives. Of course, professional standards, sometimes couched in the language of objectivity, remain necessary to deter overt biases and the mishandling of sources. Increasingly, however, historians define objectivity in relation to a community of inquiry that accommodates a diverse array of perspectives while adhering to agreed-upon methodological standards.[10]

In this context, admonitions about presentism—the alleged sin of viewing the past through the lens of the present—begin to sound rather old-fashioned.

After all, when the normative standpoint is no longer singular, neither are our ideas about what is happening in the present. The unmooring of such singular certainties, a trend associated with both the spread of "postmodern" sensibilities and the growing diversity of American life, inclines us to question how much we can transcend our own subjectivity as interpreters of the past—or the present. The very boundaries between past and present begin to blur, and the old idea of the past as a foreign country now seems like the tip of an iceberg. Like it or not, historians work within pasts that are as multiple and shifting as our presents. And although we can, and must, try to avoid projecting our own assumptions onto the past, we inevitably think more and more in terms of relevance when choosing topics of study.

In fact, since the heyday of the Niebuhr brothers—themselves sophisticated theorists of history and power—we have witnessed the gradual replacement of notions of history as objective and disembodied with notions of history as perspectival and situated. This shift accommodates a multitude of voices, even as baseline historical methods still separate the writing of history from the writing of fiction. But it also places tremendous pressure on interpretive categories such as religion and secularization. This is particularly true of work on religion in modern America, where the sheer diversity of religious groups produces myriad and often competing notions of religious authenticity.

The close attention that intellectual historians pay to conceptual and linguistic choices attunes us to the unwritten assumptions and biases that inform historical scholarship. This methodological proclivity also helps us appreciate the constructive roles that our inevitable situatedness as interpreters can play in the writing of history. A case from the contentious arena of arguments about the proper relations between church and state in the United States illustrates this point with particular clarity. Leo Pfeffer was the leading Jewish commentator on church-state relations after World War II. American Jewish leaders of the time spoke for a small non-Christian minority group that counted many unbelievers within its ranks. Like most of his Jewish counterparts, Pfeffer advocated a strict reading of church-state separation. Indeed, as head counsel for the American Jewish Congress, Pfeffer has been called "the most influential and articulate advocate, scholar, and jurist of the separation of church and state in twentieth century America." In legal briefs and countless other forums, Pfeffer argued that strict separation represented a precondition for religious vitality in a diverse democracy. According to Pfeffer, American Jews were "almost unanimous in their belief that the responsibility for religious education must rest with the family, the church and the synagogue."[11]

Historical interpreters of postwar church-state debates have generally followed Pfeffer's theological critics, such as the conservative commentator and

Lutheran-turned-Catholic priest Richard John Neuhaus, in portraying Pfeffer as a secular liberal who sought a high wall of separation in order to oust religion from the public sphere. In fact, however, Pfeffer was the son of an Orthodox rabbi and received a traditional religious education. Although he originally attended a public school, his parents became frustrated by the daily Bible readings he encountered there. They eventually sent their son to an Orthodox school, in the wake of their school district's decision to introduce a "released time" program in which students took time within the school day to attend religious lessons led by local churches and synagogues. As an adult, Pfeffer kept kosher, refrained from working on the Sabbath, and participated actively in his Conservative synagogue. On the strength of these biographical details, J. David Holcomb has argued that Pfeffer was no self-conscious agent of secularization, and indeed welcomed "religious voices in public life." This account of Pfeffer challenges the simplistic but widely believed assertion that strict separation inevitably produces what Neuhaus famously called the "naked public square," a public sphere entirely devoid of substantive religious arguments. Holcomb argues instead that Pfeffer sought—for his own, specifically religious, reasons—the creation of "a robust public sphere where all religious (and nonreligious) voices competed actively to shape American culture and law."[12]

What should historians make of Pfeffer's views, given the wider historical context? Does his emphasis on the voluntary character of religious affiliation make him the mouthpiece of a monolithic, hegemonic "Protestant secular," as the work of religious studies scholar Tracy Fessenden might appear to suggest? Should we instead echo the sociologist Christian Smith by locating Pfeffer within a cadre of "secularizing activists" who consciously set out to "marginalize religion" in American life? Or was there something more complicated—and potentially more interesting—going on with Pfeffer that might call for finer historical distinctions?[13]

We can certainly question Pfeffer's confidence that the public sphere could so easily become a neutral space or "level playing field."[14] As historians, however, we may want to refrain from automatically labeling Pfeffer a "secular liberal" or declaring his faith commitments inauthentic. The methods of intellectual history should also sensitize us to the slippage in the term "secularist" itself, which scholars apply to several different kinds of actors: those who are strongly anticlerical, those who are personally atheistic or agnostic, those who favor liberal theologies that accommodate science, and those who advocate strong church-state separation. Historians often write as if these distinct commitments, or others that inspire the label "secularist," directly entail one another. In fact, the relationships between them are considerably messier than the usual, undifferentiated application of that term implies.

In my book on Judeo-Christian discourse in modern America, I argue that the postwar United States, like so many other times and places, witnessed a battle between competing frameworks of religious authenticity. I also contend that historians should not simply reproduce the terms of that battle by assuming that one framework was true and the alternatives false. For many decades, of course, historians of American religion endorsed the voluntarist model, which holds that religion operates best when it stands apart from state institutions and does its distinctive work in public forums and private relations. Nowadays, they often treat the voluntarist model as purely ideological and deeply oppressive, a sham neutrality that masks unmarked Protestant power and creates all manner of modern ills. But what if Pfeffer's primary aim was not to privatize religion, as his critics have routinely claimed, but rather to promote it? Many advocates of strict separation argued that it would enable a host of religious systems to flourish. What if we take that stated desire seriously, whether or not we agree with the causal analysis that informed it?

Reframing Pfeffer's legacy in this way forces scholars of American religious history to see that their dismissal of the possibility that strict separation could fuel religious vitality reinscribes alternative conceptions of religious authenticity. Rejecting a voluntarist account, we end up assuming that religion cannot be genuine unless it infuses all social and political domains. In other words, we find ourselves hard-pressed to critique voluntarism without writing off Pfeffer's religion as secularism in religious garb, the proverbial wolf in sheep's clothing. What if we stepped back further from the contest and narrated it as just that: a real contest over competing notions of religious authenticity, not the exertion of hegemony by one group over all others? Although we should not ascribe equal measures of power to the postwar disputants, we would do well to avoid identifying some of them as the champions of authentic faith and portraying the others as pretenders whose motives and impact were secular rather than religious.

New Perspectives

The issue of religious authenticity brings us face to face with the coercive power of narratives. As we craft our narratives, they begin to write themselves—picking up momentum and filling in the gaps, insinuating causality and agency, making the messiness of the past seem neat and tidy. There is no question that our historical accounts do violence to the complexity of the past, even as they shine spotlights on what we hope to illuminate. And as we have seen, the category of "religion" is an interpretive lens in its own right. That lens clearly illuminates certain features of the past, but it does not free us from the coercive tendency common to all narratives. In particular, the powerful binary of the religious and the secular constantly threatens to flatten our accounts of phenomena such as secularization and religious pluralism, even as many scholars work to overcome that binary. It can exert so much interpretive pressure that it evacuates conflict from our accounts, generating narratives of secularization that assert the demise of all religion. Likewise, the religious/secular binary tends to inflect our narratives of religious pluralism so that they celebrate the triumph of religion in general. But as we have seen, secularization changes the religious landscape in ways that impact different individuals and groups in very different ways. Similarly, patterns of pluralism have divergent effects on individuals and groups. In interpreting these dynamics, historians would do well to attend carefully to how our own constructions of religious authenticity, and thus "religion" itself, shape our narrative choices.

Such subterranean claims can be harder to spot in works with an expressly revisionist bent—those that aim to expose and challenge the hidden assumptions of prior narratives. Yet these revisionist accounts inevitably rest on their own structures of assumptions, built into their very language. This tendency is clear in two recent scholarly initiatives: first, to give greater specificity to the concept of "secularity" by attending to its theological origins and character in particular contexts, and second, to explore the entanglement of religious and economic impulses. In each case, interpreters employ their own, distinctive conceptions of religion.

In the first instance, scholars have recently argued that secularity in the United States bears the marks of previous cultural configurations in which Protestantism reigned supreme. Tracy Fessenden, for example, sees the informal but powerful Protestant establishment of the nineteenth century as the relevant context for understanding American secularism. In *Culture and Redemption: Religion, the Secular, and American Literature*, Fessenden calls on scholars to "unmask the exacting religious, national, racial, and other specifications" that have been "concealed within an allegedly universal secular." In the case of the United States up to the 1920s, she finds a strong Protestant bias in the putatively neutral condition of secularity—a phenomenon she terms "the Protestant secular"—that weaves through American literature in the "long nineteenth century." Fessenden invites other scholars to trace their own narrative paths forward from the 1920s, where her account ends, thus leaving it to them to decide whether "the Protestant secular" is a useful interpretive category for subsequent periods.[15]

Fessenden wants her readers to reject "a simplified narrative of secularization-as-progress" and embrace "the interplay of different religions and different secularisms." In her final paragraph, she calls for "more nuanced assessments of the contradictions and ideological limitations of the secularization narrative." However, in the same paragraph, Fessenden argues that proponents of secularization in the United States undertook an impossible and undesirable task—namely "confining religion to a privatized sphere," in the hope that this would "ensure religious freedom and eradicate conflict." This critique carries powerful assumptions about the nature of religious authenticity. Fessenden's contention implicitly aligns her with Neuhaus and the many other Catholic (and evangelical) scholars who argue that genuine religion is public, collective, and externally binding. From that point of view, the model of religious freedom that emerged in the nineteenth-century United States was thoroughly and objectionably Protestant because it defined religion as a matter of voluntary, individual, and private affiliation rather than a binding obligation, a collective endeavor, or a public identity. From this perspective, both Protestantism's rising fortunes after World War II and the heightened church-state barrier characteristic of postwar secularism instantiated an inauthentic form of religion that squeezed out more genuine faith expressions.[16]

Fessenden's influential account also reflects a broader tendency in recent scholarship to find religion in avowedly secular spaces in the modern world. Whereas skeptics of the postwar revival argued that much of what appeared under the banner of religion was actually secularism in disguise, many scholars in religious studies now reverse the argument and emphasize the persistence of religion in the face of secularization. They contend that the putatively secular modern world remains shot through with religious content and sensibilities. Kathryn Lofton, for example, reads Oprah Winfrey, the Kardashians, Goldman Sachs, and innumerable other features of America's celebrity-obsessed, consumption-driven culture as religious phenomena.[17]

David Hollinger agrees with Fessenden on the close relationship between Protestantism and secularism in the United States but traces the distinctive character of American secularity to a more recent configuration of cultural power: the sway of "ecumenical Protestantism" over American public life in the middle decades of the twentieth century. In *After Cloven Tongues of Fire: Protestant Liberalism in Modern American History*, Hollinger uses the concept of "post-Protestant secularism" to argue that the liberal Protestant establishment achieved cultural influence at the price of its specifically religious character during 1950s and 1960s. Like Fessenden, then, Hollinger identifies a set of recognizably Protestant concerns within the American version of secularity. He, too, challenges the common tendency to sharply differentiate religious and secular domains. But Hollinger locates the transition from an overtly pious culture to a more secular one much later in time.[18]

The contrasts between the two accounts run deeper than chronology, however. Hollinger sees a mixture of peril and promise in the religious values that shaped the emerging mode of secularity. He recognizes that the views of his figures could advance imperialism and white Christian triumphalism, but he also sees that the individualistic, voluntarist approach to group affiliation that many critics now define as a form of Protestant domination could also generate antiracist and anti-imperialist sensibilities. Hollinger's approach acknowledges the perspectives of many liberal Protestants, Jews, and others who believed that secularization, in the form of de-Christianization (or perhaps de-Protestantization), expanded the circle of inclusion by creating a less overtly hostile, if not fully neutral, public culture. He argues that the liberal Protestant establishment did considerable good, as well as some harm, by conceding much of its institutional power and infusing the wider culture with its core political and social values.

A second project of the current era—analyzing religion's relation to capitalism—highlights additional scholarly disagreements over religious authenticity. What does it mean for interpreters to "take religion seriously"? On one side, adherents to the "lived religion" approach seek to bracket their own perspectives and judge the religious beliefs of historical actors on their own terms, while treating these beliefs as genuine motive forces for action rather than reducing them to economic interests or other imperatives. Other interpreters, however, focus more squarely on the effects—whether intended or unintended—of religious commitments.

An influential new analysis of the postwar religious revival illustrates the latter approach. Kevin Kruse, in *One Nation under God: How Corporate America Invented Christian America*, engages in precisely the kind of economic reduction that lived religion scholars reject, even as he recognizes the potent impact of religious commitments on the course of US history. Kruse's bold subtitle—"How Corporate America Invented Christian America"—captures the book's central argument. He argues that the image of the United States as a nation founded on Christian principles emerged from a 1930s campaign by powerful business leaders to combat the New Deal, in part by mobilizing public faith and equating Roosevelt with Stalin. In those years, "Christian libertarians" such as the Sun Oil chief J. Howard Pew Jr. deemed the welfare state dangerously secular and implicitly totalitarian. In response, Kruse argues, they developed religious constructions of American liberties to advance their business interests. Billy Graham, on Kruse's account, carried forward this tradition of seamlessly merging markets and faith. Throughout the period, powerful economic forces united evangelical Protestants and Catholics behind assertions about the nation's Christian roots.[19]

For Kruse, then, much of the postwar upsurge of religiosity can be explained away as a side effect of a conservative effort to kill off the New Deal state. He takes religious arguments seriously in terms of their effects but acknowledges no distinctively religious motives behind those arguments. Moreover, Kruse, like many US political historians sharing the profession's current fascination with capitalism and conservatism, identifies the religious Right as the only causally important expression of religion in the twentieth century. This interpretation reflects the prevailing paradigm of American political history, which holds that US political culture is essentially conservative ("antistatist") rather than liberal in character. Such an approach highlights the actions of Protestant evangelicals and conservative Catholics and renders invisible the contributions of other religious figures—also a well-worn pattern among journalists since the 1980s. Indeed, the fact that Kruse ignores "Judeo-Christian" discourse altogether, during its postwar heyday, attests to the deeply perspectival nature of all history writing. When we shine a spotlight on one corner of the historical past, we leave others in the shadows.

Innovative though these masterly works are, and compelling in innumerable ways, none of the three analyses escapes the ongoing struggle over the nature of religious authenticity. Rather, each highlights the fact that when we write about secularization and its critics, we inevitably make potent assumptions about who lost and who gained—and whose perspective should prevail in the present and future. None of these interpretive frameworks is neutral. At the end of the day, adopting a Catholic critique of secular neutrality as a corrective to the long history of Protestant hegemony simply replaces one interpretive framework with another. The same goes for rejecting an older framework of American political history that emphasizes the persistence of liberalism in favor of a new one that emphasizes the persistence of antistatism. In each case, we have simply traded one situated perspective for another. This is a form of progress, insofar as it widens the range of interpretive possibilities, but it does not bring us closer to a final, objective analysis.

So while Fessenden, Hollinger, and Kruse each suggest compelling ways of thinking about the resurgence of religion in modern America, no interpretation can remove the obligation to decide for ourselves how we will define religious authenticity and where we will locate it in our narratives. In the wake of the long era of liberal Protestant dominance over American religious history, many scholars have explicitly or implicitly adopted the viewpoint of another religious group instead. Some write as if Catholics held a privileged epistemological position, arguing that Catholic history reveals with particular clarity the oppressive and inauthentic character of Protestant definitions of religion. Some imply instead that Jews transcended all perspectives, because they saw clearly the oppressive tendencies of the Christian supermajority in the United States. Other scholars have tried to carve out a place to stand through methodological innovations: say, an ethnographic approach that privileges actors' own words and categories, or a highly theoretical mode that translates all historical phenomena into the categories of a particular conceptual framework. Still others, including myself, have sought new insights through close attention to discursive meanings.

But we should not make the mistake of thinking that any of these valuable ways of seeing the past is fully correct in its own right. The intensely perspectival nature of history guarantees that our interpretations, however insightful, remain partial. Our scholarly revisions are alternatives to existing interpretations, but they are never the final word. Yet recognizing the inescapable limits of our subjectivity can inspire a different kind of scholarly conversation that more fully acknowledges the multiplicity of perspectives without declaring one of them correct, dismissing others as purely ideological, or holding out for the prospect that some sort of final answer will emerge via synthesis. In the end, historical interpretation is just that: interpretation.

For my own part, I seek to narrate the history of religion with an eye to the underlying structure of the conflicts between groups—including their competing definitions of religion itself. Interpreters can hardly avoid using the term "religion" altogether, and thus imposing some kind of boundary. Within that boundary, however, one can leave the term's precise meaning relatively open and explore conflicts that involved alternative constructions of the category of religion. Greater sensitivity to the fact that we take sides every time we use the word "religion" can lead us to enlist anew in the struggles of the world, by challenging the intellectual constructions of the dominant powers. But it can also inspire us to see the struggle as a clash of multiple, situated alternatives. We can develop analytic categories that are hardly neutral or universal but nevertheless serve as powerful heuristic devices for understanding more clearly the stakes of particular conflicts. By doing so, we can often discern complex and often surprising lines of allegiance and influence as well as opposition.[20]

Still, this approach is no more capable than any other of providing a final, authoritative answer to the interpretation of religious history. There can be no escape into total objectivity from our limited human perspectives. As I see it, history writing is an ethical practice that involves both self-awareness of one's own perspectives and respect for—though hardly capitulation to—the positions of others. It depends on particular habits of mind and interpretive practices, as well as communal norms that support robust exchanges with others. In each case, doing history well involves striking the right balance between critical and empathetic engagement. And the historian of religion must take account of all extant perspectives, not merely those that satisfy some predetermined criterion of religious authenticity. Even the implicit assumption that every interpreter must stand squarely within a recognized faith tradition can undermine the needed diversity of perspectives. There is no correct way—or even a closed set of correct ways—to write the history of religion.

Ultimately, we will not free ourselves from the constraints of history and human subjectivity by adopting any single approach to historical narration. We will not do so, for example, by self-consciously moving "beyond the Niebuhrs," as the title of Randall Stephens's interview with Robert Orsi would have it.[21] Although Orsi is right that popular religious leaders such as Norman Vincent

Peale deserve scholarly attention, our desire for liberation from the confines of our limited human perspectives will never be fully realized—not in the arms of Peale, nor Billy Graham, nor even Oprah Winfrey. Nor can a restless longing for a position beyond the fray be stilled by pinpointing the religious in the secular, or collapsing "the binary," or using critical theory to expose the dark underbelly of the things "we liberal moderns" hold dear. All of these lines of inquiry generate worthy intellectual projects. But what if the Niebuhr brothers were on to something? What if the constraints of history are not solely "out there," to be overcome by our incessant striving, but also "in here," nestled next to all that makes us so impossibly human? Recognizing the perspectival character of historical interpretation will not provide an escape from history, but it may position us to develop more fully the resources and possibilities of the particular worlds in which we find ourselves.

NOTES

1. "The Unreal Revival," *Time*, November 26, 1956.
2. Randall J. Stephens, "Beyond the Niebuhrs: An Interview with Robert Orsi on Recent Trends in American Religious History," *Historically Speaking* 7, no. 6 (July–August 2006): 9. Intellectual historians have long led the way in analyzing figures such as Beecher: e.g., Richard Wightman Fox, *Trials of Intimacy: Love and Loss in the Beecher-Tilton Scandal* (Chicago: University of Chicago Press, 1999). Ironically, Fox also happens to be the author of the single most influential biography of Reinhold Niebuhr: *Reinhold Niebuhr: A Biography* (Ithaca, NY: Cornell University Press, 1985).
3. Quoted in George Dugan, "Methodists Map World Message," *New York Times*, September 12, 1956, 14.
4. William Lee Miller, "Piety along the Potomac," *Reporter*, August 17, 1954, 3.
5. Edward L. R. Elson, "Evaluating Our Religious Revival," *Journal of Religious Thought* 14, no. 1 (Autumn–Winter 1956–1957): 55–62.
6. Will Herberg, *Protestant-Catholic-Jew: An Essay in American Religious Sociology* (Garden City, NY: Doubleday, 1955), 14, 98–99; Reinhold Niebuhr, "Prayer and Politics," *Christianity and Crisis* 12, no. 18 (October 27, 1952): 138–39.
7. K. Healan Gaston, "The Cold War Romance of Religious Authenticity: Will Herberg, William F. Buckley, Jr., and the Rise of the New Conservatism," *Journal of American History* 99, no. 4 (March 2013): 1133–58.
8. David A. Hollinger, "The 'Secularization' Question and the United States in the Twentieth Century," *Church History* 70, no. 1 (March 2001): 132–43.
9. The very different valences attributed to secularization by its best-known early theorists of the 1960s, Harvey Cox and Peter Berger, suggest that secularization is, to a great extent, in the eye of the beholder: Cox, *The Secular City: Secularization and Urbanization in Theological Perspective* (New York: Macmillan, 1965); Berger, *The Sacred Canopy: Elements of a Sociological Theory of Religion* (Garden City, NY: Doubleday, 1967).
10. For the story up to the 1980s see Peter Novick, *That Noble Dream: The "Objectivity Question" and the American Historical Profession* (New York: Cambridge University Press, 1988).
11. J. David Holcomb, "Religion in Public Life: The 'Pfefferian Inversion' Reconsidered," *Journal of Law and Religion* 25, no. 1 (2009–2010): 57. See also Laura Levitt, "Impossible Assimilations, American Liberalism, and Jewish Difference: Revisiting Jewish Secularism," *American Quarterly* 59, no. 3 (September 2007): 807–32.

12. Richard John Neuhaus, *The Naked Public Square: Religion and Democracy in America* (Grand Rapids, MI: W. B. Eerdmans, 1984); Holcomb, "Religion in Public Life," 58.

13. Tracy Fessenden, *Culture and Redemption: Religion, the Secular, and American Literature* (Princeton, NJ: Princeton University Press, 2006); Christian Smith, *The Secular Revolution: Power, Interests, and Conflict in the Secularization of American Public Life* (Berkeley: University of California Press, 2003), 1, 48.

14. Holcomb, "Religion in Public Life," 58.

15. Fessenden, *Culture and Redemption*. Kathryn Lofton, for one, has extended Fessenden's argument up to the present. In her view, Fessenden's emphasis on "the persistent effects of Protestantism" as a powerful cultural force governing "American religious experience and identity" speaks directly to the peculiar relationship between modern individuals and "corporate matrices" that characterizes contemporary neoliberalism. Lofton, *Consuming Religion* (Chicago: University of Chicago Press, 2017), 211. See also Lofton, *Oprah: The Gospel of an Icon* (Berkeley: University of California Press, 2011).

16. Fessenden's fascinating chapter on F. Scott Fitzgerald raises the prospect of an alternative "Catholic secular" that opposed the mainstream model in the twentieth century. I develop this idea further in my book.

17. Lofton, *Oprah*; Lofton, *Consuming Religion*. Of course, the claim that religious commitments can be found throughout a secular society rests on a particular understanding of religion as a phenomenon that requires neither overt expressions of faith nor participation in religious services.

18. David A. Hollinger, *After Cloven Tongues of Fire: Protestant Liberalism in Modern American History* (Princeton, NJ: Princeton University Press, 2013). See also Hollinger, *Protestants Abroad: How Missionaries Tried to Change the World but Changed America* (Princeton, NJ: Princeton University Press, 2017).

19. Kevin M. Kruse, *One Nation under God: How Corporate America Invented Christian America* (New York: Basic Books, 2015).

20. In my own work, for example, I analyze the differences between "Judeo-Christian exceptionalists" and "Judeo-Christian pluralists" in the mid-twentieth-century United States and explore the uses and consequences of these distinct visions of religious diversity for various groups. Historians writing from the perspective of a single group cannot easily address such disagreements.

21. Stephens, "Beyond the Niebuhrs."

15

"THE ENTIRE THING WAS A FRAUD"
Christianity, Freethought, and African American Culture

Christopher Cameron

In his 1945 autobiography *Black Boy*, the famed novelist Richard Wright describes a memorable service at his grandmother's Seventh-Day Adventist church, where the minister preached a particularly vivid fire-and-brimstone sermon. The sermon was replete with "images of vast lakes of eternal fire, of seas vanishing, of valleys of dry bones, of the sun burning to ashes, of the moon turning to blood, of stars falling to the earth, of a wooden staff being transformed into a serpent." Wright notes that while he listened to the sermon he was "pulled toward emotional belief, but as soon as I went out of the church and saw the bright sunshine and felt the throbbing life of the people in the streets I knew that none of it was true and that nothing would happen." For Wright, experiencing nature and interacting with people provided a reasonable counterpoint to religious belief and was a foundation for his budding atheism. His expression of religious skepticism here is one of many throughout the text and is arguably the central theme in the story of his life before leaving the South.[1]

Richard Wright's rejection of Christianity and his exploration of black atheism in both his autobiography and multiple novels represent a key moment in African American intellectual history. The New Negro Renaissance that began in the 1920s and continued during the start of his writing career helped to inaugurate a vibrant tradition of African-American secularism. This tradition closely intersected with and influenced black movements and ideologies ranging from communism to black power to womanism and black theology. Secular thinkers such as Wright, Langston Hughes, James Forman, and Zora Neale Hurston, among others, used novels, poetry, and autobiographies to explore the meaning of atheism for black cultural and political life. Their writings constitute a critique of the idea that black people were naturally religious and evince a desire to portray a more complex and dynamic portrait of African-American culture. They likewise speak to notions of racial authenticity, positing the compatibility between blackness and religious skepticism.

Intellectual historians have devoted significantly less attention to skepticism and freethought than they have to the role of religion in American life. What works do exist tend to focus on deism in early America. This is true of classic texts such as Herbert Morais's *Deism in Eighteenth Century America*, as well as more recent work by Eric R. Schlereth, Christopher Grasso, and Kerry Walters. James Turner's *Without God, Without Creed* is one of the few in-depth historical treatments of atheism in America, yet his work stops short of exploring freethought in the twentieth century. Schlereth's *Age of Infidels* is singular in its focus on freethought among the lower classes, especially mechanics and artisans in the urban North, but aside from a brief discussion of Frances Wright, nearly all the freethinkers in his book are white males, a focus shared by most historians of American freethought.[2]

Scholars of African-American religious and intellectual history have similarly been slow to recognize the presence and significance of freethought in black cultural and political life. According to the philosopher and theologian William R. Jones, African-American humanism's place within the study of black religion "parallels the predicament of the hero in Ralph Ellison's *The Invisible Man*, who though flesh and blood, living and breathing, is treated as if he did not exist." The same holds true for other components of black freethought, including agnosticism and atheism. What little scholarship does exist has come primarily from theologians such as Jones and Anthony B. Pinn. While their works provide valuable insights into the nature of black humanism, their scholarship is aimed more at constructing a black humanist theology than exploring the historical conditions that gave rise to black freethought.[3]

There are a number of different reasons for historians' scholarly neglect of black freethought. As Barbara Savage notes in *Your Spirits Walk beside Us*, the central role of churches and religious leaders in the civil rights movement has influenced the way we see black religion and politics throughout American history. While many historians have depicted the movement as the natural progression of the black church, for Savage "in many ways, the movement is best thought of not as an inevitable triumph or a moment of religious revival, but simply as a miracle." In the years after the civil rights movement, historians have portrayed black Christianity as the central force in black political life when that was not always the case, especially during the early twentieth century.[4]

Another factor that has played a role in the lack of attention to black freethought is that black religious and intellectual history has often operated under the same political project as African-American history more broadly, namely a perceived need to use scholarship as a means of combating racism in the United States. African-American history has thus overemphasized agency, resistance, rebellion, creativity, persistence, and other "positive" themes. Many scholars have been loath to explore topics that would portray African Americans in a negative light and thus prove the racist argument that blacks are not fit to be American citizens. Even the new National Museum of African American History and Culture views its mission in part "to explore what it means to be an American and share how American values like resiliency, optimism, and spirituality are reflected in African-American history and culture." The mission of the museum aside, this trend has been changing over the past decade, with scholars such as Dylan Penningroth, LaShawn Harris, Randy Browne, and others challenging depictions of harmonious slave communities and black respectability by showing the oftentimes violent conflicts among the enslaved and black participation in underground economies. Barbara Savage likewise critiques the idea of a unified black church, arguing that the term masks "the enormous diversity and independence among African-American religious institutions and believers." More work needs to be done in this vein, showing especially the growing numbers of black thinkers who rejected monotheistic religion and embraced freethought.[5]

One of the most commonly recurring events in the writings of black atheists is the conversion narrative. Just as the moment of the new birth is usually the key turning point in the spiritual autobiographies of evangelical Christians, the conversion to atheism and agnosticism is often a pivotal moment, perhaps even the pivotal moment, in the lives of black freethinkers. Indeed, the two conversion stories often parallel one another, as many black freethinkers convert to atheism after an experience on the Christian mourner's bench. The literary scholar Michael Lackey refers to such stories by black atheists as "touchstone" narratives in his important work *African American Atheists and Political Liberation*. Lackey posits four stages to these narratives—an inability to make the leap of faith, efforts by the congregation to convert the infidel, rejection of the idea of God, and analysis of the damaging effects of religious belief. What Lackey doesn't address, however, is the way that black freethinkers use these narratives as a means of cultural critique and a way to articulate a more expansive notion of black identity. Writers such as Langston Hughes, Richard Wright, and James Forman use their experiences on the mourner's bench to reject the idea that blacks are naturally religious, criticize the perceived irrationality of many black Christians, and undermine prevailing ideas of racial authenticity.[6]

In 1940, Langston Hughes became one of the first black freethinkers to frankly discuss his path toward religious skepticism with the publication of his autobiography, *The Big Sea*. By this point, many of Hughes's critiques of Christianity were well known, as poems such as "Litany," "Who but the Lord," "Song for a Dark Girl," and especially "Goodbye, Christ" proffered harsh assessments of the ties between religion, capitalism, and racism. "Goodbye, Christ," published in 1932, gained for Hughes the enmity of black Christians throughout the nation, as he stated in the work,

> Goodbye,
> Christ Jesus Lord God Jehova,
> Beat it on away from here now.
> Make way for a new guy with no religion at all—
> A real guy named
> Marx Communist Lenin Peasant Stalin Worker ME

Eight years later, in *The Big Sea*, Hughes writes that he became a nonbeliever while still a teenager. One day there was a revival service at Saint Luke's Methodist Episcopal Church in Lawrence, Kansas, the home congregation of his Auntie Reed. He spent the entire day in church and was then forced to attend a meeting just for children that evening. All the kids who had not been saved were placed on the mourner's bench to hasten their conversion. The preacher implored the children to accept Jesus as their lord and savior, and the congregation prayed for all of them. Some went to be saved, while others just sat there on the mourner's bench. Through it all, Hughes "kept waiting to *see* Jesus." At the end of the night, there were just two people left who had not been converted, Hughes and his friend named Wesley. Eventually, Wesley could no longer take the pressure of being on the bench in the hot church and whispered to Hughes "'God damn! I'm tired o' sitting here. Let's get up and be saved.'" Wesley got up and was saved, after which Hughes "was left all alone on the mourner's bench. My aunt came and knelt at my knees and cried, while prayers and songs swirled all around me in the little church. The whole congregation prayed for me alone, in a mighty wail of moans and voices. And I kept waiting serenely for Jesus, waiting, waiting—but he didn't come. I wanted to see him, but nothing happened to me. Nothing!"[7]

In an implicit critique of the lack of personal choice and irrationality of such conversion tactics, Hughes claims that he decided to simply lie in order to get off the mourner's bench. "I began to wonder what God thought about Wesley, who certainly hadn't seen Jesus either," he recalled. "God had not struck Wesley dead for taking his name in vain or for lying in the temple. So I decided that maybe to save further trouble, I'd better lie, too, and say that Jesus had come, and get up and be saved." Just as Wesley had done, Hughes stood up and told the congregation that he had accepted Jesus into his heart and was now saved. Everyone was proud of him, especially his Auntie Reed, but he was not proud of himself and cried for one of the last times in his life that night. His aunt woke up and thought he was crying out of joy at having seen the Holy Ghost and accepting Jesus into his life. Hughes notes, however, that "I was really crying because I couldn't bear to tell her that I had lied, that I had deceived everybody in the church, that I hadn't seen Jesus, and that now I didn't believe there was a Jesus any more, since he didn't come to help me."[8]

Richard Wright's story of his fake conversion and acceptance of atheism is similar in many respects to that of Langston Hughes. Wright first became disillusioned with Christianity when he went to live with his grandmother at the age of seven. His grandmother had taken in a boarder named Ella, a local schoolteacher, and one day while she was reading on the porch, Richard asked what the book was about. Ella began to tell him the story of *Bluebeard and His Seven Wives*, and as she did so, "the tale made the world around me be, throb, live. As she spoke, reality changed, the look of things altered, and the world became peopled with magical presences. My sense of life deepened and the feel of things was different, somehow." This was one of the most exciting experiences of his young life, one that sparked his imagination and opened up limitless possibilities for him. His grandmother soon found out, however, and told Ella "'You stop that, you evil gal!' . . . 'I want none of that Devil stuff in my house!'" Richard replied that he liked the story, but his grandmother said he would burn in hell if he listened to stories, and she wanted none of that in her house. Wright uses this story for two primary reasons. First, like Hughes, he critiques the irrationality of Christian belief. After all, he was simply trying to expand his intellectual horizons, but his grandmother's religion precluded that possibility. But perhaps even more important, Wright implies that Christianity serves to divide people from one another, especially people who should have a natural affection for each other.[9]

As he grew into a teenager, the pressure on Richard to convert began to intensify. When he was thirteen, there was an upcoming revival at his grandmother's church, and the family was more anxious than ever for his conversion, because he was transferring to the local public school. He soon noticed that "the entire family became kind and forgiving," but he suspected the motives behind their behavioral change, which served to drive him away even further. A more intense pressure to convert to Christianity came when Richard's mother recovered from a stroke and began attending the local black Methodist church. He started going to Sunday school with her to meet his classmates and agreed to attend a revival a few months later. During the service, the preacher asked the mothers of the boys to come to the front of the church and implore their sons to accept Jesus. "My mother grabbed my hands and I felt hot tears scalding my fingers. I tried to stifle my disgust." His mother pleaded with him to accompany her to the altar and signal his willingness to be baptized, which in effect changed the rules of the game. Now, if he did not convert, he was not just saying that he didn't believe in God or didn't think he needed to be saved. He was saying that he did not love his mother, which was incredibly taboo in that small, tight-knit black community.[10]

In the end, he decided to bow to community pressure, even though he "had not felt anything except sullen anger and a crushing sense of shame." He confessed this to his mother, who told him that he would grow into feeling God's love over time. On the day of his baptism, he wanted to back out but said nothing and went through with the ritual. Even after he had become a member of the church, religious services continued to bore him, as they did the other boys in Sunday school. Eventually, "the boldest of us confessed that the entire thing was a fraud and we played hooky from church." Here Wright alludes to the fact that religious skepticism is likely much more prevalent among blacks than most people think. Even those who seem to be good Christians may have been faking their belief at the time of their conversion and beyond. As one friend of Wright's said to him, what they believed was not very important. "The main thing is to be a member of the church," he asserted.[11]

James Forman's experience in church was similar to that of Hughes and Wright, although his eventual move toward atheism would occur as an adult. When he was twelve he attended a revival, and some of his friends yelled out that they had gotten religion. "The older people shouted that they had got religion too," he writes. "At the age of twelve, in a Baptist tradition and setting, I did not have the courage to tell my grandmother that I thought this was all nonsense. I simply observed what had been happening around me and knew that I, too, could fabricate some tears in this emotionally charged atmosphere. So I covered my face with my handkerchief and cried, 'Lord, have mercy!' It worked. I was taken off the mourner's bench and the people talked of how many children got saved that day by the grace of the Lord." Like Hughes and Wright, Forman likely began his conversion to atheism on the day that he faked his conversion to Christianity. His move toward atheism progressed in college. In 1947, he entered Wilson Junior College in Chicago and started to develop serious questions about god. "How could he exist? What type of God was he that would allow all the injustices in the world? World wars? Killing? Prejudices? Define him. Hell was here on earth, man, for black people." He would end up dropping out of school and serving in the army before a second stint in college, this time at Roosevelt College in Chicago, completed his journey toward atheism. While enrolled in a philosophy course there, he noted, "God finally died in my conscious mind." For his course's final exam, students had to compose an essay exploring the most important thing they learned in the class. Forman wrote: "The most important things that I have learned from this class are a number of intellectual arguments which disprove the myth that there is a God."[12]

Langston Hughes, Richard Wright, and James Forman deploy the stories of their conversion to atheism to argue against the widespread notion that blacks were naturally religious. This was an idea that stretched back to at least 1835, when the Unitarian minister William Ellery Channing argued in his book *Slavery* that "the colored race are said to be peculiarly susceptible of the religious sentiment." This idea was certainly still widespread in the mid-twentieth century as well. In 1953, for example, Hughes testified before Joseph McCarthy's Permanent Subcommittee on Investigations regarding the atheist and Communist themes in his poem "Goodbye, Christ." During the testimony, Senator Everett Dirksen of Illinois asked whether Hughes thought the "Book [the Bible] is dead" and whether or not "Goodbye, Christ" was an accurate reflection of African American religious values. Dirksen claimed that he was very familiar with African Americans and knew them to be "innately a very devout and religious people." By demonstrating that conversion to Christianity was anything but a natural process, however, black atheist writers pushed back against this widespread notion. They argued that conversion to Christianity was actually the result of pressure by the community to conform. Wright portrayed these tactics as particularly underhanded when he noted his disgust that the revival preacher used the children's mothers to get them to accept Jesus. So too with Hughes and Forman, both of whom note having to lie in order to satisfy the religious community. For all three of these writers, then, accepting Christianity was actually more of an unnatural act that went against free will and individual agency. If black children were given the choice, they imply, many would reject the church and become religious skeptics.[13]

Attacking the idea of blacks as naturally religious went hand in hand with another underlying theme in atheist conversion stories, namely the articulation of a different perspective on what it meant to be authentically black. According to prevailing wisdom, if black people were supposed to be religious and most adhered to the Christian religion, then it stood to reason that being black also meant being Christian. Becoming an atheist, then, was not simply a matter of holding a different religious belief. Rather, it constituted a rejection of blackness itself. This is the reason all three of these writers felt the need to lie and say they had been converted. If they were open and honest about their skepticism, they would have been ostracized from their communities. Wright stated of his experience at the revival, "If we refused to join the church, it was equivalent to ... placing ourselves in the position of moral monsters." Zora Neale Hurston, another prominent freethinker, supports this point. "When I was asked if I loved God," she notes in her autobiography, "I always said yes because I knew that was the thing I was supposed to say. It was a guilty secret with me for a long time." This "guilty secret" eventually saw the light of day for an increasing number of black atheists after the 1930s. By coming out as freethinkers yet still forcefully championing racial equality and promoting black cultural output, African American atheists let the world know that blackness was an expansive identity that could incorporate multiple religious perspectives or no religion at all.[14]

Along with his autobiography, Richard Wright used his 1953 novel *The Outsider* to further reflect on the meaning of black atheism and notions of racial authenticity. He wrote this book after having lived in France for seven years, and the text reflects his deep engagement with the existentialist philosophy of Jean-Paul Sartre and Simone de Beauvoir. The protagonist is a man named Cross Damon, who feels trapped by his circumstances, or his facticity, as Sartre would say, including his loveless marriage and a mistress threatening to charge him with statutory rape. After a train accident where Cross is presumed dead, he flees Chicago for Harlem, where he falls in with some Communists and ends up committing three murders (Cross had already killed one man in Chicago who recognized him after the accident). Cross actually feels that his murders are justified and that for individuals such as himself, outsiders, there is no morality and anything goes. As with Bigger Thomas, the protagonist in Wright's best-known work, *Native Son*, a significant motivation for Cross Damon's crimes was his unwillingness to be dominated by the social forces and political ideologies of his time. He is determined to assert his individuality and go against the grain of modern society. In this respect, Cross and, by extension, other blacks are "no longer just America's metaphor but rather a central symbol in the psychological, cultural, and political systems of the West as a whole," according to Paul Gilroy. The story of African Americans may seem unique, Wright argues, but blacks represent the broader alienation of man in the modern world.[15]

Wright's acceptance of existentialist philosophy, as seen in *The Outsider* and other writings, marks an important component of African-American secularism, namely its broad engagement with European intellectual life. Indeed, even before leaving the United States, Wright felt that because of his upbringing in the Jim Crow South, he was already familiar with many of the themes in the work of existentialists such as Heidegger, Nietzsche, Sartre, and others. While existentialists such as Kierkegaard remained Christian, postwar existentialists in France were primarily atheists. Critics of the philosophy complained that it was just another form of bourgeois individualism, a way to ignore the problems of modernity. For Wright, Sartre, and de Beauvoir, however, bringing about the freedom of the individual could not happen without wholesale structural changes that would promote equality for women, the poor, minorities, colonized peoples, and other disadvantaged groups. As Sartre would argue in perhaps his most famous and controversial speech, existentialism was a humanism that could radically transform modern society.[16]

Contemporary reviewers of *The Outsider* by and large believed the novel to be a much inferior production to Wright's earlier works, largely because the book's atheist and existentialist themes were seen as unrelated to black life and culture. During a 1964 symposium on Richard Wright's work, featuring a roundtable with Horace Cayton, Arna Bontemps, and Saunders Redding, Bontemps claimed that "*The Outsider* was not quite up to Wright's earlier books" and speculated that the reason might have been Wright's lack of anger and his contentment in Paris. Wright wrote best when he was discontented, according to Bontemps, and the congenial atmosphere in France was not conducive to his producing great "protest literature," as James Baldwin referred to Wright's style. Saunders Redding also attributed Wright's decline to his time in France and his exposure to new ideas while there. "Existentialism is no philosophy that can be made to accommodate the reality of Negro life," Redding wrote, "and especially . . . of Southern Negro life." For Redding and other reviewers, Wright's acceptance of French existentialism, which we have seen included a secular humanist perspective, was inauthentically black and was the major reason behind his literary declension. The irony in these critiques of Wright is that the idea that there is an authentic black culture is itself an intellectual influence of nineteenth-century German Romanticism, which saw thinkers such as Johann Gottfried Herder argue that different cultures have their own distinctive characteristics. As Paul Gilroy points out, Wright's body of work was aimed at undermining this idea and showing how the racism and racial ideologies that blacks dealt with on a daily basis (and that contemporaries used to point to the uniqueness of black culture) were part and parcel of the broader challenges of modernity.[17]

The idea that atheism was foreign to black culture would remain a powerful one throughout the twentieth century. As we have seen in the writings of Hughes, Forman, Wright, and Hurston, however, there is nothing inauthentically black about atheism, agnosticism, and other forms of freethought. The same social, political, and economic conditions that undergirded African-American religious belief also propelled others into religious skepticism and nonbelief. The reasons could be largely personal, as family strife and negative experiences with religion at a young age pushed thinkers such as Hughes and Wright into rejecting monotheistic religion. The political function that the concept of God served likewise turned African-American writers and intellectuals away from Christianity, which they believed supported the racist system of Jim Crow and was seemingly ineffective at alleviating the economic and social conditions of blacks in the United States. With the onset of the Great Depression, ministers and churches should have turned their attention to bolstering the economic position of blacks in the nation, yet many ministers seemed to care only about their own personal finances. Rather than trust in a god who cannot be seen, African-American atheists argued that blacks would be better off placing their trust in each other and working together for the betterment of all mankind.

The writings and political activism of African-American atheists and agnostics should push intellectual historians toward a reassessment of early to mid-twentieth-century freethought. Historians of the movement often portray a sharp decline during the 1920s, a decline that coincided with the rise of fundamentalism and the weakening of freethought organizations such as the Manhattan Liberal Club. The prevalence of secular themes in the works of Harlem Renaissance authors, however, demonstrates that freethought often took on new forms that were not solely aimed at undermining the church. Similarly, the embrace of socialism and communism by black freethinkers such as Wright, Hughes, W. E. B. Du Bois, and Louise Thompson Patterson demonstrates this sharp transformation in American freethought. No longer were freethinkers content to simply be against Christianity. Instead, freethought complemented other political commitments, becoming more radical in the hands of black intellectuals and artists.[18]

Scholars of the black radical tradition and African Americans and the Left can likewise benefit from a more thorough engagement with the religious critiques of black freethinkers. We know a great deal about the impact of evangelical Christianity, Islam, and even African-derived traditions on black political thought, yet few scholars of black radicalism tie in their subjects' atheism to their politics. Mark Solomon's *The Cry Was Unity*, for example, does not discuss religion, and attributes the growing appeal of socialism and communism among African Americans to Caribbean immigration and the Black Belt thesis adopted by the Comintern in 1928. For Joyce Moore Turner, it was largely economic factors and racism that pushed blacks to accept socialism in New York City. And Michael Dawson posits three primary draws of Marxism to black thinkers that likewise do not touch on religion at all. This oversight in the literature on black radicalism is not due to a lack of evidence. Published collections of the writings of black freethinking radicals such as Hughes, Du Bois, Hubert Harrison, Harry Haywood, Alice Walker, Stokely Carmichael, and others abound, and they clearly tie radical critiques of capitalism, imperialism, racism, and Christianity together. In order to truly understand the genesis of twentieth-century black radicalism, intellectual historians could start with the question: How did freethought influence black political thought? Rather than try to explain away black freethinkers' religious critiques, or worse, ignore them altogether, we must take them just as seriously as we would the theology of believers. Doing so will provide us with a fuller and more accurate picture of black intellectual life and twentieth-century American thought more broadly.[19]

NOTES

1. Richard Wright, *Black Boy (American Hunger)* (1945; New York: HarperCollins, 1998), 102.

2. In this chapter, I employ Anthony Pinn and Gordon Kaufman's understanding of religion, namely ideas and practices aimed at providing an ultimate orientation and meaning for human life. Under this definition, many freethinkers can be seen as religious, and indeed, individuals such as Zora Neale Hurston and James Baldwin considered themselves religious despite their nonbelief in God. See Anthony Pinn, *Varieties of African American Religious Experience* (Minneapolis: Fortress, 1998), 3, and Gordon Kaufman, *In Face of Mystery: A Constructive Theology* (Cambridge, MA: Harvard University Press, 1993), 225; Herbert M. Morais, *Deism in Eighteenth Century America* (1934; New York: Russell & Russell, 1960); Kerry Walters, *Revolutionary Deists: Early America's Rational Infidels* (New York: Prometheus Books, 2011); Christopher Grasso, "Skepticism and American Faith: Infidels, Converts, and Religious Doubt in the Early Nineteenth Century," *Journal of the Early Republic* 22 (2002): 465–508; Eric R. Schlereth, *An Age of Infidels: The Politics of Religious Controversy in the Early United States* (Philadelphia: University of Pennsylvania Press, 2013); James Turner, *Without God, Without Creed: The Origins of Unbelief in America* (Baltimore: Johns Hopkins University Press, 1985).

3. William R. Jones, "Religious Humanism: Its Problems and Prospects in Black Religion and Culture," in *By These Hands: A Documentary History of African American Humanism*, ed. Anthony B. Pinn (New York: NYU Press, 2001), 27.

4. Barbara Dianne Savage, *Your Spirits Walk beside Us: The Politics of Black Religion* (Cambridge, MA: Harvard University Press, 2008), 2–3.

5. Pero Dagbovie argues that from the antebellum era through the 1970s, most historians of black America embraced contributionism, an approach that focused largely on the ways that blacks contributed to American political and economic life. See his *African American History Reconsidered* (Urbana: University of Illinois Press, 2010), 18. National Museum of African American History and Culture, "About the Museum," https://nmaahc.si.edu/about/museum (accessed September 17, 2016); Dylan Penningroth, *The Claims of Kinfolk: African American Property and Community in the Nineteenth-Century South* (Chapel Hill: University of North Carolina Press, 2003); LaShawn Harris, *Sex Workers, Psychics, and Numbers Runners: Black Women in New York City's Underground Economy* (Urbana: University of Illinois Press, 2016); Randy M. Browne, "The 'Bad Business' of Obeah: Power, Authority, and the Politics of Slave Culture in the British Caribbean," *William and Mary Quarterly* 68 (2011): 451–80; Savage, *Your Spirits Walk beside Us*, 9.

6. Michael Lackey, *African American Atheists and Political Liberation: A Study of the Sociocultural Dynamics of Faith* (Gainesville: University Press of Florida, 2007), 121.

7. Langston Hughes, "Goodbye, Christ," in *The Collected Poems of Langston Hughes*, ed. Arnold Rampersad and David Roessel (New York: Vintage Books, 1994), 166; Langston Hughes, *The Big Sea* (New York: Hill & Wang, 1940), 19, 20.

8. Hughes, *Big Sea*, 20, 21.

9. Wright, *Black Boy*, 39, 40.

10. Ibid., 113, 153–54.

11. Ibid., 155.

12. James Forman, *The Making of Black Revolutionaries* (1972; Seattle: University of Washington Press, 1997), 29, 55, 82.

13. William E. Channing, *Slavery* (Boston: James Munroe, 1835), 108; *Executive Sessions of the Senate Permanent Subcommittee on Investigations of the Committee on Government Operations*, vol. 2, Eighty-Third Congress, First Session, 1953 (Washington, DC: Government Printing Office, 2003), 980.

14. Wright, *Black Boy*, 154; Zora Neale Hurston, *Dust Tracks on a Road*, in *Folklore, Memoirs, and Other Writings* (New York: Library of America, 1995), 755; Qiana J. Whitted, *"A God of Justice?": The Problem of Evil in Twentieth-Century Black Literature* (Charlottesville: University of Virginia Press, 2009), 56.

15. Richard Wright, *The Outsider* (1953; New York: HarperCollins, 2003); Paul Gilroy, *The Black Atlantic: Modernity and Double Consciousness* (Cambridge, MA: Harvard University Press, 1993), 159; Robert A. Coles, "Richard Wright's 'The Outsider': A Novel in Transition," *Modern Language Studies* 13, no. 3 (Summer 1983): 58.

16. Gilroy, *Black Atlantic*, 171; Thomas R. Flynn, *Existentialism: A Very Short Introduction* (New York: Oxford University Press, 2006), 45–49; Jean-Paul Sartre, "Existentialism Is a Humanism," in *Existentialism: From Dostoevsky to Sartre*, ed. Walter Kaufman (New York: Penguin Books, 1975), 345–69.

17. "Reflections on Richard Wright: A Symposium on an Exiled Native Son," in *Anger and Beyond: The Negro Writer in the United States*, ed. Herbert Hill (New York: Harper & Row, 1966), 203, 205–7, 209; Gilroy, *Black Atlantic*, 156–57, 160, 171.

18. Rachel Scharfman argues that the golden age of freethought ended in 1915 but notes some radical new directions for the movement after the 1920s. See her "On Common Ground: Freethought and Radical Politics in New York City, 1890–1917," PhD diss., New York University, 2005, 19, 88; Susan Jacoby, *Freethinkers: A History of American Secularism* (New York: Owl Books, 2004), 151; Marshall Brown and Gordon Stein, *Freethought in the United States: A Descriptive Bibliography* (Westport, CT: Greenwood, 1978), 47.

19. Mark Solomon, *The Cry Was Unity: Communists and African Americans, 1917–1936* (Jackson: University Press of Mississippi, 1998), 4, 86–87; Joyce Moore Turner, *Caribbean Crusaders and the Harlem Renaissance* (Urbana: University of Illinois Press, 2005), 28; Michael C. Dawson, *Black Visions: The Roots of Contemporary African-American Political Ideologies* (Chicago: University of Chicago Press, 2001), 174.

Section V
IDEAS AND CONSEQUENCES

16

AGAINST AND BEYOND HOFSTADTER
Revising the Study of Anti-intellectualism

Tim Lacy

Richard Hofstadter—the most provocative of the United States' midcentury historians—prominently charted the nation's intellectual failures and problems in his 1963 work, *Anti-intellectualism in American Life*. That study earned him the Pulitzer Prize in 1964. Since then it has provided a durable framework for analyzing anti-intellectualism in politics, religion, business, and education. Historians, critics, and pundits have been writing in its shadow ever since.[1] Hofstadter's biographer, David Brown, explains *Anti-intellectualism*'s durability by describing it as "one of the most troubling criticisms of American democracy ever written." It "raised serious questions," Brown added, "about the nature and function of popular government." Further demonstrating Hofstadter's staying power, the historian David Greenberg labeled him "the Pundits' Favorite Historian" in 2006.[2]

The problem, however, is that few historians since have revised, or improved upon, the original framework and assumptions in *Anti-intellectualism*. Too often, the problems that activated Hofstadter in the 1950s, as well as his failures of analysis, have been repeated in relation to past American history or, worse, imported into the present. To make more progress on the subject of anti-intellectualism and related topics, intellectual historians must move above, beyond, and against Hofstadter. To make that move, I contend that historians must view charges of anti-intellectualism as a failure of discourse in a democracy.

This argument begins by historicizing Hofstadter. First explored are the context of production, contents, and reception of *Anti-intellectualism*. A new look at its reception by historians reveals that many original criticisms were ignored or forgotten. Historicizing the reception of *Anti-intellectualism* also involves an analysis of Hofstadter's more prominent heirs. Herein that is accomplished by a close look at three books. Those authors extended some themes in *Anti-intellectualism* and even acknowledged a few problems with the book, but were less critical than early reviewers. After this analysis I suggest how future studies of anti-intellectualism could be improved. That effort is worthwhile, because improving the study of anti-intellectualism also forwards the study of intellectual history and the history of ideas generally.

The Book

In *Anti-intellectualism*, Hofstadter posits, at base, a straightforward thesis of cyclicality: there exists an ebb and flow of anti-intellectualism in US history. American anti-intellectualism, he argues, "is older than our national identity." He focuses his study on four areas—religion, politics, business, and education—with each conceived as a social movement. Together they form an anti-intellectual tone comprising ideas, attitudes, and historical subjects within each area.[3] Also under scrutiny is the idea of democracy itself, often under guise of the term "egalitarianism." In Brown's words, *Anti-intellectualism* chronicled the "contest between intellect and egalitarianism."[4]

Hofstadter's foci grew out of his historical context and concerns. He confessed that the book "was conceived in response to the political and intellectual conditions of the 1950s," when "anti-intellectualism, only rarely heard before, became a familiar part of our national vocabulary." McCarthyism was a particular concern, and Hofstadter saw it as rooted in an older anti-intellectual, agrarian populism.[5] The 1950s, then, made the term "anti-intellectual" a "central epithet." While the term was new, he added, the force behind it was "familiar," formed out of the nation's English heritage. The renewal had occurred because of the prominence intellectuals had obtained in the Cold War administrative state.[6]

On the first of his four major social movements, religion, Hofstadter focused on Christian evangelicals, revivalists, and modernity. "The American mind," he begins in grand style, "was shaped in the mold of early modern Protestantism." The Christian religion served as "the first arena for American intellectual life" and the "anti-intellectual impulse."[7] While learning was essential to the old Protestant ministers, they also valued "the spirit" (i.e., the Holy Spirit) over book learning. Salvation came from the heart. Hoftstadter properly credits the First Great Awakening for having "quickened the democratic spirit" and given a start to "humanitarian causes," such as the antislavery cause. But it also fostered anti-intellectualism and "uprising[s] against traditional and rational authority."

Protestantism gave authority to emotion and enthusiasm, making rationality a distraction. Charles Finney, John Wesley, Francis Asbury, Dwight Moody, and Billy Sunday were exemplary for Hofstadter.[8]

When the narrative moved into the twentieth century, Hofstadter focused on two crises for Protestantism. An internal crisis produced fundamentalism as a reaction to churches that embraced "the spirit of modernism." An external crisis involved the force of ideas and figures associated with American modernity: Darwin and Darwinism, secularism, rationalism, Freud, urban culture, mixing (i.e., mongrelization), elite Progressive intelligentsia, mobility, and mass education. The fundamentalist mind-set was exemplary in the person of Billy Sunday: his "one-hundred percent mentality" brooked "no ambiguities, no equivocations, no reservations, and no criticism." Sunday was a proxy, for Hofstadter, regarding wrongheaded masculinity, ideology, and populist ideologues—all reactions to modernity and its complications of social and cultural life. Sunday and related figures relied on common sense as *better than* the judgment of intellectuals. Hofstadter called this "the crux of the matter" in relation to thought life and anti-intellectualism.[9]

When *Anti-intellectualism* moves to politics, Hofstadter starts with an irony and then brings focus to a peculiar weakness of American-style democracy. He observes that the United States was founded by intellectuals—unspecialized in education, yet "sages, scientists, men of broad cultivation . . . [and] apt in classical learning." Thereafter, however, beginning with the Jacksonian era, Hofstadter argues, the nation made its intellectuals scapegoats, servants, and outsiders. Over time "popular democracy" overtook leadership by "the patrician elite," resulting in political parties that became "vehicles of a kind of primitivist and anti-intellectualist populism" that was "hostile to the specialist, the expert, the gentleman, and the scholar." This new "egalitarian impulse" valued character over intellect, which linked it to historical religious impulses. Whereas learning was artificial, the "natural wisdom of the natural man" and "native intuition" were real, common, and accessible. The "native practical sense of the ordinary man"—that is, the "wisdom of the common man"—became, to Hofstadter, a new "democratic creed" and "militant popular anti-intellectualism." In politics, especially populism, this would result in "more men [being] pushed up from the bottom than selected from the top."[10] This was how the anti-intellectual impulse found another home in democratic politics.

Hofstadter underscored "usefulness" as the key word when the book moved to the world of business. The measure of worth in America, he argued, derived directly from a "devotion to practicality and direct experience." This extended into "almost every area of American life" as an "excessive practical bias" permeating everything. A "practical vigor" fed the propensity to hold intellectuals and the intellectual life in perpetual suspicion. Hofstadter mocked the way that the

Patent Office, for instance, seemed to contain "the true secret of civilization." An Age of Utility superseded philosophy and the Enlightenment. The "industrial era in America" gave businessmen a "central and . . . powerful" position. Little room existed for other ideals.[11] The rise of the mogul in the industrial era helped bring into prominence the notion of the self-made man. The symbolism of this mattered more than reality. That mythic, self-made position could be obtained without "formal learning or careful breeding." It involved immersion and initiation in the "cult of experience."[12]

The final major topic of *Anti-intellectualism* is education. In how that related to business, Hofstadter reminds the reader that education became a concession in the fields of accounting, engineering, law, and economics. But, in the voice of Henry C. Link (a prominent midcentury psychologist), education became a vice when it fostered a "liberal mind." Taken too far, education was "damaging" and, Hofstadter added, "mystical and irrational." A liberal or humanist education resulted in "ruthless iconoclasm," emancipating one from traditions and restraint. The introspective life of the mind and an "idolatry of reason" led nowhere productive.[13] Hofstadter idealized those very ends feared by Link, but found other trends in education that undercut intellectualism.

Those trends existed across all education levels. In terms of higher education, Hofstadter held up particular historical figures—William Jennings Bryan, Billy Sunday, Billy Graham, and Joseph McCarthy—for mockery because of their disdain for the college-educated. Hofstadter wrote somewhat admiringly of "the Wisconsin idea," which put "experts in the service of 'the people.'" It fostered "the brain-trust idea" in politics at large, manifest in the New Deal. But Hofstadter also argued that this caused conservatives, such as those listed above, to see the university as "a conspiracy against them."[14] He also critiqued higher education for fostering anti-intellectualism by mimicking the worst aspects of secondary education. Colleges and universities promoted vocationalism and job training, and were "dominated by athletics, commercialism, and the standards of the mass media."[15] In the K–12 realm, Hofstadter criticized life-adjustment education as the product of progressive educators inspired by, but corrupting, John Dewey's thought. Compulsory attendance was a "custodial function" that diminished teachers' intellectual status and role model. That diminished function resulted in "low pay and . . . [a] lack of personal freedom." Hofstadter's narrative of decline, from a pinnacle of aspiring to "selective" European ideals of "mind culture," via the 1893 Committee of Ten, to the shadowy valley of the 1947 Life Adjustment Conference (in Chicago and led by Charles Prosser), meant that educational democratization became mere "massification." That change sidelined talented students, destroyed mental discipline, and discouraged high thinking. Despite his thesis of cyclicality, he concluded that the educational system was a "failure" and "a constant disappointment."[16]

As this brief summary indicates, there is much to absorb and appreciate in Hofstadter's tome. For those who study American history while pondering the long-running failures of its education system and politics, the book perennially affirms one's pessimistic sense of the present. If you are reading it and have self-conscious intellectual tendencies, *Anti-intellectualism* summarizes and articulates your criticisms of American Protestant Christianity, business trends, ideological politicians, and the inanities of professionalized education. Hofstadter mocks the requisite historical figures for you, quoting them extensively, letting them put their feet in their mouths. *Anti-intellectualism* provides historical weight, or affirmation, to the sense of alienation and oppression felt by critics of American society. The book also affirms the prejudices of liberal elites, a point that arises, consciously and unconsciously, in a few reviews. If your politics tend toward American midcentury liberalism, Hofstadter's work walks to the edge of criticizing capitalism without crossing the Rubicon. Liberals can use Hofstadter to safely bludgeon, in the words of Lionel Trilling, the "irritable mental gestures," perpetuated by conservative pseudo-intellectuals and ideologues, "which seek to resemble ideas."[17]

While Hofstadter reflected deeply on his subject matter, he refused to anchor his terminology in a particular theory or philosophical school. He critiqued business and historical business leaders, but avoided a Marxian theory of capitalist analysis. Hofstadter criticized religion and religious leaders, but did not forward Nietzsche, Voltaire, or Niebuhr to buttress his views. He narrated the intellectual failures of politicians, yet avoided invoking Hobbes or Machiavelli to add weight to his critique of democratic institutions. In terms of education, Hofstadter dealt subtly with Dewey and bluntly with Dewey's followers, but avoided prescribing an educational theorist or philosopher to counter progressive education. The end result, historically, is that Hofstadter engaged in indirect and direct polemics, even to the point of criticizing democracy and certain aspects of capitalism, without obtaining the taint of ideology so despised during the Cold War.

Hot and Cold Reception

Although recognized as sui generis in its moment, *Anti-intellectualism*'s early reviews, academic and otherwise, were cold.[18] That early reception underscores numerous weaknesses that have often been underappreciated, or ignored, by Hofstadter's heirs. The first reviewers leveled the harshest assessments of *Anti-intellectualism* and Hofstadter's interests. They took aim at his and the book's elitism, problems of evidence and rigor, tone, and evasiveness on issues of justice. Little was made, however, by these critics of the book's embeddedness in the concerns of liberalism, capitalism and, in the perceptive words of William Appleman Williams, empire.[19] This makes sense, however, as Hofstadter and his reviewers were embedded in their times—a product of them. Despite the cold reception, the book's novelty as a work of intellectual history meant that sales numbers were excellent: 13,190 hardback copies through 1965.[20] Why? What follows is an attempt to explain this historical irony.

One of the first published reviews of *Anti-Intellectualism* was a thorough panning. The adversarial examination came from Daniel Boorstin. He accused Hofstadter of pretending to "defend the higher values of American civilization" while actually just wringing his hands about "the reputation, status, and privileges of 'intellectuals' as a separate class." The book's problems began with its introductory "exhibits," which focused, in Boorstin's words, on "the crackpot or near-crackpot right." From there Hofstadter failed to exhibit any anti-intellectual failings from the left or liberals. Boorstin saw elitism in Hofstadter's plaint about American society's failure to honor intellectuals while also vulgarizing their work. Hofstadter merely proves, again, America's imperfections while offering nothing historical on how "democratic political life" actually rectifies injustices. Hofstadter's status-conscious lament on the lack of honor for intellectuals leads him, by default, to join "the cult of alienation," a cult he himself deplored for its Bohemian, beatnik aesthetics. Boorstin concludes by calling for intellectuals and thinkers to "learn to live in and with and by and for" their community. Self-proclaimed intellectuals must lose the so-called "life of the mind" in order to gain it, and to secure democracy.[21]

The assault on Hofstadter's elitism continued with an inspection by Kenneth S. Lynn. Lynn grouped Hofstadter with the new post–World War II neo-Menckenites, who were repulsed by McCarthyism (or "populistic hysteria") and 1950s middle-class "materialistic vulgarity." The neo-Menckenites believed that the "enemies of the American mind" were "Bryanism, Babbittry, and the Bible Belt."[22] Lynn integrated that fault with a ruthless critique of presentism. Hofstadter practiced, to Lynn, "the habit of relating history to the morning headlines ... to create an elitist myth of the American past that might somehow serve as a lifeline to beleaguered intellectuals in a scary [Cold War] present." Finally, while Hofstadter denied that anti-intellectualism was treated as "anti-rationalism" in his work, particularly in its philosophical or "highbrow" sense, Lynn accuses Hofstadter of confusing "rationalism" with "intellectualism." That confusion causes certain rationalist, Enlightenment theologians (e.g., Charles Chauncy) and their conservative politics to become unintelligible in *Anti-intellectualism*.[23]

Anti-intellectualism's other early reviews, all published later in 1963, gave no indication that reception might warm, or that the book might achieve lasting acclaim from pundits and critics. Harvard's Howard Mumford Jones criticized *Anti-intellectualism* as an overly ambitious book that condensed four complex studies into one, sacrificing "the rigor of historical scholarship" in the process. Merle Borrowman, writing in the *History of Education Quarterly*, accused Hofstadter of harboring a false nostalgia for nineteenth-century curricula. Borrowman faulted Hofstadter's selection and emphases, noting that "prize examples ... tend to come from the lunatic figure." Like Lynn, Borrowman observed the fallacy of presentism—of "organiz[ing] the past in terms of a current lively personal issue."[24] David Riesman dissected the elitist drift of the work, saying it insufficiently recognized how Cold War intellectuals were "linked to power, opportunity, and privilege, and the ways in which this linkage leads to resentment." Hofstadter's "sympathies," he added, "lie too much with the Establishment to see its faults." Riesman also criticized, with Borrowman, Hofstadter's lack of a "full appreciation of the anti-intellectualism of the academic and classical curricula against which ... evangelicals were fighting in one era," in seminaries, and "Dewey and his co-workers" opposed in schools. With this, Riesman observed (correctly) that Hofstadter seemed "tempted at times to understate the injustices of the past."[25]

Riesman echoed Boorstin in pointing toward failures of democratic discourse as a key issue. There exists, argued Riesman, a "dialectic ... in which intellectualism becomes a tactic of exclusion, both of people and of themes and topics, leading to its undoing—followed by a renewal of intellect in perhaps more egalitarian and inclusive form."[26] This failure of dialectic points toward the need to fully explore those other "themes and topics" under the larger rubric of anti-intellectualism. What is avoided? What is assumed? What is out of bounds? How are intellectuals complicit in these failures of discourse?

After these early critics, the renowned Catholic historian and vocal critic of Catholic anti-intellectualism, John Tracy Ellis, signaled a turn toward increased enthusiasm for *Anti-intellectualism*. Ellis forwarded a distinction on potential reception. On academics, Ellis—who had clearly not read the earlier reviews—somewhat blithely offered that it was "difficult to see ... more than a murmur of dissent" on *Anti-intellectualism*'s main thrust. Academics would receive it in the Emersonian spirit as "a sound enterprise in self-correction," as Hofstadter hoped. Ellis foresaw "vigorous protest," however, from the general public, who would recoil from "the author's exposé ... of the more unlovely aspects" of American history.[27] It seemed "plain" to Ellis that anti-intellectualism was firmly linked to what Hofstadter called "democratic institutions and egalitarian sentiments." Rather than viewing the place of intellectuals in a mass democracy as "an insoluble dilemma," Ellis shared an outlook with Hofstadter that both "intellectual achievement" and distinction were possible. Elites could be "creative and imaginative," wrote Ellis, but also offer "enlightened leadership to the masses."[28] Inspired by Hofstadter, Ellis argued, essentially, that the efficient operation of a democratic, international, and modern American empire required an intellectual, technocratic elite. This justified, to Ellis, Kennedy's "New Frontier" brain trust. They enabled an enlightened Cold War democracy, even if its technocrats failed to fully engage all segments of the democratic populace.

News of the Pulitzer Prize came in the spring of 1964. Hofstadter, then a professor at Columbia University, won at a time when all Pulitzer Advisory Board members were appointed by Columbia University, and included university president Grayson Kirk. Perhaps this bit of context explains a surprising comment from Hofstadter, relayed in a David Brown footnote. On earning the Pulitzer, Hofstadter told Eric Foner: "I don't deserve it. I did the first time [for *Age of Reform* in 1956], but not for this book."[29] Despite this misgiving and internal politics at Columbia, *Anti-intellectualism*'s attractiveness reflected a time when the John Birch Society was news (and had broad appeal), Barry Goldwater was running for president, and the nation was still dealing with a presidential assassin influenced by "nut country."[30]

After the Pulitzer, professional analyses of *Anti-intellectualism* warmed somewhat, in the vein of Ellis's review. Rush Welter noted that "Hofstadter has taken on an impossible task," but there could be no doubt that anti-intellectualism was "part of the national experience," one that historians must not ignore. Even while Welter chided Hofstadter for often taking the side of intellectuals, he sympathized on the capaciousness of the topic. Welter noted the "protean" nature of anti-intellectualism, which created "the risk of thinking [Hofstadter] has proved more than he intended."[31] In a mildly belated July 1965 assessment, Arthur Bestor called *Anti-intellectualism* an "important book." But he also faulted Hofstadter for writing an "impressionistic treatment" of disparate, nonreinforcing themes presented as "formal history."[32] Unqualified praise was difficult to find, except from the Pulitzer's board.

Beyond Bestor, Welter, and others, the long and damning criticisms of *Anti-intellectualism* made by early reviewers were only sparingly acknowledged by Hofstadter's heirs. To summarize, those problematic areas included elitism, antiradicalism, presentism, no firm definition of anti-intellectualism, use of extreme examples, understated injustices of the past, excessive sympathy for intellectuals and the intellectual Establishment (except for unfair treatment of John Dewey), distrust for the working class, false nostalgia for historical "academic" curricula, religion treated too monolithically, and the lack of a firm distinction between ideas and psychology. And then there were other soon-to-be-major issues, not covered in *Anti-intellectualism* but in the air in the early 1960s: race, gender, and relevant contemporary critiques of class and capitalism.

Heirs and Legacies

Its long list of negative attributes makes subsequent scholarly and popular use of *Anti-intellectualism* problematic. Beyond that, the creation of a legacy of affirming heirs seems nearly inexplicable. Hofstadter's work should have started a historiography of negation and vigorous revision. But it didn't.

Despite the holes, *Anti-intellectualism*'s basic structure somehow stood. Why? It was well written. It possessed a Pulitzer. The deep grooves of irrationality and resentment narrated by Hofstadter resonated well beyond 1963. Even in his negation of American intellectual possibilities, Hofstadter affirmed liberalism and liberal technocratic leadership. Most importantly, the book served as a statement—evident in its title, *Anti-intellectualism in American Life*. It functioned as a symbol. It was a touchstone and totem for critics, academics, and elites with regard to frustrations with religion, religious leaders, business philistinism, political nonsense, and educational failures. When democracy and democratic discourse seemed to fail, commenters could refer to Hofstadter's prize-winning work. In it John Winthrop's "city upon a hill" was tragically compromised by long-running failures to acknowledge, or honor, the nation's best and brightest thinkers. Our elites had told us so, without irony. We had been warned.

Although other works utilize *Anti-intellectualism* or its themes, directly and indirectly, this section focuses on three prominent books.[33] Works by Mark Noll, Susan Jacoby, and Catherine Liu affirm the legacy of *Anti-intellectualism* and substantially expand on Hofstadter's coverage of religion, politics, cultural politics, and education. Noll's and Jacoby's works were popular, with Noll's becoming a touchstone itself for evangelicals. All three, however, either downplay or fail to acknowledge major weaknesses identified by reviewers. They underscore the need to get beyond Hofstadter and into the failures of social, cultural, and political discourse that inform their studies.

In *The Scandal of the Evangelical Mind* (1995), Mark Noll mimicked Hofstadter's style and themes, even while improving *Anti-intellectualism*'s coverage of Protestant Christianity. Like Hofstadter, Noll wrote a personal book with eyes simultaneously on the past and present. On the latter, he invoked an ominous warning from the Lebanese philosopher Charles Malik: "The greatest danger besetting American Evangelical Christianity is the danger of anti-intellectualism." In conjunction with Hofstadter, Noll saw the US context as anti-intellectual, and Protestantism therein as having acquired that national characteristic. Other acquisitions included pragmatism, populism, a focus on techniques or technology, and reliance in numerous spheres on charisma, or celebrity. In addition, for Noll, Christian piety in the United States tended to be an "inward state." These larger trends resulted in a general devaluation of intellectualism.[34]

Apart from context, Noll agreed with Hofstadter's assertion that "the evangelical spirit" was a prime mover in relation to American anti-intellectualism. That spirit among Protestant Christians led to a devaluation of learning and intellectual cultivation (the idea was that the faith was best propagated by "unlearned and ignorant" adherents). But Noll described Hofstadter's characterization as "too simple." To Noll, "the intuitions of the spirit" need not lead to a dismissal of "the mechanics of worldly learning." Noll's revision focused on how evangelical anti-intellectualism resulted from the "sometimes vigorous prosecution of the wrong sort of intellectual life" by Protestant Christians. This led Noll to explore the inner dynamics, and failings, of Christian institutions from the early republic through the 1980s.[35]

While affirming large swaths of *Anti-intellectualism*, Noll's narrative centered on declension rather than cyclicality. The irony for Noll was that Protestants had vigorously engaged the life of the mind, beginning in the late eighteenth century when evangelicals aligned "faith in reason with faith in God," via the Scottish didactic Enlightenment and commonsense rationalism. This synthesis fell apart because of "the fundamentalist influence on Protestantism." Noll emphasizes how an anti-elitist fundamentalism relied on the sermon and speech, preferred a mythical history of Christianity, emphasized *sola scriptura* (i.e., the Bible alone), used the Bible to interpret current events, exalted the supernatural over the natural (i.e., science), engaged in symbolic politics over institutional renovation, and turned political reflection into mere intuition. Noll saw a paradox at the heart of the scandal: both the lack of respect for creation and overconfidence in the heart went against biblical principles.[36]

Noll demonstrates that fundamentalism served as the causal agent of late twentieth-century evangelical anti-intellectualism. Fundamentalism degraded evangelical Protestant intellectual institutions and their contributions to the public square. Fundamentalism served, using the words of Sam Wineburg, as an "occluding" force—a "competing knowledge system"—rather than anti-intellectualism. Its adherents engaged in democratic political discourse differently owing to differing assumptions and epistemology.[37] Noll, then, extends Hofstadter's analysis while keeping the basic structure of the latter's work.

The next, most prominent affirmation of *Anti-intellectualism*'s legacy came in 2008. Susan Jacoby produced a popular history and cultural criticism that zeroed in on "unreason." In *The Age of American Unreason*, she argues that anti-intellectualism (defined as against too much learning) and antirationalism (defined as being antifactual or not using evidence) converged into a general sense of unreason. This convergence has been exacerbated by "an ignorant popular culture of video images and unremitting noise that leaves no room for contemplation or logic." Like Noll, Jacoby breaks with Hofstadter by favoring declension rather than cyclicity. Jacoby culminates in the judgment that post-1960s "anti-rationalism . . . propelled a surge of anti-intellectualism capable of inflicting vastly greater damage than its historical predecessors."[38] And *Age of American Unreason* charts the damage.

Jacoby seems to lionize Hofstadter's *Anti-intellectualism*. She opens her own work (literally, on the introduction's first page) arguing that his forty-five-year-old book "endures and provides the foundation for insights" in her book and beyond. *Anti-intellectualism* is, for Jacoby, a bedrock great book. She appropriates Hofstadter within her idiosyncratic personal ideology of "cultural conservationism," committed to preserving culture from decay and destruction. This ideology feels like elitism, except for her admiration of midcentury "middlebrow" culture. Despite acknowledging Hofstadter's thesis of cyclicality and noting an "old-fashioned fairness" in his consensus history scholarship, Jacoby persists with a polemical story of decline.[39] Her engagement with his work, furthermore, is ironically sparse in *Unreason*—a name check rather than a fundamental reference point. *Anti-intellectualism*, then, is a totem for Jacoby.

Jacoby shared Hofstadter's disposition to dispatch shallow politicians (especially conservatives and, with Jacoby, George W. Bush), preachers, fundamentalists, and Babbitt-like business people.[40] Appropriate to the book's postwar period, Jacoby delves into: "junk thought"; scientific illiteracy ("junk science"); the devolution of language, in general and in political speech (e.g., increased use of the term "folks"); and fads and "popular infotainment culture" (e.g., bad television instead of worthwhile middlebrow literary culture). Like Hofstadter, Jacoby also blamed the education system for the nation's intellectual problems. As Stephen Whitfield noted in his 1978 retrospective on Hofstadter, targets like these made *Anti-intellectualism*, and Jacoby's work by extension, "less courageous" and less challenging.[41] It played well to cultural and intellectual elites who despised conservatism. But these choices disable smarter analyses of democratic discourse. They render invisible the compromises between democracy, its dynamic American culture, and its capitalist context. The reader cannot see the deeper roots of apparent unreason in political discourse. Worst of all, the condition of "unreason" feels, in Jacoby's hands, immovable rather than contingent.

This brief look at Hofstadter's heirs and legacy concludes with Catherine Liu's *American Idyll: Academic Antielitism as Cultural Critique* (2011). Liu's study generally affirms Hofstadter's themes and work, and is the most complicated of the three analyzed here. Hofstadter's name recurs in every chapter, either as a citation or reference. Liu extends the work of *Anti-intellectualism* in her analyses of meritocracy, of the demise of liberal education and the rise of standardized testing, and of the problems of vocational and progressive education.

American Idyll accomplishes two interesting and provocative goals in relation to Hofstadter. First, Liu argues that anti-elitism is the dominant attitude of late twentieth-century cultural studies adherents. She also acknowledges the elitism in *Anti-intellectualism* by noting how it became a reference point for leftist academics concerned with academic elitism. Those cultural theorists then became "academic populists," critiquing "modernity, reason, and universalism" by imagining an academic "idyll" friendly to popular culture and antirational politics. This idealized state of mind, in cultural studies, "imagined a world of ordinary people with popular tastes and deep passions who, as fans and amateurs, could finally create a culture of their own that eluded the experts." These academic populists, to Liu, "routinized anti-elitism" and professionalized academia such that a hostility arose to the "ideals of liberal education as well as aesthetic and intellectual autonomy"—the kinds of education and autonomy defended by "thinkers like Richard Hofstadter and Theodor Adorno." The academic populists faulted Hofstadter as an overly "harsh critic of the mythologization of ordinary people" and of "populist politics."[42] In other words, the academic populists fully understood the earlier critiques of Hofstadter's *Anti-intellectualism*. But Liu faults them for not acknowledging his legitimate criticisms of education, culture, and politics.

The second goal of *American Idyll* involves Adorno. Liu places Hofstadter alongside Adorno for their "remarkably negative" conceptions, respectively, of intellectual and aesthetic autonomy. Indeed, Liu cites David Brown's biography for evidence that Hofstadter was influenced by Adorno's *The Authoritarian Personality*—aside from Hofstadter's existing attachments to the urbanity and cosmopolitanism of New York intellectual life. This connection between Hofstadter and Adorno began shortly after the 1950 publication of *The Authoritarian Personality*, and was evident in Hofstadter's pathologizing of the Far Right ("criticism in psychiatric categories," wrote Brown, paraphrasing Christopher Lasch) and his use of the term "pseudo-conservative." By the end of *American Idyll*, Hofstadter seems, loosely, like a Frankfurt school member. David Brown, however, assessed *Anti-intellectualism* as a kind of "memoir of twentieth-century American liberalism," written in the spirit of "liberal skepticism."[43] Whatever the critical muse, the reader probably would not understand the need for Liu's review of Hofstadter's place in recent cultural criticism, and similarities with Adorno, without some understanding of the original 1960s reception of *Anti-intellectualism* and subsequent attempts by others to work in Hofstadter's legacy.

While Liu's study is insightful and worthy of admiration, its focus on academic cultural studies limits its use in histories about anti-intellectualism broadly conceived. In addition, Liu accidentally reinforces Hofstadter's nostalgia for historical academic curricula by understating the injustices of twentieth-century educational institutions (e.g., the need for inclusion of students from a vast varieties of backgrounds and with special deficits and needs). Liu rightly affirms Hofstadter's criticisms of progressive and vocational education, and their nefarious consequences. But Liu offers little on how proponents of the liberal arts ideal might have negotiated conflicting social and political aspirations in recent decades. For the sake of purported anti-intellectualism in democratic discourse and inclusive institutions, the devil is in those details.[44]

New Directions

Because of the weaknesses, issues, and problems outlined by 1960s reviewers of Hofstadter's *Anti-intellectualism*, and in the work of some of his heirs, new directions are needed. If anti-intellectualism is to be, or can be, salvaged and fulfilled as a "protean" concept (borrowing Rush Welter's descriptor), a revised view of the term and its applications is necessary.[45] What follows is an attempt to move the conversation.

Charges of anti-intellectualism most often signal, in a democracy, failures of discourse. If the charge arises from a pundit or critic, that charge often disguises a logical fallacy, such as an appeal to authority, usually in psychology or psychiatry, or the simple ridiculing of an opponent. Both avoid the specifics of an argument or issue at hand. Both fallacies signal elitism and a reactionary mind, whether from the right or left. The critic's avoidance, or deflection, may be accidental or purposeful. It may also be a lack of respect for the emotion spent in, and attention given to, a particular political, social, or cultural situation. More nefariously, the charge of anti-intellectualism may also be a power play. When critics and historians do legitimately identify the potential for unreason, reaction, irrationality, ignorance, paranoia, anti-elitism, or any other term summoned by a Menckenesque or Hofstadterian analysis, it is fair to suspect failures in discourse by multiple parties. One should ask: What other issues are not being articulated in ordinary discourse? Why is there a lack of communication or miscommunication? What power dynamic is preventing recourse to reason? What fears are making unreason or irrationality an issue? Rather than viewing anti-intellectualism as an enemy or problematic of democracy, historians would be better served by viewing suspected historical formations of the same as signs or signals of deeper problematic currents. Anti-intellectualism can never then be ignored, but also never taken at face value.

In terms of theory, one direction that salvages the term "anti-intellectualism" and offers a bridge to other currents is to view it as an expansive "sensibility." Instead of pathologizing or dismissing an anti-intellectual phenomenon, a sensibility helps the historian look for and respect, at once, emotion and reason, in the context of discourse. According to Daniel Wickberg, a sensibility encompasses "perception and feeling, the terms and forms in which objects were conceived, experienced, and represented." It is inclusive of "the emotional, intellectual, aesthetic, and moral dispositions of the persons" who, in this case, exhibit an anti-intellectual sensibility (AIS). An AIS is sometimes imaginative (springing from a certain structure of experience), and at other times concrete; it can be conscious and unconscious. The AIS for which I advocate here, and the kind Wickberg outlined and for which he argued, is "capacious." That capaciousness maintains the potential protean nature of anti-intellectualism as a historical object of study. Wickberg reminded readers of William James's notion of "the sentiment of rationality" (outlined in an 1882 essay), which implies reason without the same rising above emotion and attitudes. An AIS requires emotion and reaction without believing, necessarily, that logic, syllogisms, and reason are absent.[46] Without disrespecting what universalism is present, a more plural view of "reasoning" might be employed by the historian. Hofstadter himself might approve of this approach. In the context of religion, he argued that Christianity first hosted the "anti-intellectual impulse." The term "impulse," as a motivation or a force that produces motion, points toward anti-intellectualism as a sensibility—a combination of head and heart, of reaction and outlook.[47] Because religion gave authority to emotion and enthusiasm far beyond religion, for theoretical purposes it is proper to designate anti-intellectualism a sensibility.

Future work on American anti-intellectualism might avoid the serious charge of elitism if, in the spirit of Aaron Lecklider's *Inventing the Egghead: The Battle over Brainpower in American Culture* (2013), historians worked in a bottom-up fashion, following the new social history of the 1960s. In that mode, one should ask: How are ordinary citizens, or nontraditional intellectuals, seizing, reworking, and refashioning democratic discourse? Or, what ideas, from elites or intellectuals, are being revised and reinserted in politics and culture? One does not have to subscribe to the Gramscian notion of an "organic intellectual tradition" to respect plurality in the history of thought in non-elite contexts. Rather, utilizing historical evidence from non-elite contexts might reveal, or foster respect for, what Kwame Anthony Appiah called "rooted cosmopolitans," or Homi Bhabha's "vernacular cosmopolitans." Since the terms "intellectual" and "cosmopolitan" are used interchangeably in some historical contexts, a historian can view this as exploring rooted or vernacular intellectuals.[48] A respect for differing registers and hierarchies of thought, or "moral dispositions" in Wickberg's framework, might arise from unpacking homogenizing terms such as "the working class" or "ordinary Americans." The emerging field of "agnotology" has shown promise in avoiding elitism, moving beyond Hofstadter, and explaining failures of political and social discourse.[49]

For my part, I would like to see historians use neo-Marxian, Gramscian, and critical theory tools to bridge the gap between charges of anti-intellectualism (real and purported) and problems with capitalism. Catherine Liu began a move in this direction, connecting Hofstadter with Adorno, but her focus on academia limited her inquiry. Instead of using the history of thought and stopping with cultural, psychopathological, educational, and social analysis, I would like to see an integration with economics and political economy, especially with regard to imperialism and the information economy. On the latter, for instance, has the commodification of discourse via social media cheapened democratic engagement? In sum, I think that analyses that incorporate Marxism, sensibility, rooted cosmopolitanism, and reception theory could build a new history of anti-intellectualism that steers clear of elitism, psychopathology, and run-of-the-mill liberalism.

Movement in these new directions will help correct a problem identified by David Riesman—namely, Hofstadter's understatement of the injustices of the past. By more thoroughly exploring the ratiocinations, sensibilities, and *apparent* unreason of others, a more inclusive, just, and useful history of thought may emerge. This new line of work will improve the study of the idea of anti-intellectualism by going above and beyond the work of Hofstadter, and helping Americans fully understand larger failures in democratic discourse.

NOTES

1. A Lexis-Nexis Academic search for "anti-intellectualism" or "antiintellectualism" resulted in 2,551 citations since January 1, 2001, and 537 since January 1, 2015. Since January 1, 2001, Hofstadter and anti-intellectualism (together) have been cited fifty-three times in newspapers—excluding many results from reviews of two major works citing Hofstadter (by David Brown and Susan Jacoby). This search was conducted on December 19, 2016, and excluded results with "high similarity." The earliest invocations of "anti-intellectualism" in the English language occurred in 1909 and 1921, according to the *Oxford English Dictionary*. Google's Ngram reviewer reveals a relative burst in usage of the term in the 1950–1980 period, peaking in the mid-1960s. Usage has remained at 1950 levels since the early 1980s.

2. Richard Hofstadter, *Anti-intellectualism in American Life* (New York: Alfred A. Knopf, 1963); David S. Brown, *Richard Hofstadter: An Intellectual Biography* (Chicago: University of Chicago Press, 2006), 121, 131; David Greenberg, "Richard Hofstadter: The Pundits' Favorite Historian," *Slate*, June 7, 2006, at http://www.slate.com; Aaron Lecklider, *Inventing the Egghead: The Battle over Brainpower in American Culture* (Philadelphia: University of Pennsylvania Press, 2013), 229n6. Hofstadter's work, notes Lecklider, overshadowed an important, related work by one of his students, Christopher Lasch. Lasch's

1965 book, *The New Radicalism in America*, charted the role and place of intellectuals in American life. Hofstadter likely overshadowed Lasch among reviewers, heirs, and successors because the former blamed anti-intellectualism on the public and secondary figures, while Lasch blamed intellectuals themselves.

3. Hofstadter, *Anti-intellectualism*, 6, 7, 18, 47.

4. Brown, *Richard Hofstadter*, 24–26, 125, 126, 128.

5. See also Michael Paul Rogin, *The Intellectuals and McCarthy: The Radical Specter* (Cambridge, MA: MIT Press, 1967).

6. Hofstadter, *Anti-intellectualism*, 3, 6, 20. On the English heritage of anti-intellectualism, John Erskine made a similar argument in 1915 when he wrote: "The disposition to consider intelligence a peril is an old Anglo-Saxon inheritance." See *The Moral Obligation to Be Intelligent: And Other Essays* (New York: Duffield, 1915), 3–34.

7. Hofstadter, *Anti-intellectualism*, 55.

8. Ibid., 57, 68–69, 74, 83, 84, 85, 97, 117 chaps. 3–5 passim.

9. Ibid., 117–18, 119, 123, 124, 128.

10. Ibid., 145–46, 147, 151, 154–55, 158, 160.

11. Ibid., 233, 236–37, 238–39.

12. Ibid., 253–54, 257, 264–65, 266, 269.

13. Ibid., 260–63, 270–71.

14. Ibid., 13–14, 198–200, 202, 214–15.

15. Ibid., 12–14, 60, 139, 164, 262–63, 301. See also Robert M. Hutchins, *The Higher Learning in America* (New Haven, CT: Yale University Press, 1936).

16. Hofstadter, *Anti-intellectualism*, 304–5, 310, 324, 327–28, 329–32, 343–47. Also, chap. 14 passim. See Andrew Hartman's *Education and the Cold War* (New York: Palgrave Macmillan, 2008), chap. 6, for more on the tension between Dewey and Hofstadter.

17. Lionel Trilling, *The Liberal Imagination: Essays on Literature and Society*, introduction by Louis Menand (1950; New York: New York Review of Books, 2012), xv.

18. Here is a chronological listing of every academic/near-academic review I could find: Daniel J. Boorstin, "The Split-Level Tower," *Saturday Review*, June 1, 1963, 19–20; Benjamin DeMott, "America Absolved," *New York Review of Books*, June 1, 1963; Kenneth S. Lynn, "Elitism on the Left," *Reporter*, July 4, 1963, 37–40; Howard Mumford Jones, review in *Political Science Quarterly* 78, no. 4 (December 1963): 597, 599; Merle Borrowman, review in *History of Education Quarterly* 3, no. 4 (December 1963): 223–25; David Riesman, review in *American Sociological Review* 23, no. 6 (December 1963): 1038–40; John Tracy Ellis, review in *Catholic Historical Review* 49, no. 4 (January 1964): 580–81; Ramsay Cook, review in *International Journal* 19, no. 1 (Winter 1963–1964): 99; Rush Welter, review in *Journal of American History* 51, no. 3 (December 1964): 482–83; Arthur Bestor, review in *American Historical Review* 70, no. 4 (July 1965): 1118–20; Philip Gleason, "Anti-Intellectualism and Other Reconsiderations," *Review of Politics* 28, no. 2 (April 1966): 238–42; Stephen J. Whitfield, "Second Thoughts: 'The Eggheads and the Fatheads,'" *Change* 10, no. 4 (April 1978): 65; Daniel Rigney, "Three Kinds of Anti-Intellectualism: Rethinking Hofstadter," *Sociological Inquiry* 61, no. 4 (October 1991): 434–51.

19. See William Appleman Williams, *The Tragedy of American Diplomacy* (New York: World, 1959), and Paul Buhle and Edward Rice-Maxim, *William Appleman Williams: The Tragedy of Empire* (New York: Routledge, 1995).

20. Brown, *Richard Hofstadter*, 146.

21. Boorstin, "Split-Level Tower," 19–20.

22. Lynn, "Elitism on the Left," 37–40; Wolfgang Saxon, "Kenneth S. Lynn, 78, Biographer of Hemingway and Chaplin," *New York Times*, July 3, 2001, http://www.nytimes.com/2001/07/03/arts/kenneth-s-lynn-78-biographer-of-hemingway-and-chaplin.html; Brown, *Richard Hofstadter*, 139.

23. Lynn, "Elitism on the Left"; Hofstadter, *Anti-intellectualism*, 8–9.
24. Jones, review, 597, 599; Borrowman, review, 223–25.
25. Riesman, review, 1038–40.
26. Ibid.
27. Ellis, review, 580–81; Hofstadter, *Anti-intellectualism*, viii, 140.
28. Ellis, review, 581–83; Hofstadter, *Anti-intellectualism*, 140, 407; Cook, review, 99.
29. Peter Kihss, "Pulitzer Prizes Omitted in Drama, Fiction, and Music," *New York Times*, May 5, 1964; Brown, *Richard Hofstadter*, 120, 256n34.
30. For more on both topics see D. J. Mulloy's *The World of the John Birch Society: Conspiracy, Conservatism, and the Cold War* (Nashville, TN: Vanderbilt University Press, 2014) and Edward H. Miller's *Nut Country: Right-Wing Dallas and the Birth of the Southern Strategy* (Chicago: University Of Chicago Press, 2015). On the assassination, the Pulitzer for photography went to Robert Jackson's picture of the fatal shooting of Lee Harvey Oswald by Jack Ruby.
31. Welter, review, 482–83; Brown, *Richard Hofstadter*, 139. Brown covered Welter's review but did not relay Welter's praise of the book's larger significance to historical work.
32. Bestor, review, 1118–20; Brown, *Richard Hofstadter*, 139. Here I agree with Brown's assessment of Bestor's review.
33. Each of the following books (listed chronologically) lies in the tradition of *Anti-intellectualism*, drawing from its major themes whether or not Hofstadter is directly cited: Allan Bloom, *Closing of the American Mind: How Higher Education Has Failed Democracy and Impoverished the Souls of Today's Students* (New York: Simon & Schuster, 1987); Paul Fussell, *BAD, or, the Dumbing of America* (Summit Books, 1991); Rick Shenkman, *Just How Stupid Are We? Facing the Truth about the American Voter* (New York: Basic Books, 2008); Charles P. Pierce, *Idiot America: How Stupidity Became a Virtue in the Land of the Free* (New York: Anchor Books, 2010); Lecklider, *Inventing the Egghead* (2013); Mark Bauerlein and Adam Bellow, eds., *The State of the American Mind: 16 Leading Critics on the New Anti-intellectualism* (West Conshohocken, PA: Templeton, 2015).
34. Mark A. Noll, *The Scandal of the Evangelical Mind* (Grand Rapids, MI: Wm B. Eerdmans, 1995), 11–12, 26, 55–56; Hofstadter, *Anti-intellectualism*, 48–49n8, 55–80. No mention of Lasch or any other noteworthy secular historian appears in *Scandal*. Malik's warning came in *The Two Tasks* (1980).
35. Noll, *Scandal*.
36. Ibid., 4, 83–88, 91, 98, 123–26, 152–53, 156, 158, 166, 169, 174, 175, 202.
37. Sam Wineburg, *Historical Thinking and Other Unnatural Acts: Charting the Future of Teaching the Past* (Philadelphia: Temple University Press, 2001), 242–43; Adam Laats, "Religion," in *Miseducation: A History of Ignorance-Making in America and Abroad*, ed. A. J. Angulo (Baltimore: Johns Hopkins University Press, 2016), 161, 176–79.
38. Susan Jacoby, *The Age of American Unreason* (New York: Vintage Books, 2009), xi–xii. The book was first published by Random House–Pantheon in 2008. But in this chapter I am working from the 2009 Random House–Vintage edition, which contains updates on Barack Obama after his election and inauguration.
39. Jacoby, xi–xii, xv, xvi, chap. 5 passim.
40. Jacoby's animus toward President George W. Bush and conservatives is palpable. For a more objective political analysis of historical presidential rhetoric (i.e., its substance, uses, and consequences), I recommend Elvin T. Lim's *The Anti-Intellectual Presidency: The Decline of Presidential Rhetoric from George Washington to George W. Bush* (New York: Oxford University Press, 2008). Although Lim is concerned with a decline in intellectual rhetoric, and Hofstadter's *Anti-intellectualism* is cited, Lim's work is more of a study using recent historical data than a narrative of intellectual or cultural history, hence it is not analyzed here.

41. Jacoby, xviii, 3, 22, 25, 61, 102–4, 107, 124, 173–74, 244–45, 286; Whitfield, "Second Thoughts," 66; Patricia Cohen, "Hand-Wringing about American Culture—Are Americans Hostile to Knowledge?," *New York Times*, February 14, 2008, http://www.nytimes.com/2008/02/14/books/14dumb.html; Mike O'Connor, "The Age of American Unreason," *U.S. Intellectual History Blog*, May 12, 2008, http://s-usih.org/2008/05/age-of-american-unreason.html. See also Sinclair Lewis, *Babbitt* (1922).

42. Catherine Liu, *American Idyll: Academic Antielitism as Cultural Critique* (Iowa City: University of Iowa Press, 2011), 1, 7–8, 59–60.

43. Ibid., 8, 11; Brown, *Richard Hofstadter*, 90, 140, 151, 227, 257n22.

44. Liu's book has received little professional attention. One review, by J. E. Herbel, criticized the book's construction ("elliptical") and writing style ("subjunctive mood and passive voice"). Herbel also accused Liu of "not adequately comment[ing] . . . on the elitist tendencies of critical theory itself." See Herbel, review of *American Idyll: Academic Antielitism as Cultural Critique*, by Catherine Liu, *CHOICE: Current Reviews for Academic Libraries*, May 2012: 1739.

45. Welter, review, 482.

46. Daniel Wickberg, "What Is the History of Sensibilities? On Cultural Histories, Old and New," *American Historical Review* 112, no. 3 (June 2007): 662, 664–65, 669, 671, 675, 676–77.

47. Hofstadter, *Anti-intellectualism*, 55.

48. Lecklider, *Inventing the Egghead*, 221–23, 228n8; Kwame Anthony Appiah, *The Ethics of Identity* (Princeton, NJ: Princeton University Press, 2005), chap. 6 passim; Homi Bhabha, "Unsatisfied: Notes on Vernacular Cosmopolitanism," in *Text and Nation*, ed. Laura Garcia-Morena and Peter Freifer (London: Camden House, 1996), 191–207.

49. Robert Proctor's and Londa Schiebinger's *Agnotology: The Making and Unmaking of Ignorance* (Redwood City, CA: Stanford University Press, 2008) helps by not taking ignorance for granted as a static phenomenon. In *Agnotology*, ignorance is produced and maintained, "through mechanisms such as deliberate or inadvertent neglect, secrecy and suppression, document destruction, unquestioned tradition, and . . . culturopolitical selectivity." The focus is on "how or why we don't know" rather than epistemology. Ignorance is not a void in need of rectification, as a fault in the ignorant masses, but rather a variable, multicausal phenomenon to be explained (vii, 2, 3, 24). There is a scientific tone about *Agnotology* that takes the focus off the ignorant and puts it on structures and larger forces. The promise of agnotology has already yielded one related volume on education: A. J. Angulo, ed., *Miseducation: A History of Ignorance-Making in America and Abroad* (Baltimore: Johns Hopkins University Press, 2016).

17

CULTURE AS INTELLECTUAL HISTORY

Broadening a Field of Study in the Wake of the Cultural Turn

Benjamin L. Alpers

Writing about the relationship of culture to intellectual history is a complicated task for at least two reasons. First, "culture," as Raymond Williams remarks in *Keywords*, is "one of the two or three most complicated words in the English language."[1] As we will see, even as an object of historical study, it can mean a variety of quite different things. In a sense, I could almost have written about anything and called it "culture." Second, unlike most, though not all, of the other topics addressed in this volume, culture lies at the heart of a historical subfield of its own, cultural history, a subfield that has, for at least the last three decades, a close and complicated relationship to intellectual history.

Intellectual and cultural history have grown so close to each other for at least the last three decades or so that some historians speak of them a single subfield. Though the *Intellectual History Newsletter* (*IHN*, 1979–2002)—along with the Intellectual History Group (IHG) that published it—saw intellectual history as its primary focus, the opening piece by Thomas Bender, the IHG's first coordinator, in the inaugural (Spring 1979) issue of *IHN*, described the membership of the IHG as scholars of "the intellectual and cultural history of both North America and modern Europe" and described the audience for the new *IHN* as "intellectual/cultural historians." An attached survey for a directory of members referred to "the field of intellectual and cultural history."[2] More recently, in describing the mission of their then new journal in 2004, the editors of *Modern Intellectual History* (*MIH*) proclaimed "we see no point in neatly dividing intellectual from cultural history."[3]

However, in many other contexts, historians treat intellectual and cultural history as separate subdisciplines. In that very same introductory statement, the editors of *MIH* described the bleak recent past of intellectual history, when "its natural habitat" had "been laid waste by social and cultural historians who rejected its elitism."[4] Both the American Historical Association and the Organization of American Historians still list intellectual and cultural history as separate areas of specialization. A July 2016 search of the OAH membership directory revealed that 899 of its members called themselves intellectual historians, 1,456 listed themselves as cultural historians, and 462 listed themselves as both.[5] Or to put this another way, among the US historians who make up the membership of the OAH, a narrow majority (51 percent) of self-described intellectual historians also considered themselves to be cultural historians. On the other hand, over two-thirds of the more numerous tribe of cultural historians in the OAH (68 percent) *didn't* consider themselves to be intellectual historians. To the extent that we want to make a distinction between them, cultural history seems more central to most intellectual historians than intellectual history seems to be to most cultural historians.

I should at this point probably lay my own cards on the table. I am one of those 462 OAH members who list ourselves as both intellectual and cultural historians. And I do so because, like the editors of *MIH* in their more sanguine moments, I have never seen the point in dividing the two. When people, inside or outside the discipline, ask me what kind of history I study, I have always tended to answer "twentieth-century US intellectual and cultural history," going right back to the years when I was writing my dissertation in the early 1990s. This, in turn, reflects my training. Though my dissertation adviser Daniel Rodgers is usually spoken of as an intellectual historian, he too never drew a sharp distinction between intellectual and cultural history.[6] But despite my self-understanding and my training—and, I suspect, like most of the other of those 462 intellectual *and* cultural historians in the OAH—I have some sense of what the differences are between intellectual and cultural history, or at least of the sorts of things that people have in mind when distinguishing between them.

There are in fact two rather different ways of dividing the disciplinary turf between intellectual and cultural history: by methodology and by subject matter. One of the most commonly made, broad methodological distinctions has been succinctly described by Donald R. Kelley in an essay in which he explores this difference at some length: "What is the relationship between intellectual and cultural history? An answer to this question may be found in the area between the two poles of inquiry commonly known as internalist and externalist methods. The first of these deals with old-fashioned 'ideas' (in Lovejoy's sense) and the second with social and political context and the sociology and anthropology of knowledge."[7]

But although this distinction is familiar, I actually do not think that it does a particularly good job distinguishing what we mean by cultural history from what we mean by intellectual history, at least not these days. Most US intellectual history written today is deeply contextual in its approach. Since 2013, the Society for U.S. Intellectual History (S-USIH) has been awarding a prize for the best book in US intellectual history. The first five winners—in 2016 two books tied for the award— were concerned with context: Jennifer Ratner-Rosenhagen's *American Nietzsche* (2012), Ajay K. Mehrotra's *Making the Modern American Fiscal State* (2013), Ruben Flores's *Backroads Pragmatists* (2014), Sarah Bridger's *Scientists at War* (2015), and Daniel Immerwahr's *Thinking Small* (2015).[8] Indeed, the 2004 opening editorial in the first issue of *MIH* declared that the journal would focus on scholarship that deals with the interaction between text (broadly understood) and context.[9]

But if we cannot draw a hard and fast methodological line between cultural and intellectual history, we nevertheless should acknowledge the ways in which cultural history has inflected intellectual historical practice over the last three or four decades. Cultural history plays a key role in what has emerged as the standard narrative about the changing status of intellectual history in this country. Intellectual historians all know this story. Having risen to a central place in the field of history during the 1940s and 1950s, the subfield of intellectual history was dealt a severe blow in the 1960s. The rise both of history-from-below and of quantitative methodologies boosted the fortunes of social history. Though social history was not new—like intellectual history its roots as a subfield lay in the early twentieth century—it came to be seen, for a time, as both the most methodologically up-to-date and the most authoritative subfield in our discipline. By the 1970s, intellectual history seemed elitist and increasingly irrelevant to many historians. The kind of big, unifying themes of the heyday of US intellectual history, captured by the phrase "the American mind," seemed out of place in a time that Daniel Rodgers would later dub the "Age of Fracture."[10] In the midst of this apparent crisis of authority, a group of US intellectual historians gathered near Racine, Wisconsin, in December 1977, to discuss the state of the subfield. The Wingspread Conference (named for the Frank Lloyd Wright– designed house in which it took place) became a watershed in the subfield. The conference volume that emerged from Wingspread, *New Directions in American Intellectual History* (1979), played a key role in setting the agenda for the subfield in the years ahead.[11] The *Intellectual History Newsletter* in part grew out of Wingspread. *IHN*, in turn, spawned *Modern Intellectual History* (2004–), which has become the leading English-language journal in intellectual history. In the decades since Wingspread, virtually all onetime gatherings of US intellectual historians, including the symposium that led to this volume, have referenced Wingspread in their statements of purpose.

Even in 1977, at the time of Wingspread, culture seemed to be one of the lifelines available to US intellectual history. "History of Culture"—along with "Definitions" and "History of Ideas"—would be one of the three sections into which John Higham and Paul Conkin, editors of *New Directions*, organized the Wingspread papers for publication. To a number of the Wingspread participants, cultural history seemed like a response to the challenge of social history that could be embraced by intellectual historians. Thomas Bender, for example, argued that intellectual history could renew itself by focusing on the "cultures of intellectual life," the particular institutions, communities, and networks developed among American intellectuals that shaped changing American "structures of discourse." The goal would be a new "social history of ideas," a phrase that both echoed Merle Curti's 1943 suggestion of a "social history of American thought" and seemed to relocate intellectual history *as* social history.[12]

The 1980s and 1990s proved to be an era of great growth for cultural history, as a "cultural turn" that had begun in the 1970s swept history and the humanities in general. By the time that *Modern Intellectual History*, an institutional grandchild of Wingspread, hosted a forum in 2012 on the state of US intellectual history, the subfield seemed to participants to be in a period of great health. And many of them saw cultural history as key to the resurgence.[13] So conventional was the wisdom of the narrative I have just sketched that Leslie Butler, in her piece for the *MIH* forum, could even write that the story of American intellectual history's decline and resurgence, "rescued in part by the linguistic and cultural 'turns' that swept the entire discipline of American history in the 1980s and 1990s," had "become trite with the retelling."[14]

However, all of this seemed less clear in the years between Wingspread and *MIH*'s twenty-first-century optimism. In 1996, the *Intellectual History Newsletter* published a symposium on "Intellectual History in the Age of Cultural Studies."[15] Thirty-two scholars published short pieces in response to a call put out by Casey Blake. Blake's charge to his fellow historians was celebratory but anxious. An "extraordinary renaissance" had taken place in intellectual history since Wingspread, Blake suggested. But "the intellectual history revival of the late seventies and eighties has subsided," as graduate students were now turning away from intellectual history to cultural history or cultural studies. Mid-career scholars, too, were turning to more "culturalist" projects. Though Blake insisted that he was not trying to "register some status anxiety among intellectual historians, nor to bemoan the passing of a golden age of intellectual history," the framing question of the symposium was full of anxiety: "Does intellectual history have a future in an age of cultural studies?"[16]

The decision to frame the question in terms of "cultural studies" rather than "cultural history" was significant. While cultural history was a subdiscipline of history that was often presented in the pages of *IHN* as allied with, or even identical to, intellectual history, cultural studies was an interdisciplinary practice that was largely found outside history departments and that seemed to be on the rise in the 1990s. The thirty-two scholars who responded to Blake's call generally focused on cultural studies. But some wrote, instead, about cultural history. And at least two contributors—Deborah J. Coon and Dorothy Ross—treated the two as equivalent.

If few contributors echoed Blake's sense that intellectual history was threatened by "culturalism," many expressed doubts about cultural studies as a substitute for intellectual history. Joyce Appleby, John Toews, Mary Kupiec Cayton, Paul Jerome Croce, and Deborah J. Coon all suggested that cultural studies tended to devalue the role of the individual, as it located culture in totalizing webs of meaning. The study of individuals, they each suggested, is central to the practice of intellectual history. The Foucauldian notions of culture that many of the symposium's participants associated with cultural studies stood in stark contrast to Thomas Bender's earlier understanding of the "cultures of intellectual life" in *New Directions*. The networks that interested Bender were local and provided the context for individual thought and action that, in turn, shaped the networks themselves. But the problem of cultural studies for intellectual historians was not simply its different focus. A number of scholars in the 1996 *IHN* Symposium simply questioned the quality of most work in cultural studies. "Cultural studies began as a salutary effort to enliven disembodied academicism," wrote Jackson Lears, "but it has turned into a ludicrously anti-intellectual enterprise." "The trendiness of continental ideas" was, for Bruce Kuklick, "not so much threatening as intellectually embarrassing."[17]

But despite the sometimes negative assessments of cultural studies in the symposium, none of the participants felt that cultural studies was a serious threat to the future of intellectual history. Dominick LaCapra, George Cotkin, Jackson Lears, Donald R. Kelley, James Livingston, Alan Lawson, and Dorothy Ross all suggested that intellectual history could learn some important things from cultural studies, whether that was greater attention to popular culture, a greater concern for questions of race and gender, or greater consideration of the theoretical perspectives that drove much work in cultural studies. Others, such as Martin Jay and Wilfred McClay, argued that the rise of cultural studies would lead intellectual historians to productively sharpen the differences between their subdiscipline and that of the culturalists.

The participants were almost evenly split on the question of whether cultural *history* and intellectual history were one and the same field. Daniel Rodgers, Joan Rubin, Andrew Ross, Nikhil Pal Singh, John Toews, and Richard Wightman Fox argued for the identity (or at least the continuity) of the two historical subfields. Martin Jay, Carolyn Dean, Donald R. Kelley, Mary Kupiec Cayton, Deborah J.

Coon, and David Hollinger, on the other hand, suggested that intellectual and cultural history were distinct from each other.

What then characterized, or should characterize, intellectual history? Though the scholars in the *IHN* Symposium did not entirely agree in their answers to that question, one of the most common themes was the importance of close reading of texts, which Dominick LaCapra, George Cotkin, Michael Steinberg, John Toews, and Dorothy Ross all mentioned as a defining aspect of intellectual historical practice. And while a handful of participants in the symposium suggested that intellectual history was interested in particular sorts of thinkers—namely, intellectuals—more saw the field as taking a capacious view of the sorts of people and texts the subfield should concern itself with. Daniel Rodgers, for example, praised the cacophony of Americans' thinking that had replaced American thought or the American mind as the object of US intellectual history. Noting the wide variety of topics then being pursued by his graduate students, Rodgers concluded, "They have found Americans thinking everywhere, with the most intense seriousness, under the most trying circumstances, and with historical consequences. That seems to me the essence of the matter."[18]

By the time of the 2012 *MIH* forum, the anxieties of 1996 about cultural studies had largely dissipated. Participants saw the "cultural turn" as having lifted the fortunes of intellectual history in the decades since the 1970s and having significantly inflected intellectual-historical practice. David D. Hall—who contributed both to *New Directions* and to the 2012 *MIH* forum on the state of US intellectual history—identified a number of key features of these changes, including "the interplay of 'high' and 'low' and how ordinary people received and acted upon stories or representations"; "an awareness of the mediations that all texts undergo and the politics that drives these mediations"; "a description of culture as practice" and an attendant "focus on narrative or 'discursive' structures as a form of action"; and "recasting politics as a struggle against certain representations (say, of race and gender)."[19] Many of these changes reflect things that participants in the 1996 *IHN* Symposium had associated with cultural studies. And to the extent that they have come to shape intellectual history of the last two decades, the changes that Hall identified support the views of those scholars who, in 1996, had seen no clear line between intellectual and cultural history.

But if methodology does not define a clear difference between the two subfields, perhaps their objects of study do. And this brings us back to the question with which I began: what exactly is culture? What makes it, in Raymond Williams's assessment, "one of the two or three most complicated words in the English language"? This is not the time or place to detail the complicated early history of the term, but rather to focus on a number of meanings that it has taken on in English, especially over the last two centuries or so, that constitute the things historians tend to mean when we talk about culture. Two in particular stand out. First, "culture" can mean "the works and practices of intellectual and especially artistic activity."[20] In the nineteenth and early twentieth century, "culture" in this sense principally meant *high* culture. But the referent shifted over time. By the mid-twentieth century, critics were distinguishing between lowbrow, middlebrow, and highbrow culture, and writing about popular and mass culture and the differences between them. Especially when contrasted to intellectual history, which in its heyday in the 1940s and 1950s focused on formal thought and elite intellectuals, cultural history is more likely to be about folk, popular, or mass culture. This is one sense it which intellectual historians in the 1970s felt that social and cultural history were overtaking their subfield. Both were instances of "history from below," which had come to have more intellectual salience than the study of elites.

But since the nineteenth century, "culture" has also been used to refer to "a particular way of life, whether of a people, a group, or humanity in general." This is a meaning often associated with anthropology, though, as Raymond Williams points out, in cultural anthropology, "culture" is more often associated with "material production, whereas in history and cultural studies the reference is primarily to signifying or symbolic systems."[21] And since at least the 1970s, culture in this sense has been a frequent object of study by historians. Because of his emphasis on symbolic systems, the anthropologist Clifford Geertz became particularly important for intellectual historians making the cultural turn. It was Geertz, for example, whom the European intellectual historian Robert Darnton cited in a 1980 essay on the state of intellectual and cultural history as "offer[ing] the historian what the study of *mentalité* has failed to provide: a coherent concept of culture." Geertz's definition of culture, cited by Darnton, is "an historically transmitted pattern of meanings embodied in symbols."[22]

Darnton's turn to Geertz reflected the especially strong role that the anthropologist played in the intellectual life of Princeton University's history department, of which Darnton was a member at the time.[23] In 1970, Geertz had moved from the University of Chicago to the Institute for Advanced Study, just down the road from Princeton University.[24] When I was a graduate student at Princeton in the late 1980s and early 1990s, Geertz was still an enormous intellectual presence, reflected both in the way many members of the department wrote history and the way those of us who thought of ourselves as intellectual and/or cultural historians understood our own practice. In particular, Geertz's essay collection *The Interpretation of Cultures* (1973) could be found in many of our carrels. His concept of "thick description" as an interpretive goal and his famous reading of a Balinese cockfight were especially salient for us.[25]

My own work has tended to reflect those methodological changes identified by David Hall and to embrace culture as a subject, both in the sense of looking at, among other things, artistic works and in the sense of thinking about historically transmitted patterns of meaning embodied in symbols. But my work always attends to individuals thinking within those patterns of meaning. My current major project, tentatively titled *Happy Days: Images of the Pre-sixties Past in Seventies America*, explores the ways in which American cultural producers in the 1970s, working in a variety of media, thought about and represented the American past as a way of processing and understanding more recent changes in American culture and society that we associate—and they associated—with the sixties. To give you a sense of the project, let me sketch an argument I make about Paul Schrader and the figure of the hard-boiled private investigator as a man from the past in 1970s neo-noir films.

Though classic film noir was a product of Hollywood in the 1940s and 1950s, until the 1960s, the critical conversation about film noir as such was largely confined to France, where the term had been coined in 1946. The first American article on film noir was written by Paul Schrader, then a young film-school graduate and film critic, who was already beginning to toy with the idea of making movies rather than writing about them. In November 1971, Schrader curated a film noir series for the first Los Angeles International Film Exposition. His screening notes for that series were published the following spring in *Film Comment* as "Notes on Film Noir," kicking off a vigorous American critical discussion of film noir that continues to this day.[26] Most of "Notes on Film Noir" consists of Schrader's attempt to identify the essence of noir while denying that he is offering a definition, as "it is almost impossible to argue one critic's descriptive definition against another." Instead, Schrader attempts to identify what factors brought about film noir, to describe its distinguishing stylistic and thematic features, and to identify how noir changed from what he saw as its start in 1941 to what he saw as its conclusion in 1953.

Three aspects of Schrader's understanding of film noir in "Notes" are particularly interesting to me as an intellectual historian thinking about the 1970s. First, Schrader emphasizes the relationship between the past, the present, and the future in film noir. He writes that "a passion for the past and present, but also a fear of the future" is "perhaps the over-riding *noir* theme." A particular kind of focus on the past was important in many film noirs: "the narration creates a mood of *temps perdu*: an irretrievable past, a predetermined fate and an all-enveloping hopelessness. In *Out of the Past* Robert Mitchum relates his history with such pathetic relish that it is obvious there is no hope for any future: one can only take pleasure in reliving a doomed past."

Second, Schrader especially praised what he saw as classic noir's final phase, which ran from 1949 to 1953. "The *noir* hero," wrote Schrader of this period, "seemingly under the weight of ten years of despair, started to go bananas." The films of this phase, wrote Schrader, were "the most aesthetically and sociologically piercing," as they "finally got around to the root causes of the period: the loss of public honor, heroic conventions, personal integrity, and, finally, psychic stability." What Schrader saw as the qualities of the late noir hero and late noir's particular kind of social criticism would later come to be reflected in the new noir movies of the seventies.

The third moment in "Notes" that I find particularly interesting occurs early in the essay. Schrader pauses to address the status of film noir in America at the beginning of the seventies and makes a bold prediction about the place of noir in that then-young decade:

> Hollywood's *film noir* has recently become the subject of renewed interest among moviegoers and critics. The fascination *film noir* holds for today's young filmgoers and film students reflects recent trends in American cinema: American movies are again taking a look at the underside of the American character, but compared to such relentlessly cynical *films noir* as *Kiss Me Deadly* or *Kiss Tomorrow Goodbye*, the new self-hate cinema of *Easy Rider* and *Medium Cool* seems naive and romantic. As the current political mood hardens, filmgoers and filmmakers will find the *film noir* of the late Forties increasingly attractive. The Forties may be to the Seventies what the Thirties were to the Sixties.[27]

Not only was the particular past, the 1940s, that produced the films that we call "noir" important to Schrader, but so was its relationship to his 1970s present. Like many of his fellow Americans, even at the start of the seventies, Schrader saw the sixties as a distinctive and transformative era, but one that had in many ways come to an end. Classic film noir had reflected, perhaps had even helped constitute, a forties that was more cynical, curdled, harder than the sometimes hopeful radicalism of thirties American culture, even in the face of the Great Depression. The renewed interest in noir, which Schrader observed and, as a screenwriter, would actively help encourage, similarly reflected and constituted the new, more cynical decade in which Schrader wrote and its relationship to the transformative decade that preceded it. As Schrader had suggested in "Notes on Film Noir," in the early seventies, noir had begun to interest not only filmmakers and critics, but also audiences, perhaps especially those who felt the hardening political atmosphere most intensely.[28] Schrader's analysis of film noir not only shaped the American critical conversation about classic film noir, but it also had a profound impact on filmmakers, who soon began to make what would later be called "neo-noirs."

I see in Schrader's analysis of film noir—and in the neo-noir movies that appeared after it in the seventies—an instance of a broader cultural phenomenon in that decade. In order to grapple with a period of rapid and profound change in American society and culture—what we tend to simply call "the sixties," though we historians, at least, argue about its temporal boundaries—Americans in the seventies often turned to earlier periods of the past. Even during the 1970s, American cultural critics proclaimed that the decade was marked by an unusual wave of nostalgia for earlier eras, especially the 1950s. But nostalgia was only one of the modes in which seventies Americans represented and repurposed the pre-sixties past.

Both Schrader's analysis of classic film noir and the neo-noir films that followed in its wake grew, in part, out of a nostalgia for Hollywood's own past. But filmmakers' and critics' attitudes toward that past were often more than simply nostalgic. Take, for example, Robert Altman's *The Long Goodbye* (1973). The film was adapted from Raymond Chandler's final novel, published in 1953 and set in 1950. Altman and his screenwriter Leigh Brackett, herself a veteran of classic noir and the screen's first Raymond Chandler adaptation, having cowritten the screenplay for *The Big Sleep* (1946), decided to set their film in 1970s Los Angeles and to reimagine Chandler's PI hero, Philip Marlowe, as a kind of man from the past. Altman would refer to him as "Rip van Marlowe." The film opens with Marlowe (Elliott Gould) waking up in bed, nearly fully clothed. For the rest of the film, Marlowe seems out of step with his world. He drives a late-model car. Unlike every other character in the film, he dresses in a drab suit and tie. He tries to uphold values of loyalty and honor that otherwise seem to be absent in the world of the film. *The Long Goodbye* received a mixed critical reception. But prominent critics both among the film's admirers, such as the *New Yorker*'s Pauline Kael, and among its detractors, such as the *Village Voice*'s Andrew Sarris, understood it as commenting on the figure of the private investigator, a midcentury Hollywood model of effective masculinity who no longer fit in post-sixties America. And *The Long Goodbye* is only one of many 1970s neo-noirs with contemporary settings that feature protagonists who are, like Altman and Gould's version of Marlowe, men whose older value systems, in various ways, no longer function in the 1970s as they once did in the past.[29]

My work on Schrader and film noir in the 1970s certainly reflects intellectual history's passage through the age of cultural studies. I do all five things that David Hall associated with the cultural turn in intellectual history: I deal with an interplay between "high" (serious film criticism) and "low" (film noir); I look closely at the mediations that film noir underwent in the 1970s and the politics that drove those mediations; I treat narrative and discursive structures as a form of action; and I consider the politics of the representation of masculinity in seventies neo-noir and film criticism. And yet, I think my current project is still recognizably intellectual history. I read texts closely. I am interested in individuals thinking in a variety of media. And ultimately I concern myself with what Leslie Butler has identified as the core focus of intellectual history in the early twenty-first century: an interest in the circulation of ideas in the public sphere.[30]

As recently as the 1980s, the cultural historian Warren Susman, himself a participant at Wingspread and one of the authors whose essays appeared in *New Directions*, could note that "when I argue that Mickey Mouse may in fact be more important to an understanding of the 1930s than Franklin Roosevelt, audiences snicker."[31] Today audiences, at least in the field, would not find such a claim particularly shocking. That Susman titled the collection of essays for which he is best known, and which appeared just before his untimely death in 1985, *Culture as History* is a measure of the boldness of the place of culture in his work at the time it first appeared in the period spanning from the 1960s through the first half of the 1980s.

Many intellectual historians, and probably most of us who also identify as cultural historians, are, broadly speaking, intellectual children of Susman. We now like to think there are no limits on the kinds of texts that we study. However, while intellectual historians are notionally open to every sort of text, most of us still tend to feel most comfortable dealing with the written word.[32] Though there are certainly intellectual historians who have taken popular music seriously, whether in works focused on music, such as Lewis Erenberg's *Swinging the Dream* (1998) and Michael Kramer's *The Republic of Rock* (2013), or in books with a nonmusical focus, such as Jefferson Cowie's *Stayin' Alive* (2010), which incorporates rich readings of Bruce Springsteen in its discussion of 1970s American culture, more of us need to consider popular music as an important source for intellectual history. The same is true for most other visual and performing arts. Motion pictures seem to be well incorporated into intellectual history. But we venture less frequently into painting or sculpture. And those of us who study the recent past are often not as sophisticated in our considerations of television as we ought to be.

In 1980, the European intellectual historian Robert Darnton surveyed the place of intellectual history in history departments and journals in the United States. He suggested that the subfield had not actually lost ground as so many scholars at the time feared. From the evidence of course listings, dissertations, and scholarship in major journals, intellectual history seemed to have held fairly steady through the 1970s. Yes, social history, alone among the subfields, had grown in size during the previous decade. But it had done so to a great extent at the expense of political history. "The importance of intellectual history has fluctuated very little," Darnton concluded, "so little, in fact, that its practice seems to belie the jeremiads of its practitioners." But, Darnton cautioned, one would be wrong to accuse worried intellectual historians of "false consciousness" about the state of their subfield: "the importance of intellectual history has declined relative to that of social history; and although intellectual historians may be just as active as ever, some of them may have an accurate intuitive sense of momentum running down, of innovation passing into other hands."[33]

Today the situation seems to be almost precisely the opposite. As nearly everyone in the subfield attests, intellectual history in the early twenty-first century is enjoying a new period of self-confidence. Few intellectual historians worry today that our subfield lacks a mission or that historians outside of intellectual history are disdainful of our work. However, materially things look rather grim. In December 2015, the American Historical Association's *Perspectives on History* published the results of a survey of subfield specialties in the AHA's *Directory of History Departments, Historical Organizations, and Historians* (formerly the *Guide to History Departments*) during the last forty years. Since 1975, intellectual history was one of five subfields that had suffered the most serious decline in its share of faculty. While over 10 percent of historians had identified as intellectual historians in 1975, by 2015, only around 5 percent did.[34] But among the subfields that had enjoyed the largest increase between 1975 and 2015 has been cultural history.[35]

But while cultural history might provide young intellectual historians with a few more jobs in a generally grim academic job market, this is not the main way that the study of culture, in its various meanings, has contributed to the rising self-confidence of intellectual history over the last decade or two. Rather, understanding culture as, in a sense, a—or perhaps the—central object of intellectual history has made our subfield broader and more diverse and of generally greater interest to other historians and, at least occasionally, the public at large.

NOTES

I would like to thank the editors of this volume, Raymond Haberski Jr. and Andrew Hartman, as well as Angus Burgin, David Sehat, Daniel Wickberg, and the other participants in the Dangerous Ideas Symposium at IUPUI for their comments and suggestions on an earlier draft of this chapter.

    1. Raymond Williams, *Keywords: A Vocabulary of Culture and Society* (New York: Oxford University Press, 2015), 49.

    2. Thomas Bender, Editorial Note on the Intellectual History Group, *Intellectual History Newsletter* 1 (1979): 1–2, 19.

    3. Editorial, *Modern Intellectual History* 1 (2004): 2.

    4. Ibid., 1.

    5. The 462 were overlapping.

    6. In a 1988 essay in which he expresses some concern about the waning coherence of intellectual history as a subfield, David Hollinger cited Daniel Rodgers as a leading figure

in what Hollinger called "the Popular Culture Program," which, Hollinger suggests, is what scholars who distinguish between intellectual and cultural history mean by the latter. Hollinger's sanguine conclusions about the future of intellectual history in this essay are in part based on his pleasure at Rodgers's focus on the transatlantic flow of ideas—rather than popular culture—in his then current project, which would eventually become *Atlantic Crossings* (Cambridge, MA: Harvard University Press, 1998). David Hollinger, "Science and Philosophy as Subject Areas within 20th-Century American Intellectual History," *Intellectual History Newsletter* 10 (April 1988): 18–23.

7. Donald R. Kelley, "Intellectual History and Cultural History: The Inside and the Outside," *History of the Human Sciences* 15, no. 2 (2002): 1.

8. Jennifer Ratner-Rosenhagen, *American Nietzsche: A History of an Icon and His Ideas* (Chicago: University of Chicago Press, 2012); Ajay K. Mehrotra, *Making the Modern American Fiscal State: Law, Politics, and the Rise of Progressive Taxation, 1877–1929* (New York: Cambridge University Press, 2013); Ruben Flores, *Backroads Pragmatists: Mexico's Melting Pot and Civil Rights in the United States* (Philadelphia: University of Pennsylvania Press, 2014); Sarah Bridger, *Scientists at War: The Ethics of Cold War Weapons Research* (Cambridge, MA: Harvard University Press, 2015); Daniel Immerwahr, *Thinking Small: The United States and the Lure of Development* (Cambridge, MA: Harvard University Press, 2016).

9. Editorial, *Modern Intellectual History* 1 (2004): 1.

10. Daniel T. Rodgers, *Age of Fracture* (Cambridge, MA: Belknap Press of Harvard University Press, 2011).

11. John Higham and Paul K. Conkin, eds., *New Directions in American Intellectual History* (Baltimore: Johns Hopkins University Press, 1979).

12. Thomas Bender, "The Cultures of Intellectual Life: The City and the Professions," in Higham and Conkin, *New Directions*, 181–95, esp. 191–92.

13. See particularly Thomas Bender, "Forum: The Present and Future of Intellectual History Introduction," *Modern Intellectual History* 9 (2012): 149–56; Leslie Butler, "From the History of Ideas to Ideas in History," *Modern Intellectual History* 9 (2012): 157–69; Joan Shelley Rubin, "Nixon's Grin and Other Keys to the Future of Cultural and Intellectual History," *Modern Intellectual History* 9 (2012): 217–31; and, somewhat more critical in its support, David Hall, "Backwards to the Future: The Cultural Turn and the Wisdom of Intellectual History," *Modern Intellectual History* 9 (2012): 171–84.

14. Butler, "From the History of Ideas," 157.

15. "Symposium on Intellectual History in the Age of Cultural Studies," *Intellectual History Newsletter* 18 (1996): 3–69.

16. Casey Nelson Blake, editor's introduction, ibid., 3–4.

17. Jackson Lears, "Against Anti-Intellectualism," ibid., 20–21; Bruce Kuklick, "Intellectual History at Penn," ibid., 62–64.

18. Daniel Rodgers, "Thinking in Verbs," ibid., 21–23.

19. Hall, "Backwards to the Future," 178–79.

20. Williams, *Keywords*, 52.

21. Ibid., 52–53.

22. Robert Darnton, "Intellectual and Cultural History," in *The Past before Us: Contemporary Historical Writing in the United States*, ed. Michael Kammen (Ithaca, NY: Cornell University Press, 1980), 347–48.

23. Geertz's influence on intellectual history extended well beyond the Princeton department, however. In the 1996 *IHN* Symposium on Intellectual History in the Age of Cultural Studies, George Cotkin, Robert Orsi, and Mary Kupiec Cayton, none of whom had any direct connection to Princeton, all cited the influence of Geertz on intellectual historical practice.

24. The two institutions are entirely unaffiliated with each other, but there has long been a strong flow of ideas between them.

25. Clifford Geertz, *The Interpretation of Cultures* (New York: Basic Books, 1973), esp. chaps. 1 and 15.

26. Paul Schrader, "Notes on Film Noir," reprinted in *The Film Noir Reader*, ed. Alain Silver and James Ursini (New York: Limelight, 1996), 53–63.

27. Ibid., 53. Schrader had lost his job as film critic for the *Los Angeles Free Press* following his negative review of *Easy Rider*.

28. The film noir scholar Paul Arthur dates his interest in noir to this period "in which the rebellious energies of the 1960s began to splinter and ebb." Arthur recalls that in the early 1970s, noir movies "struck a responsive chord with an increasingly besieged segment of the radical protest movement" through an "identification with the plight of noir protagonists." See Paul Arthur, "Murder's Tongue: Identity, Death, and the City in Film Noir," in *Violence and American Cinema*, ed. Paul Arthur and J. David Slocum (New York: Routledge, 2001), 172.

29. Some other examples include *Joe* (1970), *The Friends of Eddie Coyle* (1973), *The Yakuza* (1975), *Night Moves* (1975), and *Rolling Thunder* (1977).

30. Butler, "From the History of Ideas."

31. Warren Susman, *Culture as History* (New York: Pantheon, 1984), 103.

32. Charles Capper has noted that in 1970s, "literature and art, major components of 1950s and 1960s American intellectual history and its ally American Studies, were largely left behind." See Capper, "One Step Back, Two Steps Forward," in "Symposium on Intellectual History in the Age of Cultural Studies," 66–68.

33. Darnton, "Intellectual and Cultural History," 335–36.

34. The Wingspread generation might take some comfort in the fact that one of the other fastest declining subfields has been social history, which had seemed so dominant in the 1970s.

35. Robert B. Townsend, "The Rise and Decline of History Specializations over the Past 40 Years," *Perspectives on History* (online edition), December 2015, https://www.historians.org/publications-and-directories/perspectives-on-history/december-2015/the-rise-and-decline-of-history-specializations-over-the-past-40-years.

18
ON THE POLITICS OF KNOWLEDGE
Science, Conflict, Power

Andrew Jewett

How can US intellectual history contribute to the overall academic enterprise and to public discourse? In the current spate of self-reflections by intellectual historians, many contributors have focused, in whole or in part, on the field's relationship to cultural history. They have generally urged greater attention to the circulation and reception of ideas, as these are taken up and translated across multiple discursive contexts. It is particularly important, discussants have stressed, to explore the noncanonical texts and actors that certain modes of intellectual-historical work have ignored.[1]

It would be easy—if contrary to most authors' intentions—to conclude from these writings that a high wall divides the wide-open spaces of "cultural" phenomena from a narrow, hermetic realm of "high" intellectual history: the domain of formal, organized thought by philosophers, political theorists, scientists, literary scholars, theologians, and other professional traders in ideas. This spatialized image of two distinct territories also recurs in informal, day-to-day discussions of the state of intellectual history. It suggests both an analysis of intellectual history's diminished status since the 1950s and a professional strategy in response to that diminution: intellectual historians have overlooked the cultural realm and can recuperate their lost influence by refocusing their attention there.

But this account of the field's present situation is much too simple. For one thing, as Leslie Butler and others recognize, intellectual historians have always addressed broad cultural sensibilities as well as specialized texts and their makers. Until quite recently, many scholars called themselves "intellectual and cultural historians," or "intellectual and social historians," or simply historians, period, as with Richard Hofstadter. The felt need to differentiate intellectual and cultural history by assigning a separate social domain to each is a relatively new phenomenon, and it is not clear that the main impetus comes from those identified as intellectual historians.[2]

The two-spheres model also tends to imply a theory of historical change holding that ideas become socially efficacious—and thus worthy of historians' attention—only when they move "outward" or "downward" from the cloistered space of formal thought into the cultural domain. In fact, however, our historical analyses routinely challenge that model. In this essay, I want to discuss a body of scholarly work that interprets the historical influence of ideas quite differently, with important ramifications for intellectual history's role in the academic firmament.

At present, we lack a well-established label for the transdisciplinary discourse I describe here, or even a sense that it constitutes a coherent whole. But the phrase "the politics of knowledge" reveals its contours. Interpreters of the politics of knowledge examine how the articulation, circulation, acceptance, and instantiation of knowledge claims have shaped the distribution of power among actors in particular settings. Such studies represent a major growth area across the disciplines, including intellectual history. Although knowledge claims constitute only one part of the discursive terrain that intellectual historians explore, much work undertaken by US intellectual historians today fits under the rubric of the politics of knowledge.[3]

Scholars from many other disciplines and subdisciplines also participate in the burgeoning conversation on the politics of knowledge. These include cultural and political historians; historians of policy, social movements, philanthropy, and education; historians of race, gender, sexuality, disability, and other axes of inequality; students of American political development; political and social theorists; historical sociologists; sociologists of knowledge; historians and philosophers of science and medicine; scholars in religious history, religious studies, and science and technology studies; and historically minded thinkers in virtually all of the disciplines and professional schools who study the past trajectories of their own fields.[4] Few of these figures see themselves as engaged in a single, common enterprise, but lines of affinity and webs of shared references connect their work. The study of the politics of knowledge represents an intellectual commons or trading zone wherein scholars with similar preoccupations exchange—if currently in a largely haphazard and decentralized way—their findings, insights, and techniques.[5]

Research on the politics of knowledge matters for this volume in two ways. First, such work rebuts the two-spheres image of separate discursive domains and the associated presumption that ideas make a difference only when they infuse popular discourse. This truncated conception of social change rightly ascribes agency to ordinary individuals but ignores the equally real power of elites. Second, work on the politics of knowledge highlights the practical, contemporary importance of the topics that many intellectual historians address. In an age when chasms of belief divide societies around the globe, the everyday effects of the politics of knowledge become clearer by the day. Hot-button issues such as abortion, biotechnology, climate change, and religious liberty involve deep conceptual disagreements that require close scrutiny and cannot be neatly reduced to sociological categories.

By foregrounding the "invisible" sources of inequality—the diffuse but consequential operations of power across multiple discourses—studies of the politics of knowledge challenge the misguided but all too common assumption that studying the history of ideas means ignoring or whitewashing the deep inequalities that have structured societies past and present. In fact, intellectual historians have much to say about how "knowledge work" has intersected with other forms of power in particular contexts. We can scarcely understand a world in which formal knowledge systems have exercised substantial influence without the intellectual historian's close attention to rhetorical connotations, unstated assumptions, and cultural resonances.[6]

Naturalization and Denaturalization

Rather than positing clearly bounded discursive territories, work on the politics of knowledge tends to break down spatial metaphors and to highlight complex, sprawling networks of claims, assumptions, actors, institutions, and practices. Interpreters of the politics of knowledge often analyze the popular circulation, reception, and translation of ideas. Yet they also show that systematic thinking shapes the world in other ways as well. Ordinary citizens rarely followed suit when Kennedy-era policy makers embraced modernization theory, or George W. Bush's cabinet took cues from Leo Strauss, or economists omitted environmental degradation in their cost-benefit analyses. In each case, a knowledge framework gained efficacy without structuring popular discourses. Studies of the politics of knowledge demonstrate that the popular appeal of an idea does not always translate into historical influence, and conversely, that unpopular ideas often have profound effects. These works acknowledge the highly complex structures of institutional and discursive power in modern societies.

Moreover, even if one seeks to conceptually distinguish a realm of formal thinking from another world of cultural and social forces, work on the politics of knowledge reminds us that traffic between these realms is typical, not exceptional. Scholars and other individuals move constantly through "high" and "low" domains; and institutions—schools, universities, religious organizations, and the state, among others—cut across the putative boundary.[7] Disciplinary scholarship and theological argumentation are importantly different from everyday chatter, but to a surprising degree the differences center on form rather than content. Formal thoughtways do not simply shape or feed into public discourses, in a unidirectional process. Rather, they take much of their shape from the translation of pervasive cultural preoccupations into the idiosyncratic terms of particular traditions of reasoning. Knowledge workers routinely "thematize" items of common sense and questions of shared concern. In short, "high" intellectual discourses operate inside cultural and social frames, not apart from them.

We can better understand this interpenetration of discourses by examining the opposing dynamics of "naturalization" and "denaturalization" that shape the politics of knowledge. Though these terms may be unfamiliar to many historians, the basic concepts are not. Across the centuries, scholars and other intellectuals have frequently worked to "denaturalize" social institutions and prevailing assumptions by describing them as contingent human constructions, not preexisting features of the natural world.[8]

The rapid expansion of the social sciences in the late nineteenth- and early twentieth-century United States offers a clear example of the denaturalizing impulse. That growth reflected, in part, a widespread desire among left-leaning scholars to challenge the inexorable "economic laws" that classical economists found embedded in the structure of the world. Pioneering social scientists often adopted a historical, historicist approach. They not only advocated political alternatives to economic laissez-faire but also explained how and why that system had been culturally naturalized—elevated to the status of an unquestionable, unchanging truth, a matter of received wisdom and common sense—in the nineteenth century.[9]

Likewise, many scholars today explore the naturalization of various phenomena they deem contingent, chosen, and malleable rather than permanent, imposed, and unchanging. Free-market ideology is again a common target, but legions of critical scholars also trace the naturalization of racial hierarchies, class distinctions, gender categories, colonial relations, liberal universalism, secularism, national identities, and other formations. The "anti-essentialist" bent of much recent scholarship represents both an extension of the denaturalizing impulse to entirely new categories of social phenomena and a theoretical generalization from long-standing scholarly inclinations.

Because naturalization and denaturalization efforts profoundly shape the distribution of power and resources in modern societies, scholars cannot understand those societies without looking closely at the natural and social sciences and employing the tools of intellectual history, among other resources. Let us first consider the importance of the sciences as subject of historical analysis. Here, it is worth noting that there are actually two possible alternatives to naturalization. Critics can argue that some other pattern is natural and innate. Or they can contend that nothing is fixed in that particular area (or perhaps any area) of social reality, and that unconstrained human choices determine the outcome. We might call these strategies re-naturalization and denaturalization. But each of the two dynamics makes scientific work a crucial object of scholarly study.

Science is deeply intertwined with social processes of naturalization, denaturalization, and re-naturalization. Scientists seek to delineate the contours of nature—to identify the features of what exists and to mark the boundaries between what human beings can conceivably change and what they must simply accept. As scientific theories have gained traction over the centuries, it has grown increasingly difficult for competing views of reality to retain their credence. Today, denaturalizing an interpretive framework that bears science's imprimatur can be daunting; scientists often set the terms on which alternatives can even be considered. Of course, the authority of science is not, and cannot be, absolute. But it is strategically central in societies that define politics in secular, depersonalized terms. In such societies, science is widely seen as the final arbiter within its own sphere, specifying which features of the world a political regime can seek to alter and which it cannot.

To understand the dynamics of naturalization, denaturalization, and re-naturalization, we must also look to the past. Of course, such dynamics also occur in the present, but for obvious reasons most scholarly studies address earlier eras. Although naturalization is an ongoing process, it is hard to discern which current patterns will eventually gain the status of naturalized common sense and which will remain contested. Scholars seeking to denaturalize a social pattern typically turn to history, in order to explain when and how that pattern attained its unquestioned status. Employed in this manner, historical research begins to resemble cultural anthropology, with its relativizing tendency to challenge the universal validity of prevailing practices and beliefs. Such work has normative implications, suggesting the possibility of making different choices in the future. For instance, if earlier generations of Americans learned to see the Irish, Italians, and Jews as white, then surely their successors today can change their own conceptions of human difference. To take another example, I have argued that scholarly views of science and values in the United States changed substantially in the mid-twentieth century, and thus might change again in the future. In such denaturalizing efforts, contingency and possibility become the keynotes of historical argumentation.[10]

But not just any mode of historical analysis will do, if we seek to understand processes of naturalization and the countervailing dynamics. We must draw, at least in part, on the methods of intellectual history. For naturalization is at base a mental process, even in cases where an absence of institutionalized alternatives helps to authorize the prevailing mind-set. Naturalization requires conceptual closure: a group of actors comes to believe that a significant feature of the world is as it is, will always be so, and could not be otherwise. Naturalization often involves the disappearance of the capacity to even imagine, let alone embrace, alternatives to the prevailing pattern. Studying naturalization processes thus directs scholars' attention to conceptual changes—to developments in formal thought and cultural assumptions. Histories of naturalization, denaturalization, and re-naturalization are always in large part intellectual histories, whether they take that name or not.

Such historical accounts have proliferated of late. Since the 1960s, numerous Western scholars have sought to denaturalize assumptions about the social world that even their most radical predecessors took for granted. In the Progressive period, critical scholars typically challenged free-market orthodoxies and invidious class distinctions. After World War I, many targeted racial hierarchies as well. But they took for granted much that now seems questionable and dangerous to new generations of critics, including the coherence and stability of national cultures, the desirability of industrialized mass production, and the superiority of science to other ways of knowing—or, as a critic might say, deciding.

As these foundational assumptions have come under fire, our scholarly understandings of "politics" have expanded apace. Virtually every thought and action now appears political, in an academic climate where many interpreters view all forms of knowledge and the associated institutional patterns as exercises of human will that distribute power differentially to actors. Indeed, critical scholars have denaturalized the very boundary around politics itself. They have stressed the eminently political consequences of declaring some social phenomena "political"—susceptible to collective intervention—while naturalizing others as unchanging features of the given world. Scholars have redefined element after element of modern life as mental, cultural, and fungible rather than material, structural, and stable. The scientific enterprise has faced particular scrutiny, owing to its practitioners' constitutive assumption that some features of the world are found, not made. But whatever the subject matter, today's expansive understanding of politics points to dynamics that intellectual historians are particularly well equipped to assess.[11]

Symmetry, Conflict, and Context

Within what social settings and power dynamics did past knowledge claims operate? It is at this nexus, I believe, that intellectual historians have the most to contribute to research on the politics of knowledge—and at the same time, the most to learn from interpreters in other fields. In recent years, the intensified denaturalizing campaign across the disciplines has generated thousands of intellectual histories, of varying quality and sophistication. When social scientists excavate the past trajectories of their disciplines, they write intellectual history by examining bygone arguments, ferreting out the underlying assumptions and sensibilities, and finding links to wider contexts. So do literary critics tracing shifts in university curricula, historians of science exploring changing understandings of objectivity, natural scientists tracing the theoretical development of their fields, theologians grounding themselves in traditions of interpretation, and students of politics following the careers of key ideological elements, to name just a few.

Despite this wellspring of enthusiasm for the study of ideas, however, the phrase "intellectual history" continues to generate widespread suspicion. The field suffers from stereotypes and resentments dating back to the mid-twentieth century, when intellectual history and other dominant modes of historical writing anchored the academic establishment and transparently advanced a centrist, anti-populist liberalism. Today, many leading history departments seem to be outsourcing the study of key intellectual domains—the natural and social sciences, religion, philosophy, education—to other academic programs and disavowing responsibility for these elements of the past.[12]

I find this tendency extremely unfortunate. An adequate understanding of the politics of knowledge depends on a strong central field of intellectual history and a steady flow of ideas between its practitioners and their counterparts in other disciplines and other historical subfields. The professional field of intellectual history is, among other things, an invaluable clearinghouse or commons for the work of all scholars concerned with past expressions of knowledge. Trained intellectual historians also bring detailed knowledge of the past contexts—not just ideational but also cultural, social, economic, and political—in which knowledge claims have emerged and operated.

At the same time, however, intellectual historians can also take important cues from other scholars, who have often been quicker to grasp the high-stakes conflicts that swirl around knowledge systems and the interpretive value of not analytically privileging some forms of knowledge over others. Combining these interpretive strengths with the intellectual historian's distinctive forms of expertise promises richer, more complex accounts that capture the intricate politics of knowledge in modern societies.

Some intellectual historians regard their work as a form of explicitly normative cultural criticism. This goal, though laudable, can encourage oversimplification as scholars recommend or decry ideas developed in the past. All too often, the cultural critic posits an undifferentiated cultural space, occupied by a single "we" and dominated by a sensibility or theory that is not only wrong and dangerous but also hegemonic—and thus responsible for present-day ills. But this is rarely, if ever, an adequate description of an actual society, whatever its efficacy as a rhetorical strategy. Against the image of a homogeneous culture, studies of the politics of knowledge tend to foreground discursive conflicts and negotiations, without assuming even rough equality—let alone cultural sameness—between the participants.

Of course, the "politics" metaphor imposes its own limitations, especially when that term is decoupled from sophisticated understandings of discursive power. Generally, however, studies of the politics of knowledge account for complex institutional structures and competing modes of power. As compared with the mode of cultural criticism described above, these works offer a different sort of guidance for the present day: not so much suggestions for what to think but rather illustrations of how our words—including the historical narratives we craft—tend to shape the world around us. What effects might flow from particular arguments today, in our own institutional and cultural contexts? Intellectual history can offer powerful examples—often cautionary tales—of how ideas operate in wider social settings. This approach does not rule out writing intellectual history as normative cultural criticism. Indeed, it can help us sharpen our critiques, making them more targeted and less sweeping. Oversimplification has its advantages in the rough-and-tumble of cultural combat, but it does not necessarily serve historians well in their professional writings.

A second analytical shortcoming often associated with the stance of the cultural critic is a tendency to obscure the socially situated character of one's own diagnosis and prescription. Cultural critics often claim the mantle of universal human truth, placing themselves outside historical struggles rather than openly locating themselves within those struggles. In short, they often engage in re-naturalization. Here, too, studies in other disciplines offer crucial insights. The field of science and technology studies is particularly attuned to the value of interpretive reflexivity—the practice of applying the same critical-historical methods to the institutions and ideas we favor as to those we deplore. This is not to say that scholars must abandon all distinctions between truth and falsehood. However, they should not assume that their own preferred views have taken hold because they shone with the light of pure truth, whereas the alternatives gained their power solely from illicit interests or institutional imperatives. Sociologists of science speak of "symmetry": interpreters should invoke the same *kinds* of contextual factors in explaining the trajectories of theories currently deemed true as they do in analyzing the historical careers of discredited falsehoods. To my mind, an intellectual history aimed at denaturalizing a prevailing cultural pattern should offer not a simple ideology critique, but rather a symmetrical analysis that acknowledges the social, cultural, and institutional factors operating on all sides of contentious matters. To proceed otherwise is to risk becoming a mere debunker rather than a careful analyst—and thereby to fatally skew one's understanding of how ideas have worked in the world.[13]

Among intellectual historians and their counterparts in other fields, the prevailing modes of cultural criticism also tend to portray conflict—especially in the current era—as suppressed and subterranean rather than open and persistent. We currently have at hand several kinds of homogenizing master narratives that erase conflict, especially for the period since World War II. One account, following the "organizational synthesis" of the 1970s and 1980s, anchors American history since the late nineteenth century in the growth of bureaucratic organizations, managerial professionals, and technical rationality. A related interpretation likewise highlights the growing cultural dominance of a morally vacuous, bureaucratic mind-set but identifies that sensibility as the result of concerted action by an ascendant "new class," not the by-product of functionally driven structural shifts. A third interpretation instead traces the dominance of technical rationality to the secularizing tendencies of the professional-managerial class, rather than its institutional roles or class interests per se. Meanwhile, a different kind of homogenizing narrative locates a decisive paradigm shift in the 1960s and 1970s, from an earlier hegemonic outlook to a new one (most often secularism, multiculturalism, individualism, or neoliberalism). All these interpretations tend to obscure persistent, substantive conflicts in the world of thought. By contrast, scholars in other fields have often been more attuned to the persistence of competing outlooks than have intellectual historians. I find accounts of conflict—if always between unequal combatants—more plausible, and thus more reliable, than totalizing consensus or hegemony narratives. Here, too, intellectual historians can find important resources in the work of other chroniclers of the politics of knowledge.

At the same time, intellectual historians bring to the table valuable resources that are seldom found among other scholars. As compared with most counterparts in other fields, trained intellectual historians often have richer and more nuanced understandings of the many overlapping contexts in which knowledge claims emerge and circulate. Students of the politics of knowledge routinely argue that "external" factors shape knowledge claims. Yet few scholars outside history departments are trained to analyze the full array of intellectual, cultural, political, economic, and social dynamics that shape knowledge systems. Even professional historians struggle to understand these complex dynamics on a transnational scale, but within national or regional boundaries they are well equipped to situate ideas fully in their contexts. It is hard to imagine that adequate accounts of the politics of knowledge will emerge without the participation of those trained in the careful study of historical details, tendencies, and methods. Scholars need more than the mere principle of contextualism; they also need intimate, detailed familiarity with particular historical contexts.

Such content knowledge is particularly important for those who aim at a fully symmetrical or reflexive analysis rather than a one-sided, debunking approach that selects only one feature of a multidimensional historical setting. Many intellectual histories undertaken outside history departments—and some produced within them—amount to simplistic ideology critiques of allegedly biased, interested forms of knowledge, written from the standpoint of a self-evidently purer and higher truth. And even those studies that do take a symmetrical approach tend to adopt blocky, monocausal explanations of intellectual change if they are not informed by a deep knowledge of the historical contexts in question.

Also important for students of the politics of knowledge is the institutional space of intellectual history itself. The field's conferences and journals provide sites of exchange for the historical studies of knowledge systems that continually appear across the disciplines. The dispersed character of intellectual-historical writing—the fact that it takes place in numerous disciplinary communities—presents dangers as well as opportunities. Disciplinary boundaries can hinder communication and lead interpreters to miss or ignore relevant bodies of literature. At their best, intellectual historians maintain an institutional nexus that facilitates the cross-disciplinary transfer of insights and methodological tools, while contributing their own deep knowledge of historical settings and training in the careful use of evidence.[14]

Science and Power

Intellectual histories of the sciences demonstrate the need to tether claims about knowledge and its political effects to careful historical analysis, in order to get a handle on the intricacies of power and its multifarious operations in the worlds of thought and argumentation. The case of the scientific disciplines illustrates the insights that can be gained by combining detailed knowledge of historical contexts with analytically symmetrical explanations and a sensitivity to conceptual conflict. The past few decades have brought rafts of critical histories, written by scholars across the disciplines, that highlight the cultural work performed by knowledge claims in the natural or social sciences. These studies have traced the rise of scientific disciplines and their relations to systems of expertise and instruments and ideologies of control. Since the late nineteenth century, the universities and disciplines have come to anchor a knowledge-intensive, institutionally dense political economy. Broader relations between science and religion have also shifted, as the social sciences gained authority and researchers across the sciences claimed a greater need, and a greater ability, to bracket value commitments.

How should we understand the rise of science as a political phenomenon? Given the centrality of the sciences to processes of naturalization, denaturalization, and re-naturalization, especially in the twentieth century, it is particularly important to avoid misrepresenting their cultural influence. It is tempting, but ultimately inadequate, to reduce the politics of knowledge to a simple, straightforward narrative in which putatively objective scientists magnify the power of elites by embedding dominant interests in hegemonic, totalizing systems of "official knowledge." As the best work in the field illustrates, the scientific disciplines have not been merely machines for laundering, as it were, structures of domination by obscuring their contingent, human origins and stamping them with the label "natural." The sciences have produced many other kinds of power effects as well.[15]

Of course, we should neither deny the potent influence of scientific claims on social structures nor ignore their sometimes baldly ideological character. Scholars can say very little about knowledge and power in the modern world without attending to the scientific disciplines and research-centered universities that coalesced in the nineteenth century. The conclusions of the natural sciences, and in some areas the social sciences, wield an authority rarely enjoyed by other knowledge systems. Indeed, by the late nineteenth century, "science" became virtually synonymous with "knowledge" in many intellectual circles. Numerous scholars, tracing such developments, have shown in great detail how the natural and human sciences reproduced social inequalities.

Although science has been highly influential and occasionally nefarious, however, we should note four kinds of complications, stemming from central features of the naturalization, denaturalization, and re-naturalization processes. First of all, scientific claims typically remain open to active contestation, both within and beyond the universities. The naturalization process is often partial and relative rather than absolute. Forms of knowledge gain ascendance among certain social groups but not others. Even within these spheres of influence, the cultural embrace of a broad knowledge system can be partial rather than total. In the United States, for example, science now holds special authority in universities, courtrooms, public schools, and the media. At the same time, many politicians proudly tout their rejection of Darwinism and anthropogenic climate change. A plurality of the citizenry likewise rejects these basic scientific concepts—without blinking an eye at the application of physics to airplanes and bridges, or biology to medicine.

It is too simple, then, to conclude that "science" in general has become unquestioned common sense in our day. Scientific knowledge claims are enormously variegated. Each has its own distinctive politics and topography of influence, and these change substantially from time to time and place to place. Moreover, a knowledge system such as science can exert authority by default, rather than through active acceptance. In the United States, the Constitution's church-state provisions give scientific theories a structural advantage in public arguments, but theologies at odds with many scientific tenets also remain extremely influential. Scholars should question sweeping claims about the naturalization of belief systems, or even particular tenets, across entire societies.

A second counterpoint to reductive, debunking narratives in which scientists simply launder elite power is the observation that contests within the natural and human sciences often reflect the interests of multiple, competing elites—and sometimes even those of marginalized groups. Today, for example, biologists' widespread rejection of clearly demarcated "races" reveals a strong desire to equalize power and undermine white privilege, although other scientific theories cut the opposite way politically. Such internal conflicts are even more typical in the social sciences. For example, although historians sometimes argue that American social science emerged as an ideological adjunct to modern capitalism, most of the early social scientists actually deplored key features of a market-based society, even as they failed to fully transcend their own middle-class norms. Since the 1960s, moreover, demographic and cultural changes in the universities have allowed members of disadvantaged groups to participate much more directly and effectively in academic debates. Social relations, and thus social conflicts, operate inside the disciplines as well as beyond them.

Third, naturalization dynamics are hardly the exclusive province of scholars donning the mantle of science. Religious figures constantly offer influential claims about what is true and unchanging in society and nature. So do politicians and business leaders—and even the scholarly critics who deplore the ideological effects of science's putative value-neutrality. Merely by using language, we constantly naturalize (or re-naturalize) the concepts implied by our words. Even when we explicitly seek to problematize one of those concepts, we reify many others in the process. Every sentence we utter encodes, or requires for its legibility, silent assertions of the form "X is real"—and often also "Y is not real." In any imaginable society, multiple systems of common sense will compete in some respects and overlap in others, leaving scientific claims open to contestation. All else being equal, science has typically garnered more credibility and deference in modern societies than other ways of knowing. But all else has rarely been equal. Precisely because scientific claims have political effects—because they tend to promote particular distributions of power—they inspire scrutiny and challenge.

And the challengers inevitably engage in some form of re-naturalization, offering competing assertions or assumptions about the contours of the given world.

A fourth complication is that formal knowledge claims of the type offered by scientific researchers and other scholars usually connect to power relations in indirect, mediated, and contingent ways. There are exceptions, of course. The political ramifications of social scientists' constructions of race, gender, and class, for example, are fairly straightforward. But scientists, theologians, and other thought workers usually exercise their discursive power in much more complex ways. These figures operate within established traditions of reasoning that include distinctive—and typically unstated—material inferences: assumptions about causes and effects in the world, including the practical implications of each tradition's own theories and concepts. Such inferences—contingent, and often unconscious, translations of practical matters into more or less abstracted, scholarly terms—are typically invisible, and sometimes counterintuitive, to actors standing outside the traditions in question. It often takes careful, detailed study to discern the commonsense background assumptions that a particular group of scholars takes for granted.

A failure to understand the complexities of disciplinary translation may explain the critique of intellectual history as a form of academic navel-gazing whose practitioners systematically ignore power relations in the "real world." On the one side, the charge resonates because it contains a kernel of truth. Many intellectual histories, whether written by professional historians or other scholars, focus solely on abstracted ideas and their producers. Some of the authors fail to recognize the importance of disciplinary translations, or insist on principle that these translations do not exist or are unimportant or irrelevant. It should be obvious that I disagree with this approach. But other authors of intellectual histories leave the particular assumptions of their subjects unanalyzed because they implicitly share them. And a third group simply chooses to leave the task of analyzing and narrating such phenomena to other scholars.

In an ideal world, none of these three approaches would diminish the professional status of intellectual history, although the social theory implied by the first would draw sustained—and I think valid—criticism. But many critics, for their part, fail to see that intellectual historians *are* writing about an important aspect of power relations in the world, whether they point that out or not.[16] Scholars' formal, abstract claims are connected, though in mediated and contested ways, to material inferences—including not only their own inferences but also those of other scholarly communities and various non-scholarly actors. For this reason, formal arguments produce practical effects, even when they do not transparently ratify or attack a particular structure of domination. Processes of thought and argumentation are both complex and consequential, if hardly all-encompassing.

It is a mistake to dismiss studies of general philosophical concepts (epistemologies, metaphysical frameworks) or technical disciplinary constructs (structural-functionalism, process theology) as inattentive to power and inequality. Both formal thinking and the study of its history are modes of political action, if often indirect and mediated ones. And such work cannot be simply delegated to other disciplines. The guild of professional historians cannot understand the past unless some of its prominent members employ—and, of course, constantly hone—the methods of intellectual history.

The histories of the social sciences and affiliated philosophies of knowledge illustrate the importance of understanding disciplinary translations. It is crucial to grasp how traders in formal thought have made social conflicts their own by converting nonprofessional discourses into the distinctive terms of their traditions of reasoning. To understand the effects of a particular formal argument, we must discern what both its architects and its audiences thought was at stake, politically. We must recover not only the contours of a given system of formal thought and its institutional settings but also the structures of material inferences that prevailed in and around it at the time.[17]

It bears repeating that when we examine the social sciences and related epistemologies, we cannot think too superficially or literally about their political effects. The statement "Economic regulation leads to totalitarian politics" has straightforward implications. But what about a more abstract assertion, such as "Human beings are not isolated, atomic individuals; they are enmeshed in webs of social relations"? Here, the political meanings depend on the connotations of key terms and on external structures of causal assumptions—assumptions about human psychology, the capacity of institutions to reshape behavior, and much more. Many knowledge claims and systems relate even less obviously to political matters, yet still produce political effects. To understand the politics of knowledge, historians cannot simply single out the past scholars who overtly addressed leading issues of today, such as race, gender, the environment, or economic policy. All actors, including those outside the universities, can translate political questions into more or less abstract intellectual discourses via contingent and ever-shifting structures of linguistic connotations and "causal stories" about actions and their effects. These assumptions are key elements of the contexts in which thought workers operate.

Indeed, even the simplest disciplinary translations feature hidden complexities and contested assumptions. Witness how today's climate scientists jump seamlessly from the assertion that human beings are largely responsible for global warming to a series of additional, increasingly specific claims: that we must collectively act to limit or reverse global warming, that we must do so in large part by shifting resources away from carbon-based energy production, that we must employ the regulatory power of the federal government to do so, and that we must adopt X, Y, and Z regulatory actions in particular. For discussants like myself who share the inferences that sustain this chain of reasoning, science itself seems to demand a specific set of political actions. But other sets of inferences suggest that climate scientists seek to overthrow capitalism, or despise coal workers, or hope to subordinate national sovereignty to a global regime, or fail to see that their proposed actions will undermine freedom and prosperity, or simply choose their professional self-interest over the common good.

These inferences can change dramatically over time. In 1950, for instance, most US scholars and activists thought it was progressive to view humankind as a single unit rather than erecting sharp boundaries between racial and national groups. Today, the perceived politics of universalism differ markedly, especially in the academy. To take another example, most early twentieth-century radicals assumed that science inevitably aided their cause, whereas many now argue that only religious frameworks pointing beyond the spatiotemporal order can authorize substantive challenges to the status quo. These cases remind us once again that general ideas carry particular—if invariably multiple and often unstable—political meanings in specific historical contexts.

Even the most abstract conceptions, such as metaphysical systems, exhibit these tendencies. In the early twentieth century, for example, many US progressives began to believe that a metaphysical view of reality as composed of discrete, elemental particles was reactionary rather than radical. That model's perceived tendency to legitimize economic laissez-faire increasingly overshadowed its earlier, anti-monarchical connotations. Progressive thinkers now reasoned that holistic, interconnected conceptions of reality reflected the bonds of mutual obligation that characterized healthy societies. However, holism has had many potential meanings and created strange bedfellows. After all, the Nazis were holistic thinkers, too. Both perceptions of metaphysical holism's effects and its actual effects have varied over time, depending on many factors external to that framework itself. Because of the ubiquity of such political translations, the power effects of knowledge claims can be highly tangled and often counterintuitive in retrospect.[18]

Of course, historians should not overestimate the impact of formal knowledge production. Disciplinary frameworks, or knowledge claims more generally, do not simply determine social reality. Intellectual historians, like other scholars, risk attributing too much causal power to the phenomena they study. Still, the multiplication and circulation of formal knowledge claims that characterize our world have clearly made a difference in history—or rather, many differences. Knowledge work is a key feature of the broad matrices of change and causation that all historians interpret from their various specialized angles. "Immaterial" forces are seldom determinative in themselves, but the same holds true for other dimensions of historical change. Ideas structure action alongside institutions and other instantiations of power.

These four caveats about the influence of scientific claims and epistemologies apply to other knowledge systems as well. If it is too simple to say that science became all-powerful in the twentieth century, we should likewise resist claiming total hegemony for any alternative framework, be it possessive individualism, theological liberalism, secularism, neoliberalism, a system of gender roles, or something else. Scholars can acknowledge the contested, mediated, and contingent character of these frameworks without obscuring the asymmetries of power that have made some discourses far more influential than others.

The key, as always, is to dig deeply into specific historical dynamics and contexts, using interpretive tools developed by intellectual historians and their counterparts in other fields. Intellectual history, with its linguistically and contextually sensitive treatments of past texts and arguments, helps illuminate the complex effects of the modern era's proliferating knowledge claims—and thus the wider structures of power and conflict in which knowledge systems have participated. To omit formal ideas and their champions from the picture is to fundamentally misrepresent social action and historical change.

NOTES

1. A particularly sophisticated and compelling version of this argument appears in Sarah Igo, "Toward a Free-Range Intellectual History," in *The Worlds of American Intellectual History*, ed. Joel Isaac, James T. Kloppenberg, Michael O'Brien, and Jennifer Ratner-Rosenhagen (New York: Oxford University Press, 2017): 324–42. Other takes on the relationship between intellectual and cultural history include Leslie Butler, "From the History of Ideas to Ideas in History," *Modern Intellectual History* 9, no. 1 (April 2012): 157–69; David D. Hall, "Backwards to the Future: The Cultural Turn and the Wisdom of Intellectual History," ibid., 171–84; James T. Kloppenberg, "Thinking Historically: A Manifesto of Pragmatic Hermeneutics," ibid., 201–16; and Joan Shelley Rubin, "Nixon's Grin and Other Keys to the Future of Cultural and Intellectual History," ibid., 217–31.

2. Butler, "From the History of Ideas," 160. By contrast, Igo discerns a widespread retreat from broad cultural discourses in the wake of the 1970s.

3. Some of these studies come from authors trained in both intellectual history and history of science or science and technology studies: e.g., S. M. Amadae, *Rationalizing Capitalist Democracy: The Cold War Origins of Rational Choice Liberalism* (Chicago: University of Chicago Press, 2003); Amadae, *Prisoners of Reason: Game Theory and Neoliberal Political Economy* (New York: Cambridge University Press, 2015); John Carson, *The Measure of Merit: Talents, Intelligence, and Inequality in the French and American Republics, 1750–1940* (Princeton, NJ: Princeton University Press, 2007); Jamie Cohen-Cole, *The Open Mind: Cold War Politics and the Sciences of Human Nature* (Chicago: University of Chicago Press, 2014); Sarah Igo, *The Averaged American: Surveys, Citizens, and the Making of a Mass Public* (Cambridge, MA: Harvard University Press, 2007); Andrew Jewett, *Science, Democracy, and the American University: From the Civil War to the Cold War* (New York: Cambridge University Press, 2012); Rebecca M. Lemov, *World as Laboratory: Experiments with Mice, Mazes, and*

Men (New York: Hill & Wang, 2005); and Joy Rohde, *Armed with Expertise: The Militarization of American Social Research during the Cold War* (Ithaca, NY: Cornell University Press, 2013). Other studies include Howard Brick, *Transcending Capitalism: Visions of a New Society in Modern American Thought* (Ithaca, NY: Cornell University Press, 2006); Angus Burgin, *The Great Persuasion: Reinventing Free Markets since the Depression* (Cambridge, MA: Harvard University Press, 2012); David C. Engerman, *Modernization from the Other Shore: American Intellectuals and the Romance of Russian Development* (Cambridge, MA: Harvard University Press, 2003); Engerman, *Know Your Enemy: The Rise and Fall of America's Soviet Experts* (New York: Oxford University Press, 2009); Ellen F. Fitzpatrick, *History's Memory: Writing America's Past, 1880–1980* (Cambridge, MA: Harvard University Press, 2002); John S. Gilkeson, *Anthropologists and the Rediscovery of America, 1886–1965* (New York: Cambridge University Press, 2010); Nils Gilman, *Mandarins of the Future: Modernization Theory in Cold War America* (Baltimore: Johns Hopkins University Press, 2003); David Paul Haney, *The Americanization of Social Science: Intellectuals and Public Responsibility in the Postwar United States* (Philadelphia: Temple University Press, 2008); Jonathan Scott Holloway, *Confronting the Veil: Abram Harris Jr., E. Franklin Frazier, and Ralph Bunche, 1919–1941* (Chapel Hill: University of North Carolina Press, 2002); George M. Marsden, *The Twilight of the American Enlightenment: The 1950s and the Crisis of Liberal Belief* (New York: Basic Books, 2014); Patrick J. McGrath, *Scientists, Business, and the State, 1890–1960* (Chapel Hill: University of North Carolina Press, 2002); Jon H. Roberts and James Turner, *The Sacred and the Secular University* (Princeton, NJ: Princeton University Press, 2000); Ron Robin, *The Making of the Cold War Enemy: Culture and Politics in the Military-Intellectual Complex* (Princeton, NJ: Princeton University Press, 2001); Daniel T. Rodgers, *Age of Fracture* (Cambridge, MA: Belknap Press of Harvard University Press, 2011); Christopher Shannon, *A World Made Safe for Differences: Cold War Intellectuals and the Politics of Identity* (Lanham, MD: Rowman & Littlefield, 2001); Jeffrey Sklansky, *The Soul's Economy: Market Society and Selfhood in American Thought, 1820–1920* (Chapel Hill: University of North Carolina Press, 2002); and many of the essays in Nelson Lichtenstein, ed., *American Capitalism: Social Thought and Political Economy in the Twentieth Century* (Philadelphia: University of Pennsylvania Press, 2006).

4. A sampling of works by scholars in other historical subfields includes Laura Briggs, *Reproducing Empire: Race, Sex, Science, and U.S. Imperialism in Puerto Rico* (Berkeley: University of California Press, 2002); Carl N. Degler, *In Search of Human Nature: The Decline and Revival of Darwinism in American Social Thought* (New York: Oxford University Press, 1991); Leah N. Gordon, *From Power to Prejudice: The Rise of Racial Individualism in Midcentury America* (Chicago: University of Chicago Press, 2015); Khalil Gibran Muhammad, *The Condemnation of Blackness: Race, Crime, and the Making of Modern Urban America* (Cambridge, MA: Harvard University Press, 2010); Alice O'Connor, *Poverty Knowledge: Social Science, Social Policy, and the Poor in Twentieth-Century U.S. History* (Princeton, NJ: Princeton University Press, 2001); and Daryl Michael Scott, *Contempt and Pity: Social Policy and the Image of the Damaged Black Psyche, 1880–1996* (Chapel Hill: University of North Carolina Press, 1997). Of course, historians of science write in this vein as well: e.g., Christopher J. Phillips, *The New Math: A Political History* (Chicago: University of Chicago Press, 2015); Paul Erickson, *The World the Game Theorists Made* (Chicago: University of Chicago Press, 2015); Paul Erickson, Judy L. Klein, Lorraine Daston, Rebecca Lemov, Thomas Sturm, and Michael D. Gordin, *How Reason Almost Lost Its Mind: The Strange Career of Cold War Rationality* (Chicago: University of Chicago Press, 2013); Michael D. Gordin, *The Pseudoscience Wars: Immanuel Velikovsky and the Birth of the Modern Fringe* (Chicago: University of Chicago Press, 2012); Anne Harrington, *The Cure Within: A History of Mind-Body Medicine* (New York: W. W. Norton, 2008); Jennifer S. Light, *From Warfare to Welfare: Defense Intellectuals and Urban Problems in Cold*

War America (Baltimore: Johns Hopkins University Press, 2003); Erika Lorraine Milam, *Looking for a Few Good Males: Female Choice in Evolutionary Biology* (Baltimore: Johns Hopkins University Press, 2010); Gregg Mitman, *The State of Nature: Ecology, Community, and American Social Thought, 1900–1950* (Chicago: University of Chicago Press, 1992); Katherine Pandora, *Rebels within the Ranks: Psychologists' Critiques of Scientific Authority and Democratic Realities in New Deal America* (New York: Cambridge University Press, 1997); Philip J. Pauly, *Biologists and the Promise of American Life, from Meriwether Lewis to Alfred Kinsey* (Princeton, NJ: Princeton University Press, 2000); Robert N. Proctor, *Value-Free Science? Purity and Power in Modern Knowledge* (Cambridge, MA: Harvard University Press, 1991); and Mark Solovey, *Shaky Foundations: The Politics–Patronage–Social Science Nexus in Cold War America* (New Brunswick, NJ: Rutgers University Press, 2013). Representative studies by historically minded social scientists and philosophers of science include John G. Gunnell, *Imagining the American Polity: Political Science and the Discourse of Democracy* (University Park: Penn State University Press, 2004); Philip Mirowski, *Machine Dreams: Economics Becomes a Cyborg Science* (New York: Cambridge University Press, 2002); David H. Price, *Anthropological Intelligence: The Deployment and Neglect of American Anthropology in the Second World War* (Durham, NC: Duke University Press, 2008); George A. Reisch, *How the Cold War Transformed Philosophy of Science* (New York: Cambridge University Press, 2005); George Steinmetz, ed., *The Politics of Method in the Human Sciences: Positivism and Its Epistemological Others* (Durham, NC: Duke University Press, 2005); and a number of the essays in Christian Smith, ed., *The Secular Revolution: Power, Interests, and Conflict in the Secularization of American Public Life* (Berkeley: University of California Press, 2003). The intellectual historians David C. Engerman and Joel Isaac have pushed back on the simplistic "Cold War determinism" that animates many works in the latter category: Engerman, "Rethinking Cold War Universities: Some Recent Histories," *Journal of Cold War Studies* 5, no. 3 (March 2006): 80–95; Isaac, "The Human Sciences in Cold War America," *Historical Journal* 50, no. 3 (2007): 725–46. Debates over this theme also reverberate through Joel Isaac and Duncan Bell, *Uncertain Empire: American History and the Idea of the Cold War* (New York: Oxford University Press, 2012). In *Science, Democracy, and the American University*, I issue a somewhat different challenge to the common practice of reading epistemological value-neutralism as merely a tool for turning interests into ideologies.

    5. Science and technology studies (STS) offers another institutional space in which these scholars can interact, and it sustains an unusually self-reflective dialogue on methodological and interpretive issues. However, many historians have been wary of that field's association with controversial (and widely misunderstood) interpretive frameworks such as social constructionism and actor-network theory. Moreover, many STS scholars address contemporary rather than historical topics. A series of collaborative volumes has also fostered exchanges between intellectual historians, historians of science, and internal historians of the nonhistorical disciplines: e.g., Robert Adcock, Mark Bevir, and Shannon C. Stimson, eds., *Modern Political Science: Anglo-American Exchanges since 1880* (Princeton, NJ: Princeton University Press, 2007); Roger Backhouse and Philippe Fontaine, eds., *The History of the Social Sciences since 1945* (New York: Cambridge University Press, 2010); Backhouse and Fontaine, eds., *The Unsocial Social Science? Economics and Neighboring Disciplines since 1945* (Durham, NC: Duke University Press, 2010); Backhouse and Fontaine, eds., *A Historiography of the Modern Social Sciences* (Cambridge: Cambridge University Press, 2014); JoAnne Brown and David K. van Keuren, eds., *The Estate of Social Knowledge* (Baltimore: Johns Hopkins University Press, 1991); Craig Calhoun, ed., *Sociology in America: A History* (Chicago: University of Chicago Press, 2007); Theodore M. Porter and Dorothy Ross, eds., *The Cambridge History of Science*, vol. 7, *The Modern Social Sciences* (Cambridge: Cambridge University Press, 2008); Ross, ed., *Modernist Impulses in*

the Human Sciences, 1870–1930 (Baltimore: Johns Hopkins University Press, 1994); and Mark Solovey and Hamilton Cravens, eds., *Cold War Social Science: Knowledge Production, Liberal Democracy, and Human Nature* (New York: Palgrave Macmillan, 2012). So, too, have the annual conferences of groups such as the Society for the History of Recent Social Science.

6. Although most commentators today are sanguine about intellectual history's status, especially as compared to the situation in the 1970s, I find continued resistance among other historians to the study of formal thought systems—science, theology, philosophy, literary theory—unless they straightforwardly address questions of sociological difference or political disputation. This resistance might help explain intellectual history's omission from Eric Foner and Lisa McGirr, eds., *American History Now* (Philadelphia: Temple University Press, 2011), after its inclusion in Foner's earlier volume *The New American History* (Philadelphia: Temple University Press, 1997).

7. Daniel T. Rodgers has written about the centrality of movement and circulation: Daniel T. Rodgers, "Paths in the Social History of Ideas," in Isaac et al., *Worlds of American Intellectual History*, 307–23. See also his introduction to Rodgers, Bhavani Raman, and Helmut Reimitz, eds., *Cultures in Motion* (Princeton, NJ: Princeton University Press, 2014).

8. A classic exploration of such phenomena is Robert M. Young, "The Naturalization of Value Systems in the Human Sciences," *Problems in the Biological and Human Sciences* 6 (1981): 63–110. For an illustration from US history see Andrew Jewett, "Naturalizing Liberalism in the 1950s," in *Professors and Their Politics*, ed. Neil Gross and Solon Simmons (Baltimore: Johns Hopkins University Press, 2014).

9. This tendency is evident in the canonical histories of the US social sciences, which helped to establish the study of the politics of knowledge as a major preoccupation of intellectual historians: Mary O. Furner, *Advocacy and Objectivity: A Crisis in the Professionalization of American Social Science, 1865–1905* (Lexington: University Press of Kentucky, 1975); Thomas L. Haskell, *The Emergence of Professional Social Science: The American Social Science Association and the Nineteenth-Century Crisis of Authority* (Urbana: University of Illinois Press, 1977); and Dorothy Ross, *The Origins of American Social Science* (New York: Cambridge University Press, 1991).

10. Jewett, *Science, Democracy, and the American University*. A classic study of the "whitening" of immigrants is Matthew Frye Jacobson, *Whiteness of a Different Color: European Immigrants and the Alchemy of Race* (Cambridge, MA: Harvard University Press, 1998).

11. Among historians, Paula Baker influentially advocated this conceptual expansion in "The Domestication of Politics: Women and American Political Society," *American Historical Review* 89 (1984): 620–47. Mark B. Brown makes a compelling case for delineating a space of formal, organized "politics" within the broader category of actions with "political" effects: "Politicizing Science: Conceptions of Politics in Science and Technology Studies," *Social Studies of Science* 45, no. 1 (2015): 3–30. However, the phrase "politics of knowledge" is sufficiently widespread and resonant that I employ it here.

12. Both within and beyond history, meanwhile, many critical scholars feel obliged to distance themselves from the phrase "intellectual history," often by adopting Foucault's term "genealogy" or dubbing themselves cultural historians. Yet the differences in practice are frequently minimal.

13. David Bloor famously articulated this symmetry principle in *Knowledge and Social Imagery* (Boston: Routledge and Kegan Paul, 1976).

14. This intermingling is evident, among elsewhere, in the pages of *Modern Intellectual History* and the *Journal of Intellectual History* and at conferences of the Society for U.S. Intellectual History.

15. Helpful studies of the complexities of scientific authority include Ellen Herman, *The Romance of American Psychology: Political Culture in the Age of Experts* (Berkeley:

University of California Press, 1995); Anne Harrington, *Reenchanted Science: Holism in German Culture from Wilhelm II to Hitler* (Princeton, NJ: Princeton University Press, 1996); Theodore M. Porter, *Trust in Numbers: The Pursuit of Objectivity in Science and Public Life* (Princeton, NJ: Princeton University Press, 1995); and Steven Epstein, "The Construction of Lay Expertise: AIDS Activism and the Forging of Credibility in the Reform of Clinical Trials," *Science, Technology & Human Values* 20, no. 4 (1995): 408–37.

16. Note, for example, Edward A. Purcell Jr.'s observation that the fortunes of the black civil rights movement inspired his study of deep shifts in epistemology and political theory: *The Crisis of Democratic Theory: Scientific Naturalism and the Problem of Value* (Lexington: University Press of Kentucky, 1973), ix.

17. This is not to say that a single scholar, let alone a single study, must address all facets of the situation. The overarching task falls to scholarly communities in the round.

18. Harrington, *Reenchanted Science*; Linda Sargent Wood, *A More Perfect Union: Holistic Worldviews and the Transformation of American Culture after World War II* (New York: Oxford University Press, 2012).

CONCLUSION
The Idea of Historical Context and the Intellectual Historian

Daniel Wickberg

One of the most familiar rhetorical moves for historians is to insist on seeing a person, text, or phenomenon "in historical context." The notion that historical explanation involves contextualization is such an ingrained reflex among historians that it is often taken for granted; it is one of the elements that, by virtue of their ubiquity and consensus, constitute the "common sense" of the profession. And because it is part of this common sense, it has gone largely unanalyzed as an epistemological strategy. Everybody knows what it is to invoke historical context. As a consequence, nobody really questions context *as* context. The invocation of context is a way to move the understanding of a phenomenon from abstract, formal, and rationalist understanding to concrete, specific, historical understanding. Instead of imagining a person, event, or idea as autonomous and defined by its inherent meaning, historians seek to root that person, event, or idea in larger historical structures or "contexts." All historians make this move; contextualization is a genre convention, part of what allows us to recognize written history when we read it. But given the ubiquity of the concept, or perhaps because of that ubiquity, there is very little analysis, either in the writing of historians or in the philosophy of history, of the meaning of the concept of "context."[1]

I want to suggest that if we have a clearer idea of context, some of the old debates that have characterized the field of intellectual history for the past half century might be put aside, and we might give to the field a new analytical precision. The result would be to expand the kinds of approaches that will allow us to better understand the substance and functions of ideas, thought, and thinking in the past. As intellectual historians have turned toward a more capacious understanding of the field—beginning to welcome the return of long-range history of ideas, moving toward a more thoroughly transnational study of thought, embracing popular and fugitive texts and beliefs as legitimate objects of study, and considering the reception of texts and ideas as well as the conditions of their creation and origin—the commitments forged by besieged intellectual historians in the 1960s, '70s, and '80s have received renewed critical attention.[2] The accommodation of intellectual history to the dominance of social history in the discipline in the 1970s and '80s, and the surprising potency of the Anglo-American linguistic turn in the writings of Quentin Skinner and his followers, have set the terms in which intellectual history has been practiced and discussed in recent decades.[3] Given this recent move toward a "big tent" of intellectual history, it seems appropriate to reconsider how we might think about so-called contextualism, the tradition of the history of ideas, and the variety of methods associated with the turn to discourse, culture, and language. One way to do this is to think more rigorously about what historians are up to when they invoke "context" as the condition of historical understanding of thought, thinking, and ideas.

While historians of American thought have been influenced in recent decades by models of discourse and collective patterns of thought and language, rather than, say, analysis of single authors, intellectual biography, and the centrality of individual texts, they have received their version of Cambridge school "contextualism" rather indirectly. Few Americanists read Quentin Skinner, the most highly regarded theoretician of the Cambridge school historians.[4] The term "Cambridge school" refers to a group of British historians of political thought who came to prominence in the 1960s and '70s: Peter Laslett, John Dunn, J. G. A. Pocock, and Skinner most notable among them. Within the circles of European intellectual historians, and especially among historians of political thought and theory, Skinner and the Cambridge school have been highly influential. Pocock's version of Cambridge-school practice is best known to Americanists, given its prominence in the debates about republicanism that structured an older generation's understanding of American revolutionary ideology.[5] And Pocock's approach, in practice, was much more concerned with collective languages of politics than the theoretical statements associated with Dunn and particularly Skinner, which seemed to foreground the interpretation of individual thinkers and texts. Skinner's famous 1969 article "Meaning and Understanding in the History of Ideas," became the focus of a wide-ranging debate among a variety of scholars on "contextualism" in the history of ideas.[6] That debate has shaped the thinking about context, often in misleading ways, so is worth attending to in order to clear the ground for a better understanding of the role of context in intellectual history. Despite the fact that historians of American thought have not generally been followers of Arthur Lovejoy or Leo Strauss, nor Skinnerians in any explicit sense, their orientation toward the history of thought has been shaped by this debate, although obliquely.

In part, the misunderstanding lies in matters terminological and polemical. Skinner's "Meaning and Understanding" was a full-fledged attack on a field he designated as "the history of ideas"; he characterized that field broadly in a way that conflated schools of thought and intellectual approaches that were quite distinct. Thinkers such as Leo Strauss, C. B. MacPherson, Carl Becker, Ernst Cassirer, and Arthur Lovejoy were lumped together with scholars of literature such as F. R. Leavis and R. S. Crane as exhibiting a set of common dispositions, despite the fact that they had widely different views about how to think about ideas, and some of them were far more "historical" in their approach than others. While Skinner's real concern was with an ahistorical method of treating political thought, and his primary quibble was with resident scholars in the field of political theory, by characterizing his intervention as one addressed more broadly to historians of ideas, he suggested that the entire field was guilty of a kind of ahistorical generalization. According to Skinner, the history of ideas, as a field of study, was committed to a false search for intellectual coherence in the patterns of thought found in the past, the imposition of abstract and universal typologies on historical particulars, or the reduction of texts to mere ideological expressions of social and economic conditions. Only the method he was advocating provided a proper "historical" understanding, in contrast to what he described as the prevailing "orthodoxies" of the history of ideas. Despite the fact that he recognized scholars such as MacPherson as committed to understanding ideas in terms of their social and economic "contexts," he argued that their form of contextualism shared an ahistorical understanding with scholars such as those who believed that classic texts could be read in terms of their internal logic; both sought to reify an understanding of the meaning of the text and its content independent of the intentions of its author. Marxist-derived categories of analysis, such as "bourgeois ideology," invoked social and economic contexts as a means to interpret ideas historically, but imagined some transhistorical force at work in producing ideas. The conclusion that Skinner drew was that social and economic conditions that were not understood as such by historical actors could be no part of the relevant context for understanding their ideas historically.

There is some irony in the fact that Skinner himself reified the orthodoxies of the field he designated "the history of ideas" in order to distinguish his preferred method from what he pictured as the dominant orientation of the field, regardless of the stated intentions of its practitioners—some of whom surely thought of themselves as historians of ideas, and some of whom surely didn't. The only legitimate form of historical understanding of ideas and texts for Skinner, and those who followed him, was one that sought to reconstruct the intentions of authors in terms of the meanings and understandings available to them in their tightly bounded community of contemporaries. For Skinner, the history of ideas was the history of their use in arguments, and the reconstruction of those uses involved a reconstruction of their author's intentions in terms of linguistic conventions available to them in the world in which they wrote.[7] Situating an author and/or a text in terms of a longer intellectual tradition that he or she could not have been aware of, and therefore could not intend to contribute to, was an illegitimate move that could only prevent or distort proper historical understanding. Thinking of John Locke, for instance, in terms of the development of liberalism would be applying a category of which Locke had no understanding, and an intention that he could not have had. The "mythology of prolepsis," said Skinner, was the propensity of historians of ideas to find later meanings present in earlier texts. Skinner went as far as suggesting that those who wrote the history of intellectual traditions, developing through time, were engaged in essentially the same practice as those who built abstract and universal models of political theory that were then applied to all times and places. Thinking in terms of traditions of thought such as liberalism, Marxism, idealism, or empiricism was, for Skinner, an anti-contextual practice. It substituted historians' categories for the historically existing contexts.

This is not the place to enter into a full-scale critique of Skinner and the Cambridge school. Others have done that with varying degrees of success, from a variety of different positions.[8] What I want to stress here is the historical outcome of Skinner's intervention. The debate that followed on Skinner's 1969 article ended up being widely characterized as a debate between Cambridge school "contextualists" and their critics, who were characterized as "anti-contextualists." The Skinnerians appropriated the name of contextualism for themselves, with the implication that all historians of ideas who didn't share their particular linguistic preoccupations and methodological commitments—who did not put "use" and authorial intention at the center of their reconstructions, who did not set out to discover the linguistic conventions of a bounded time and place—were enemies of contextual understanding. To be clear, Skinner did not argue this, but in the broader scholarly culture of intellectual historians, this was the result; "context" became a kind of shorthand for the particular method associated with Skinner. Because Skinner had distinguished his method from a singular set of orthodoxies he claimed represented the rest of the field, it was easy to conflate those who were genuinely opposed to historical and contextual analysis with those contextualists who simply didn't subscribe to Skinner's particular version of historical context.

Some critics, such as David Harlan, John Patrick Diggins, and Dominick LaCapra, might fairly be characterized as advocates for a vision of great ideas and classic texts that transcend their contexts, and fierce critics of what they regarded as the limiting forms of Skinnerian contextualism.[9] In the field of political theory and philosophy, there really was a sharp line between those who approached it historically, and those who wanted to treat it as an object that contained timeless concerns and problems. As an intervention in the field of political theory on behalf of a historical approach to the subject, Skinner's argument was salutary. And just to complicate things, in the field of philosophy, the term "contextualism" does designate a particular epistemological theory, and there are many epistemologists who reject it as a form of epistemological relativism.[10] There are places in contemporary scholarship where there are real and critical battles between contextualists and anticontextualists. The discipline of history, I think, is not one of these places; it is hard to be a historian without being some kind of contextualist.

Not all critics of the Cambridge school were opposed to contextual understanding, especially those who regarded themselves as historians. Like the supporters of the proposed American constitution, who appropriated the title "Federalism" from the critics of a centralized national state, made it their own, and left their opponents with the name of "Anti-Federalists," the contextualists dominated the Anglo-American study of European ideas, and left their critics— no matter how deeply committed to various ideas of context—to be designated anti-contextualists.[11] Talk of linguistic conventions, illocutionary force, and local meanings came to be associated with contextualism writ large, and advocates for various other methods of contextual understanding struggled to get a foothold in the central practice of the field. Arthur Lovejoy, for one, had been a deeply contextualist historical thinker, but in the wake of Skinner and the dominance of Cambridge school historians, his work was repeatedly characterized as unhistorical and committed to abstract decontextualized "unit ideas" that remained the same throughout history. Lovejoy, having died in 1962, was unable to defend his version of the history of ideas against this caricature.[12]

The primary reason that forms of contextualism that differed from Cambridge school positions were unable to get a strong hearing is the generally held commonsense idea that historical context is a unitary, singular, fixed thing. In this view, either you're for contextualism or against it. And if there are only two camps—those who want to contextualize, and those who are committed to formalist or intrinsic methods of understanding—then the ownership of contextualism by the Cambridge school hides the varying forms of context that may well not be commensurate with one another. If contexts are plural, on the other hand, then the debate in intellectual history turns out to be entirely different from the debate between textualists and contextualists, formalists and historicists, internalists and externalists. It suddenly becomes a debate among varieties of contextualists. Almost all historians can agree on the idea that some form of contextual understanding is necessary if we are to understand thinking, ideas, and thought as historical phenomena. Not all historians, on the other hand, think that the specific methods outlined and practiced by Skinner and those of like mind are the exclusive method of historical understanding of ideas. Without denying the legitimacy or power of the Skinnerian approach, intellectual historians can be sure there are forms of contextual understanding that are fundamentally different from those offered by Skinner.

Before I outline (and argue for) what I take to be a pluralist understanding of the idea of context, I want to suggest that there are good reasons, baked into the intellectual history of the idea of historical context, for the confusion about whether the idea refers to a singular unified whole or to the possibilities of multiple or plural understandings—whether there is one form of context or many. While the term "context" has a long and complex history, the term "historical context," along with its twin "cultural context," is of relatively recent vintage, rising in use steadily since the 1930s (see figure 19.1).

Prior to the 1930s, historians rarely used the phrase "historical context" to refer to the particular elements of a past era. Its saliency has been contemporaneous with the turn in historians' discourse away from the commitment to "objectivity" and the embrace of varieties of cultural and historical relativism. The writings

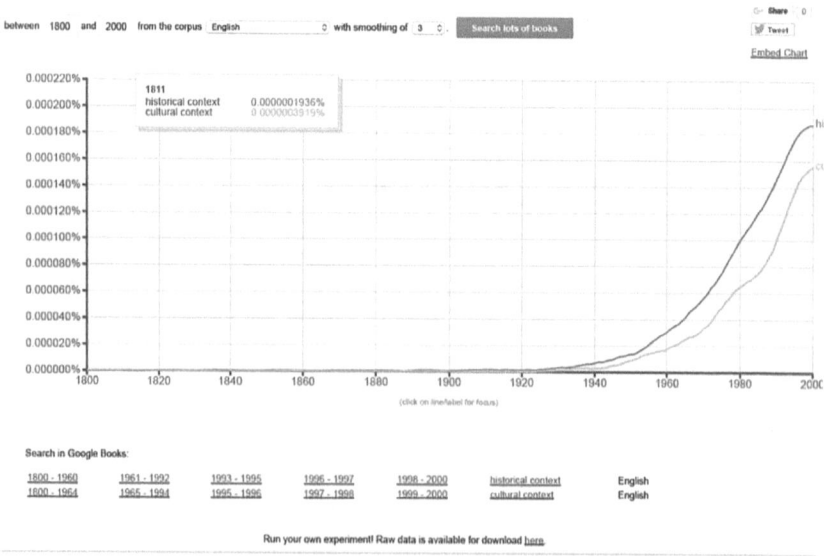

FIGURE 19.1 Google Ngram "historical context" and "cultural context"

of historians in the 1930s such as Carl Becker, Charles Beard, R. G. Collingwood, and Herbert Butterfield, who turned away from ideals of objectivity, progress, rational order, historical metaphysics, and epistemological foundationalism, were consonant with a conceptualization of context. The idea of context, in its use by historians, then, is closely associated with historicist notions that challenge older Enlightenment-derived ideas of universal rational order and foundational certainty, of what Beard called "that noble dream" of historical objectivity and positive knowledge. To think contextually is to think relativistically, concretely, and pluralistically, rather than to look for abstract principle, general law, and uniform models of human behavior. Historicism, since its nineteenth-century inception, has been a key component of a modernist sensibility. The modern concept of historical context is part of this sensibility—it seeks a situating of objects in the specific conditions of particular times and places, and looks at such objects not as free-standing, abstract entities with a formal internal structure, but as objects deriving their life and meaning from the elements around and outside them. In this sense, the emergence of the idea of historical context in the twentieth century is part and parcel of what Morton White famously called "the revolt against formalism" in modern social thought.[13]

But like those practitioners of White's antiformalism, the twentieth-century historians who followed them often advocated a kind of organicism or cultural holism as a solution to the emptiness of formalist understanding. They imagined the environment of any action as a single totality into which it could be placed. Hence, the idea of context could express both a pluralist, relativist sensibility, *and* embrace a notion that historical objects had a singular holistic environment. Context meant relativistic understanding of ideas, texts, and actions, but it was a relativism based on the idea that each distinct historical era or culture—each context—was a unified seamless whole into which those ideas, texts, and actions could be placed. It was culturally and historically relativistic, but epistemologically realistic and universalistic. What it took away with one hand—the commitment to universalist, rationalist, objectivist standards—it gave back with the other; ideas and actions were historically relative and could only be understood in terms of their contexts, but each context was a singular, uniform and comprehensive object in the world, and could be known as such. The tension between these two aspects of contextual and historicist thinking continues to the present. The intellectual historian Peter Gordon, for instance, in his recent critique of contextualism, argues, among other things, that the premises of contextualism "support the view that, for any given idea, there is *one and only one* historical context that both enables and exhausts its meaning."[14] This notion of particular historical contexts as objects whose identity in the past is singular, sits hard against the general relativism and epistemological constructivism of historical thinking at large.

Given all this, it is scarcely a wonder why the term "context" in the present seems to hide contradictory assumptions. And yet, as a term of art for historians, it is indispensable. What follows is an attempt to spell out more clearly a conception of "context" that is analytically useful for intellectual historians, and both builds upon and clarifies our practice. It does so by abandoning the notion that a historical context is somehow a given unitary thing that existed in the past, and affirming that it is primarily a tool that allows us to think historically about ideas as past objects. It replaces a mistaken ontology with a commitment to methodological pluralism. My definition of historical context has six components: question-dependency, plurality, contiguity, relationality, placement, and relative stability. If all that sounds a little dense and abstract, I hope the reader will stick with me. Too often the philosophy of history is ignored by historians, and the work of historians is ignored by those who would have something philosophical to say about it.[15] I hope my argument here can mediate between historians interested in methodology, and philosophers of history interested in the conceptual basis of historical knowledge.

My first proposition is that contexts are question dependent. They are not simply "out there" in the historical past, waiting to reveal themselves to us. The relevant context will arise out of the questions we ask; since it is not an object to be unearthed, but a tool for finding historical relationships, its parameters are inevitably shaped by the direction in which we are pointed by the questions we ask. If I ask, for instance, what led to changes in curricula in American higher education in the later nineteenth century, I will call forth a set of conditions, abstracted from the potential whole of what was going on in the nineteenth century: what will appear relevant might be particular scientific and religious changes; institutional shifts and the rise of professions premised on technical expertise; the experience of Americans with education abroad; changes in the student body and its demands; the rise of state universities, etc.[16] I think it unlikely that the relevant context would include passage of the Fourteenth Amendment, the rise of urban machine politics, the development of vaudeville, Chinese Exclusion, and the invention of the bicycle. We might ask other questions that bring these contexts into sight, but they play little or no part in our necessarily selective choice of relevant contexts for a question about changes in university curricula. Out of the buzzing undifferentiated mass of historical existants, an orderly context is shaped by the questions we ask about the past; it does us little good to throw everything that was contemporary into the hopper and hope that a context will emerge out of it. The idea that by contextualizing first we will come to know what to ask gets it backwards. It implies that we can find a context without knowing what might possibly be relevant to the concerns that we have.

My second proposition is that contexts should be understood as plural, rather than singular. What makes contexts plural is that we have many different questions we might ask about past objects, and each question will generate a different context as a means to answer it. There is no one singular "historical context" for any given object of analysis. Every object has multiple relevant contexts. The notion of context as a singular historical formation is owing to a species of realism or objectivism—the idea that there is one single historical context "out there." It is tempting to think of *the* historical context, as if it involved a past that was passively waiting for us to place an object in it, and thereby make sense of it. Any historical phenomenon, person, text, institution, event has always more than one single historical context—the phrase "put it in its historical context" is misleading, since it seems to imply that there is such a singular definite context for any object of analysis. But we can think of multiple contexts for any phenomenon. The Emancipation Proclamation can be seen in relationship to Lincoln's antislavery thought, the broader ideologies and internal conflicts of the Republican Party, military strategy during the Civil War, the shifting role of executive authority and the understanding of the Constitution during the Civil War, Lincoln's personal biography and family life, ideas about race and citizenship in the nineteenth century, black emancipation movements both before and after, the colonization movement, foreign relations, westward expansion and Republican policy, the growth of market capitalism and wage labor relations, the diffusion and transmission of information in the nineteenth century. Each of these potentially forms a separate context.

It is, again, tempting to think that if we just expanded our view, we would see that each of these "subcontexts" in reality belongs to a comprehensive general context that would include them all. But the Annales school dream of "*histoire totale*" floundered precisely because it is impossible to successfully formulate an inclusive general context of this kind; something must always be left out, and such a general context with uneven temporal and geographic features cannot be made coherent.[17] Even the best historians fall into the trap of imagining a singular comprehensive context. When James Kloppenberg, in his otherwise salutary effort to open intellectual history to a fully pluralist and pragmatic hermeneutical approach, defined the contextual practice of historians, for instance, he did so in a way that strongly implied the existence of a general context:

> A series of concentric circles helps explain the diverse objects of analysis in intellectual history. Place a particular text at the center, and arrange around it an ever-widening set of circles that trace the contexts surrounding any text, whether it is a published work of philosophy or political theory, a diary entry or an anonymous pamphlet, an advertise-

ment or a material object, such as a quilt or a sofa, in which numerous cultural currents collide.

Intellectual historians begin at that center, with that text, and work outward toward historical understanding. Different historians will concentrate their energies on different circles as a practical matter of research strategy. Some will study individual thinkers, others philosophical debates, others the texts produced by members of social movements, and others the circulation of ideas among ordinary people. But the broader discursive community of intellectual historians should encompass work in all of those circles, from the most minute to the most expansive.[18]

On the one hand, Kloppenberg affirms the notion of plural contexts for any historical object; on the other, the metaphor of "concentric circles" suggests that each of these contexts can be neatly fit into one that is wider and more expansive, that each context is really part of the one big context. When I say that contexts are plural, I mean this in a way that is different from the vision of Kloppenberg's additive contexts, snuggled inside one another like Russian dolls; I mean plural in the sense that they are not necessarily coherent or consistent with one another, that they cannot inevitably be seen as subsets of a larger set, that they are potentially incommensurable, because they rest on alternative conceptions of the ways in which the world is organized.[19] The idea that it would be theoretically possible to bring "the entire context" to bear on an object of historical analysis seems, from this view, wrong.

My third proposition is that historical contexts involve contiguity in time and space. To put an object in some kind of context is to situate it not in terms of analogy, abstract type, or universal law, but in terms of what preceded, what was contemporaneous, and what followed within a specific designated place or social entity. Time spans of contexts can be short or long—the events of a day, month, or year, on one hand, and of centuries on the other. Similarly, spatial range of contexts can be narrow or wide—a neighborhood, a nation, or a set of transnational spheres. Because the concept of context is so abstract—even as it points us toward concreteness—it hides the extent to which it refers to such a wide range of historical conceptualizations. But this, too, is part of the fact that contexts are not unitary but plural. The tendency is to think that contiguity in time and space is, like Goldilocks's judgment, "just right"—that contexts are the same kinds of things, even as we know that periodization, for instance, really varies historiographically, and we don't divide the past up into equal blocks of relevant time. But if the term "context" can refer to something as broad and extensive as "the modern West," on the one hand, and as narrow as "Chicago in August of 1934," on the other, it's clear that it really does not designate any *specific* range of contiguity in time or space. Rather, it refers generally to the idea of contiguity in time and space, leaving the question of the size and extent of a context unspecified. This is partly why there can be no singular general context for an object; the various contexts refer to different time scales and different spatial extents that cannot be made coterminous. At some level, the choice of how to limit the range of a particular context—how to specify where it begins and where it ends—must be arbitrary, driven by established convention, or arising out of the needs of the specific contextualizing practice. Context cannot be limited to mere contemporaneity, as the Skinnerian version of contextualism would suggest it is, partly because the idea of what is contemporary to any object requires some notion of a contiguous time frame. The way in which time and space are configured in the definition of any given context is highly variable, but limited by the notion of contiguity. For instance, classical Roman political theory is not a context for early modern European political theory, but the recovery and interpretation of the classical tradition, its status as a continuing intellectual tradition through time and space, does form a context for later political thought.[20] Traditions, reinterpreted and maintained through time, are a form of context if they are "live" for given historical actors and exist in contiguous time and space. An unknown, unread, lost text from a distant past cannot be a part of a later context. A designation of temporal and spatial aspects of a context are necessary, but not sufficient, to establish a particular historical context; the introduction of other parameters (political entities, institutions, social categories, religions, etc.) give more specific shape to any designated context.

The fourth proposition is that context is a relationship, not a substance. That is, when we contextualize an idea, an actor, or a text, what we are doing is establishing some kind of relationship between the object and aspects of its environment. It is not simply the historical past of a particular era "out there," already formed as a historical given. To describe something as a context is to establish a relevant relationship, and is hence analytical rather than merely descriptive. The purpose of describing a context is to develop an interpretation of an object by showing its relationship to aspects of its historical environment. We can be engaged in "thick description," à la Geertz, in an effort to root meaning in environment, or we can be setting up a set of causal conditions as context; we can be imagining traditions of thought into which we can situate our thinker or text, or we can be demonstrating how a receptive audience for a particular idea was formed. All these uses of context involve an analytical relationship. Hence, contexts are really tools of analysis, rather than independent objects in the world. We would not describe some historically existing phenomena as a context if it did not help us to make sense of the object we are contextualizing.

Fifth, when we speak of a context, we mean a means of centering an object in a setting. In the actual past, the things we end up calling contexts are not distinct things from the objects, persons, text, or ideas that they are invoked to explain. Historical reality is undifferentiated in this way. A context cannot be identified or made without having an object to place in it. By metaphor we might think of this as foregrounding an object in a landscape, placing a gem in a setting, or putting a picture in a frame. That is, in order to contextualize we must start with an abstracted entity, and place that entity in a centered relationship with historical phenomena that exist outside of the boundaries of that abstracted entity. Here Kloppenberg's notion of contextualization as a centering practice is apt, but I would stress further the artifice involved in defining a bounded entity in the past, abstracting it from history, and then re-placing it in the center of an environment called into being by the questions we have asked. This is very much the opposite of the image of contextualization as returning an object to where it presumably belongs in its place of origin, as if we were simply placing a jigsaw puzzle piece in order to complete the puzzle.

Finally, when we create a historical context for an object, we do so in a way as to create an illusion of stability in the past. While actual historical phenomena are fluid and dynamic, contextualization is a way to contain that dynamism. Even when we picture a context as changing or developing in time, that change occurs within a stabilizing framework. For instance, conventions of periodization allow us to give a kind of unity and fixity to past eras, to characterize them as having consistent structures, patterns of thought, and conditions of life. While all historians are concerned with change, just like other analysts we need a way to hold constant some environmental variables, and context allows us to do that. For historians, context is the epistemological equivalent of the laboratory for laboratory scientists—it gives us a stable space in which we can place an object or relationship so that we can say something meaningful about it. But the difference between a context and a laboratory points to the differences between historians (and other social scientists who share the orientation toward concrete, particular, and contextual understandings) and natural scientists. The laboratory is a space in which variables can be controlled by isolating a phenomenon or relationship from its concrete occurrence in nature. It is an environment that allows for abstraction. Context, on the other hand, is a way of specifying, but also controlling, the environment in which actual ideas and events have occurred. Its mode of stabilizing points toward concreteness.

How does this conception of context as a tool of analysis, rather than a picture of historical reality, have specific implications for intellectual historians? The tendency of intellectual historians is to foreground thinking, patterns of thought, and ideas as the objects that need to be contextualized. Most American intellectual historians are what I have elsewhere called "fusionists," who believe that intellectual history is not different in kind or approach from other forms of history (e.g., social, political, economic, cultural), but is really a matter of emphasis—choosing to focus more on thought, but relating it to a vision of reality in which thinking is necessarily and always bound up with non-ideational matters.[21] For these historians, contextualizing ideas and thinking is a matter of situating ideas in relation to institutions, social and economic changes, the particular interests of various groups, the political and policy environment. The object/context distinction is imagined largely as a distinction between foregrounded ideas, and backgrounded matter, or contexts of non-ideational reality. The tendency is then to imagine this particular arrangement of ideas and their contexts in terms of realism: the idea that a picture of reality is arrived at by putting ideas into a non-ideational context. But this is no more (or less) "real" than picturing ideas in relation to other ideas. Since contexts are question dependent, they never provide us with a simply historical reality. There is no empirical or logical reason why we should prefer one mode of contextualization over another, why it is better to put ideas in a political context, for instance, than in a philosophical context. Some questions will push us toward political contexts, others toward philosophical contexts—one result is not "more accurate" than the other; both are equally "exclusionary" in foregoing some contexts at the expense of others. Unless we believe that politics is somehow more essentially causative and significant as a context than, say, religious beliefs—that power has universal metaphysical priority over faith—there is no stronger case to be made for the priority of political over religious contexts in historical analysis. This is particularly appropriate to note, since the current fashion in intellectual history leans strongly toward the foregrounding of political intellectuals, policy history, and the world of public action.[22]

We come full circle back to Skinner and his form of contextualism, because the kind of context that Skinner pointed to was decidedly *not* the material social, economic, and political context of a given text. In fact, Skinner rejected a method that would identify such contextual forces as the condition of textual meaning and historical understanding. Instead, he embraced the notion that the specific kind of relevant context was the immediate environment of meaningful conventions and collective understandings—that historical contexts were, in some basic way, ideational in nature. To understand the meaning of a text as a linguistic act was to understand what its authors intended, what they thought they were doing. I would designate these Skinnerian contexts as one kind of context among many. The method is salutary in opening intellectual history to the idea that thinking is a matter of context as well as text; it is limiting by claiming for itself the sole authority of "historical understanding."

Since history changes as the questions we ask about the past change, a truly pluralistic and open form of historical inquiry will make room for a variety of questions. Once we give up the idea that there are contexts as singular, comprehensive, and unitary objects in the past, that they specify some consistent range of time and space, that we need simply place our texts and objects into them, we open up our practice to the possibilities of thinking about ideas as contexts for other ideas, and, contra Skinner, intellectual traditions as contexts. What appears from one angle to be a text, from another is a context. Thinking about intellectual history this way allows us to multiply the kinds of historical thinking and ways of knowing that are possible. In the "big tent" version of intellectual history we will have many varieties of contexts. It seems, perhaps, we already do.

NOTES

My thanks to all the participants in the S-USIH "Dangerous Ideas" Symposium in Indianapolis and especially to the organizers of that remarkable meeting, Andrew Hartman and Raymond Haberski. For particularly helpful insights by participants in the symposium that have aided me in my revisions of the original draft, I want to acknowledge Benjamin Alpers, Angus Burgin, and Andrew Jewett. Thanks also to Ashley Barnes, Charles Hatfield, Annelise Heinz, and Eric Schlereth for their comments and suggestions.

1. For instance, the concept of "context" is touched on only briefly in a recent work that represents a wide-ranging critique of historical epistemology, Allan Megill, *Historical Knowledge, Historical Error: A Contemporary Guide to Practice* (Chicago: University of Chicago Press, 2007), 214. There are exceptions to this general disregard of the idea of context, but even they fail to analyze the concept in ways that reflect historians' practice broadly conceived. See, for instance, Martin Jay, "Historical Explanation and the Event: Reflections on the Limits of Contextualization," *New Literary History* 42, no. 4 (Autumn 2011): 557–71; Mark Bevir, "The Role of Contexts in Understanding and Explanation," in *Begriffsgeschichte, Diskursgeschichte, Metapherngeschichte*, ed. Hans Erich Bödecker (Göttingen: Wallstein, 2002); Peter Gordon, "Contextualism and Criticism in the History of Ideas," in *Rethinking Modern European Intellectual History*, ed. Darrin M. McMahon and Samuel Moyn (New York: Oxford University Press, 2014), 32–55; Edward Baring, "Enthusiastic Reading: Rethinking Contextualization in Intellectual History," *Modern Intellectual History* 14, no. 1 (April 2017): 257–68.

2. On long-range intellectual history see David Armitage, "What's the Big Idea? Intellectual History and the *Longue Durée*," *History of European Ideas* 38, no. 4 (December 2012): 493–507; Darrin M. McMahon, "The Return of the History of Ideas," in McMahon and Moyn, *Rethinking Modern European Intellectual History*, 13–31. On the move toward a more capacious understanding of intellectual history see Sarah E. Igo, "Toward a Free-Range Intellectual History," in *The Worlds of American Intellectual History*, ed. Joel Isaac, James T. Kloppenberg, Michael O'Brien, and Jennifer Ratner-Rosenhagen (New York: Oxford University Press, 2017), 324–42. A recent example of an important work that is both transnational and concerned with ideas extended through longer periods of time is James Kloppenberg, *Toward Democracy: The Struggle for Self-Rule in European and American Thought* (New York: Oxford University Press, 2016). A good example of the recent interest in reception history, and in the use of texts such as comic books and the letters of ordinary people, as well as the writings of intellectuals, is Jennifer Ratner-Rosenhagen, *American Nietzsche: A History of An Icon and His Ideas* (Chicago: University of Chicago Press, 2012).

3. The key text for understanding the reorientation of intellectual history in the 1970s and '80s is John Higham and Paul Conkin, eds., *New Directions in American Intellectual History* (Baltimore: Johns Hopkins University Press, 1979). For the current standing of this reorientation see "Forum: The Present and Future of American Intellectual History," *Modern Intellectual History* 9, no. 1 (2012): 149–248; and my critical evaluation, Daniel Wickberg, "The Present and Future of American Intellectual History," *U.S. Intellectual History Blog*, April 3, 2012, at http://us-intellectual-history.blogspot.com/2012/04/present-and-future-of-american.html; Angus Burgin, "New Directions, Then and Now," in Isaac et al., *Worlds of American Intellectual History*, 343–64.

4. An example of the way Skinner was treated by Americanists—in this case critically—can be found in David Harlan, *The Degradation of American History* (Chicago: University of Chicago Press, 1997), although Harlan is highly idiosyncratic in his view of what intellectual history should do. Skinner was referred to by several of the contributors to the Higham and Conkin volume cited above, including David Hollinger and Gordon Wood, but was figured as part of a general orientation seeping into the field that included figures like Thomas Kuhn and Clifford Geertz. Many political theorists and Europeanists followed Skinner; few Americanists did. One strong exception is the Constitutional historian Saul Cornell, who has drawn heavily on Skinner. See, for instance, Saul Cornell, "Meaning and Understanding in the History of Constitutional Ideas: The Intellectual History Alternative to Originalism," *Fordham Law Review* 82, no. 2 (2013): 721–55.

5. On the influence of Pocock on American historiography see Daniel T. Rodgers, "Republicanism: The Career of a Concept," *Journal of American History* 79, no. 1 (June 1992): 11–38; Joyce Appleby, *Liberalism and Republicanism in the Historical Imagination* (Cambridge, MA: Harvard University Press, 1992). Pocock's most influential work among Americanists is J. G. A. Pocock, *The Machiavellian Moment: Florentine Political Thought and the Atlantic Republican Tradition* (Princeton, NJ: Princeton University Press, 1975).

6. Quentin Skinner, "Meaning and Understanding in the History of Ideas," *History and Theory* 8, no. 1 (1969): 3–53. Another early theoretical statement of Cambridge school methods, often cited along with Skinner's "Meaning and Understanding," is John Dunn, "The Identity of the History of Ideas," *Philosophy* 43, no. 164 (April 1968): 85–104.

7. Quentin Skinner, "A Reply to My Critics," in *Meaning and Context: Quentin Skinner and His Critics*, ed. James Tully (Princeton, NJ: Princeton University Press, 1988), 283.

8. Here the literature is vast. A sampling is available in *Meaning and Context*, ed. Tully, cited above. For a more recent critique see Michelle Clark, "The Mythologies of Contextualism: Method and Judgment in Skinner's *Visions of Politics*," *Political Studies* 61 (2013): 767–83. An overview and assessment of Skinner's work and the debates surrounding it is Kari Palonen, *Quentin Skinner: History, Politics, Rhetoric* (New York: Cambridge University Press, 2003).

9. Harlan, *Degradation of American History*; John Patrick Diggins, "The Oyster and the Pearl: The Problem of Contextualism in Intellectual History," *History and Theory* 23, no. 2 (May 1984): 151–69; Dominick LaCapra, "Rethinking Intellectual History and Reading Texts," *History and Theory* 19 (1980): 245–76. Other historians, such as Hayden White, truly were neoformalists, who believed that the use of context in historical writing was itself a formal element of narrative; but despite White's prominence, his position was always on the extreme margin of historians' practice. White's oeuvre is extensive and complex, but it reveals a turn away from historical practice to historiographical critique and philosophy of history in largely formalist terms. See, in particular, Hayden White, *The Content of the Form: Narrative Discourse and Historical Representation* (Baltimore: Johns Hopkins University Press, 1990). For a discussion of his work as a whole see Herman Paul, *Hayden White* (London: Polity, 2011). For a recent discussion of the relationship between

Skinner and White see Martin Jay, "Intention and Irony: The Missed Encounter between Hayden White and Quentin Skinner," *History & Theory* 52, no. 1 (February 2013): 32–48.

10. Keith DeRose, *The Case for Contextualism: Knowledge, Skepticism and Context*, vol. 1 (Oxford: Oxford University Press, 2009).

11. On the Federalist/Anti-Federalist distinction see Alison L. LaCroix, *The Ideological Origins of American Federalism* (Cambridge, MA: Harvard University Press, 2010); Jack Rakove, *Original Meanings: Politics and Ideas in the Making of the Constitution* (New York: Alfred A. Knopf, 1996).

12. Daniel Wickberg, "In the Environment of Ideas: Arthur Lovejoy and the History of Ideas as a Form of Cultural History," *Modern Intellectual History* 11, no. 2 (August 2014): 439–64.

13. *Oxford English Dictionary*, s.v. "context"; Peter Novick, *That Noble Dream: The "Objectivity Question" and the American Historical Profession* (New York: Cambridge University Press, 1988), 250ff; on the development of "the historical sensibility" and its relationship to new forms of epistemology in the late nineteenth and early twentieth centuries see James T. Kloppenberg, *Uncertain Victory: Social Democracy and Progressivism in European and American Thought, 1870–1920* (New York: Oxford University Press, 1986), 107–14; Morton White, *Social Thought in America: The Revolt against Formalism* (New York: Viking, 1949).

14. Gordon, "Contextualism and Criticism," 44.

15. On the historical relationship between history and philosophy in the post–World War II era see Kerwin Klein, *From History to Theory* (Berkeley: University of California Press, 2011), 35–58.

16. Laurence R. Veysey, *The Emergence of the American University* (Chicago: University of Chicago Press, 1965); Jon H. Roberts and James Turner, *The Sacred and the Secular University* (Princeton, NJ: Princeton University Press, 2000); Julie Reuben, *The Making of the Modern University: Intellectual Transformation and the Marginalization of Morality* (Chicago: University of Chicago Press, 1996); Andrew Jewett, *Science, Democracy, and the American University: From the Civil War to the Cold War* (New York: Cambridge University Press, 2012).

17. André Burguière, *The Annales School: An Intellectual History*, trans. Jane Marie Todd (Ithaca, NY: Cornell University Press, 2009), 133–62.

18. James Kloppenberg, "Thinking Historically: A Manifesto of Pragmatic Hermeneutics," *Modern Intellectual History* 9, no. 1 (2012): 202.

19. I am using the term "incommensurable" here in a way that is derived from Kuhn's notion of the incommensurability of paradigms or scientific theories. The debate surrounding this concept is long-standing and very complex. In ways that I cannot develop in this paper, I mean it to refer to a historical object that has multiple contexts that cannot be translated into a single common account; the vocabulary by which those contexts are described, and the objects and relations they designate, are, at some level, mutually exclusive. See Thomas S. Kuhn, *The Structure of Scientific Revolutions*, 4th ed. (Chicago: University of Chicago Press, 2012), xxx–xxxiii, 147–49; Eric Oberheim and Paul Hoyningen-Huene, "The Incommensurability of Scientific Theories," *The Stanford Encyclopedia of Philosophy*, Spring 2013 edition, ed. Edward N. Zalta, http://plato.stanford.edu/archives/spr2013/entries/incommensurability/.

20. Caroline Winterer, *The Culture of Classicism: Ancient Greece and Rome in American Intellectual Life, 1780–1910* (Baltimore: Johns Hopkins University Press, 2002).

21. Wickberg, "Present and Future of American Intellectual History."

22. Leslie Butler, "From the History of Ideas to Ideas in History," *Modern Intellectual History* 9, no. 1 (2012): 157–69. For an argument that politics and power should be the framework for intellectual history (and are not sufficiently so in the current environment)

see Andrew Jewett's chapter in this volume, "On the Politics of Knowledge: Science, Conflict, Power." I think Jewett is clearly making a case for something that is already the de facto condition of contemporary practice, although he projects it as a direction counter to current practice. There is a much bigger debate about the role of political and public life as the dominant frame for intellectual history. My view, which I cannot sufficiently develop here, but is implicit in my argument, is that insisting on either the practical reasons (i.e., it will make intellectual history more relevant to what others are concerned with) or the metaphysical reasons (i.e., power is the primary substance of human relations that can be invoked to explain all other phenomena) for foregrounding political contexts is a limiting movement that unnecessarily narrows the field of intellectual history and is at odds with a pragmatic approach open to the larger possibilities of variety. Politics, power, and public life are but one context among many.

Contributors

Benjamin L. Alpers is Reach for Excellence Associate Professor at the Honors College of the University of Oklahoma. He is the author of *Dictators, Democracy, and American Public Culture* and is currently at work on a book tentatively titled *Happy Days: Images of the Pre-sixties Past in Seventies America*. He is the editor of the *U.S. Intellectual History Blog*.

Angus Burgin is an associate professor of history at Johns Hopkins University and the author of *The Great Persuasion: Reinventing Free Markets since the Depression*, which won the Merle Curti Award for Intellectual History and the Joseph Spengler Prize for the History of Economics. His articles have appeared in *Modern Intellectual History*, *History of Political Economy*, and *The Worlds of American Intellectual History*, and he is coeditor of *Modern Intellectual History* and co-executive editor of the book series Intellectual History of the Modern Age at the University of Pennsylvania Press.

Christopher Cameron is an associate professor of history at the University of North Carolina at Charlotte. He is the author of *To Plead Our Own Cause: African Americans in Massachusetts and the Making of the Antislavery Movement*. In 2014, he founded the African American Intellectual History Society, an organization dedicated to fostering dialogue about researching, teaching, and writing about black thought and culture. He was the first editor of the society's blog, *Black Perspectives*, and was elected the society's first president. Cameron is currently completing a history of African American secularism from the nineteenth century to the civil rights era.

Ruben Flores is an intellectual and cultural historian who studies US and Mexican history. He is an associate professor of American studies at the University of Kansas and the former associate director of KU's Center for Latin American and Caribbean Studies. His book, *Backroads Pragmatists: Mexico's Melting Pot and Civil Rights in the United States*, was awarded the best-book prize from the Society for U.S. Intellectual History in 2015.

K. Healan Gaston is a lecturer in American religious history at Harvard University and the author of *Imagining Judeo-Christian America: Religion, Secularism, and the Redefinition of Democracy*, forthcoming from the University of Chicago Press. Other publications have appeared in the *Journal of American History* and the *Harvard*

Theological Review, among others. Gaston is the past president of the Niebuhr Society and served as senior adviser to Martin Doblmeier on his film *An American Conscience: The Reinhold Niebuhr Story*.

Raymond Haberksi Jr. is a professor of history and the director of American studies at Indiana University–Purdue University Indianapolis (IUPUI). He is the author of five books, including *God and War: American Civil Religion since 1945* and *Voice of Empathy: A History of Franciscan Media in the United States* for the American Academy of Franciscan History. He is at work on a monograph about the US Catholic bishops' pastoral letter, *The Challenge of Peace*. With a group of his colleagues from around the country, he founded the Society for United States Intellectual History in 2011, a professional organization that grew out of an award-winning blog that he has contributed to since 2009.

Andrew Hartman is a professor of history at Illinois State University. He is the author of *A War for the Soul of America: A History of the Culture Wars*, and *Education and the Cold War: The Battle for the American School*. Hartman was the founding president of the Society for U.S. Intellectual History (S-USIH), has written for the *U.S. Intellectual History Blog* since its inception in 2007, and was the Fulbright Distinguished Chair in American Studies at the University of Southern Denmark for the 2013–2014 academic year. He is currently writing a third monograph, titled *Karl Marx in America*.

Jonathan Holloway is the author of *Confronting the Veil: Abram Harris Jr., E. Franklin Frazier, and Ralph Bunche, 1919–1941* and *Jim Crow Wisdom: Memory and Identity in Black America since 1940*. He edited Ralph Bunche's *A Brief and Tentative Analysis of Negro Leadership* and coedited *Black Scholars on the Line: Race, Social Science, and American Thought in the 20th Century*. He is currently working on a new book, *A History of Absence: Race and the Making of the Modern World*. He is the provost of Northwestern University and a professor of history and African American studies.

Andrew Jewett is a visiting associate professor at Boston College and the author of *Science, Democracy, and the American University: From the Civil War to the Cold War* (Cambridge University Press, 2012). His current book traces anti-expert sentiment among American intellectual and political leaders and ordinary citizens since the 1920s.

Amy Kittelstrom is the author of *The Religion of Democracy: Seven Liberals and the American Moral Tradition* (Penguin, 2015). She is a professor of history at Sonoma State University and currently serves on the editorial board of the *Journal of American History*. Her next book will provide a deep history for the twentieth-century writer James Baldwin.

Tim Lacy is the author of *The Dream of a Democratic Culture: Mortimer J. Adler and the Great Books Idea* (2013). He earned his Ph.D. at Loyola University Chicago and is a cofounder of both the *U.S. Intellectual History Blog* and the Society for U.S. Intellectual History. Lacy is wrapping up a manuscript on "great books cosmopolitanism" before embarking on a long-term project about post-war anti-intellectualism. He lives in Chicago and has recently taught courses and seminars for Loyola University Chicago, Monmouth College, and the Newberry Library.

James Livingston has taught history for many years in a wide variety of settings, including one small liberal arts college, five large state universities (Illinois State University among them), two maximum security prisons, and a community/county college. He is currently a professor of history at Rutgers University. He has written on an equally wide variety of topics, from Marxism, pragmatism, and feminism to *South Park*, Amy Winehouse, and *The Little Mermaid*. Also Heidegger. His most recent book is *No More Work: Why Full Employment Is a Bad Idea*. He has written for *In These Times*, the *New York Times*, the *Los Angeles Times*, the *New Republic*, the *Nation*, the *Chronicle of Higher Education*, the *Christian Science Monitor*, *Dissent*, and other publications. The online magazine he edits, *Politics/Letters*, has published ten issues.

Kevin Mattson teaches American intellectual, cultural, and political history at Ohio University. He is the author of numerous books, including *When America Was Great: The Fighting Faith of Postwar Liberalism*; *Intellectuals in Action: The Origins of the New Left and Radical Liberalism, 1945–1970*; *Rebels All! A Short History of the Conservative Mind in Postwar America*; and *What the Heck Are You Up to, Mr. President?* He is on the editorial board of *Dissent* magazine and writes regularly for *Democracy Journal*.

Christopher McKnight Nichols is the director of the Oregon State University Center for the Humanities and as associate professor of history at Oregon State University. Nichols is a 2016 Andrew Carnegie Fellow. He authored *Promise and Peril: America at the Dawn of a Global Age*, coedited the *Wiley-Blackwell Companion to the Gilded Age and Progressive Era: The Making of Modern America*, coedited and coauthored, with Charles Mathewes, *Prophesies of Godlessness: Predictions of America's Imminent Secularization from the Puritans to the Present Day*, and was the senior editor of the two-volume *Oxford Encyclopedia of American Military and Diplomatic History*. Nichols is at work on three book projects on the history of the United States' relations to and with the world.

Natalia Mehlman Petrzela is an associate professor of history at the New School and the author of *Classroom Wars: Language, Sex, and the Making of Modern Political Culture*. She is currently working on a history of fitness culture in the postwar

United States. Her writing has appeared in multiple scholarly journals and in popular venues such as the *Washington* Post, the *New York Times, Slate,* the *Chronicle of Higher Education, Public Books,* and *Refinery29.* She is a host of the Past Present podcast, a contributor to the History Channel, and the cofounder of the wellness education program Healthclass2.0. She holds a B.A. from Columbia University and a M.A. and Ph.D. from Stanford.

Kevin M. Schultz is a professor of history, religious studies, and Catholic studies at the University of Illinois at Chicago, where he has taught since 2007. His books include *Buckley and Mailer: The Difficult Friendship That Shaped the Sixties*; *Tri-Faith America: How Postwar Catholic and Jews Forced America to Live Up to Its Protestant Promise*; and *HIST: A Textbook of American History*, fifth edition. An award-winning teacher and author, he served as the president of the Society for U.S. Intellectual History from 2014 to 2018.

David Sehat is an associate professor of history at Georgia State University. He is the author of *The Jefferson Rule: How the Founding Fathers Became Infallible and Our Politics Inflexible* and *The Myth of American Religious Freedom*, which won the Frederick Jackson Turner Award from the Organization of American Historians. He is now writing a book about the American secular tradition titled *Politics after God*.

Lisa Szefel is an associate professor of history at Pacific University and the author of *The Gospel of Beauty in the Progressive Era: Reforming American Verse and Values*. She has published essays on US intellectual and cultural history in the *Montreal Review, Callaloo,* and the *New England Quarterly*. Her current book projects include *"Think or Die!": A Prize to Ezra Pound, Treason, and the Fate of Democracy in Cold War America*.

Daniel Wickberg is an associate professor of historical studies and the history of ideas at the University of Texas at Dallas and the past president of the Society for U.S. Intellectual History. He is the author of *The Senses of Humor: Self and Laughter in Modern America* and numerous articles on intellectual and cultural historiography and methods. His current book project is tentatively titled *The Idea of Tradition in a Culture of Progress: Thinking about the Past and Future in Post–World War II America*.

Acknowledgments

We would first like to thank the contributors to this volume. Their intelligence and passion have made working on this book a joy.

Ray's institution, Indiana University–Purdue University Indianapolis (IUPUI), has been crucial to this project. An Indiana University New Frontiers / New Currents grant awarded through IUPUI significantly helped the development of this volume by allowing most of the contributors to gather in Indianapolis for a few days in July 2016. For their considerable help and support winning and implementing that grant, we thank Jason Kelly, the director of IUPUI's Arts and Humanities Institute (IAHI), Megan Lizarme in the Institute for American Thought, Mary Cox and Edith Millikan in the dean's office of the School of Liberal Arts, the dean himself, Thomas Davis, for writing a letter supporting our efforts to the administration, and George Cotkin, an emeritus professor of history at Cal Poly San Luis Obispo, for writing a letter supporting our efforts in the profession.

As part of this grant, a few contributors to the volume joined Ray in leading a public discussion that traced the intellectual history of contemporary debates. Making that event possible, Cassie Stockamp, the president of the Indianapolis Athenaeum and its foundation, provided our group space in the beautiful building that houses a significant part of Indianapolis's past. We are grateful for her enthusiastic support. As the volume neared publication, Jason Kelly once again stepped up to help us by contributing funds from the IAHI. Likewise, we would like to acknowledge the generosity of Paul and Catherine Nagy, who also provided financial support toward the publication of this book. IUPUI's American Studies doctoral program has already greatly benefited from the Nagys' magnanimity, and Ray is truly grateful for their interest in US intellectual history. Andrew's institution, Illinois State University—specifically Research and Graduate Studies, the College of Arts and Sciences, and the Department of History—generously kicked in to help support the publication of this book as well.

Families participate in endeavors such as this, and Ray wants to thank his wife, Shenan, and his daughter, Devon, for their encouragement and love. During the week that we hosted our contributors in Indianapolis, Ray's parents, Ray and Alice Haberski, came out from New York to help out. During their stay, Ray's dad joined our mini-conference for a couple of sessions, which was a thrill for Ray, who had a chance to introduce his colleagues and friends to the guy who first got him fired up about history.

Andrew would like to thank his family as well. Without Erica's love and support, being an academic would be much more difficult. Without Asa and Eli, there might be more time for academic work, but life would be far less meaningful.

We dedicate this book to our friends and advisers, Charles C. Alexander and Leo P. Ribuffo. We continue to strive to live up to their lofty standards.

Index

1960s: as subject for intellectual history, 39–41; intellectual atmosphere of, 40–41

abolitionism, 137–138
academia: and black experience, 71–72; and judicial interpretation, 28–29; and US foreign policy, 213; careerism in, 67, 256; inequality within, 67–68; nonwhite labor force of, 80–82; overlap with consulting, 169; professionalization of, 56–57, 60, 63–67; shift to careerism in, 62; white maleness of, 88; whiteness of, 75–79
academic job market, 3, 12, 14, 282
Adorno, Theodor, 19–20, 264
African American historiography, and uplift, 241
African Americans, and health care, 91
American history, significance of intellectual history in, 17–20
American ideas, used against American power, 110–111
American neutrality, 204
anti-contextualists, 308–309
anti-intellectualism, 6; and capitalism, 267; and logical fallacies, 265; as sensibility, 266; as signal of deeper currents, 265–266; charges reflecting failure of discourse, 253
antiracism, in African American thought, 64–65
antisemitism, in academia, 59–61
atheism, 6
authenticity, 39; as object of historical inquiry, 231; of religious experience, 231; of religious experiences, 223–226; religious, 227–228
authority, questioned, 44; social, 43
automation, effect on capitalism, 172–174

Baldwin, James, 40, 49, 73–74, 83; atheism of, 249n2
Bay, Mia, 64, 88
Beard, Charles, 141, 311
Beard, Mary, 141
Beecher, Henry Ward, 225
Bender, Thomas, 1, 41, 271, 274, 275

Berger, Raoul, 27–28
Billy Lynn's Long Halftime Walk, 183–184, 194–196
black culture, as source for feminist philosophy, 88
black experience, recognition of, 71–72
black intellectuals, 5; individuality, 75; public, 72–74
black students, 75–76; protests by, 77–79
black studies, 77
Blake, Casey, 18, 274–275
bodies, as objects of historical interest, 88–89
Boorstin, Daniel, 258
Borrowman, Merle, 259
Bourne, Randolph, 185, 190–192, 210–211
Brest, Paul, 27–29
Brick, Howard, 39
Brooks, David, 126, 128, 159
Brown, David, 253–254, 264
Buchanan, Pat, 155, 211
Buckley Jr, William F., 39, 149, 155, 159, 226
Butler, Jonathan, 78
Butler, Judith, 18–19, 89
Butler, Leslie, 274, 281, 285

capitalism, 20; and religion, 234–235; and repression, 143; conflict with freedom and justice, 171; corporate, 19, 133, 142–144, 152, 167–168, 170–176; corporate, faith in prior to 1960s, 42; corporate vs. laissez-faire, 46; industrial, 133–134
Cavell, Stanley, 16, 202–203
centrism, Democratic, 152
Chicago, University of, 108, 174
church-state relations, 229–231
Civil Rights movement, 26–28, 47
Civil War, 22, 208; historiography of, 141
class, and intellectual history, 114; in America, 154
class conflict: and race, 141; in America, 135, 139–143. *See also* IWA; Left; Marx
Clinton, Hillary, 119, 122, 125
Coates, Ta-Nehisi, 64–65, 74
Cochran, Thomas, 167–168

329

Cold War, 43, 47; end of, 151; technocracy during, 260–261. *See also under* liberalism
Cole, Arthur, 167, 168
Collingwood, R. G., 16, 19, 311
communism, African American, 248
Conkin, Paul, 2, 17, 274
conservatism, 5, 24–34; 60s and 70s, 150; 80s and 90s, 151; 90s and 00s, 152–155; and literary modernism, 146–148; as temperament, 157–159; contemporary, 155–159; media sympathizing with, 150, 154–156; motivations, 154; post WWII, 146–149, 160; religious, 151
Constitution, U.S., 22; living, 23; (invented) reverence for, 24–25 (*see also* fundamentalism, legal); popular understandings of, 33–34
consumerism, as danger, 147–148. *See also* materialism
context, 6; and political meaning, 23–24, 26–27, 30–34; as central for historical study, 305; as epistemological strategy, 305; as relationship, 315; as subject for intellectual history, 273; as subject of cultural history, 272; as tool, 312; contiguous, 314–315; historical and cultural, 310–311; historical significance of, 16–17; ideational, 317; more clearly defined, 312; of translated works, 114; of U.S. in world, 198; placement within, 316; plural, 309–311, 313–314; question dependent, 312; stability of, 316; understood on the terms of the historical subject, 307–309; use of, 317–318
conversion narratives: and identity, 241–245; to atheism, 241–245
Coon, Deborah J., 275
Cornell, Saul, 32
Cotkin, George, 275, 276
Cowie, Jefferson, 281
cultural and intellectual history, 2, 18; boundaries, 285–286; common ground, 271–272; divided by methodology, 272; divided by subject matter, 272; mutual influence, 273
cultural studies, and historical research, 275–276
culture: as object of historical study, 276–277; as survival strategy, 73
Curti, Merle, 66, 67, 201, 274

Darnton, Robert, 13, 277, 281–282
Debs, Eugene V., 132–133, 139
denaturalizing social institutions and assumptions, 288–290

Dewey, John, 3, 19–20, 57, 88, 105, 107, 109, 190
Diggins, John Patrick, 134–136, 190, 308
diplomatic history, broadening scope and techniques, 198
disciplinary translation of intellectual history work, 297–299
disciplines, academic, 11
diversity, aims of, 76–79; as essential element of national identity, 107–108; in Mexico, 106–107; in Peru and Ecuador, 107–108
Douglass, Frederick, 64
Drucker, Peter, 168–171, 173–175
Du Bois, W. E. B., 63–64, 140–142; socialism of, 248; use of Marx, 142
dualism, Cartesian. *See* bodies
Dunn, John, 306
Dunning, William Archibald, 141

economic history, 11–14
economists, Austrian, 174
Ecuador, building school system in, 107
education, anti-intellectualism in, 264
efficiency, inhumanity of, 170–171
egalitarianism, 17
Eisenhower, Dwight D., 41–42, 223, 225
Eliot, T. S., 148
Ellis, John Tracy, 259–260
Ellison, Ralph, 75, 240
entrepreneurship, 5; apparent decline of, 167–168; as function, 174–175; bipartisan appeal of, 163; rise of, 164–166, 175–176
Esalen Institute, 94–95
existentialism, 246–247
explanation, as task of intellectual history, 39–40

Faust, Drew Gilpin, 187
feminism: "crunk," 88. *See also* women; women's health.
Fessenden, Tracy, 230, 232–33
film noir, 278–280
First International, 138
Fonda, Jane, 92–100
foreign policy: 19th-century, 208–209; assumed to align with good of the world, 213; early American, 202–207; entangled with economic concerns, 205; foundation of isolationist tradition, 206–207; role of ideas in, 214–215
Forman, James, conversion to atheism of, 244

INDEX   331

Fountain, Ben, 183, 194–195
freedom, 4, 38; as unifying theme of 1960s, 47–50; competing uses of, 47–50; liberal concepts of, 126. *See also* individualism
freethought: African American, 240–248. *See also* atheism; secularism
Friedan, Betty, 39, 40, 50n3, 100
fundamentalism: and evangelical anti-intellectualism, 262; and historical change, 33–34; and its relationship to the past, 24–25; legal, 21–22

Geertz, Clifford, 65, 277, 315
gender, 5, 87–89
Gettysburg Address, 186–188
globalism, 152
Gordon, Peter, 311
Graham, Billy, 223
grand strategy, 212; as epistemology, 213–14
Greif, Mark, 92, 97
Griffin, Stephen, 33
gym culture, history of, 92–100; inclusion of women in, 94; sexuality and, 93

Hall, David D., 1, 65, 278, 280
Hartz, Louis, 135
Harvey, George, 211–212
Haskell, Thomas, 1, 11–12, 16–17, 19, 20, 65
Hegel, G. W. F., 14–16
Herberg, Will, 226–227
Higham, John, 1, 17, 274
historicism, 311
history. *See* American history, diplomatic history, intellectual history, social history, transnational history
Hofstadter, Richard, 6, 286; affirming preconceived notions, 257; context, 254; durability of analysis of, 253; elitism of, 258; lack of rigor in, 259; on business, 255–256; on education, 256–257, 263–265; on politics, 255; on religion, 254–255; reception of, 257–265; tone of, 258
Hollinger, David, 1, 2, 16–17, 32, 68n7, 227, 233–234, 276
Hughes, Langston, conversion to atheism, 242–243
Hurston, Zora Neale, atheism of, 245

identity, 4–5; African American, 246–248; American, 18, 23, 25, 46, 202–203; and physical fitness, 90–91; and war, 184–188; creedal, 202–203

Immerwahr, Daniel, 169, 273
imperialism, 188–190: American, 110–111; Mexican, 111
indigenous peoples, 202, 205
individualism, 44–45, 135–140, 143, 147–149, 165
industrial production, inhumanity of, 170–171
inequality, 144; and knowledge work, 287
innovation, 166–168; centrality of, 173–175
intellectual: as category, 89; as gendered term, 86–88
intellectual history: and American history, 61–62; and anti-intellectualism, 157; and church history, 61–62; and international political history, 105; and political history, 110–111; as normative cultural criticism, 292–293; as tool for analyzing ideas and categories, 227–229; complicating political history, 112; contribution to public discourse, 285–287; cultural history as subfield, 274; current vibrancy, 282; in crisis, 1; in dialogue with social history, cultural history, 2–7; in the age of cultural studies, 280–281; individual thinkers as subjects, 275; interdisciplinary, 65–67; mid-20th century crisis in, 273; of American foreign policy, 199; of economic concepts, 165–166; of emotions, 159; of religious experience, 224–226; of scientific knowledge, 295–297; personal accounts of, 12–14; popular appeal of, 3–4; rejected by legal originalists, 31–34; relation to philosophy, 56–59; relation to social history, 59; relationship to culture, 15–20; relationship to politics, 17–18; relationship to work, 15–16; scale of, 39–41; significance of, 7, 66–67; subjects of, 87–88; transnational methodologies, 113–116; turn to discourse, culture, and language, 306; unique resources of, 293–294, 300
interpretation, textual, 21–34. *See also* fundamentalism; legal realism
interventionism, and support for liberty, 213–214. *See also* isolationism; neutrality; nonintervention
isolation: as context, 204–207; geographic, 202, 217–218n16
isolationism: American traditions of, 201; and incapacity for foreign intervention, 207; and self-interest, 208–212; and simultaneous expansionism, 207; idealistic, 211; interwar, 201; political, 199; protectionist, 199–200; traditions of, 212

isolationist imperialism, 210
IWA, 138–139. *See also* socialism

Jacoby, Russell, 72
Jacoby, Susan, 262–263
James, Alice, 56; contribution to William James's work of, 58
James, William, 3, 18–20; and American unity, 60; on importance of philosophy, 55; on professional philosophy, 56; social context of, 57–58. *See also* pragmatism
Jazzercise, 97–98
Jefferson, Thomas, 22, 47, 205
Johnson, Andrew, 208
judiciary, U.S., and political change, 26–28
just war theory, 185, 192–195

Kelley, Donald R., 272, 275
Kennedy, John F., 90–91, 125
Kirk, Russell, 48, 148–49
Kloppenberg, James, 18, 32, 33, 137, 313–14, 316
Knight, Frank H. 167–68
Kolko, Gabriel, 142
Kruse, Kevin, 234–35
Kuhn, Thomas, 11–12, 16, 39, 320n19

Labor: as political force, 126; in academia, 80–82
LaCapra, Dominick, 275–276, 308
language, 15; as a historical source, 2
Lasch, Christopher, 2, 90, 92, 264
League of Nations, 211
Lears, Jackson, 190, 275
Left: in the academy, 142; international, 137–140; New, 142–143; U.S., 5, 122, 134, 136–144
legal realism, 24
Lerner, Gerda, 87–88
liberal arts, political significance of, 148–149
liberal humor, 129
liberalism, 5, 261; Cold War, 135–136, 257; complex, 123–128; early American history of, 62; emphasizing complexity, 130; in America, 134–144. *See also* Protestantism
libertarianism, 199
limits of U.S. power, 204
Lincoln, Abraham, 17, 22, 138, 147, 186–188
Liu, Catherine, 263–265
Lodge, Henry Cabot, 209–211
love, 38; as political force, 49–50
Lovejoy, Arthur, 307, 309
Lynn, Kenneth S., 258

management theory, 169–176
Marcuse, Herbert, 15, 95, 142–143

marketplace of ideas, 17–18
Marty, Martin E., 24, 28
Marx, Karl, 15, 133, 137–138
Marxism, 134, 141; and health, 95. *See also* communism; materialism; socialism
materialism: as explanatory principle, 120–122; capitalist and Marxist, 159. *See also* consumerism; Marxism
May, Henry, 1, 39–41
meaning, as subject of historical study, 2–3
Menafee, Corey, 81–82
metaphor, 19–20
Mexico: as source for Sáenz's pragmatism, 109; immigration from, 104; institution building in, 106; public schooling in, 106; relations with U.S., 110–113; state-sponsored research in, 110. *See also* Sáenz, Moisés
Missett, Judi Sheppard, 97–98
modernism, literary, 146–149
modernity, anti-intellectualism as response to, 255
money, as metaphor, 19–20
Monroe, James, 205–206
Monroe Doctrine, 210–212
Mumford, Lewis, 19–20, 173
Myrdal, Gunnar, 141

NAACP, 140
narratives, constraining thought, 231–236
Nash, George, 146
naturalization of contingent phenomena, as object of study, 288–290
neutrality, 203, 209. *See also* isolationism; nonintervention
New Critics, 147–148, 160
New Deal, 26, 234, 256; opponents of, 47
Niebuhr, Reinhold, 124, 126–128, 225–227, 236–237
Noll, Mark, 261–262
nonintervention, 203. *See also* isolationism; neutrality
norms, social, faith in prior to 1960s, 43
nostalgia, 280

Obama, Barack, 48, 122, 128–130; and black community, 123–124; and liberalism, 123–126; style of, 125
objectivity, 228
originalism, U.S.: criticisms of, 28–30, 31–33; legal, 21–22; modern origins of, 27–29; "new," 31–33
Orsi, Robert, 225, 236

Peale, Norman Vincent, 223, 225
Peru, building school system of, 108
Pfeffer, Leo, 229–231
philosophy: and social science, 63–64; extradisciplinary, 65–66; individual, 55–56; individual and professional, 57, 65–66; individual vs. professional, 58–59; practical applications of, 106–108; privilege in, 59–61; privilege within, 67; secular orientation of, 61
pluralism: necessity of, 128; of perspectives, 229
Pocock, J. G. A., 306
political history, becoming the domain of political science, 11
political science, 11
politics, expanding implications of, 290
politics of knowledge: among elites and private individuals, 287; and power, 291–294, 300; and social context, 291–294, 300; as object of intellectual history, 286–287
populism, 17; 21st century, 153–159; and white nationalism, 125; economic, 120–122
pragmatism, 19, 137; and Church power, 112; early history of, 55–56; history of, 3; in Latin America, 106–108; mediated influence overseas of, 109. *See also* James, William; Sáenz, Moisés; Dewey, John
privilege: class, 58; male, 86
Progressive Era, 23
protest, 77–79, 81
"Protestant secular," 232
Protestantism: evangelical, and anti-intellectualism, 262; liberal, 225
public opinion, 17

race, 5; and social order, 43, 49. *See also* black culture; black experience; black intellectuals; black students; black studies
racism, 141; as political motivator, 153–154; driving U.S. politics, 120–121; in academia, 59–61
radicalism, African American, and religion, 248
Rakove, Jack N., 30, 32
Rankine, Claudia, 74–75
rationality, faith in prior to 1960s, 41–42; weakened faith in, 45
Ratner-Rosenhagen, Jennifer, 66–67, 273
Reagan, Ronald, 150–151
recognition: and capitalism, 170; compensatory, 83–84; failures of, 73

Reconstruction, historiography of, 141–143. *See also* Civil War
Reed, John, 139–140
reflexivity, 292
reform-focused isolationism, 209
religion, 5–6; 1950s resurgence, 223–224; 1950s revival, 226; African American, 240–244; African American "natural" tendency toward, 245–248; and capitalism, 234–235; and civil rights movement, 240–241; and community, 242–244; and conflict, 236; and national redemption, 226; and pluralism, 236; and social order, 43; as category, 224–226, 228; failure to ameliorate racism, 247–248; public and private, 233–235; publicness as authenticity, 233; role in public sphere, 229–231
Republican Party, 152–153, 153–154
Riesman, David, 259
rights, as premise for social order, 44–45
risk, 167. *See also* uncertainty
Robin, Corey, 157
Robinson, Armstead, 76–79
Rodgers, Daniel T., 34, 46–47, 165, 201, 272–273, 275
Ross, Dorothy, 1, 275–276

Sanders, Bernie, 48, 119–122, 211. *See also* materialism; socialism
Sáenz, Moisés, 105–112
Schlesinger Jr, Arthur, 126, 148
schooling, aims of, 108
Schrader, Paul, 278–280
Schumpeter, Joseph, 149, 166, 168, 174
science as a political phenomenon, 295
sciences, role in naturalization, denaturalization, 289–290
secularism, African American, 239–241, 248; rising with religiosity, 226
secularization, narratives of, 227–228, 232; opening up new spaces for religion, 234
self-consciousness, 15–16
sexuality, 93
Sherry, Michael, 186
Skinner, Quentin, 32, 306–310, 317–18
slavery, reconciliation for, 83–84
Smith, Bonnie, 87
social history, 11; growth of, 1–2
social norms, embodying unjust power relations, 45, 49; weakened, 44
social order, challenged, 45
social science, practical applications of, 106–108

social science research, political effects of, 298–299
socialism, 126–27, 132–34, 137, 142; African American, 248
sociological jurisprudence, 24
Solum, Lawrence B., 31–33
sovereignty, popular, 206
spheres of influence, 210
state, role of under capitalism, 171
states, and intellectual history, 114–115
Susman, Warren, 1, 16–17, 19, 281
symmetry, in history of ideas, 293

taxation, as contribution to national project, 46
theory of truth, 20
think tanks, conservative, 46
transnational history, of American Civil War, 137–138
transnationalism: accounting for multi-directional flow of ideas, 111; as lens, 115–116
transnationalism studies: enriched by intellectual history, 105; focused on immigration, 104
Trilling, Lionel, 128, 135–36, 148
Trump, Donald, 121, 128–130, 152, 155–156; as protectionist isolationist, 200
Twain, Mark, 185, 188–190

uncertainty, 165–168, 174
unilateralism, 203
unity, American, 46, 60
utopianism, 132–134. *See also* socialism

Viereck, Peter, 159–160

Walzer, Michael, 185, 193–194
war, 5; and media, 195–196; and national identity, 184–188; and national unity, 191–192; and the power of the state, 185; and the state, 190–192; as consumer product, 183; as norm, 192–196; satirized, 189–190
Washington, George, as isolationist, 204
wealth, equally distributed, 42–43
wellness: as lay philosophy, 89; early definitions, 90–91; negative aspects of, 92, 100; of women and nonwhite people, 91
Welter, Rush, 17, 260
West, Cornel, 64, 72
Williams, Raymond, 271, 276–277
Williams, William Appleman, 207, 210, 213, 258
Wilson, Woodrow, 23–24, 141, 219
Wingspread Conference, 1–2, 11, 273–274
Wisconsin, 67, 256
Wisconsin, University of, 66–67
women: in academia, 59–60. *See also* gender
women's health, as political movement, 95–100
Woodward, C. Vann, 126, 206
work, 15–16
World War I, 210
World War II, 47, 192
Wright, Richard: conversion to atheism, 243–245; existentialism of, 246–247; on atheism and racial authenticity, 246–247; rejection of Christianity of, 239; socialism of, 248

yoga, 94

www.ingramcontent.com/pod-product-compliance
Lightning Source LLC
Chambersburg PA
CBHW051207300426
44116CB00006B/461